Although Donald Cammell's credits consist of a very few titles as a film director – *Performance* (1970), *Demon Seed* (1977), *White of the Eye* (1987) and *Wild Side* (1995) – he remains one of the most fascinating of British filmmakers.

This book explores Cammell's key works, including unmade projects, and considers his themes and interests, his collaborators and productions, and his life.

MEDIA, FEMINISM, CULTURAL STUDIES

The Poetry of Cinema
by John Madden

The Sacred Cinema of Andrei Tarkovsky
by Jeremy Mark Robinson

Jean-Luc Godard: The Passion of Cinema / Le Passion de Cinéma
by Jeremy Mark Robinson

Liv Tyler
by Thomas A. Christie

The Cinema of Richard Linklater
by Thomas A. Christie

Walerian Borowczyk
by Jeremy Mark Robinson

Stepping Forward: Essays, Lectures and Interviews
by Wolfgang Iser

Wild Zones: Pornography, Art and Feminism
by Kelly Ives

'Cosmo Woman': The World of Women's Magazines
by Oliver Whitehorne

Andrea Dworkin
by Jeremy Mark Robinson

Cixous, Irigaray, Kristeva: The Jouissance of French Feminism
by Kelly Ives

Sex in Art: Pornography and Pleasure in Painting and Sculpture
by Cassidy Hughes

The Erotic Object: Sexuality in Sculpture
From Prehistory to the Present Day
by Susan Quinnell

Women in Pop Music
by Helen Challis

Detonation Britain: Nuclear War in the UK
by Jeremy Mark Robinson

Julia Kristeva: Art, Love, Melancholy, Philosophy, Semiotics
by Kelly Ives

Luce Irigaray: Lips, Kissing, and the Politics of Sexual Difference
by Kelly Ives

Helene Cixous I Love You: The Jouissance *of Writing*
by Kelly Ives

Feminism and Shakespeare
by B.D. Barnacle

THE CINEMA OF DONALD CAMMELL

DEATH. AND SEX. ART. AND MADNESS. MAGIC. AND PERFORMANCE.

Jeremy Mark Robinson

The Cinema of
DONALD CAMMELL

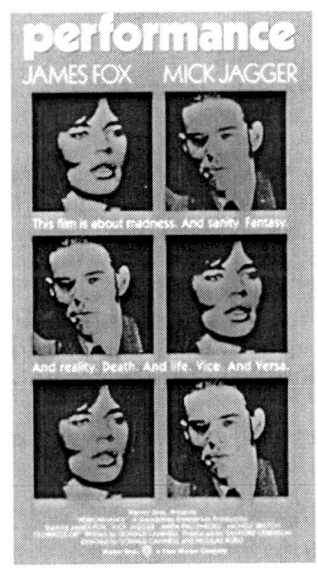

DEATH. AND SEX.
ART. AND MAGIC.
MADNESS. AND
PERFORMANCE.

Crescent Moon

Crescent Moon Publishing
P.O. Box 1312
Maidstone, Kent
ME14 5XU, Great Britain
www.crmoon.com

First published 2015.
© Jeremy Mark Robinson 2015.

Printed and bound in the U.S.A.
Set in Rotis SemiSans, 10 on 14pt.
Designed by Radiance Graphics.

The right of Jeremy Mark Robinson to be identified as the author of this book has been asserted generally in accordance with sections 77 and 78 of the Copyright, Designs and Patents Act 1988.

All rights reserved. No part of this book may be reprinted or reproduced, stored in a retrieval system, or transmitted, in any form or by any means, electronic, mechanical, photocopying, recording or otherwise, without permission from the publisher.

British Library Cataloguing in Publication data available for this title.

ISBN-13 9781861712820 (Pbk)
ISBN-13 9781861715029 (Pbk)
ISBN-13 9781861714992(Hbk)

CONTENTS

Acknowledgements 10
Picture Credits 10
Abbreviations 11

1 Donald Cammell 19
  Film Career • Donald Cammell Biography • Influences and Associations • Donald Cammell and Jean-Luc Godard • Cinema in the 1960s
2 *Performance* 59
3 Cultural Echoes of *Performance* 156
4 *Demon Seed* 220
5 *White of the Eye* 242
6 *Wild Side* 274
7 Other Movie Projects 299

Appendices 308
   Nic Roeg • *The Man Who Fell To Earth* • Syd Barrett • *One Plus One* • *Fitzcarraldo* • *Boogie Nights*
   Critics On *Performance* • Fans On *Performance* 334
Filmography 337
Bibliography 347

ACKNOWLEDGEMENTS

To the authors and publishers quoted.
To the copyright holders of the illustrations.

PICTURE CREDITS

Goodtimes Enterprises. Warner Bros. Paramount. Studio Canal/ Universal. Canyon/ Fantoma/ Mystic Fire. Landau/ Elstree Film. Columbia. Cinema 5. Cinerama Releasing. MGM. United Artists. GFD/ Universal. Warner-Pathé. Casey/ Eldorado/ Paramount/ Warner. TriStar. October Films. David Del Valle. Nu Image, Inc. Tartan Films. Film Designs Ltd. Festival Films. Frank Mazzola. Melvin Simon Productions. Cannon Screen/ Palisades Entertainment.

ABBREVIATIONS

B   *Performance* by Mick Brown
M   *Performance* by Colin McCabe
U   *Donald Cammell* by R. and S. Umland

Donald Cammell and Anita Pallenberg, during the making of Performance (1970), Cammell's best-known movie.

Following pages: posters of the four films Cammell directed.

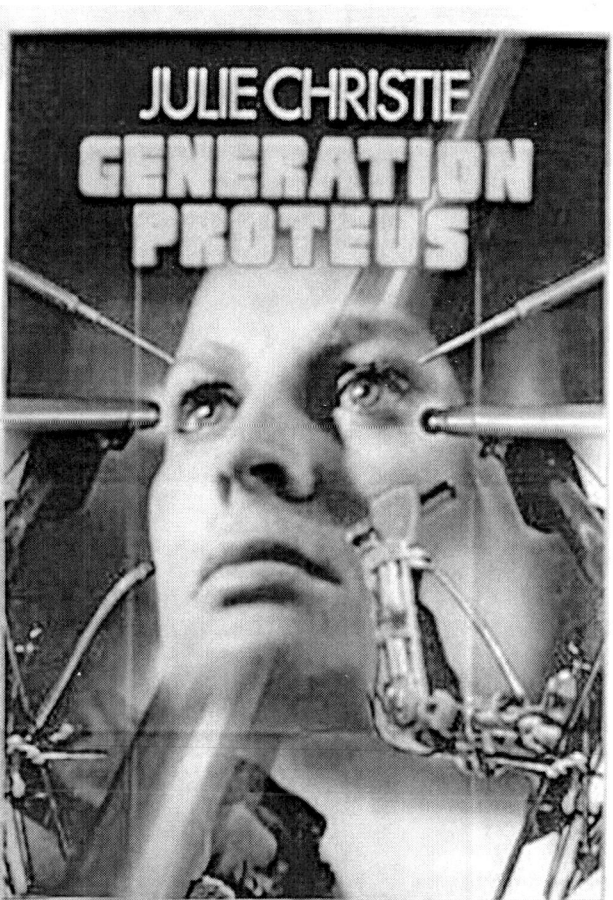

DONALD CAMMELL

1

DONALD CAMMELL
☆

DONALD CAMMELL: BIOGRAPHY

Donald Seton Cammell, born in Edinburgh on January 17, 1934, was the son of Charles Richard Cammell (b. 1890), and his second wife, Iona Katherine Lamont Macdonald (b. 1903). Cammell was born in the Outlook Tower in one of the most historic parts of Edinburgh (the tower contained a famous *camera obscura*). Cammell senior had inherited his money from the Cammell Laird shipbuilding company. Both Cammell's parents were Scottish;[1] they had married in 1932. Cammell had a brother, David, and a half-brother.

Donald Cammell was described by friends as witty, intellectual, magnetic, attractive, intense, an æsthete, and something of a control freak.[2] He was famously fascinated by death, and suicide, which became perennial themes in his cinema (but he wasn't alone among filmmakers – Ingmar Bergman, Woody Allen, Francis Coppola, Jean-Luc Godard, Ken Russell and Carl-Theodor Dreyer come to mind).

Donald Cammell was a creative, artistic child from an early age: he studied at Westminster public school, Shrewsbury House School,[3] Bryan Shaw,[4] the Royal Academy (he won a scholarship), and in Florence (where he studied with Pietro Annigoni, a leading portrait painter).[5] Cammell's roots, then, and his education, are distinctly upper-class and privileged (as well as bohemian and artistic – and English). Just look at the list of schools and colleges he attended: he was a very highly educated guy, and was already moving in culturally sophisticated circles by his late teens.

Donald Cammell was thus another product of the British art school tradition: the art schools of the 1950s and 1960s were breeding grounds for numerous pop musicians, for example, from John Lennon, Pete Townshend, and Bryan Ferry to the punk rock scene (Joe Strummer, Adam Ant, Chrissie Hynde, Jordan, etc).[6]

In the 1950s Donald Cammell set up as a portrait painter in Flood

---

[1] However, Cammell seems a very 'English' artist, perpetually associated with London (and later with L.A.).
[2] M. Brown, 1999, 34.
[3] Cammell had been sent to Fort Augustus, to a prep school/ boarding school (Abbey School), but hated it so much his mother brought him home. Something traumatic seems to have happened at Fort Augustus, including perhaps abuse: for Cammell, it was a 'trauma point', and he ran away from the school (when he was 8, around 1942-43) twice at least (U, 33, 260).
[4] Donald Cammell left home when he went to Byran Shaw art school, said Cammell's brother David: he moved out when he went to live in Earl's Court with some friends and a girlfriend, Rita (U, 37).
[5] In Firenze, Donald Cammell did the usual art student thing of studying the fabulous art in the Uffizi, the Pitti, and the Medici churches, etc. And he hung out with fellow artists, including Beat poet Harold Norse (U, 41). Norse described meeting Cammell looking like 'a medieval Florentine', 'a breathtaking youth'.
[6] Many of punk's leading lights came from the British art school scene: Fay Fife, the Rezillos and Jo Callis (the Human League) from Edinburgh; Budgie (the Banshees), OMD, Deaf School and Echo and the Bunnymen from Liverpool; the Mekons, Gang of Four, Scritti Politti and Soft Cell from Leeds; the Psychedelic Furs' Richard Butler from Epsom; Hazel O'Connor, the Selecter and the Specials from Coventry; Joe Strummer and Lene Lovich from Central, London; Glen Matlock, Lora Logic (X Ray Spex) from St Martin's School of Art; Adam Ant, Wire, Monochrome Set, and Albertine of the Slits from Hornsey.

Street, Chelsea (Cammell would be associated with West London often after this – Chelsea, Kensington, Earl's Court and Notting Hill).[7] A precocious talent from an early age, Cammell was already earning good money as a painter by the age of nineteen (£3,000/ $4,500 a year, Cammell said). As actress Barbara Steele put it, Cammell had the painter's lifestyle down pat (getting the right lifestyle was important to Cammell – and it's certainly a vital ingredient in his most famous work, *Performance*). When the lure and potential of painting began to wane for Cammell (he wasn't that keen on becoming a society painter), he moved into filmmaking (but he still continued to paint portraits into the 1970s [U, 59]).

A huge influence on his life, Donald Cammell's father Charles Cammell was an intellectual, an æsthete, a highly educated critic and poet. Cammell grew up in a bohemian, artistic atmosphere. Among the visitors to the Cammell household was the infamous arch magician, charlatan, pornographer and mountaineer, Aleister Crowley (Crowley was then living in a house near the Cammells in Devon).[8] Cammell's father had met Crowley in 1936. His book about Crowley was published in 1951: *Aleister Crowley: The Man: The Mage: The Poet;* it was out-sold by one of the standard texts on Crowley, by John Symonds. (Cammell senior and Crowley fell out during WW2). According to Charles Cammell, Crowley 'had no sense of humour, friendship or virtue of any kind, and was grossly sensual and unscrupulous'.[9]

Although Donald Cammell did not talk much about Aleister Crowley, he did joke about being dangled on the knee of the Beast himself (Crowley called himself the 'Great Beast' and the press dubbed him 'the wickedest man in the world'). Cammell's brother David reckoned that Cammell wasn't at all religious or a mystic: he was a realist. Crowley was simply a great character for Cammell, and Crowleyania was 'all a load of tosh' (B, 56). Cammell recalled his childhood house in 1971:

> I was brought up in a house where Magick was real. My old man, Charles...
> filled with magicians, metaphysicians, spiritualists and demons. I was
> conditioned by my father, by his books (that library...), by Aleister Crowley.

The Umlands have identified some Gnostic influences in Donald Cammell's cinema in their biography of Cammell – the Gnostic beliefs in the 'fall' into matter, for instance, the idea that the world and the flesh is corrupt, that the world was created by a demiurge – the Devil.

Certainly Gnostic and Manichean religious beliefs chime with Western

---
[7] He painted Princess Margaret's portrait, for instance.
[8] The Cammell family had moved out of London, like many others, to avoid the bombing.
[9] Quoted in U, 30.

magic at many points. It's classic dualism – good and evil, flesh and spirit, sin and redemption. On this basis, one could find Gnostic religious beliefs in numerous filmmakers, from Ingmar Bergman and Pier Paolo Pasolini to Jean-Luc Godard and Robert Bresson.

In Paris, Donald Cammell and his girlfriend Deborah Dixon led the bohemian, artistic lifestyle, mixing with folk like Amanda Lear (Salvador Dali's mistress and later a singer), Roman Polanski, Anita Pallenberg (they met in 1964),[10] 'Stash' Klossowski (Balthus's son, a painter), and Joseph Balsamo (who acted in Jean-Luc Godard's *Weeekend*). (Also in Paris, Cammell appeared in *La Collectionneuse* (1967), *un film de* Eric Rohmer).[11]

Paris was then as now one of the best places in the world to see movies; indeed, it may be *the* film capital of the Western world, even more than Los Angeles. Anita Pallenberg recalled that she and Donald Cammell loved films, and loved to talk about them. Cammell's partner Deborah Dixon said 'we went to the cinema a lot' (U, 61). Cammell adored movies, his first wife Maria Andipa recalled: 'we used to see every film that was playing. Donald loved movies' (U, 48).

After living in Paris in the late 1960s, Donald Cammell moved to Hollywood in 1969, where he remained for the rest of his life (he also moved to New York City for a while).[12]

Spain was a favourite place to visit for Donald Cammell; so was Morocco, and South France (he had a place in the 1960s near St Tropez); and he said he thought of Paris as home. But it was in Tinseltown that Cammell spent most of his later life (and where he died).

In Morocco, Donald Cammell and his girlfriend Myriam Gibril would visit Paul Bowles (a visit to Bowles in Tangiers was essential for any artist or writer going to North Africa). In the 1960s, Morocco was a popular destination for the Western intelligentsia and bohemians – John Paul Getty, Jr, William Burroughs, Brion Gysin, Brian Jones, Led Zeppelin, Christopher Gibbs, Robert Fraser, Comte Jean de Breteuil and many others visited the Maghreb.

The three essential books on Donald Cammell and *Performance* are: *Performance* by Mick Brown, *Performance* by Colin McCabe, and *Donald Cammell* by R. and S. Umland.

The Umlands' book is required reading on Donald Cammell, full of

---

[10] Anita Pallenberg said she'd met Donald Cammell through his girlfriend Deborah Dixon, because she'd been hanging out in Paris with a bunch of Americans (U, 66). At the time, Pallenberg was modelling.
[11] Eric Rohmer wanted representatives of the 'Sixties Generation' in his movie, according to Sally Shafto, hence the casting of Donald Cammell and other painters and critics (U, 63).
[12] That was when he was exploring abstract painting.

incredible detail and years of painstaking research.13 I'm not wholly convinced by their psychoanalyzing of Cammell's personality, though. It's an unusual approach to an artist (but not unknown). And you can bet that Cammell would have summat to say about it if he were still alive!

The TV documentary *Donald Cammell: The Ultimate Performance* (1998), produced by Kevin Macdonald, Chris Rodley and David Cammell, is fascinating viewing. It includes interviews with many of the key players in Donald Cammell's life and career, with contributions from Cammell. 14

L.A.

I can see the attraction that living in Los Angeles had for Donald Cammell. As I write this in a hotel on Sunset Boulevard, I can see the Hollywood Hills outside, the neons on Sunset Strip, the palm trees, the traffic cruising along the boulevard ceaselessly, etc. Yep, the weather's great (usually), the sun shines, living costs are cheap (or rent is), it's by the sea, and it's one of the centres for the global film industry. Yes, there are plenty of things to do, people to meet, parties or openings to go to, and all the rest of it. However, if you are *not* part of the entertainment industry (and, although L.A. is often dubbed a 'one industry town', there are plenty of other industries here), you are no closer to getting a movie made than if you lived in Buttfuck, Iowa.

Outside of the movie, TV and porn industries, La-La Land is just like anywhere. Oh, there are more helicopters circling overhead, more sirens wailing throughout the night, and more poverty and crazy folk than in many cities of the world, but it's just another place.

But the whole Southwest of America does have two terrific advantages over Britain: it is warm and it is cheap. Do you really want to go back to cold, rainy, dreary Britain after the Mediterranean climate and desert and palm trees of The Angels? L.A. is like Spain (*the* favourite overseas destination of the British), but they speak English! (Actually, L.A. seems more than half Mexican/ Hispanic to me, and Spanish is the norm).

RELATIONSHIPS.

Donald Cammell's many romantic relationships included Deborah Dixon, a fashion model, with whom he lived in Paris in the 1960s;15 actress Barbara Steele (when she was a painter at Chelsea art college) in the 1950s; singer Eartha Kitt; actress Jill Ireland; Anita Pallenberg, girlfriend of

---

13 However, some of the Umlands' terminology is a little bewildering: they call '69' the 'reciprocal genital-oral sexual position' (244). Eh?!
14 Donald Cammell is featured in other documentaries, including *Empire of the Censors* (1995) and *Hollywood UK* (1993).
15 They met in New York City, where Cammell had gone following the break-up of his marriage.

Brian Jones and Keith Richards and star of *Performance*; Michèle Breton (who also appeared in *Performance*, as Lucy); Myriam Gibril, a model and actress in the 1970s; Susan Bottomley (known in the Andy Warhol period as 'International Velvet' [U, 166]); actress Patti D'Arbanville; Cammell was linked by rumour to actresses Jacqueline Bisset and Faye Dunaway; he married Maria Andipa, a Greek actress (six years older than Cammell) in 1954, and had a son, Amadis Aeneas Antony Cammell;[16] his second marriage was to China Kong, the daughter of Marlon Brando's lover Anita Kong. Cammell had met Kong in 1974: he was 40, she was 14 (teenage women are recurring elements in the Cammellverse, including in *Performance*).[17] They were married in 1978.[18]

Through Deborah Dixon, Donald Cammell was introduced to Anita Pallenberg, Brian Jones and the Rolling Stones coterie. Dixon, a model from Texas, was an important influence on Cammell's life and work; friends said they made quite a formidable pair (they met in Gotham in November, 1959, and lived together through the 1960s).

In the late 1960s, Donald Cammell's circle included: the art dealer Robert Fraser, the Stones set (Brian Jones, Mick Jagger, Keith Richards, Anita Pallenberg and Marianne Faithfull), designer and antiquarian Christopher Gibbs, photographer Michael Cooper, the Ormsby-Gores, Kenneth Anger, Tara Browne, the Guinness heir, and Suna Portman. Many of these people were linked with *Performance*; others included Pallenberg's drug dealer, 'Spanish Tony' Sanchez and ex-criminal David Litvinoff.

DEATH AND DEPRESSION.

Donald Cammell committed suicide on April 24, 1996, aged 62, in his home in the Hollywood Hills.[19] He shot himself in the forehead and, as contemporary accounts (and the legend) have it, died slowly, over some forty minutes. His lover at the time, China Kong, told how Cammell seemed almost euphoric, and asked her to bring him a mirror, so he could observe his own death. She recalled how she was in another room, on the phone, and Cammell brought in some papers to her, which absolved her of any part in his suicide. Then she heard a gunshot. She said he wasn't in any

---

[16] Donald Cammell's relationship with his son Amadis was troubled: Cammell and Maria broke up during the pregnancy, and Cammell only saw his son once after the final meeting with Maria in 1961 (U, 52).
[17] Donald Cammell called Patricia Kong 'China' in homage to China Machado, a fashion model in the 1960s that Cammell had tried to seduce but failed (U, 60). According to an anonymous person quoted in the Umlands' book, 'no worldly, bohemian artist and intellectual like Donald would deign to have a girlfriend named "Patty"' (U, 173). Shit, what's wrong with the name Patty?!
[18] The liaison between Donald Cammell and the teenage Kong had made Marlon Brando furious – because Kong was the daughter of one of his good friends, Anita Loo. Brando threatened to have Cammell deported (from California), and also charged with legal action which might have included statutory rape (U, 172).
[19] Donald Cammell lived with China Kong at 9032, Crescent Drive, in the Hollywood Hills.

pain. (B4 he shot himself, Cammell gave Kong some documents that included his will (dated Dec 28, 1992),[20] a letter to the police in which he stated that he had shot himself, and a personal letter for China, absolving her from any involvement.)

Myriam Gibril said that Donald Cammell's depressions[21] became too much when they were dating. 'You can only listen to someone say they want to kill themselves so many times. You say, come on, let's move on. But it was no, I have to kill myself' (B, 44).

Apparently Donald Cammell had something of an obsession with guns (one acquaintance said Cammell often carried a gun in his bag); he was known to suffer from depression (Kenneth Anger remarked how Cammell seemed to have a kind of cosmic sadness, and many friends spoke of the darkness or melancholy at the heart of Cammell). In the later years, he called the dark side of his personality 'the uncensored Don';[22] he became depressed over the way that *Wild Side* had been taken over by the studio (Nu Image), that he was very poor, and that his wife, China, had started an affair with a younger man, John Ganem – ironically the guy that Cammell had hired to re-edit *Wild Side*[23] (China had co-written *Wild Side* with Cammell).[24] Cammell had been talking about suicide in the weeks before his death.[25]

> He could be this charming Donald, then all of a sudden sink into this dark, dark mood [said Myriam Gibril]. We were staying in New York and one day he told me he was going to go to the roof of the building and jump. (B, 44)

According to some reports, Donald Cammell had seriously contemplated suicide at least twice before 1996: in the August of 1995, when China Kong had left him, and in December, 1992 (the letter which Cammell gave to Kong in which he stated to the authorities that he had shot himself was dated Dec 28, 1992).

Donald Cammell's gun fetishism has been over-done by critics, who inevitably relate it to his suicide. Have you looked at any movie billboards

---

20 Some say his will was dated Dec 28, 1992.
21 Donald Cammell tried drugs (such as lithium) initially, it seems, to deal with his recurring depressions: by the late 1950s, he had experimented with most drugs.
22 The 'uncensored Don' would do crazy stuff, recalled Drew Hammond, 'like get up in the middle of a movie theatre and start doing a little dance, or he would sing opera in Italian' (B, 49).
23 Cammell's brother David stayed with him when he was depressed over China Kong's departure; David Cammell said that Cammell 'was certainly talking about suicide' (B, 50).
24 One reason Kong may have left Cammell was the same with Myriam Gibril – the sinister side of Cammell, the depressions where he would say nasty things (B, 49).
25 However, Kong insists that Donald Cammell didn't kill himself because he was depressed about *Wild Side* or his film career. Yes – it doesn't seem a sufficient reason for suicide (Cammell was a veteran of the film business, where failed movies are common).
Kenneth Anger said he had discussed 'the philosophy and morality of suicide' many times with Cammell, including with reference to Aleister Crowley's statements in *Liber LXXVII*, in which the Beast said: 'man has the right to live by his own law... to die when and how he will'.

and posters recently? You will see guys with guns everywhere: every fucking poster advertizing the latest action flick or thriller features a photo of the star with a friggin' gun! Drive down Sunset and there're pix of macho stars hefting guns all over.

And in movies themselves, guns are fetishized to an extraordinary degree: in every Western you've ever heard of or seen, in every action-adventure pic and blockbuster pic, in 1940s *film noirs*, in Hong Kong action pictures, in historical pictures from the Elizabethan era through Napoleonic Wars to the two World Wars, in the French New Wave pix, and in every thriller and murder mystery made since 1895.

And Donald Cammell is not the only film director fascinated by guns: John Milius, Paul Schrader,[26] Martin Scorsese, John Woo and Steven Spielberg[27] were others (and many in the Japanese animation industry, such as Mamoru Oshii, Katsuhiro Otomo and Kenji Kamiyama). Indeed, the 'movie brat' or 'New Hollywood' generation were well-known for their gun fetishism, and regularly went to fire guns at gun clubs and shooting ranges (such as at the Oak Tree Gun Club in L.A.'s Newhall Pass district).

---

[26] Paul Schrader's paranoia and gun fetishism are well-known – especially in the 1970s, the period when he was writing *Taxi Driver*.
[27] Steven Spielberg had a large collection of guns, something he kept quiet about, perhaps because possessing firearms was not in keeping with his media image (A. Yule: *Steven Spielberg*, Little, Brown, Boston, MA, 1996, 446).

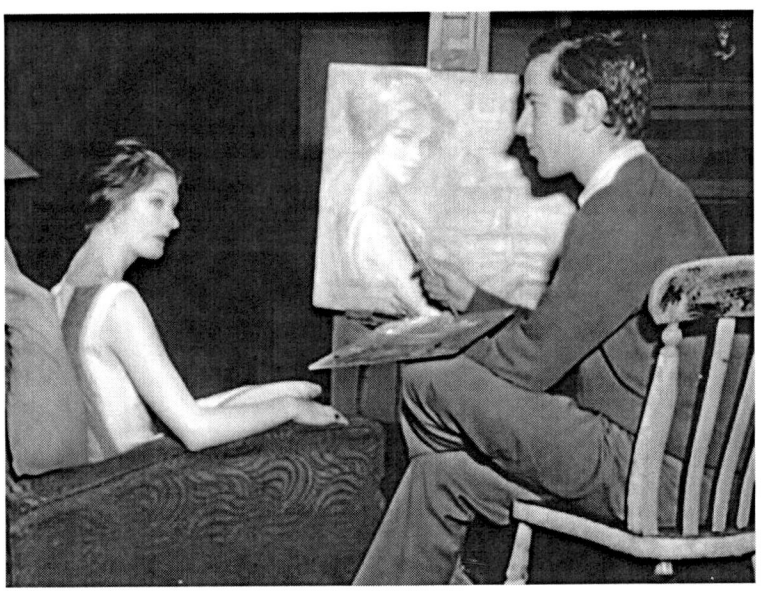

Donald Cammell in 1957, as a society painter

Maria Andipa and Amadis, Donald Cammell's wife and son

Donald Cammell and Deborah Dixon

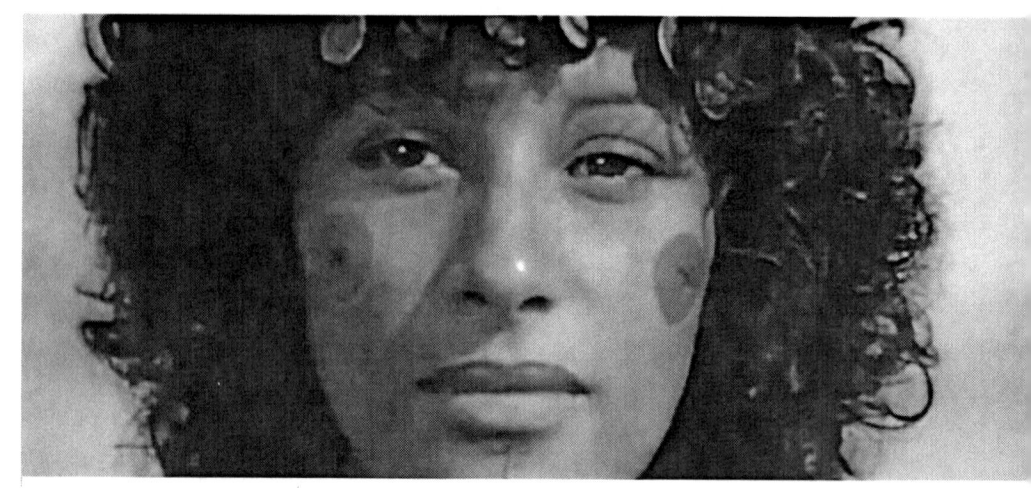

Myriam Gibril (in The Argument, 1971).

DONALD CAMMELL: FILM CAREER

As a writer and director, Donald Cammell's credits consist of a very few titles: he directed *Performance* (1970), *Demon Seed* (1977), a sci-fi chiller starring Julie Christie, *White of the Eye* (1987), a bizarre American thriller, *Wild Side* (1995), a kind of erotic thriller, and *The Argument* (1999). His scripts which were made into films include the above five movies, plus *Duffy* (Robert Parrish, 1968), *Tilt* (Rudy Durand, 1978)[28] and *R.P.M.* (Ian Sharp, 1997).

Otherwise, Donald Cammell's film career is a story of scripts that didn't get made, a series of setbacks, false starts, of possible then abandoned projects (but that's a familiar story with most filmmakers – every filmmaker has a drawer full of unmade projects).

So where does one put Donald Cammell as a filmmaker and screenwriter in the grand scheme of things? Well, as a British filmmaker, he's certainly not in the front rank, along with Alfred Hitchcock, David Lean, Charlie Chaplin or Michael Powell. But Cammell doesn't fit in with his contemporaries, either, with the Ridley Scotts, the Alan Parkers, the Hugh Hudsons and the Adrian Lynes of British or international cinema. Cammell is in a category of his own, I think, like Ken Russell or Derek Jarman, filmmakers who created their genres, their own rules, their own idiosyncratic ways of doing things.

♣

A number of aspects strike one immediately when considering the four feature films that Donald Cammell directed: (1) they all have contemporary settings (with *Demon Seed* in the some futuristic period); (2) three were set in North America, and made in America (and *Performance* would've ended up in Gotham if Cammell'd had his way); (3) they all feature sex and violence; (4) they were made with American money by American studios (Warners; MGM; Nu Image), except for *White of the Eye* (though the money was still American); and (5) they all have elements of thrillers and film noir (they can all be classed as thrillers).[29]

NIC ROEG.

Although *Performance* is usually seen as Nic Roeg's film (partly because of Roeg's subsequent success in cinem) – it does have Roeg's visual stamp on it, and his allusive, kinetic editing style – Donald Cammell's

---

28 Donald Cammell worked on 1978's *Tilt*, starring Brooke Shields, Charles Durning and Ken Marshall, as a writer.
29 In this respect, you could say that Donald Cammell's range as a filmmaker was rather limited, being only contemporary-set thrillers.

influence should not be under-estimated (for more on Nic Roeg, see the Appendix). Although Cammell's ventures into mainstream filmmaking did not perhaps fulfil his potential, his films are extraordinary. Certainly, as his subsequent movies show, his views and methods have been far stranger than Roeg's (and Roeg is classed as one of the more unusual film directors in British cinema from the 1970s onwards).

Donald Cammell resented the fact that Nic Roeg seemed to have benefitted much more from *Performance* than he did.[30] After all, Roeg went on to critical successes (if not box office hits) such as *Walkabout* (1971), *Don't Look Now* (1973), *The Man Who Fell To Earth* (1975), *Bad Timing* (1979), *Eureka* (1981), *Insignificance* (1985), *Castaway* (1986), and *The Witches* (1989). His later theatrically-released work includes *Cold Heaven* (1991), *Two Deaths* (1995) and *Puffball* (2007). TV work includes *Heart of Darkness* (1994), *Full Body Massage* (1995), *Samson and Delilah* (1996), and an episode of *The Young Indiana Jones Chronicles*.

Born Nicholas Jack Roeg on August 15, 1928 in London, Roeg has been married three times (Susan Stephen, 1957-77, actress Theresa Russell, 1982-early 2000s, and Harriet Harper, 2004-present). He has six children. Roeg, popular with critics in the 1970s (*Don't Look Now* and *The Man Who Fell To Earth* became, like *Performance*, cult films),[31] fell from critical favour in the late 1980s. I began to lose interest in Roeg's films, which seemed over-rated in the end (like Peter Greenaway's or Derek Jarman's movies), and to go over the same ground, and lacked inspiration. There was always a tendency in Roeg's works too for pretending to be high art, or self-consciously arty – you can see it in *Bad Timing* or *Castaway*. In short, Roeg is not Pier Paolo Pasolini or Walerian Borowczyk.

Sometimes it's simply the cameraman in Nic Roeg being self-consciously affected. There are shots in *Castaway*, for instance, of a boat from underwater, which can seem pointless. And *Bad Timing* is a misjudged exploration of erotic desire (and badly miscast, too, with Art Garfunkel trying to convince in a romantic, erotic role). It was territory which Donald Cammell explored better in *Wild Side* – and in *Performance* of course.

Meanwhile, interest in Donald Cammell remained at the cult level for most of his life; he was seen as a legendary figure, until interest in his life and work increased in the late 1990s. (The legendary status of Cammell is reminiscent of Terry Malick, who by the 2000s had only directed four

---

[30] Donald Cammell knew Nic Roeg prior to *Performance*, and asked him to shoot *Performance*; it was also Cammell who suggested that they direct the film together (because Roeg said he wanted to move into directing. At the time, he was gearing up for *Walkabout*, but elected to delay *Walkabout* in order to make *Performance*). The disagreements between Cammell and Roeg occurred during the editing of the film. But for the shooting, they had been very close, Roeg said.
[31] *The Man Who Fell To Earth* is a kind of follow-up to *Performance*, or at least displays its influence.

movies, yet was revered as a God-like genius by some.)

Donald Cammell, however, is still not a well-known name outside of cult film circles. People may have heard of *Performance*, and certainly of Mick Jagger, but they probably haven't seen it (how often is *Performance* screened on television or cable? Not often). As to Cammell's other movies, no.

On *Performance*, Nic Roeg (then 40) was the film industry professional (dressed in blazer and tie, which he continued to sport for the rest of his career), having been a cameraman on movies such as *Far From the Madding Crowd* (1967), *The Caretaker* (1963), *The Masque of the Red Death* (1964), *Fahrenheit 401* (François Truffaut, 1966), *A Funny Thing Happened On the Way To the Forum* (1966) and *Petulia* (1968),[32] while Donald Cammell (aged 34) was the novice writer-turned-director.[33] Cammell said it worked very well, having him work with the actors, and blocking the scene, then Roeg coming in to figure out how to shoot it.

❈

Donald Cammell does seem to have been one of those artists and filmmakers who appeared to scupper his projects deliberately, or unconsciously. There were times, for example, when Cammell could've capitalized on offers or opportunities, but seems to have created excuses or problems where none needed to exist.

Certainly, as a filmmaker, Donald Cammell did not fulfil his potential. It's impossible to estimate exactly what Cammell might have produced had he taken up every opportunity and followed them through to completion. He didn't wanna be a 'director for hire', I don't think (although he was something like that on *Demon Seed*), but he did have the talent and skills and imagination to create some startling movies.

But Donald Cammell was not your regular filmmaker. Plenty of filmmakers can be difficult, temperamental, mercurial, moody, and all the rest, but with the right production team and the right producers and the right project, they can flourish. (Besides, some film directors have prospered as hired hands – the really crafty veterans in the studio system in Hollywood, for instance, knew exactly how to adjust a movie project to suit themselves as well as making the studios happy. In the end, I guess Cammell didn't want to play that game, or operate like that).

---

[32] Nic Roeg's other work as DP includes second unit and uncredited work on *Doctor Zhivago*, *Judith*, *The Sundowners*, *Bhowani Junction*, *Lawrence of Arabia* and *Casino Royale*.
[33] It's common film industry practice to team up a first-time director with an experienced director of photography (and other heads of department). The classic instance is of course *Citizen Kane*.

DUFFY AND *THE TOUCHABLES*.

Donald Cammell's second script, *Duffy* (Robert Parrish, 1968), a heist comedy starring three Jameses (Coburn, Mason and Fox), had not been an entirely happy experience for Cammell; for his next film, he was determined to have control. His first script, *The Touchables* (Robert Freeman, 1968), was written with his brother David, about a rock star who's kidnapped by female fans. The film was released in 1968 by 20th Century Fox, and had been rewritten by Ian La Frenais. Cammell's brother David said that there was little of Donald Cammell in the final movie – director Freeman hadn't liked what Cammell had brought to the script (U, 71). 'Nothing of what Donald or I wrote remains in the finished film', David Cammell remarkd (ibid.).[34]

On *Duffy*, Donald Cammell had been fired after writing the script, and the producers and studio hired another writer;[35] it's not uncommon for writers to be hired then fired. Cammell was then re-hired, and ended up staying around for the whole shoot. It was here that Cammell formed a strong friendship with James Fox, who would play such a pivotal role in *Performance*. Originally, Clive Donner had been due to direct *Duffy*, but had left during preproduction. The shoot was also delayed, because of political unrest in the Middle East (the production moved to Spain, and began filming in August, 1967 [U, 68]).

As directed by Robert Parrish and produced by Martin Manulis for Columbia, *Duffy* was another of those films of the mid-to-late 1960s which tried to capitalize on the pop culture boom in Britain and failed (as films which try desperately hard to be hip and trendy often do). Donald Cammell dismissed *Duffy* as a fluffy piece:

> it's not a serious movie, more of a bon bon, very carefree. Not worth discussing. (*Video Watchdog*, 1996)

❈

Donald Cammell survived in the lean years by directing pop promos from time to time,[36] writing scripts, and living off development deals. He wrote many scripts, and auctioned them off; his partner China Kong collaborated on most of Cammell's scripts after *Demon Seed*.

Unfortunately, Donald Cammell wasn't able to capitalize on *Performance* (unlike Nic Roeg); Cammell did not, like other successful first-time

---

34 Linked to *The Touchables* was a script called *Privilege*, which Anita Pallenberg said she had worked on with Donald Cammell (U, 71). No relation to the 1967 movie *Privilege*, it also featured a rock star (partly inspired by Brian Jones).
35 Harry Joe Brown, Jnr co-wrote *Duffy*. The script, then titled *Avec Avec*, had been sold to Columbia in 1965 (U, 66).
36 Donald Cammell directed some music videos, primarily in the 1980s, including U2's 'Pride (In the Name of Love)', and The Hooters' 'All You Zombies'.

directors, get to make a much higher budget or higher profile film. He wasn't going to be a 'director for hire', but would only originate his own projects. Also, his films were interferred with by the studios (which has happened to the greatest filmmakers, such as Orson Welles): not only *Demon Seed*, but also *White of the Eye* and *Wild Side* (the latter was restored by Cammell's editor Frank Mazzola and China Kong, to Cammell's original intentions, and released in 1999. Mazzola used a workprint on video as a guide to the restored *Wild Side*).

Phenomenally talented, Donald Cammell refused to compromise: he decided, after *Demon Seed*, that he would only direct films from his own scripts. The bad experience of shooting *Demon Seed* had completely turned Cammell off the idea of working on other people's projects. MGM hadn't liked the film, and Cammell had been one of 100s of other filmmakers whose work was altered by a studio. Studio interference would dog Cammell to the end, when his last film, *Wild Side*, was taken away from him and re-edited by the studio, Nu Image.

Deborah Dixon remarked that Donald Cammell had a way of alienating people who could help him: although he was uncompromising and determined, it worked against him in the end (U, 256). China Kong commented that Cammell 'was unique. He was what he was and he didn't change that, or apologize for it'.[37] Myriam Gibril remarked: 'People sell out every day of their life, they compromise. Donald wouldn't compromise' (B, 43).

Vartkes Cholakian said in 2003 that Donald Cammell

> always had this 'fuck you' attitude. It was like he was always wanting to be fucking around with somebody. Everything always had to be on his terms. He always had to be the dominant one. (U, 205)

---

[37] C. Kong in B. Pendreigh, *Scotland On Sunday*, June, 2000.

SOME INFLUENCES AND ASSOCIATIONS

Donald Cammell's favourite films (from a 1990s list) included *Naked* (1993), *The Conformist* (1970),[38] *Nouvelle Vague* (1990), *Throne of Blood* (1957), *The Discreet Charm of the Bourgeoisie* (1972), *Ivan the Terrible* (1946), *Tokyo Decadence Topaz* (1991), *Blade Runner* (1982) and *Dr Strangelove* (1963).[39] Those are mostly movies that regularly feature among top ten lists of fans, critics, and filmmakers. And the filmmakers are revered too: Akira Kurosawa, Stanley Kubrick, Bernardo Bertolucci, Sergei Eisenstein and Luis Buñuel. *Nouvelle Vague* is an odd choice for a Jean-Luc Godard picture – one might've expected to see, in the light of Donald Cammell's cinema, *Pierrot le Fou* or *Breathless* or maybe *Weekend* (all of which, and others, have many links to *Performance*). *Tokyo Decadence Topaz* (1991), written and directed by Ryu Murakami, is an unusual choice, but the subject matter – sadomasochism among rich clientele in the life of a Tokyo hooker – certainly chimes with some of Cammell's interests. As for *Naked*, a dreadful, dull, social realist, Mike Leigh picture about a repellent, alienated, British, outsider figure, it simply cannot be placed alongside (or anywhere near) movies like *Dr Strangelove* or *The Throne of Blood* or *The Conformist*.

Jean Cocteau was a big influence on Donald Cammell, as he has been on so many filmmakers (Francis Coppola, Jean-Luc Godard, Kenneth Anger, Orson Welles, Tim Burton, Ken Russell, and the Disney Studios), in particular his *Orpheus* movies. Cammell's brother David recalled that Cammell had been fascinated by Cocteau's *Blood of a Poet* (1930). Maybe it's significant that a man puts a gun to his head and shoots himself in *Le Sang d'un Poète* – and not once, but *twice* (suicide as romantic martyrdom).

And of coure the Cocteau World has many elements which would appeal to Donald Cammell: the mirrors, of course, the eyes (closed, with paper eyes attached to the eyelids), the dressing-up, the camp humour, the Surrealist juxtapositions, the pretentious disquisitions on art and poetry, and the stylized, self-conscious cutting.

Key among Donald Cammell's literary influences were William Burroughs, Georges Bataille, Jean Genet, Jorge Luis Borges and Antonin

---

[38] *The Conformist* was a key film for the 'New Hollywood' generation. Filmmakers such as Francis Coppola, Paul Schrader, Joel Schumacher, Sydney Pollack and Martin Scorsese cited it as an influence. Cinematographers such as John Bailey and Michael Chapman admired Vittorio Storaro's work on that film immensely. Bailey (DP on *American Gigolo, Ordinary People, Cat People* and *The Big Chill*, among others) said (in 1984) that he'd seen *The Conformist* probably 25 times. For director Adrian Lyne, *The Conformist* 'is probably the best single film ever made. It's the perfect blend of visual and performance' (in J. Gallagher, 1989, 167).

[39] Like many others, Cammell admired *Diary of a Country Priest* (Robert Bresson, 1951); the priest Cammell identified as a poet-martyr (U, 87). Bresson is regularly cited as a big influence by many filmmakers, including Jean-Luc Godard, Andrei Tarkovsky and Paul Schrader.

Artaud. All of those writers are of the *avant garde*, European and mid-20th century ilk, the kind of authors regularly exalted by the intelligentsia.

Burroughs, Bataille, Genet, Borges *et al* foreground magic, mystery, sex, violence, avant gardeism, modernism, etc. Many writers, artists and filmmakers have been influenced by them – J.G. Ballard, Pier Paolo Pasolini, Jean-Luc Godard, Kenneth Anger, David Cronenberg, etc. They are, it has to be said, a distinctly *masculine* bunch of writers, who exalt a masculinist point-of-view throughout their works. That applies to their treatment of women, homosexuality, and politics. Their ancestors are Friedrich Nietzsche, J.-K. Huysmans, Arthur Rimbaud and the Marquis de Sade.

The fiction of William Burroughs (1914-97),[40] needless to say, hasn't led to many film adaptions, for obvious reasons (budget being one of the chief ones,[41] as well as the explicitly violent and sexual content). When *The Naked Lunch* appeared from First Independent (in 1991), based on Burroughs' cult 1959 novel, it was much more a commentary on Burroughs' fiction and an exploration of the writer and Burroughs' works' cultural impact than a direct adaption.[42]

William Burroughs was a favourite author with many rock acts, including David Bowie, Patti Smith and Frank Zappa (and bands such as Steely Dan and Soft Machine took their names from Burroughs). The cut-up technique, developed by Brion Gysin and Bill Burroughs, influenced some of Britain's foremost writers (including J.G. Ballard and Michael Moorcock), as well as Donald Cammell and Nic Roeg.[43] Certainly the cut-up process influenced the rapid montage style of editing in *Performance*, and Nic Roeg's subsequent movies (it's one of the self-conscious literary modes of High Modernism – you can see it in T.S. Eliot's *The Waste Land*, for instance, a poem that many have cited, including Burroughs and Federico Fellini, as being very cinematic).

Jorge Luis Borges (1899-1986) is alluded to a number of times in *Performance* – Rosebloom reads Borges's *Ficciones*, Turner reads from Borges' *El Sur* (*The South*), and Borges of course appears in the bullet-view shot at the end. (Borges is also quoted in *Demon Seed* – from *The Wall and the Books*). Borges' story *The Enigma of Edward Fitzgerald* is cited (British poet Fitzgerald had translated Omar Khayyám's *Rubaiyat* – providing another link with Persia). The Borgesian themes – of the double, of mirrors,

---
40 William Burroughs is referred to in *Performance* by Pherber.
41 Director David Cronenberg remarked that if you made *The Naked Lunch* in total, it would be a $400-500 million movie.
42 David Cronenberg and co. delivered a mixture of themes and motifs filmed in Canada from not only *The Naked Lunch* but other Burroughs books, combined with aspects of Burroughs' life (much of it stemming from Ted Morgan's biography of Burroughs, *Literary Outlaw*). The result was not wholly satisfying, to say the least.
43 Nic Roeg had seen *The Cut-Up*, Burroughs' and Anthony Bird's film,

of labyrinths and works-within-works, of reality and dream, of time – are all central to Cammell's cinema.

Antonin Artaud (1896-1948) is a favourite of the European cognoscenti, a classic *avant garde* artist who appeared in films such as *The Passion of Joan of Arc* and *Napoleon.* Best known now for his 'Theatre of Cruelty' theories, Artaud had a troubled life: addicted to opium, he had a number of nervous breakdowns, and spent a lot time in clinics in Europe, undergoing electric shock therapy and insulin therapy. It was Anita Pallenberg who introduced Artaud into the *Performance* screenplay.

DONALD CAMMELL AND JEAN-LUC GODARD

It would be possible to discourse at length on the affinities between *Performance* and the 1960s films of Jean-Luc Godard. Donald Cammell, like many young filmmakers of the time, certainly knew Godard's pictures (he had met one of Godard's cinematographers, Raoul Coutard, in Paris). The links between *Performance* and Godard's *One Plus One* are numerous, of course: the Rolling Stones, London, music, counter-culture, etc. But there are many other similarities between *Performance* and Godard's pictures: to mention just a few:

(1) Editing: Jean-Luc Godard's editing style is one of the most distinctive and influential aspects of his cinema, and it certainly influenced Donald Cammell and Frank Mazzola The jump cuts, the discontinuities, the flashbacks and flashforwards, it's all there in Godard's cinema. (And also the very long take – though Godard's camerawork is far more sophisticated than Cammell's).

(2) Violence. Both filmmakers have an obsessive fascination with violence (and violent people, such as gangsters). In both filmmakers' work, violence threatens to erupt suddenly.

(3) Suicide. Both Cammell's and Godard's characters toy with suicide (Jean-Paul Belmondo kills himself in *Pierrot le Fou*, for instance; when she saw the film, Godard's sister thought Godard was seriously thinking about suicide. Cammell quoted *Pierrot le Fou* in *White of the Eye*).

(4) Gun fetishism. There are guns in every Jean-Luc Godard movie, as in Donald Cammell's (but Godard loved to stage gun battles in a deliberately silly and unrealistic fashion).

(5) Design. The interior of 81, Powis Square house in *Performance* is a Moroccan hashish den style, but there are also plenty of Godardian, Pop Art touches, such as the posters and murals on the walls. *Performance* also cuts to close-ups of some of these images, exactly as in a Godard movie.

(6) Sex. Both filmmakers loved to put sex in their films, and neither could be bothered to film a regular, missionary-position sex scene to save their lives. There has to something outside of the norm going on – either anal sex, or S/M, or summat else (and in a Godard film, characters *talk* about having sex far more than they actually *have* sex. So very *French*).

(7) Women. Both Donald Cammell and God-Art loved to put beautiful actresses in their movies (two at the same time in bed if possible for Cammell!) – and Godard, partly because he made many more films than Cammell, featured many more hypnotic women than Cammell, including Anne Wiazemsky, Myriem Roussel, Juliette Binoche, Bridget Bardot, and the Goddess of the French New Wave, Anna Karina.[44] Both filmmakers liked very young women (Cammell dated China Kong when she was 14 and he was 40!), and both liked to put 'em nude on screen.

(8) Unconventional narrative structures: Jean-Luc Godard simply could not produce a straight-ahead story; he said he had tried to, but his films somehow never came out like that. Donald Cammell quoted Godard's famous saying that a movie has to have a beginning, a middle and an ending, but not necessarily in that order.

(9) Genre. By the same token, neither Donald Cammell nor Godard could deliver a straight genre picture; they simply *had* to subvert the genre.

(10) Music. Both Cammell and Godard employ pop music and found music, and use music in unusual ways. By the 1990s, the maestro had proved to be among the most distinctive filmmakers in his use of music. *No one* handles music the way Godard does. (For instance, Godard will happily cut off music instantly, or introduce it halfway through a motif. Take the opening of *Performance*: had Godard mixed the sound for it, he wouldn't have *faded* the two or three pieces of music in and out, he would simply have *cut* abruptly from silence to full volume).

(11) Dressing up: Jean-Luc Godard's movies are full of people dressing and undressing (and also taking baths, or preening themselves in mirrors); *Performance* makes dressing up and play-acting and taking on roles a major ingredient.

(12) Mirrors – like the human face, mirrors are tailor-made for cinema. They are a central motif in many filmmakers' work (Orson Welles, Jean Cocteau, Ingmar Bergman and Ken Russell come to mind). I can't think of

---

[44] Michélle Breton appeared in Jean-Luc Godard's *Weekend* and *Performance*.

another filmmaker who's included more scenes of actors looking at themselves in mirrors than Godard: if an actor's at a loss what to do in a scene, the director will tell them to fool around with the mirror. Meanwhile, in *Performance*, Donald Cammell self-consciously made mirrors a primary symbol.

Other films by Jean-Luc Godard of this period, apart from *Weekend*, *Pierrot le Fou* and *One Plus One*, have affinities with *Performance*: *La Chinoise*, for example, in which a bunch of Parisian students plot global revolution and the assassination of a political figure (the Cammellian correspondences run from the decor, with the walls painted red, to the painter character Serge Kirilov who holds a gun to his head). Or *Made In U.S.A.*, which features Anna Karina as a female private eye (the sort of role one wishes that a film producer had given to Anita Pallenberg *circa* 1967-68. It's such a pity that Pallenberg didn't have a whole movie built around her; *Performance* is the closest we get, I guess).

After enumerating the affinities between Donald Cammell and Jean-Luc Godard's films, however, there are just as many differences between the two filmmakers:

(1) Godard was *far* more politicized than Cammell, and put far more political discussion into his films;

(2) Godard drew on literature, philosophy and painting more than Cammell;

(3) Godard wasn't interested in drugs much at all, as Cammell was (though the tobacco consumption in all of Godard's films is phenomenal – actors had to be able to dangle a cigarette permanently from their lips);

(4) magicke, Aleister Crowley and Kenneth Anger didn't possess the same significance for Godard as they did for Cammell; however, French *avant garde* artists like Antonin Artaud, Georges Bataille, Jean Cocteau and André Breton chime with both directors;

(5) Godard was intensely passionate about cinema, while Cammell often wasn't that bothered about it (Cammell would never have made *Histoire(s) du Cinéma*, Godard's eight-part essay/ documentary/ love letter to the movies of the 1990s);

(6) Donald Cammell loved North America much more than Jean-Luc Godard, who maintained the most passionate love-hate relationship with it in the entire history of cinema (Godard visited the States a lot, but he would never settle there, like Cammell did);

(7) and finally Godard was far, far more productive than Cammell. In the 1960s alone, Godard helmed an astonishing amount of films, all of which were very high quality, and some were masterpieces. Godard couldn't

have stood being as inactive as Cammell appeared to be: he wouldn't be able to sit around in the Hollywood Hills month after month without getting a movie made. Godard is simply a total natural when it comes to making films, and he has, extraordinarily, produced at least one film every single year, from the late 1950s onwards (not counting short films, TV films, commercials, etc).

CINEMA IN BRITAIN AND NORTH AMERICA IN THE 1960s

Although Donald Cammell went to Hollywoodland to live and work, he did not became one of many British filmmakers who wound up making films within the North American film industry, filmmakers who seldom returned to Britain to make films with 'British' subjects.

Many British directors in the 1970s-1990s went to Hollywood, or made movies that looked to the North American market: Nic Roeg, John Boorman, Stephen Frears, Alan Parker, Richard Attenborough, Bill Forsyth, Julien Temple, Neil Jordan, Terry Jones, Richard Marquand, Mike Figgis and John Schlesinger. Donald Cammell was kind of part of that group, but not really: Cammell didn't 'belong' to any group.

These filmmakers may have started out making small-scale films centred on 'British' culture, but eventually they moved towards Hollywood. The Land of the Free meant bigger budgets, bigger stars and a larger audience. Only a few British film directors remained largely loyal to 'British' subject matter and 'British' cinema: Ken Russell, Ken Loach, David Leland, Peter Watkins, Terence Davies, Lindsay Anderson and Mike Leigh.

Filmmakers such as Alan Parker, Hugh Hudson, Adrian Lyne, Roland Joffé, Ridley Scott and Tony Scott had no qualms about going 'commercial', about aiming for big budget feature filmmaking in the North American style. Parker, Lyne, Hudson and the Scotts were the film directors that did much of their groundwork in helming TV commercials. Whether they directed their films in Britain (such as *Alien* (Ridley Scott) or *The Wall* (Alan Parker)), the product was distinctly North American. Virtually all of Tony Scott's works as director are American, in either feel, theme, location, finance or actors. One wouldn't think that the 1986 film *Top Gun* that Scott helmed, the gung-ho, fighter pilot, all-American, action movie, was directed by a Brit. Nor for that matter other Scott-directed flicks, such as

Beverly Hills Cop II, Days of Thunder, True Romance, The Hunger or *The Last Boy Scout*.

Adrian Lyne (*9 1/2 Weeks, Jacob's Ladder, Foxes*) was the director who most embodied the British Film Director Gone (to) Hollywood scenario of the 1980s and 1990s. With his black bomber jacket and blond, wavy hair, Lyne was the epitome of the arrogant, laid-back, sexist advertising director made good. Lyne directed the fatally overrated *Fatal Attraction*, the *Fame*-style dance flick *Flashdance*, and the equally vacuous and flashy *Indecent Proposal*.

Alan Parker embraced the North American feature industry wholeheartedly (*Birdy, Fame, Angel Heart, Mississippi Burning, Evita*). Stephen Frears, one of the many British directors that eventually went Stateside, said that Parker's solution to 'international' filmmaking created a 'real mess... his solution is absolutely rubbish'.[45]

Early on in their careers, it might have been possible to differentiate between the films directed by Neil Jordan, Stephen Frears, John Boorman and Alan Parker, but later on they merged into an Anglo-American conglomerate.

One could perhaps pick out a Nic Roeg film, for its distinctive multi-faceted editing, and Ridley Scott's use of the camera (long lenses, *film noir* lighting, smoke), but most major British filmmakers (Joffé, Hudson, Attenborough, Parker) did not have distinctive qualities (or even themes). A Donald Cammell movie, meanwhile, has a number of distinctive elements, one of the key being rapid, allusive, poetic montage.

The traffic between Britain and North America was largely one way. When British directors did return to Britain to make films about British subjects, the influence of Hollywood was prominent.[46] A number of North American filmmakers, including Stanley Kubrick, Terry Gilliam, Richard Lester, Ray Harryhausen, Jim Henson and Joseph Losey, came to Britain in the 1960s and 1970s and made films there. Some of them stayed permanently (Henson, Lester, Harryhausen, Kubrick, Losey, Gilliam), and were embraced by the British film world (it was good for prestige and PR to have an American genius, such as Kubrick, or an American eccentric, such as Gilliam or Lester, on the doorstep).

Stanley Kubrick is the intriguing case. After making standard Hollywood fare such as *The Killing* and *Spartacus*, Kubrick moved to England and spent most of his life near St Albans, Hertfordshire, North of

---

[45] In J. Hacker, 177.
[46] Donald Cammell, went the other way: he moved to North America, and three out of his four features were not only made in America, they were set in North America. Not only set in America, they featured American characters and American themes (in *Demon Seed*, though, Julie Christie plays the character British). As with Ken Russell, all of Cammell's movies were paid for and made by American companies.

the capital. Kubrick's maverick stance[47] meant his production team conducted Hollywood-style filmmaking from England. Though films such as *Dr Strangelove, Lolita, 2001: A Space Odyssey, Barry Lyndon, The Shining* and *Full Metal Jacket* were made in British studios, they were all part of Hollywood cinema of the 1960s-80s. Even when the subject matter seemed to be 'British' (such as in *Barry Lyndon* or *A Clockwork Orange*), Kubrick's cinematic approach was distinctly North American and Hollywood (though Hollywood absorbed European cinema stylistically, as with Martin Scorsese, Francis Coppola and Robert Altman). And of course, the finance was always North American (from Warners).

Then there are the mavericks and oddballs, such as Ken Russell, Derek Jarman, Sally Potter, Terence Davies and Peter Greenaway, who embraced (European) art cinema techniques while somehow remaining quintessentially 'British'. Jarman and Russell, in particular, have seen themselves as carrying aloft the flame of 'British' high culture (Russell in classical music, Jarman in painting). Their films exalt a particular kind of 'Britishness', that is rooted in 'British' high art. Nostalgic but also anarchic; poetic and stylized. For Russell, Jarman, Greenaway *et al*, cinema is regarded as a popular but also 'high' artform, which embraces (and is seen as a part of) dance, classical music, literature, poetry, painting and theatre. But the mavericks are neither 'British' nor North American but *avant garde*, 'international' or 'European'. Often these filmmakers pursued uneven, maverick film careers.

Donald Cammell doesn't fit in with that group, either: you wouldn't class Cammell as either an 'American' filmmaker, or a 'British' filmmaker, or even an 'international' or 'European' filmmaker (Jean-Luc Godard is very much, he insists, not a *European* filmmaker, but a *French* filmmaker).

And Ken Russell is a genre all of his own, a simply incredible, all-round filmmaker who between 1965 and 1977 was on fire with cinematic output. And while Donald Cammell is an astonishing talent, he sadly doesn't have the body of work that might have put him up there with the greats. As with Orson Welles or Carl-Theodore Dreyer in the latter part of his film career, you just wish that Cammell had been able to produce *more* films (in particular, a historical movie, such as his story about Lord Nelson, or something that *wasn't* a thriller set in the contemporary world).

It was much more common for North American directors to visit Britain on a short-term basis, to use the studios and technical facilities: in the 1970s and after, these included Steven Spielberg, James Cameron and George Lucas. The influx of North American money into Britain reached its

---

47 Some would also add his fear of flying.

height in 1968, with £31.3 million ($46m) being spent by the North American subsidiaries (*Performance* was one film which benefited from this North American money). Another reason for so much American investment in European film production was subsidies. A U.S. movie might receive subsidies from 3 countries – Italy, France and Britain, say.

In 1967, 90% of film production money spent in Britain was North American[48] (and it's still the case: movie franchises which seem 'British' – such as *James Bond* and *Harry Potter* – are of course funded by the U.S. dollar). Other financial issues, such as the exchange rate, play a role.[49]

In the Sixties, the main North American film companies operating in Blighty were Disney, Universal, Columbia, 20th Century Fox, Warner Brothers, Paramount, MGM and United Artists. In other words, of the major North American studios. The money pouring into Britain from the North American studios often resulted in self-indulgent and expensive productions. Of the 12 films that Universal made between 1967 and 1969 in Britain (Universal spent around £30 million/ $45m), most were financial disasters: *Work Is a Four-letter Word, Charlie Bubbles, A Countess From Hong Kong, Three Into Two Won't Go* and *Can Hieronymous Merkin Ever Forget Humppe and Find True Happiness?* This despite the directorial talents of Charlie Chaplin, Peter Hall, Karel Reisz, Jack Gold and Joseph Losey. There were also expensive (largely) British flops (such as the musicals *Star!, Dr Doolittle* and *Goodbye Mr Chips*).

The number of North American directors working in Britain at that time was huge: Stanley Kubrick, Roger Corman, Richard Brooks, Billy Wilder, Richard Fleischer, Sidney Lumet, William Friedkin, Delbert Mann, Stanley Donen, George Stevens, Otto Preminger, Fred Zinnemann, James Ivory, Sam Peckinpah, John Huston, Anthony Mann, William Wyler, Joseph Losey and Richard Lester.

There were also many other international directors working in the United Kingdom: Roman Polanski (*Repulsion* [1965], *Cul-de-Sac* [1966]) and *Macbeth* [1971]), François Truffaut[50] (*Fahrenheit 451* [1966], a version of Ray Bradbury's sci-fi story with Oskar Werner and Julie Christie, future star of *Demon Seed*), Jean-Luc Godard (*Sympathy For the Devil/ One Plus One*, 1968), his movie featuring the Rolling Stones, and Michelangelo Antonioni (*Blow Up*, 1967). It took an outsider, Antonioni, to explore, from a detached but interested (and highly idiosyncratic) perspective, the cultural landscape of Britain in the late 1960s, producing one of the great 'British'

---

48 R. Murphy, 1992, 258.
49 And American companies had money frozen in Europe after WWII.
50 François Truffaut didn't enjoy shooting in Britain, though, and *Fahrenheit 451* turned out to be the only film Truffaut made outside France.

films of the era (with, of course, North American money – from MGM). [51]

Roman Polanski had come to London with his producing partner, Gerard Brach.[52] He chose to direct a horror film first (*Repulsion*) because, as he put it, he needed to make some bread, and thought a horror flick would attract money. His second feature, *Cul-de-Sac*, was shot on location at Lindisfarne Castle. It was a disastrous shoot, Polanski recalled, because the cast and crew were isolated from everything at the castle, and got sick of each other. Polanski liked shooting in Britain enough, though, to direct another film there – a stunning interpretation of *Macbeth*, shot on many British locations including Lindisfarne Castle, Bamburgh Castle and North Wales.

The king of indie cinema, Roger Corman, produced his famous Edgar Allan Poe adaptions of the early-mid Sixties in Britain, taking advantage of a clause in the studio contracts that enabled him to use anything in the scene dock. So, shooting *The Masque of the Red Death* at Shepperton Studios, Corman was able to pull out the big, lavish sets that had been constructed for a historical drama that had recently shot there (probably *Becket*, Corman said). Thus, *The Masque of the Death* had some of the highest production values for a Corman film (which were famously produced on minuscule budgets and very short schedules). Cinematographer on the Poe movie, Nic Roeg, remembered that Corman was very inspired by the large sets, and was thinking up ideas for new films which would incorporate them (Corman is an endlessly inventive filmmaker – the film director as producer and showman, always with a keen eye on exploiting resources and budgets to the maximum).

While the 'kitchen sink' films, the new TV documentaries, and the 'angry young men' plays brought a new, socially conscious approach to filmmaking in the 1960s, the view of Britain as a series of out-moded cultural clichés and social stereotypes was still very much at large, in movies like *My Fair Lady, Oliver, Chitty Chitty Bang Bang,* the *Carry Ons* and *Mary Poppins,* the Britain of country houses and castles, tea shops, aristocrats, Cockneys, and the images of London which always included the Houses of Parliament and Big Ben, Tower Bridge, Buckingham Palace and Trafalgar Square. (And a'course, those clichés are still being trotted out 30, 40, 50 years later!).

Performance partakes of some of those cultural stereotypes, but it also self-consciously avoids them: it is a London film and a British film which

---

[51] On some viewings, *Blow Up* can appear a classic, on others it exhibits all of the hallmarks of the European art movie: slow (very slow), pretentious, silly, banal, over-self-conscious, sexist, with a smug self-aborption and the conviction that it is so very, very 'intellectual' or 'important'.

[52] Roman Polanski had met Donald Cammell in Paris, in around 1962-63. Cammell had offered Polanski a script called *Just a Jacknife Has Macheath, Dear*, about Jack the Ripper. But Polanski declined making it (U, 65).

doesn't pander to the stereotypes found in the typical North American movie made about or set in Britain.

The North American studios pulled out Britain nearly all at the same time, 'leaving the British film industry flat on its back'.[53] And it hasn't ever really recovered. The end of the 1960s was the end of one of the great periods in British cinema (previous ones included 1933-37 and 1944-49). The end of each of these highpoints saw a series of expensive costume dramas and blockbusters (in the late 1960s, it was costly pictures such as *The Battle of Britain, Half a Sixpence, Goodbye My Chips, Alfred the Great, Far From the Madding Crowd* and *Ryan's Daughter*, which may have hastened the departure of the Hollywood studios). The global recession, plus over-spending, were key reasons. According to Tino Balio (in *Hollywood in the Age of Television*), the 1969-71 recession and its aftermath nearly caused Hollywood to collapse.[54]

Fewer and fewer British films were made in Britain during the Seventies and early Eighties: in 1971 there were 98 British films registered; in 1976, there were just 70; by 1981, there were only 36 (a very low number, considering the size and former significance of Britain as a filmmaking centre).[55] In the Eighties, an average of 46 films were made per year, with a revival in production during 1983-85, and a slump between 1988 and 1991. Private investment in films was on the up. The resurgence of North American studios' activity in Britain was due partly to the strong dollar, 100% first-year capital allowances, and the increase in worldwide audiences and markets.[56] However, North American investment in British film production declined during the 1980s, from $220m (£142 million) in 1984, to $125 million (£67.8m) in 1993.[57]

---

53 K. Richards, 1997, 167.
54 T. Balio, 1990, 259f.
55 L. Wood, 1983, 143.
56 *BFI Handbook*, 1993, 18.
57 *BFI Handbook*, 1994, 25.

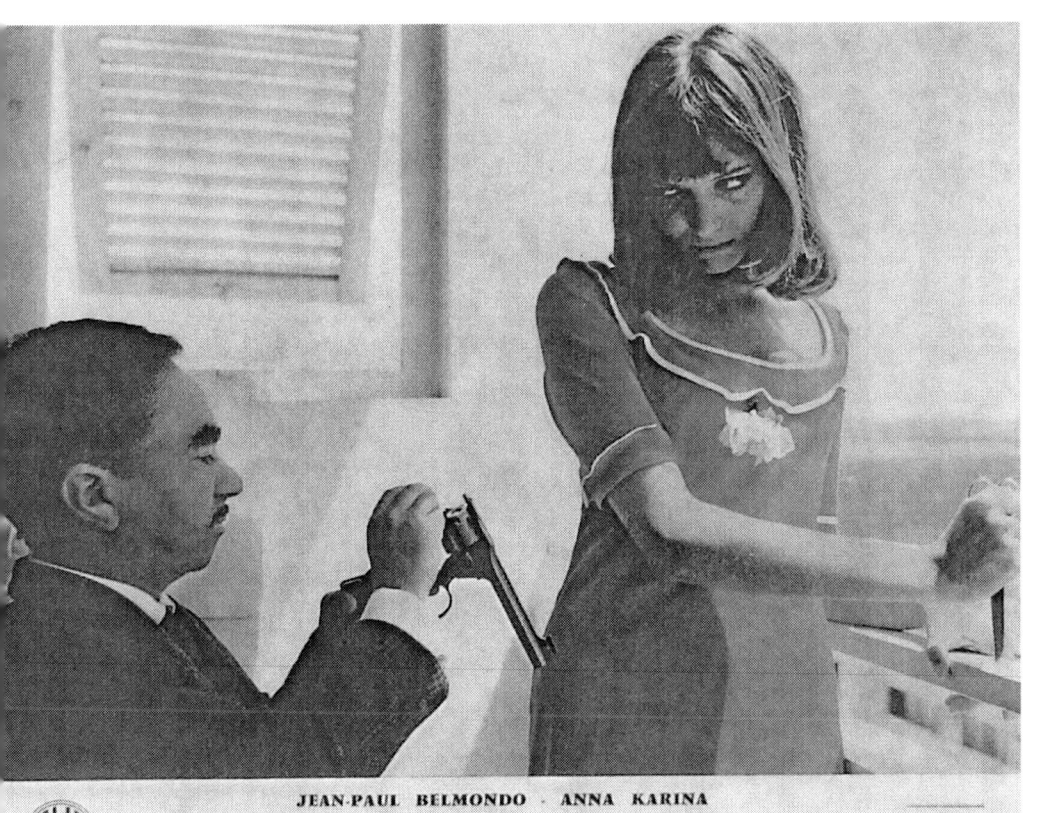

This page and the following pages: some influences on Donald Cammell, and some of the figures he's been associated with.

Jean-Luc Godard (above).

Jean-Luc Godard directing Contempt
with Brigitte Bardot

Kenneth Anger, above. With Donald Cammell, below.

A cult film if ever there was one: an image
from Scorpio Rising (Kenneth Anger, 1963)

Images from the films of Kenneth Anger (including Spring Equinox, Inauguration of the Pleasure Dome, and Lucifer Rising).

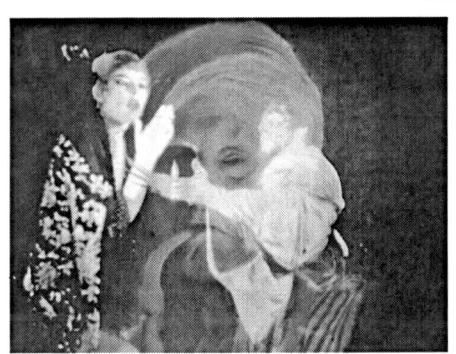

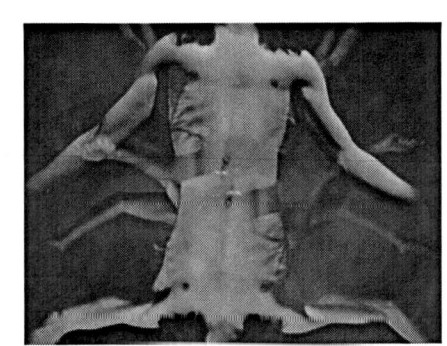

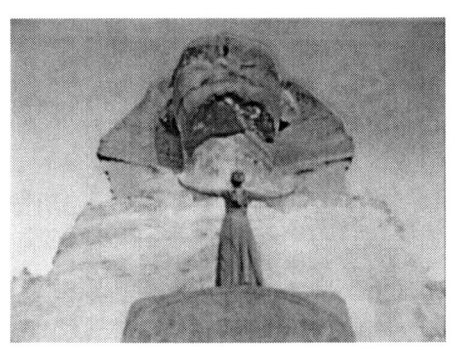

Scenes from Lucifer Rising (Kenneth Anger, 1981), featuring Donald Cammell as Osiris and his girlfriend Myriam Gibril as Isis.

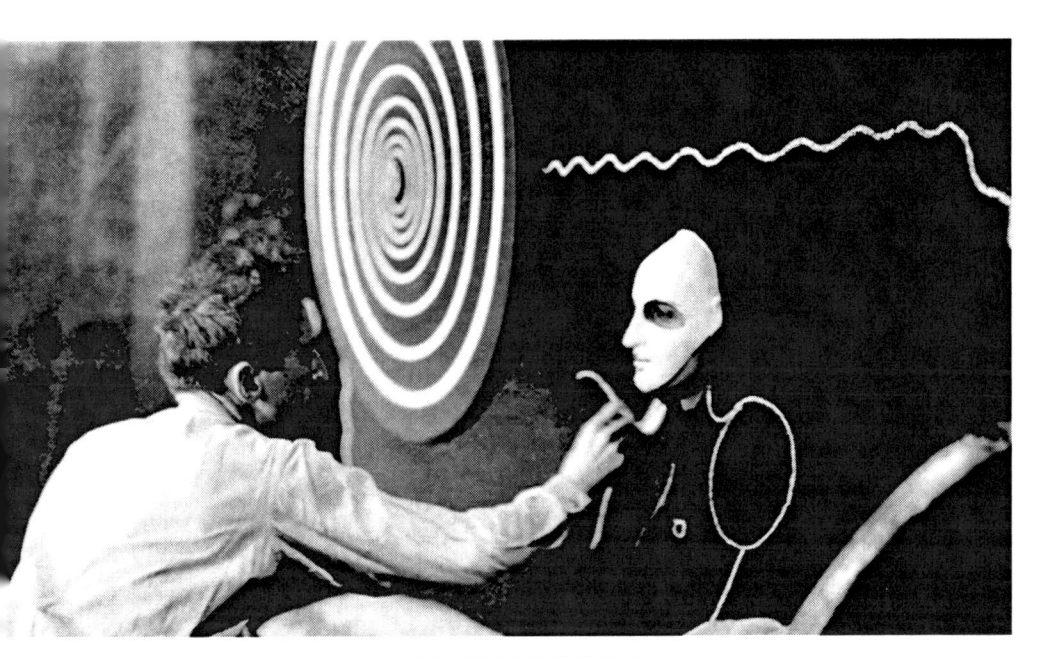

A key influence on Donald Cammell's cinema: the incomparable Jean Cocteau.

From 1930's Blood of a Poet (above).

From one of Cocteau's Orpheus films (below)

Susannah York in a PR shot for Duffy

Aleister Crowley

One of the icons of the Sixties, the cover of Sgt Pepper's (above), which features everyone's favourite crazy British magician, Aleister Crowley (below).

Some literary/ artistic influences on Donald Cammell.
Clockwise from top left: Antonin Artaud. Géorges Bataille. Jean Genet. Jorge Luis Borges and William Burroughs.

PERFORMANCE

Vice. And Versa.

Mick Jagger — And Mick Jagger
James Fox — And James Fox

See them all in a film about fantasy. And reality. Vice. And versa.

performance.

James Fox / Mick Jagger / Anita Pallenberg / Michele Breton

2

PERFORMANCE
☆

PERFORMANCE: INTRO

Performance (1970), co-directed by Donald Cammell and Nic Roeg (b. 1928), written by Cammell, starred James Fox, Anita Pallenberg and Mick Jagger; Roeg also acted as DP. Among the supporting cast were Michèle Breton, Ann Sidney, Johnny Shannon and Anthony Valentine. 'A perverted love affair between Homo Sapiens and Lady Violence', was how Jagger and Cammell described *Performance* in their telegram to the president of Warners, Ted Ashley.[1]

Performance was produced for Warner Brothers by David Cammell (Cammell's brother) and Sandy Lieberson; Richard Burge was assistant director; Jack Nitzsche composed the music, and Randy Newman was music director; Robert Lynn was production manager; Mike Molloy operated the camera; it was edited by Anthony Gibbs, Brian Smedley-Aston and Frank Mazzola; John Clark and Peter Young were art director and set dresser; Christopher Gibbs[2] was design consultant (for Turner's house); Deborah Dixon was costume consultant; the costumes were by Emma Porteous and Billy Jay; make-up was by Paul Rabiger and Linda De Vetta; Helen Lennox did the hair; Anabelle Davis-Goff was the script girl; sound recordist was Ron Barron; and the sound editor was Alan Patillo.

One of the producers on *Performance* was Sandy Lieberson, then an agent with Creative Management Agency.[3] Lieberson had asked Donald Cammell to come up with a movie that would put together Mick Jagger and Marlon Brando (U, 98). The script, called *The Liars*, was given to Brando, but, as Lieberson explained, Brando was too busy with other projects, so it was reworked for James Fox (B, 22). Lieberson[4] would go on to produce films with David Puttnam for their Goodtimes Enterprises, including movies such as *The Final Programme, Mahler, Lisztomania, Stardust, That'll Be the Day, The Rolling Stones Rock and Roll Circus, Bugsy Malone* and *Glastonbury Fayre*.

Performance was a tale of a gangster on the run who goes to ground in the basement of a reclusive pop star's mansion in London's Powis Square, Notting Hill. Like 1966's *Blow-Up* (directed by Michelangelo Antonioni, written by Antonioni, Tonino Guerra and Edward Bond), *Performance* has become a classic portrayal of late 1960s (British) pop culture, and of the London scene.

Performance is recognized as one of the Great British Gangster Movies,

---

1 Cammell and Jagger also employed the lingo later taken up for one of the posters for *Performance* in the letter: 'fantasy. And reality. Vice. And versa', etc.
2 Christopher Gibbs was an antiques dealer in Chelsea whose social circle included the photographer Cecil Beaton.
3 Donald Cammell had met Lieberson during the making of *Duffy*.
4 Lieberson later worked at Goldcrest, and Fox.

yes.

And one of the Best British Films of the 1960s, yes.

And one of the Finest British Pop Music Films, yes.

But it is also one of the Great London Movies. *Performance* is a piece which captures the feeling, the texture, the atmosphere of being in London (and living in London) so skilfully, so poetically. 5

❈

The scenario in *The Performers* script (one of the early versions of *Performance*), has the gangster Corelli hiding from the authorities in an Earl's Court house where rock star Haskin lives. Simon, the 17 year-old girl also in the house, is a young Pherber; meanwhile, the groupie Pherber shows up and has an affair with Corelli.

The Performers also introduced new characters, some of 'em seemingly drawing inspiration from real people in the Chelsea boho set, such as Lindy Sue-Dixon, another jet-setting hippy, 'a dirty little Jew (in a quite literal sense), a stupendous musician, and Turner's best friend' (as Donald Cammell put it), and a Robert Fraser-influenced art dealer called Alexander. These characters show up in the last act of *The Performers* treatment, and they would've altered the dynamics of the people at the rock star's home considerably.6

The first 30 minutes of *Performance* depicts a stereotypical gangster narrative, complete with Cockernee gangster slingo ('slag', 'grass', 'guv', and so on), as James Fox's Chas Devlin goes about his business as a bully boy (a 'performer') working for the firm (the 'firm' being the Brit term for a criminal gang).

So far so (relatively) ordinary; when James Fox's Chas Devlin heads for Notting Hill, the film changes dramatically, diving into underground and counter-culture, drug culture, and pop culture, and becomes far more interesting. There are evocations of drug trips, smoking pot, and magic mushrooms, portrayed in the cinematic style of the time (disorientating jump cuts, crash zooms, bizarre montages, and other 'psychedelic' effects). *International Times* (September, 1970) dubbed *Performance* 'probably the heaviest movie ever made – a kaleidoscope of transvestitism, sado-masochism, deaths, bad fly, trips, etc'.

During Chas Devlin's hallucinations, Turner becomes the gangster boss Harry Flowers, in the 'Memo To Turner' sequence, clad in a suit, with slicked-back hair, crooning to his mob and encouraging them to strip off, to 'turn on, tune in, drop out'.

---

5 Other Great London Movies include: *The Ladykillers, The Elephant Man, Great Expectations* (1947), *The Day the Earth Caught Fire, Blow-Up* and *London*.
6 There was also a drug bust at the end of *The Performers*.

By the end of *Performance*, Chas Devlin has literally swallowed the psychedelic, demonic, counter-culture lifestyle whole (he's eaten the mushrooms, and apparently shot 'himself', shown in an extraordinary point-of-view shot of a bullet hurtling down his throat or through his brain). Turner has swapped places with Chas, or Turner and Chas have become one (the ending is deliberately ambiguous); the fusion of the rock star and criminal persona is shown driving off in the gangster firm's boss's white Rolls-Royce;[7] a point-of-view shot of Turner/ Chas approaching the Roller has Flowers saying 'hello, Chas'; it's followed by a shot of the car moving off (with Mick Jagger, not James Fox, glancing out of the window).

❂

Performance has created many legends: such as: it had no name stars (other than Mick Jagger), it was shot on location, seemingly far from the controlling gaze of the American studio and was made by some in the crew who were (practically) beginners. That's not true at all, of course: Hollywood studios have numerous ways of keeping control of movies on location. Besides, filming in central London, one of the biggest cities on the planet, wasn't exactly far from studios and offices and producers! If Warners had really wanted to control every day of shooting on *Performance*, they could've done. And the crew were professionals.

Although some might have been surprised that North American studio Warners[8] would have backed a film such as *Performance*, it's worth recalling that the Hollywood studios made huge investments in the British film industry in the 1960s, and also came to Britain to produce American movies. But when Hollywood teetered on the brink of collapse, in the late 1960s and early 1970s, when it suffered enormous losses, the American studios pulled out of Britain *en masse*, and the British film industry has never really recovered.

Performance got the green light during the 'Swinging London' era, a time of optimism and energy. If it wasn't so rare to have a bunch of filmmakers seemingly let loose far away from the studio, unsupervised, with money to spend, so they could experiment and get up to whatever they liked, it would be much rarer in the years afterwards. In the blockbuster era (1975 to the present), the suits would be far less likely to let filmmakers get away with doing whatever they wanted (although it would still happen from time to time: *Heaven's Gate, Apocalypse Now* and *1941* being some examples from the late 1970s).

Performance may have been part of Warners' attempt to capitalize on

---

[7] The Roller might also be a reference to Jean Cocteau's *Orpheus*, which has the figure of Death riding in a Rolls-Royce.
[8] Warners were hoping for 'a Stones version of *A Hard Day's Night*', according to an early memo.

the emerging youth market, which movies such as *Easy Rider* and the Beatles movies had done. Without big stars or big construction crews, *Performance* might have been seen by a Hollywood studio as a relatively small investment. A film that could be produced for a low budget, in other words (well, not *that* low – it was between $1.5 and 2.08 million), but which could recoup its costs. After all, it had plenty of the elements that were tailor-made to appeal to a young audience: rock music, rock stars, gangsters, sex, violence and drugs.

❀

When people discuss *Performance* and the legends that've grown up around it, they're not really talking about a movie, or even about Donald Cammell or Mick Jagger: focussing on *Performance*, is really an excuse to discuss what they did in the 1960s. I have to admit it's the same for me: everybody loves talking about the Sixties, whether you were there or not (or can remember or not). Too much acid? Too many dr*uuuu*gs? Who cares: it's fun talking about the Sixties, and important, too: so much changed in contemporary Western culture in that decade.

PERFORMANCE RUMOURS

Performance is one of those movies which over the years has generated a few rumours, like *Apocalypse Now, The Exorcist, The Wizard of Oz* or *Citizen Kane.*

• One of the rumours is that filming *Performance* made such a negative impression on James Fox that he abandoned acting, only returning years later.[9] Fox later remarked: 'people think *Performance* blew my mind... my mind was blown long before that.'

• Another rumour had a possessive, jealous[10] Keith Richards[11] hanging around outside the film set, waiting to pick up Anita Pallenberg and take her home.[12]

• One rumour had Warners closing down the film after they'd seen the

---

[9] James Fox did admit that it took a while to get the experience of making *Performance* out of his system. It was partly to do with the death of his father, and smoking DMT. Terence Stamp also left acting around the same time (1969), going to India and only returning in 1978, for the *Superman* movies.
[10] Keith Richards wasn't happy about Anita Pallenberg being an actress: he offered her £20,000 ($30,000) not to appear in *Barbarella*.
[11] Keith Richards thought that Cammell was 'a wanker' (according to Stones aide Tom Keylock).
[12] Keith Richards, according to Ian Stewart, wouldn't go into the Lowndes Square house, but would send messages in to Anita Pallenberg from his car outside. Richards certainly wasn't keen on Pallenberg being involved with the production, and was reluctant to contribute to the film's music.

bath scene rushes. Nope: Hollywood studios don't look at rushes, they haven't got time (and some filmmakers don't, either).

- Another rumour was that art dealer Robert Fraser did something bad which got him banned from the set (Anita Pallenberg was staying in Fraser's apartment at 23, Mount Street, London during filming).
- Another rumour was that the actors were really having sex. Oh fuck, how many times have we heard that one?
- Another rumour was that the cast and crew really were taking drugs during filming.[13] Well, wow, *really*? Actors and filmmakers taking drugs! Never! Surely not! Oh, who gives a FUCK?
- *Performance* was another of those movies which *looked* like some of it was improvised. But it wasn't.[14] No. It was all worked out beforehand, according to Mick Jagger:

> it was shot just like a regular movie. You had to know what you were doing before you got on camera, it wasn't just a question of improvising for hours and hours. (1975, 169)

- My own favourite rumour surrounding *Performance* was when Donald Cammell was too out of it to direct and Satan himself showed up (looking, curiously, like Aleister Crowley in a red fright wig).

Unfortunately, the Devil misunderstood the nature of pretence in acting and filmmaking in a Hollywood movie, and during the cocaine orgy scene he banged half the cast and crew until they were raw, and fried the other half into pillars of sulphur. The house in Belgravia exploded, and Satan transferred the rest of the shoot to the seventh level of Hell.

♣

Performance has become known as a legendary, out-of-control movie during production. But the shoot is nothing alongside *Cleopatra, Heaven's Gate, Intolerance* and *Apocalypse Now*, for instance. (The scale and craziness of those movies is *truly* legendary! But *Performance* is three people in a house in London!).

Performance is one of those movies which people *want* to believe in the legends, they *want* to have myths sprouting up around the movie. One of these is that Warner Brothers sat on the movie for two years. Well, yes, *Performance* was shot in 1968, but that meant it would normally have been released in 1969 (possibly in Spring, 1969).[15] So *Performance* was a

---

13 Bearing in mind some of the collaborators on *Performance*, such as Anita Pallenberg and Mick Jagger, it was predictable that rumours would fly about possible drug-taking. But that was why you cast Jagger in the first place, because of the marketing potential.
14 Unusually, much of the film was shot in sequence.
15 *Performance* wasn't held up that long, really – it's normal for Hollywood studios to release films sometimes a year or more after they are ready. There are numerous reasons (and not all are tied to money). In the event, *Performance* would probably not have been ready to release before Spring, 1969 at the earliest.

year late, but no more, and maybe not even that. The New York premiere was on July 30, 1970, and the London premiere was in January, 1971.[16]

It's like saying that *Apocalypse Now* is a 1976 movie because it started shooting in 1976, or maybe *Apocalypse Now* was really a 1968 movie, because that was when John Milius and George Lucas were developing it. Nah. *Apocalypse Now* is a 1979 movie because that's when it was officially released (and, besides, the filmmakers were working on it right up until the last minute. Also, many movies are *really* put together during the *editing* and the *post-production*, and *not* when they are shot. And *Performance*, with its elliptical, poetic editing style, is certainly a movie that was largely constructed in the editing room).

There are famous cases of Hollywood studios sitting on films. Harry Cohn was furious with Orson Welles for making *The Lady From Shanghai* the way he did (and for cutting his star Rita Hayworth's hair short, and dyeing it platinum blonde). So Cohn delayed the film's release from 1946 to 1948.

MAKING *PERFORMANCE*

Performance wasn't an experimental movie shot on Super-8 film stock by two or three friends over a weekend. It might have *looked* a bit like that at times. But no: it was an American-backed drama shot on 35mm stock with a crew that included camera teams, sound teams, costume departments, hair departments, make-up departments, art departments, electricians, drivers, caterers, script girls, runners, production managers, ADs, producers, etc.

✤

According to Donald Cammell, getting the key people on board *Performance* was relatively easy: Cammell said that each person he asked said yes: Sandy Lieberson to produce, Mick Jagger and James Fox to star, and Nic Roeg to co-direct (in R.J. Libin, 10). This is something that's easy to overlook, but the casting process and hiring the right people can be a nightmare. It must've made Cammell (and the rest of the team) feel good that they had two of the main actors secured, Fox and Jagger.

---

[16] It was a charity event in Leicester Square, at the Warner Cinema, attended by many celebrities. Mick Jagger wanted the proceeds to go to Release, a charity run by Caroline Coon for legal cases of young people charged with drug possession. *Time Out* devoted an issue to the movie.

If both had declined, there were other actors who could've done it, of course, but very few would have fitted the 1970 movie as well as James Fox and Mick Jagger. Who would you cast, from that period, to play Turner, for instance? Very difficult (remembering too that the actor would be required to sing and dance, and do nude scenes – those requirements alone would inevitably mean many actors would pass – just as they would now as then). It might have held the movie up for months finding the right actors.

And 99% of film directors, too, would not have been happy sharing directing duties with someone else, let alone a novice director (some directors would never even consider it for a moment). So Nic Roeg's contribution – not only dealing with the technical side of filmmaking – was essential.[17]

✤

Performance began principal photography on July 29, 1968,[18] and ended on October 11, 1968. The initial budget for *Performance* was £1,300,000 ($2.08 million).[19] According to Philip Norman, the initial budget for *Performance* was $1.1 million for an 11 week schedule (2012, 299), with $100,000 for Mick Jagger (plus 7.5% of the gross. I think Norman must mean 1.1 million in GB pounds). Others say the shoot was twelve weeks, because it went over-schedule by 8 or 9 days, at a cost of $150,000 (B, 207). Re-shoots took place in the following days (U, 105). Sandy Lieberson reckoned the final cost was $1.5 million. The rough cut of *Performance* was ready by February, 1969, and was shown to the suits at Warners in Burbank.

Donald Cammell walked off the set once or twice, according to some, and lost his temper[20] a number of times (including yelling at Mick Jagger).[21] Anita Pallenberg said in 2004 that Cammell 'was a very difficult director to work with', and for a first time director acted 'very much like a prima donna' (U, 104).

✺

LOCATIONS.

Performance was made mainly in London (and in West London in

---

[17] Sandy Lieberson said that Donald Cammell felt a little unsure about his ability to direct a movie (he was 34 when *Performance* was filmed in 1968), and welcomed having someone working alongside him who could deal with the technical aspects of filmmaking.
[18] Mick Brown said it was July 22, 1968, beginning with the countryside scene of the Rolls-Royce car at Effingham Junction.
[19] Some critics have suggested that $400,000 was the agreed budget, for an 11 week schedule (J. Smith, 2010, 46). But that's too low. Sandy Lieberson said the budget was £1.1m, and it was finalized in L.A.
[20] Anita Pallenberg remembered that it was Donald Cammell who lost his temper most during the shooting of *Performance*, and that he (and Nic Roeg) would act like prima donnas, yelling and slamming doors (while 'the actors were like little lambs' [B, 198]).
[21] There were big arguments between Jagger and Cammell, according to Jagger – because Jagger thought that Cammell didn't quite know what he was doing.

particular). The London locales[22] of *Performance* are wonderfully crummy, evoking the hard, masculine London that's still as gritty and grey as it was in Dickensian movies (and still is today in many parts). Powis Square, for instance, has been cleaned up since 1968, and like similar areas of London has been turned into a bourgeois, residential area with high rents. But plenty of other areas of London still look today as scuzzy and bohemian as the ones in the movie.

❂

The interiors of Turner's house were filmed at 93,[23] Lowndes Square in Belgravia (thus much of *Performance* was filmed in Belgravia, a far more upmarket location than Notting Hill);[24] the exterior was 25, Powis Square, W11 (Notting Hill, standing in for 81, Powis Square); the basement and garden scenes of Powis Square were filmed in an empty house at 25, Hyde Park Gate (again, a more upmarket locale than Notting Hill), rented for the movie; the mews where the chauffeur is tortured was Queen's Gate Mews (also in West London); standing in for Paddington station was Kensington Olympia station (the buffet); the Latin Quarter club in Wardour Street stood in for the 'Hayloft Club'; the Thomas a'Beckett pub in Old Kent Road was used (including for the telephone scene between Tony Farrell and Chas); Joey Maddocks' betting shop was 469, Fulham Road (now a hairdresser's); Harry Flowers' office was shot in Mayfair, at 115, Mount Street (now an art gallery), for the exterior. In Wardour Street in the West End the production used a Chinese restaurant for the Flowers' office scenes. The scene in Harry Flowers' bedroom were shot in Kensington, at the Royal Garden Hotel. The pub was the *Black Swan* at Effingham Junction in Surrey.

❂

RE-SHOOTS.

Among the sequences that Donald Cammell wanted to re-shoot was the love scene between Chas Devlin and Lucy, in order to draw attention to 'the genuine moment of tenderness and compassion between these two that is the whole point of the scene'. (Cammell added the scene where Pherber injects herself with heroin, saying that it's B12 vitamin. 'I thought I was being really cool and nobody knew about it,' Anita Pallenberg recalled).

It's a pity that David Cammell, Nic Roeg, Donald Cammell and the team weren't able to re-shoot some of the scenes; as the editing process continued, the editing team discovered that parts of the film would be improved with some re-shooting. That's normal during editing, and some

---

22 Location scout for *Performance* was producer David Cammell.
23 According to Mick Brown, it was 15, Lowndes Square.
24 Once an illegal gambling club, and owned by Lenny Plugge. Also, Lowndes Square wasn't far from Mick Jagger's home in Cheyne Walk.

filmmakers, most famously Woody Allen, have a re-shoot clause put into their contract (Allen has famously re-shot movies almost entirely, a very rare privilege – as in the case of *September* (1987)).

Re-shoots can be relatively expensive – bringing back the major talent, for instance – but it's often only for one or two days. Clearly, Warner Brothers decided they wanted to be rid of *Performance*,[25] a troublesome project for them, and weren't eager to put any more money into it than the bare essentials to get it completed (again, that's very common).

It's a pity, because a few judicious re-shoots can really lift a movie, punching up scenes which aren't quite complete, or making the narrative clearer at particular points. In the case of the Chas-Lucy lovemaking, for instance, you can see that the editors have inserted looped lines over shots which show the back of actors' heads (there are quite a few parts of *Performance* which are patched up with off-screen dialogue. But that happens on 100s of movies).

❈

Elements that were dropped from the script (from the two scripts of *Performance*) included: Chas Devlin's assistant Mojo; more of Mrs Gibbs (the cleaner/ cook);[26] the sequential narrative of Chas doing his frighteners job; more characters arriving at the house; and perhaps the biggest ingredient, a drug bust (clearly based on the famous Redlands police raid involving some of the Rolling Stones coven – there's a jokey reference to it with the Mars Bars on the doorstep of Powis Square).

A drug bust would have been an intriguing element in *Performance*, but it would have diluted the claustrophobic, hothouse atmosphere of the Powis Square scenes. It would also have introduced the law and the establishment again, which had already been achieved in the courtroom scenes[27] (though the cops and the detectives would likely have been portrayed as corrupt – certainly Anita Pallenberg and Keith Richards thought so, when they were set up and raided by the law throughout the Seventies).

❈

David Litvinoff was billed as an adviser on *Performance*, particularly on the criminal elements. Litvinoff was friends with the Krays[28] (whom Donald

---

25 *Performance* was not a big, expensive picture that everybody – the front office, the investors, the studio heads – would be clamouring to have released (so they could recoup). However, Warners did want the movie out as soon as possible.
26 Probably named after design consultant Christopher Gibbs. There is also Anthony Gibbs, the film editor.
27 And in that feeble scene with the bobby on the beat who attempts to accost one of Joey's guys fleeing from Chas's place.
28 When *Performance* was being written, the Krays were arrested (in May, 1968), on charges of murder. As if life was imitating art, there was a lengthy (and costly) trial of the Krays in London.

Cammell never met),[29] and ensured that the script was accurate in its depiction of the criminal underworld. The scene where the chauffeur has his head shaved was based on a true story, which Litvinoff had been involved in (according to legend, Litvinoff wound up tied to the railings outside his house, hanging upside-down). Litvinoff committed suicide with sleeping pills at Christopher Gibbs' house. Another advisor on the underworld aspects of *Performance* was Tommy Gibbons, who owned the Thomas a'Beckett pub in the Old Kent Road (where James Fox trained), and that led Cammell to Johnny Shannon, who was cast as Harry Flowers.

✪

The script was not always adhered to in the second half of *Performance*; Anita Pallenberg recalls how James Fox would show up every day, having learned the script, but they wouldn't follow the script. But the second half of *Performance* isn't a free-for-all total improvization. Oh, no. If you look at it closely, from the point-of-view of dramatic development and narrative structure, it's pretty neatly worked out, right down to the multi-level ending.

But it can *appear* like improvization or a free-wheeling kind of narrative (that's one of the marks of really good art, that it can appear as if it's just happened). There is plenty of spontaneity on view, of course, but the filmmakers have already established a clear set of guidelines and modes of behaviour which the actors are working within.

ANITA PALLENBERG AS PHERBER

Anita Pallenberg's (b. Apl 6, 1944) Pherber[30] is a playful, erotic Ariel, aiding Turner's exploration of altered states of consciousness, dressing Chas Devlin up as a woman and feeding him magic mushrooms. Pherber has a wicked, teasing attitude towards Chas, whom she sees through immediately (and both she and Turner play along with Chas from the outset).

Anita Pallenberg's Pherber sports shoulder-length, blonde hair, a groovy wardrobe (she first appears in an enormous fur coat,[31] and runs

---

[29] Harry Flowers may have been inspired by Ronnie Kray (U, 102). Jimmy Evans, another East End criminal, was cited by Donald Cammell as an influence on the characterization of Chas.
[30] In *The Liars* script, Pherber, an odd name, was called Pilar and Phoebe.
[31] In her first encounter with Chas, Pherber teases him by lying on the bed with her legs open under the fur coat. Forget the continuity error here – suddenly Pherber's legs are bare; she was wearing tracksuit pants before (*Performance* is full of such continuity filips).

through a lavish array of costumes),[32] such as gauzy, white dresses, tight, pink pants and a white, frilly top (when she's straddling Chas, tending his wounds), a close-fitting, white dress, a purple silk dress, a slinky, black dress, and when she's photographing Chas for the passport photo, she's wearing a purple pants suit with gold, stacked heels. It helps too that Pallenberg is gorgeous to look at, and has a fabulous body (and she plays many scenes topless or partially nude).

Donald Cammell described Pherber (in *The Liars* version of *Performance*) as:

> very direct, spontaneous, pithy, funny, rather arrogant, ironic more by accident than design, and at the same time elliptical and evasive when it comes to any question about herself – sort of automatically secretive' (B, 174)

For Donald Cammell, Pherber is someone who likes to manipulate and control people, yet who also feels the need for being controlled herself, something that Turner can no longer provide, but which Chas offers.

We should remember that the three principal actors in *Performance* were young: Anita Pallenberg was 24, Mick Jagger was 25 and James Fox was 29 at the time of filming.[33]

If you look at *Performance*, you can appreciate just how good Anita Pallenberg is. And the more you see *Performance*, the more you recognize that Pallenberg is simply sensational. Her fee was $37,500 (what a bargain! – especially when you consider the 100s of movie stars paid millions for performances which bore you after 15 seconds).

You only have to think of other models-turned-actors who might have been cast primarily for their looks, to see how much Anita Pallenberg achieved. Let's not name names, but there are many actresses who are cast principally for their attractive appearance who can't act. Actually, it was Tuesday Weld who was first chosen for the part (but apparently broke her shoulder when Donald Cammell's girlfriend, Deborah Dixon, attempted to help with Weld's back trouble). Marianne Faithfull had been initially announced as starring opposite Mick Jagger, but she left the film when she became pregnant.[34] Mia Farrow has also been considered (for the role of

---

[32] So few film critics ever mention hair, make-up and costumes in their crrriticism of movies. But they are so important – and in this movie, which celebrates the counter-culture and hippy fashions of the late Sixties, the hair, make-up and costumes had to be as spot-on as a costume drama set in Napoleonic or Elizabethan times. So although the DP Nic Roeg and editors Gibbs, Smedly-Aston and Mazzola (among other technicians) should be praised, so should Emma Porteous and Billy Jay (wardrobe); Paul Rabiger and Linda De Vetta (make-up); and Helen Lennox (hair).

[33] So it's ironic that James Fox's Chas was the one being manipulated by Pherber and Turner, even tho' he was older.

[34] Anita Pallenberg had become pregnant before the movie was due to start, but she had an abortion (according to Philip Norman, so it wouldn't jeopardize her acting in the movie [1984, 310]). It wasn't a great way to go into filming the movie.

Lucy).35

Anita Pallenberg recalled (in 2004) that Donald Cammell had come to her and begged her to do the part, but she had resisted:

> They had already started shooting by then and Donald came to me and he really wanted me to do it, insisted that I do it. I was very involved in my relationship with Keith by then, and he didn't want me to do it, he didn't like Donald. I had been trying to get pregnant so it meant that part of my life would be put on hold. I went into the picture pretty cold right from the start. (U, 103)

You have to acknowledge that *Performance* would be far less of a movie if Anita Pallenberg wasn't in it, and wasn't one of the inspirations behind it. The character of Pherber is clearly based on her, so even if she hadn't appeared in the movie, her influence would still be vital. 36

And, let's not forget, Anita Pallenberg was also instrumental in writing the script for *Performance*: Pallenberg recalled that she, Donald Cammell and Cammell's girlfriend Deborah Dixon had worked on the screenplay on the beach in the South of France: 'we wrote it sitting on the beach in St Tropez,' Pallenberg said in 2004 (U, 99).

For Anita Pallenberg, filming *Performance* wasn't a non-stop party of drugs N sex N rock N roll. *Nah!* It was regular filmmaking. Which means, as anybody who's ever been involved in filming knows, a *lot* of waiting around:

> *Performance* was about what was going on at the time – the kind of attitudes; relaxed, cool, groovy. The *ménage à trois*, the dressing up. But what I remember most is just sitting around for hours and hours waiting for Nic Roeg. It was the most tedious thing I've ever done. (B, 162) 37

Towards the end of *Performance*, Pherber crashes out, maybe from the drugs, or maybe she's exhausted herself, or maybe the filmmakers decided they wanted to concentrate on other characters. So after Pherber has made love with Lucy, she falls asleep, and is asleep in quite a few scenes. But you miss Pherber when she's not around, because she's such a primal force in the movie.

---

35 Mia Farrow couldn't make it when she broke her ankle. Farrow, an actress with her own idiosyncratic style and look (as well as famous liaisons – Frank Sinatra, André Previn), would've added another layer of glamour and real-life fame to the movie.
36 Donald Cammell agreed that Pallenberg was one of the key influences on the film in an interview.
37 Of course, having already been on some film sets, Pallenberg should've known there would be a lotta waiting around! She recalled: 'I was getting stoned most every day, because of the boredom and tedium. Nic Roeg would take about seven hours to set up a shot, so I'd get stoned basically' (B, 224-5).

JAMES FOX AS CHAS DEVLIN

Watching *Performance* again, I was struck by just how incredibly *good* James Fox is. (Born in May 19, 1939 in London, he was 29 at the time of filming). All three principals deliver sensational performances in *Performance* – Fox, Mick Jagger and Anita Pallenberg. But in many ways, this is Fox's movie: he is absolutely superb in both aspects of Chas Devlin, first as the narcissistic, racist, sexist, working class,[38] tough gangster, with just the right amount of sarcasm and menace (and he looks the part too, having worked out in the gym).[39] Fox was cast against type, a decision that paid off handsomely. A movie such as *Get Carter*, which starred Michael Caine, is often trotted out as one of *the* British gangster movies, and it is, but I'd say Fox is easily the equal of Caine in *Get Carter*, and Richard Attenborough in *Brighton Rock*. Fox is simply sensational; yep, as good as Robert de Niro in *Raging Bull* or Al Pacino in *Dog Day Afternoon* or *The Godfather*. That good? Yes, Fox is.

Secondly, James Fox charts Chas Devlin's deconstruction at the hands of Pherber and Turner brilliantly, delivering a performance that is brave and revealing, going pretty far for an actor. As well as plenty of physical acting, Fox also portrays many layers to Chas's spiralling into unknown territory. Much of the credit must go to the writers, of course: you need great scriptwriting first, to be able to explore this kind of psychological realm, and that goes to Donald Cammell, Deborah Dixon and Anita Pallenberg (but only Cammell has screen credit). And the two directors of course contributed enormously. [40]

It's clear, too, that the cast have worked together, and with the director, to create some of the details in these roles: in other hands, these characters might not have turned out quite so fascinating and multi-layered. Anita Pallenberg must be applauded here, because both Turner and Chas are given back-stories, but Pherber, as scripted, is more of vaguely-described presence.

There are all sorts of quirky bits of actorly business in *Performance*, all the way through. Sometimes it's the editors who have enhanced the eccentricity of the acting – by taking out the local sound, for instance, or introducing pauses and/or ellipses. *Performance* is filled with such oddities, which you can only really grasp after a few viewings. *Performance* is not a

---

[38] Class was a bigger issue in the early version of *Performance*, in *The Performers* script.
[39] Cammell wrote the roles of Chas and Turner very much with James Fox and Mick Jagger in mind, and of course Pherber for Anita Pallenberg (and probably also Lucy for Michèle Breton).
[40] The interaction of the actors off-screen also played a part: Pallenberg recalled how she and Jagger would tease Fox. In the scene in the kitchen where the magic mushrooms are introduced and Chas asks about a Polaroid camera, Pallenberg seems especially teasing. I wouldn't be surprised if Cammell had taken Pallenberg to one side and instructed her to be as devilish as possible to Fox. It's the kind of thing that filmmakers do from time to time.

movie which serves everything up for the viewer on a single screening (which's one of the definitions of a cult movie, that you have to see it many times).

James Fox called himself 'a rather privileged hippie' when he hung around the fringes of the pop, movie and celebrity worlds. 'I was in that slightly druggy, slightly rock and roll environment'. Meeting the Rolling Stones in Rome (then on tour) was the beginning of a bohemian period for Fox and his girlfriend Andee Cohen, when he was hanging out with Anita Pallenberg, Robert Fraser, Marianne Faithfull, Donald Cammell and Christopher Gibbs.[41] Fox and Cohen became friendly with Jagger and Faithfull, and would visit their Cheyne Walk home (the way that Jagger's Turner teases Fox's Chas in a friendly manner in *Performance* certainly draws on their relationship which included, according to Cammell, 'a little romance').[42]

James Fox was the son of theatrical agent Robin Fox and actress Angela Worthington. He has five children; he married Mary Elizabeth Piper in 1973. One of his brothers is Edward Fox, another actor with numerous credits, and his brother Robert Fox is a film producer. Fox was educated at Harrow, and served in the Coldstream Guards. As well as Andee Cohen, he also dated actresses Sarah Miles, Ann Sidney and Anjelica Huston.

Prior to *Performance*, James Fox had appeared in *The Servant* (1963), *Those Magnificent Men In Their Flying Machines* (1965), *Duffy* (1967), *King Rat* (1965), *The Chase* (1966), *Isadora* (1968), and *Thoroughly Modern Millie* (1967); his first appearance in a film was in 1950, in *The Miniver Story*.

Following *Performance*, James Fox would often continue to play the upper-class, stiff upper lip characters that he is known for (it's a stereotype that Hollywood cinema perpetuates). After his nearly ten year absence from commercial cinema,[43] Fox appeared in films such as *A Passage To India* (1984), *Runners* (1983), *Greystoke* (1984), *Absolute Beginners* (1986), *The Russia House* (1990), *Patriot Games* (1992), *The Remains of the Day* (1993), *Heart of Darkness* (1994), *Anna Karenina* (1997), *Mickey Blue Eyes* (1999), *Sexy Beast* (2000), *The Golden Bowl* (2000), *The Lost World* (2001),

---

41 John Michel, Robert Fraser, Michael Cooper, Marianne Faithfull, Suna Portman, Kenneth Anger, the Ormsby-Gores, Tara Browne, Tony Sanchez and others were part of this set, as well as the Stones. (Fraser's art gallery in Cork Street and the Indica bookstore were other centres of the scene).
42 Donald Cammell wondered if there wasn't some macho rivalry between Mick Jagger and Jimmy Fox (and perhaps some jealousy on Jagger's part, because Fox really did look sensational). Cammell remembers that 'there was a tremendous tension between them. They were both scaring themselves, and scared of looking absurd' (B, 201).
43 For part of this troubled period, James Fox took up Christianity. Fox joined the religious sect the Navigators after visiting South America for months after the *Performance* shoot. But he kept in contact with the entertainment world. Fox has always maintained that his mind was 'screwed up in lots of different ways prior to *Performance*' and that, ironically, he felt more in control when he was playing the character of Chas, because of the disciplines of making art (B, 204).

Agatha Christie's Poirot – Death on the Nile (2004), *Suez: A Very British Crisis* (2006), *Midsomer Murders* (2010-), *Merlin* (2012), *Charlie and the Chocolate Factory* (2005), *Law & Order: UK* (2011), *Cleanskin* (2010) and *The Great Train Robbery* (2013). Much of Fox's later work has been on British television.

❂

Chas Devlin is a familiar figure in 1960s cinema: the successful, single white guy, the ultimate bachelor, with his neat pad and smart clothes. James Bond. Our Man Flint. Harry Palmer. The Persuaders. And so on. He embodies post-WW2 Britain emerging from the grey, repressive, rationing days of the Fifties into the more glamorous, permissive and affluent Sixties.

As Stephen Farber noted, Chas Devlin re-arranges the magazines on his coffee table, does exercises, chooses cufflinks from a neat array in his drawer, emtpies the ashtray, has a girlfriend that's probably one of many, and

> only when he takes his gun out from a hiding place in the Contempo bathroom can we distinguish him from the Playboy Club's ideal swinging bachelor.[44]

Chas Devlin is a classic gangster, narcissistic, self-absorbed, self-confident, street-wise, tough, well-dressed, lusty and violent. [45]

MICK JAGGER AS TURNER

Apart from *Performance*, undoubtedly his best role in a fiction film,[46] Mick Jagger, 25 at the time of filming (he was born on July 26, 1943 in Dartford, England) has appeared in *Ned Kelly* (1970), *Gimme Shelter* (1970), *One Plus One* (1968), the very wonderful send-up of the Beatles by the Rutles (1978), *Freejack* (1992), *Bent* (1997), *The Man From Elysian Fields* (2001) and *Shine a Light* (2008). The concert films, such as *Gimme Shelter*, *Let's Spend the Night Together* and *Shine a Light* (and also the unreleased *Cocksucker Blues*), have become the most celebrated of Jagger's appearances on film; ironically, Keith Richards' cameo in the wonderful

---
44 S. Farber, 161.
45 Chas is 'redeemed by his initiation into an exotic, bi-sexual, drug-oriented underworld; his mystical vision is a drug-induced hallucination', as Stephen Farber put it (161).
46 Certainly Turner in *Performance* was tailor-made for Jagger – as it was. 'Having been cast as an androgynous, sex-mad rock god, Mick was strangely impressive in the role,' opined Christopher Sanford (173).

Pirates of the Caribbean movies will have been seen by more people than all of Jagger's appearances put together *and then some* (Richards tried and failed to persuade the Mouth to appear in *Pirates*).

Mick Jagger's Turner's lifestyle in *Performance* clearly derives from certain pop stars of the day, including Brian Jones,[47] Jim Morrison and Jimmy Page: the darkened rooms, the candles, the incense, the *fin-de-siècle* furnishings, the air of decadence and dissolution (*Decadence* might be an alternative title for *Performance*, particularly in reference to Symbolist and Decadent art of the *fin-de-siècle* in France and Austria).

According to Mick Jagger (in 1971), in *Performance* there were two things that were important:

> There's the sexual thing – not only physically sexual but the interrelating of the sexes and the interchanging of roles. And the role of violence and the role of women, vis-a-vis the role of violence of a man. (*Time Out*)

'I think Turner is a projection of Donald's fantasy or idea of what I imagine how I am,' Mick Jagger remarked in 1971. (In fact, Jagger said that he based the character on Brian Jones, yes, but also partly on Cammell himself, 'though I don't think he knew').

According to Marianne Faithfull, she told her then-boyfriend Mick Jagger to make Turner a combination of Brian Jones (paranoia, androgyny, drugs, self-torture) and Keith Richards (cool, drugs, self-torture).[48] Faithfull said she helped Jagger to put the character of Turner together[49] (not realizing that for Anita Pallenberg, a combination of Jones and Richards would be verpaintingy attractive).[50]

For Mick Jagger biographer Philip Norman, 'at its core, *Performance* was a study of Mick's unsettling effect on other males, especially those who considered themselves most unassailably macho' (312). According to Anita Pallenberg, Turner talked liked Jones, but it was more 'the way Mick would have liked to see himself'. Altho' Jagger dyed his hair black like Keith

---

[47] A film was made about Brian Jones in 2005, entitled *Stoned*. A virtual remake of *Performance* (with nods to numerous other 1960s movies such as *The Servant, Blow Up* and *Cul-de-Sac*), *Stoned* tried hard to please with rapid editing depicting the usual mix of rock 'n' roll, nudity, drug-taking, wild parties and bickering in pop bands, but was scuppered by the central failure of so many of these decline and fall stories set in the pop music world: the people are *boring*. In short, *Stoned*, like many another rock biopic, didn't capture what was amazing and charismatic about Brian Jones in the first place. Instead, Jones came across as a needy, lazy, weak, vulnerable and manipulative guy who squanders his talent. Also, *Stoned*, despite a fine cast (that included Monet Mazur as Anita Pallenberg and David Morrissey), didn't have the star power trio at the heart of *Performance*: Mick Jagger, Anita Pallenberg and James Fox.

[48] As Marianne Faithfull put it in her autobiography, using Brian Jones alone wasn't enough: 'So we thought what about Brian and Keith? Brian with his self-torment and paranoia and Keith with strength and cool' (B, 215).

[49] According to Philip Norman, it took some time (and plenty of discussion with Donald Cammell and Nic Roeg) for Mick Jagger to work out how to play Turner, a personality that had no resemblance at all to Jagger. In the end, 'as always, his mimic's gift came to his rescue', Norman noted, and Jagger simply mimicked Keith Richards and Brian Jones.

[50] Marianne Faithfull: 'Mick, by playing Brian and Keith, would be playing two people who were extremely attractive to Anita, and who were in turn obsessed with her' (B, 216).

Richards' hair, there wasn't much of Keef in the role for Pallenberg (B, 216).

Pop stars going into retreat and turning to mysticism and magic were a theme of other films of the time, such as *Stardust* (1974),[51] and bands like the Who and the Beatles who discovered (usually Eastern) religion. *Performance* turns into a disturbing account of the demonic other, the Jungian shadow, the *doppelgänger* or double. Chas and Turner gradually switch roles, each subsuming the other.

Altho' Turner is inspired by Mick Jagger, the character's far removed from the real Jagger of the 1960s. For instance, it would've been impossible for Mick to be a recluse in the middle of London! (In Mustique, maybe). Band members would've been popping round (and recording or jamming), managers too (Andrew Oldham or later Allen Klein), roadies, road managers, lawyers, publicity agents, accountants, drug pushers, journalists, and all the rest of the entourage. Meanwhile, fans (not all female) would be hanging on the doorbell, or sneaking into the back garden, maybe even some ex-girlfriends carrying babies. And don't forget the *paparazzi!*

If you look at any rock star biography or documentary, you'll notice that they are surrounded by *lots* of people pretty much all the time. But Turner is very much, as Mick Jagger insisted, Donald Cammell's *view* of what a rock star was like.

Mick Jagger took up a solo career, beginning with his first album *She's the Boss* (1985). It featured Pete Townshend, Herbie Hancock, Jan Hammer and Jeff Beck. (Subsequent solo outings included *Primitive Cool, Wandering Spirit* and *Goddess in the Doorway*). Keith Richards, meanwhile, has released far less solo material, but he has been involved with numerous musical collaborations.

Mick Jagger was not a druggie. At all. Altho' he was surrounded by many heavy users (including Anita Pallenberg, Keith Richards, Marianne Faithfull, Brian Jones *et al*, in the era of *Performance*), he indulged only in a very moderate way. Jagger was on a health kick right from adolescence (it had been instilled in him by his father Joe, among others).

For the 11-12 week shooting schedule, Mick Jagger was the antithesis of the vain, unreliable rock star: he turned up on time, knew his lines, and did whatever the co-directors asked him to do. According to Sandy Lieberson, 'it was a *very* happy shoot', and the crew and cast found Jagger friendly and unpretentious. [52]

---

[51] An underrated movie, *Stardust* was the sequel to *That'll Be the Day*: both are cracking British pop movies, for me superior to the Beatles' movies *Help!* and *A Hard Day's Night. Stardust*, for instance, portrays the paranoia, megalomania and outright lunacy of the rock star rising and spectacularly falling better than many other movies, including candidates such as *The Wall*.

[52] Happy except for the times when Donald Cammell lost his temper: many have attested to Cammell's rages – he reduced Mick Jagger to tears a number of times during the making of *Performance*, and Anita Pallenberg said he was often frustrated or angry on the set.

When he needed to be, Mick Jagger could be as professional and as amenable as anyone. *Of course* – because Jagger is a hugely successful entertainer, and you can only become that good for that long if you're *really* determined and driven. (Jagger also took over part of the business of running the Rolling Stones empire).

Mick Jagger lost interest in *Performance*, and didn't turn up to the London première in January, 1971 (he was in Paris at the time – ensconced with Bianca Pérez-Mora Macias, whose antipathy towards Anita Pallenberg was perhaps strong enough to persuade her man to stay away).

THE REST OF THE CAST

Casting Johnny Shannon as Harry Flowers was a risk – he was not an actor (his background was in boxing and printing).[53] But Shannon had the look, the voice and the attitude to make Flowers convincing.[54] But it was a risk not casting a known character actor for this crucial role, particularly one where the actor has to be the boss of your star, and to command a gang. It's the kind of part you'd make sure was cast with an actor well-known for playing heavies or authority figures – Jack Palance,[55] say, or Gene Hackman.

Michèle Breton (b. 1951) was pretty much an unknown when she appeared in *Performance* at the age of 17 years-old.[56] However, she had appeared in one of the best movies ever – the incomparable *Weekend* (as one of the gang of hippy anarchists at the end)[57] – and an Italian TV version of *The Odyssey* (*Odissea*, 1967). The role of Lucy seems to draw on Breton's personality. But after *Performance*, Breton did little of note acting-wise. So the casting of Breton in a big role in a Hollywood movie was unusual (she got the role partly because she was tupping the director – she was living with Cammell at the time: Breton recounted that she'd met Cammell in St Tropez, and ended up in a *ménage-à-trois* with him and his

---

[53] Shannon said he didn't realize that Harry Flowers was meant to be gay. It was all a bit of a joke at first.
[54] However, Johnny Shannon's voice was among those dubbed for the American release of *Performance*.
[55] Jack Palance was cast as Grissom, the Joker's employer in 1989's *Batman*, because, as director Tim Burton explained, 'who can be Jack Nicholson's boss?' Only Palance seemed to fit the bill.
[56] Lucy is Pherber at seventeen, Cammell noted in his 'The Performers' treatment.
[57] *Weekend* was filmed in September and October, 1967.

girlfriend Deborah Dixon in their Paris home). [58]

And while Michèle Breton is an appealing, somewhat kooky presence in *Performance*, she is far, far eclipsed by three people giving the best performances of their careers – Anita Pallenberg, James Fox and Mick Jagger. Indeed, nobody stands a chance when compared with them. Pallenberg recalled in 2004 that shooting *Performance* probably wasn't a happy experience for Breton: 'It was quite stressful for her, I think. She seemed overwhelmed by the whole thing' (U, 104).

❂

Colin MacCabe draws attention to the fact the two women in *Performance* are both non-British: one is French, the other is Italian-German. As Chas Devlin puts it, they are 'foreign'. The women may represent 'a series of possibilities erotic and exotic which break the frigid and fetishised world of Old England' (M, 46).

Clearly Donald Cammell and co. were thinking along these lines: originally, both Pherber and Lucy were going to be played by American actresses (Tuesday Weld and Mia Farrow). That aligns them with Chas Devlin's real-life destination: the 'land of opportunity'. The women embody Escape, the Dream, the Unknown. As Americans or French or Italian-Germans in Olde Englande, they are part of the new cosmopolitan city, a city which draws people from everywhere. A global city, borderless.

DRESSING UP: THE LOOK OF *PERFORMANCE*

There's a huge amount of dressing up in *Performance*: there's a room of lavish clothes on racks at Powis Square, and plenty of mirrors in every room. Characters are often taking off and putting on clothes. Putting on or removing wigs. Admiring themselves in mirrors. The dressing up runs the gamut from childish play to explorations of those issues beloved of postmodern theorists: identity, masks, individuality, psychology.

Deborah Dixon, the costume consultant (and Donald Cammell's girlfriend),[59] is an important collaborator in *Performance*: the costumes (by Emma Porteous and Billy Jay) are one of the memorable aspects of the

---

[58] After *Performance*, Breton said she'd drifted into drug-taking: 'it was very sad' (B, 33). It's an unhappy story for Breton: she told Mick Brown that after *Performance* Cammell had driven her back to Paris, but told her to leave after a few days. The slide into drugs was consuming: 'I was taking everything that was going. I was in a very bad shape, all fucked up' (B, 34). Breton wandered to Spain, Afghanistan, India, and Italy, ending up in Berlin.

[59] Donald Cammell and Dixon had split up in November, 1967.

movie. If you had to pick five movies which capture the fashion scene in London/ Britain in the 1960s, *Performance* would undoubtedly be one of them (plus *Blow Up* and the Beatles' films). And Dixon also helped to write the script, along with Anita Pallenberg.

As well as costumes and dressing up, hair is also foregrounded in *Performance* (hair was by Helen Lennox): the principals play around with wigs, sometimes so they look like each other (culminating in the fusion of Chas and Turner at the end), while one of Chas's punishments for the lawyer's chauffeur is to shave his head (as well as tying him up).

❂

The production design in *Performance* was by John Clark and Peter Young, with Christopher Gibbs on hand as an adviser. The interior of the Powis Square house is decorated in a groovy Indian and Arabic manner, with hangings around beds, dark red walls, Moorish and Islamic patterns.[60] It might be a harem in Baghdad (Persia is of course one of the imaginary destinations in the film). The origin of the style is of course Morocco[61] – Morocco being a favourite destination with rock acts of the time (such as the Stones and Led Zeppelin), as well as Brion Gysin, William Burroughs, the Beat poets, and many other literati and bohemians. Some observers have described Turner's pad as a recreation of 1, Courtfield Road in Londinium, where Anita Pallenberg and Brian Jones lived. When Pallenberg moved to Cheyne Walk (a Queen Anne house) with Keith Richards in 1969, she decorated it in the style of 'replicas of Moroccan hashish dens' (Mick Jagger also lived in Cheyne Walk).

---

[60] During the drug hallucination scene, the lighting is shifted to a golden and yellow hue, enhancing the unreality.
[61] The 'Gibbsian Moroccan manner' as Donald Cammell described it in an early version of the script. Christopher Gibbs had also designed Brian Jones's place at 1, Courtfield Road, London. Many of the props and furnishings for *Performance* were bought by Gibbs in Morocco. 'I wanted something mysterious and beautiful and unexpected, exotic and voluptuous and far away from pedestrian; some hint of earthly paradise', Gibbs explained.
The big room at Turner's home was art-directed by Christopher Gibbs, John Clark and Peter Young to be a snapshot of rock-n-roll-dom and London bohemia: it contained: a piano, an organ, a chandelier, a pile of stones, a maze of mirrors, newspapers, a fish tank, maps, a pile of cushions and mattresses... A sort of rock star version of Mrs Havisham's digs in *Great Expectations*.

THE SHOOTING STYLE

> Any technique that works is OK; if you stir things up relentlessly you'll get results. And I went for it all the way. I thought the sparks were flying. They were all performers – and the idea of performance was alive and well and embodied by the title.
>
> Donald Cammell (B, 196)

Performance is very much of its time in its use of the camera: there are handheld shots, whip pans, and crash zooms. For instance, the camera often zooms out from extras in the background, to reveal one of the main actors in the foreground. There's an ethnic slant to some of these crash zoom shots, too: some of those people in the background are non-white: the black guy in the car hire firm; a black dancer in the nightclub; an Indian wearing a turban on the street behind the telephone kiosk where Chas calls Harry Flowers. It's the 'foreign' element which Chas, embodying white, working-class England, fears.

❂

During one of Harry Flowers' tirades, the 1970 film shifts into black-and-white and a reverby soundtrack – the kind of device usually reserved for a film entering an individual's mindscreen (presumably of Chas Devlin). A similar trope is employed later, when Chas is given drugs.

Characters turn to the camera and talk (a technique that really took off in the 1960s, in movies such as *Alfie* (1966). Well, this was re-invented for the *n*-th time, 'cos actors have been doing that since D.W. Griffith's time).

You seldom hear of Donald Cammell being described as an 'actor's director' like, say, Robert Altman, Ingmar Bergman or Francis Coppola (and according to the accounts of his directing style, he wasn't, really). But, boy, some of the performances in Cammell's movies are terrific: Cammell had a way in particular of drawing out performances from actors they didn't know they had in them. Among the outstanding performances are: James Fox, Anita Pallenberg, David Keith, Anne Heche, Steve Bauer and Christopher Walken.

According to Christopher Gibbs, Donald Cammell used a technique quite common in show business: creating tension between actors in order to obtain a different sort of performance. Cammell liked things to be intense during shooting (like many filmmakers). His brother David recalled that Cammell liked to push people beyond their potential – sometimes to tears, as in the case of Mick Jagger. 'That's what's interesting about his films; the actual making of them was a very intense experience'. Marianne Faithfull called *Performance* 'a psycho-sexual laboratory', in that Cammell was orchestrating real and imagined romantic relationships in *Performance* among the circle surrounding the Rolling Stones.

THE EDITING STYLE IN *PERFORMANCE*

The dense editing style on *Performance*, one of its key aspects, became one of the foundations of Donald Cammell's filmmaking. *Performance* was edited by Cammell and his editors in two locations: in Los Angeles, with the aid of Frank Mazzola, while Nic Roeg went to work on *Walkabout*; but the first editing sessions of *Performance* had been supervised by Anthony Gibbs in London (assisted by Brian Smedley-Aston). Roeg would employ this kind of editing in his subsequent films, but it was Cammell and Gibbs who were largely responsible for its development on *Performance*. (Gibbs said that he had disagreed with Cammell about the re-editing of *Performance*, to cut it down and also take out some of the violence. Critics have credited Mazzola with the editing of *Performance* (Mazzola said he was only really responsible for the first half of the film), but that down-plays the crucial involvement of Gibbs and Smedley-Aston, who were the first editors: they would have been responsible, for instance, of putting together the first rough cut of the film, and also the completed version for the first preview in Santa Monica in July, 1969).

Anthony Gibbs had worked on *Tom Jones*, one of the films celebrated for its New Wave editing style. He also cut *A Taste of Honey, The Knack, Petulia, The Girl With Green Eyes* and *The Loneliness of the Long Distance Runner*. So Gibbs was a very talented editor by the time he worked on *Performance*. Afterwards, Gibbs had an impressive list of editing credits, which included *Walkabout, Fiddler On the Roof, Jesus Christ Superstar, Rollerball, Juggernaut, A Bridge Too Far, Dune, Agnes of God, The Man Without a Face* and *Ronin*. Have a look at the cutting in *Jesus Christ Superstar*, for instance: you may hate Andrew Lloyd-Weber and Tim Rice's musical, but the film (shot by British DP Doug Slocombe) is technically brilliant.

The first half was slow, Frank Mazzola recalled, and most of the work that he and Donald Cammell did on *Performance* was on the first half of the film. Mazzola did some minor cuts in the second half, he said. But they ran out of time. *Performance* was re-edited by Mazzola and his team on the Sam Goldwyn lot, where Mazzola had been cutting *Macho Callahan* for producer Joe Levine.[62]

The 1970 movie was re-edited a number of times before it was approved by John Calley and Warners. However, parts of it were cut out before it was released. *Performance* as it is, is not, then, a 'director's cut', or the version that Donald Cammell and Frank Mazzola prepared. It was Ted Ashley who ordered further cuts.

Frank Mazzola remarked that you could do anything to *Performance*, editing-wise, and it would work. That's a revealing comment: it meant that the film has reached a very good state of being, that it could be cut and re-cut, but would still work. You can apply this to other movies: *Citizen Kane* could be edited backwards, and it would still work (of course, it famously opens with the death of its protagonist). Similarly, *Performance* could open with Chas's death, or Turner's death, or could be switched around in different forms, and it would still be compelling. (Films with a similar editing style to *Performance* include *F For Fake*, *Sunless*, *Mirror*, and any Jean-Luc Godard movie).

✣

Warners – what a surprise – rejected the first cut of *Performance*, demanding (1) that the first four reels be compressed, and (2) that what they saw as the prime pull of the film (Mick Jagger) should appear much earlier (they also objected to the sex and violence).[63] Sex and violence can relatively easily be toned down or cut out, but it was Jagger that Warners wanted to focus on. The film was edited again, and rejected again.[64] Warners' front office saw the film as primarily a Mick Jagger vehicle, a chance to get one of the hottest pop stars of the time, with a guaranteed music audience, into a trendy, 'Swinging London'-style film.

As Frank Mazzola and Donald Cammell worked on the film, they experimented with flashbacks and flashforwards, reprising motifs, and cutting dialogue lines in half. Some sequences had rapid montages, such as the parallel action of Chas and Dana having sex and the Rolls Royce at the start of the film (the second edit had over 50 cuts, the first had only two).

Frank Mazzola had acted in *Rebel Without a Cause* and had been editing for 13 years before working on *Performance*. Mazzola's love of improvisatory jazz may also have influenced the cutting of *Performance*. Mazzola said editing *Performance* with Donald Cammell was an inspiring

---

[62] Another link with Jean-Luc Godard – Levine had produced *Contempt* (1963), one of the best movies about movies ever.
[63] James Fox reckoned that it was the violence that Warners objected to more than the sex, and they weren't sure if the movie was commercial (U, 105).
[64] The earlier cuts of *Performance* don't exist anymore – at least, at present; they might see the light of day in the future (they are probably in some film vault in Nebraska or Ohio). The first half of the film in the Autumn, 1969 cut was much longer, and depicts Chas's job in a more linear manner.

experience. You can see why: *Performance* is, among other things, an editor's movie, like *Citizen Kane* or *Vivre Sa Vie* or *Sunless*, a movie in which editing is foregrounded, and a movie in which the editing style is central to the picture's impact.

> He liked to talk a lot in the editing-room [Mazzola recalled]. He'd pick up a book and start reading – Borges or something like that – and then he'd come over and look at what was going on and start talking and the energy would rise. I would be cutting all of a sudden, the film would just take over. It was like stepping into a world of magic. Things would start flying through my hands. I could feel the electricity in the film going through my teeth. The film took on its own life and I was trying to chase it. Everything we tried worked. (B, 68)

Performance opens with stock footage of a jet,[65] announcing its strangeness from the beginning. Why a jet? What does it have to do with the rest of the movie? Is it a reference to the space race, big news in 1967-68? To technology? To the modern world? To speed? To flight? To transcendence?

Or maybe it's a BANG! WOW! way of opening a movie.

The rapid montage of images and the electronic soundtrack[66] announce *Performance* as not your average Hollywood movie. As David Bordwell has pointed out, this kind of montage is a highly self-conscious form of narration. Donald Cammell recalled how Warners Bros. and the producers wanted to get to Mick Jagger quicker, and wanted the gangster story to be compressed.[67] This was one of the reasons for the rapid montage style that was developed. There are many ways of cutting a picture down, which *every* movie has to do, because rough cuts *always* come in too long (the rough cut of *Apocalypse Now*, for instance, was over four hours long; Woody Allen says that his films tend to come in at two and a half hours for the rough cut and around 85 to 90 minutes for the final cut).

Film critics (and film fans) generally don't understand how movies are edited: the first assembly (also known as the rough cut) puts together everything that was shot, in the order it appears in the script. Rough cuts are typically absolute murder for the director and the team to watch, and are *always* too long.

No movie gets to a rough cut stage and stays there. The rough cut is

---

[65] The footage is probably bought from one of those companies dealing in stock footage – there are other examples of stock footage in *Performance* (such as the black-and-white images of children playing in the streets).
[66] The soundtrack here employs the treated white noise/ wind fx and syntheszer fx favoured at the time by bands like Tangerine Dream or Pink Floyd.
[67] Frank Mazzola said that they were cutting down two thousand foot reels of film, for the first 2 reels of *Performance*, not thousand foot reels – so it meant that they cut down 6,000 feet of film in a short time (U, 110).

simply the first stage in a long process of editing (and editing is very much a *process* – the only way to do it is to actually *do it!*). In the case of *Performance*, the first cut/s were rejected by the studio, and the previews were disastrous. So Donald Cammell and his editorial team went back and re-cut it, at least twice (this is, however, quite common, and it drives plenty of people nuts!).

The first stages of editing *Performance* had been done in Great Britain, but some of the movie was edited in L.A. Nic Roeg was involved, but at some point there was a disagreement about the movie, and Roeg decided he'd had enough, and left. He also wanted his name off the picture. That was a big problem, not least because Donald Cammell and Roeg had worked so well in pre-production and during shooting. (And that kind of action creates all sorts of bad feeling, which nobody needs).

One method of shortening a picture is to lose scenes altogether. Another is to compress scenes down to the bare essentials of plot and narrative. Another is to combine two scenes. All sorts of approaches have been tried,[68] but the solution of Anthony Gibbs, Brian Smedley-Aston and Frank Mazzola was to employ the modernist, New Wave editing style, of flashforwards, flashbacks, jump cuts and parallel action. So, in a way, the disastrous previews and the negative response from Warner Bros. enhanced the movie, I think, because it led to further editing time, and the filmmakers trying out new ways of editing the movie.

Undoubtedly many movies are *really* made in the editing suite. It's common knowledge that movies are made at least three times: 1. during writing, 2. during shooting, and 3. during editing and post-production (you can add other processes, such as casting, or design). In the case of *Performance*, this is very true. As with pictures like *Apocalypse Now*, *The Godfather 2* and *Annie Hall* (to chose two of the directors I've already mentioned), *Performance* is a movie which was radically rewritten in the editing suite.

The editing style that Anthony Gibbs, Brian Smedley-Aston and Frank Mazzola developed on *Performance* is not 'scattershot' editing, as some film critics dub it, and it's not Eisensteinian montage, either. It could be defined as intuitive editing, or poetic editing, or dream-like editing. You can find the same techniques being employed in the films of Stanley Kubrick, Oliver Stone and Jean-Luc Godard (Godard, I would argue, is a key influence on this kind of editing – *Breathless* was hugely influential).

Quite a lot of the time, the editing style in *Performance* is simply leaving out the pauses between cuts, but the flow of images is still conventional continuity editing.

---

[68] James Cameron apparently shortened every single shot, an unusual way of doing it, on *The Terminator*.

What the editing style led to in *Performance* was a reliance on, among other things, flashforwards and flashbacks which were not complete scenes – i.e., a flashback as a memory scene, which would explain a character's back-story. Rather, the flashes forward and backward comprised short shots. And what made these inserts particularly striking was that the filmmakers would place them *two or three shots* ahead of a scene, or sometimes even longer, and they would repeat this a number of times. It meant that the viewer was picking up suggestions of scenes which might not arrive in their full form for a minute or two.

The other major editing technique was to combine scenes by intercutting them. A tried and tested formula in cinema since its early days, of course, but once again Gibbs, Smedley-Aston and Mazzola cut out establishing shots, explaining shots, or shots which would make it clearer to the audience exactly what was going on. *Performance* encourages the viewer to keep up, and assumes that the viewer will know what's happening without having to labour it.

Performance also combines many more scenes than your average narrative movie (American or European): it's not only the opening scenes of the Rolls Royce driving through the countryside and Chas Devlin and his girlfriend Dana getting freaky that are combined, but many others.

The editing style in *Performance* not only uses flashforwards and flashbacks, but uses them repeatedly, within the same scene. It's actually pretty complex – compared that is, to a regular Hollywood movie. For instance, in the scenes at 15-30 minutes, when Chas is out and about putting the frighteners on several small businesses, the film cuts from them to Chas with Harry Flowers back at HQ, then back to Chas earlier that day: but it does this more than once.

Confusing? Not really: because what this rapid, intuitive style of in *Performance* cutting demonstrates is that most film editing, called continuity editing, is so routine, so predictable.

Audiences can keep up: and it's surely one of the aspects of *Performance* that has helped to prevent it from dating badly (unlike many other movies of the period). It's still faster and more complex than most movies released today.

There are also optical effects in *Performance*, such as freeze frames, and step-motion (when film is slowed down, but not shot for slow motion). There is full slow motion too. There are giant close-ups of the magic mushrooms,[69] and shots through the viewfinders of the Super-8 camera and the Polaroid camera.

Some of those opticals and different camera speeds, like the unusual

---
[69] The film revels in giant close-ups – of nipples, of mushrooms, of ears, of faces, of mouths.

camera angles or camera movements, do all have the appearance of a first-time director, someone trying out what movies can do. It's movie-making as the best train set anyone could have, as Orson Welles put it. However, *Performance* isn't flashy (usually) for the sake of being showy; the self-consciously arty or tricky or showy effects work because they contribute towards the overall substance of this particular film, with its themes of identity, disguises, dressing up, bohemia and altered states.

Those eccentric effects might be out of place in a romantic comedy-drama about a couple splitting up during a divorce and getting back together, when the movie focuses on emotions and sit-com or soap opera-style melodrama. But in a movie about drugs and rock music and gangsters and guns and hippies, it fits.

✺

But editing is always a trade-off, because there are so many ways to edit a movie. So although the re-edit that Frank Mazzola did with Donald Cammell reduced the running time and sharpened up the first half of *Performance*, it also changed the movie. What was lost, according to Sandy Lieberson, was a lot of the details of the criminal underworld of London, with its homosexual, narcissistic, and violent subculture. The portrait of Chas Devlin, for instance, was much deeper in the original cut, and the story was perhaps stronger, Lieberson noted (B, 82).

Some movies get restored, but it's a costly and time-consuming business, and usually movies're only restored if there's a guarantee of revenue at the end of it all. Some restorations are prestige projects (*Lawrence of Arabia, Spartacus, Othello, Touch of Evil*), but *Performance* unfortunately doesn't fit into either a commercial or a prestige category. Even in the era of home video and DVD, which has encouraged some restorations, *Performance* still slips thru the cracks.

So although it would be amazing to see both the first complete cut, and Donald Cammell's and Frank Mazzola's cut, and all of the deletions demanded by Warners, and the censors, and even the rough cut or the workprint, it's not likely it's gonna happen.

One of Donald Cammell's favourite movies, and a huge cult movie (and, like *Performance*, a Warner Brothers production – tho' with a budget of $25.4 million more!), *Blade Runner*, was released in a big restoration version in 2007. The *Final Cut* of *Blade Runner* was developed between 2000 and 2002, led by restoration producer Charles de Lauzirika (who worked on other Ridley Scott movies), and was then abandoned for some years (while the legal situation was ironed out). It was taken up again in 2006, and finally released in 2007. As well as the 'final cut' itself, a bunch of new documentaries were commissioned (headed up by *Dangerous Days*), and the workprint was also released.70

PAINTING

The influence of painting upon Donald Cammell's cinema shouldn't be under-estimated: after all, Cammell had studied to be a painter, and had set up a painter's studio in Chelsea in London. It's clear he could have had a comfortable career as a painter, had he continued with the society portraits he undertook.

The influences of painting on the films of Donald Cammell is easy to spot: there are scenes in *Performance*, for instance, which were intended by Cammell as *hommages* to Francis Bacon (the room with the red carpet and entangled naked bodies).71 Cammell is one of many, many filmmakers who have drawn on the history of painting: Cecil B. DeMille (with his 'Rembrandt lighting'), Vincente Minnelli (who made a film about Vincent van Gogh, and drew on the Impressionists for *An American In Paris*), and Cammell's British contemporaries, such as Derek Jarman (another painter-turned-director like Cammell), Ken Russell, and Peter Greenaway (who believes that painting is far superior to cinema, that cinema lags far behind painting).

Another reference to painting in *Performance* is the first time that Turner is shown – not as a pop star, but as a painter, spraying72 the walls of his Powis Square home (like a visualization of the Rolling Stones' song 'Paint It Black').73 And it can't be a coincidence that Turner takes his name from Britain's greatest artist, J.M.W. Turner. And Harry Flowers has a painting that he shifts around his office, as if trying to find the best spot to hang it. This particular painting is of an eighteenth century man on a horse dressed in the red jacket of a hunting party.

---

70 The *Blade Runner Final Cut* was a restoration job in the digital age – the film was restored using all sorts of digital technology, including being scanned at a high resolution. As well as cleaning up the print, many elements were added or subtracted with digital tools: for instance, the cables that held up the spinners.
71 Francis Bacon is a darling with the intelligentsia, particularly in Britain. For me, he's powerful but over-rated. The most famous use of Bacon's art in movies is probably the credit sequence of *Last Tango In Paris* (1972).
72 The spray painting scene had been filmed b4 principal photography began (by Nic Roeg), as a way of including Mick Jagger in the production, and helping to persuade him to do the whole movie.
73 Action painting and Abstract Expressionism is referenced here (in particular, the hero of Abstract Expressionism, Jackson Pollock), and also in the red paint that Joey and his chaps chuck around Chas's flat (standing in, as it does in other films, for blood. In *Andrei Roublyov*, the Russian epic Andre Tarkovsky directed in 1965, mud is thrown at white church walls. In Walerian Borowczyk's *Three Immoral Women* a Renaissance painter hurls mud at a wall).

Why this painting? Maybe because it alludes to Olde Englande, the now-vanished past that maybe never existed in the first place. Plus it's a picture of an aristocrat, embodying the upwardly-mobile desires of working class gangsters: when they get a bit of money, they buy a decent motor, like a Jaguar, or a Rolls Royce. And the first time the Rolls Royce car is shown (and the last time too) is out in the British countryside, as if the gang boss is playing at being an aristocratic man of leisure, driving to his country estate. It's about crime and gangsterism as the ultimate expression of advanced capitalism, and the tendency, at least as portrayed in the movies, was for gangsters to aspire to an upper-class lifestyle. Two years after *Performance*, *The Godfather* completely nailed the depiction of gangsters as the ultimate capitalists, in a movie intended by director Francis Coppola to be an exploration of the rise of corporate America.

This was part of a trend among rock stars too. The mega-earnings of British supergroups such as the Beatles, the Stones, the Who and Led Zeppelin was reflected in the lifestyles of the band members. They started to purchase fish farms, banana farms, huge mansions and estates. A 'rock aristocracy' was created, containing a hundred or so megastars who had multiple homes, private jets, personal bodyguards, stretch limos, classic car collections, guitar collections, and all manner of business investments (Mick Jagger and Keith Richards were very much part of this trend; indeed, Jagger actively pursued an upwardly-mobile lifestyle, which culminated in his knighthood – which for some is as *un*-rock 'n' roll as you can get!).

This conspicuous wealth and consumption worked against the notion of rock 'n' roll being about rebellion, angst, youth and anarchy. Same with gangsters: can you be a rebel if you're buying into conventional society big time? Maybe, if you've stolen everything you got, and you've killed people to get it.

Being a millionaire became the goal – 'having it all'. The opulent homes, cars, tennis courts, swimming pools, jacuzzis, saunas, jets, Roll-Royces and Cadillacs and so on, were the usual trappings of the rich and famous in the post-WWII era. The investment in farms, estates, land, livestock *et al* in rural areas evoked a nostalgic luxury, a back-to-the-land gentrification. South London rebels, born on 'the streets', became countrified gentry. The hell-raisers became pseudo-aristocrats. In Paul and Linda McCartney's case the gentrification was given a New Age/ ecological overtone – the espousal of vegetarianism, the hippy ideals. With many of the rock aristocracy, the new wealth meant indulgence on a grand scale, including drugs, drink, travel, sex, parties, etc.

♣

There's a section of *Performance* on the Death of Painting: two guys visit the Powis Square house (dressed like Russian peasants, or dervishes – they were played by the Myers twins, London scenesters), to sell a painting to Turner. The filmmakers comment cuttingly on the death of painting by having Turner buy the frame, but not the painting (the frame is placed in the closet where Turner winds up, dead. He's just another frame, a hollow shell. As Lucy or Pherber remarks, Turner only buys the frames).

The painting is by René Magritte[74] (Magritte, like Salvador Dali and the other Surrealists, was popular in the hippy, bohemian world of the late 1960s – and still is). Used for album covers, posters, costumes and stage designs – the Surrealists were (and are) favourites with students, rock musicians, and avant gardists.

MUSIC

The music for *Performance* was by Jack Nitzsche,[75] with Randy Newman credited as music director. Both Newman and Nitzsche went on to contribute to movie soundtracks, with Newman moving into the big league with music for films such as Disney-Pixar's *A Bug's Life*, *Toy Story*, *Monsters, Inc*, *The Frog and the Princess* and *Seabiscuit*, among many others. Nitzsche wrote the music for the much-acclaimed and very wonderful *One Flew Over the Cuckoo's Nest*, *Personal Best*, the infamous New York cop movie *Cruising*, another cult movie, this time about a bunch of young American kids, *Stand By Me*, *9 1/2 Weeks*, *The Jewel In the Nile*, *The Crossing Guard*, and also *BlueCollar* (1978), an underrated drama that Paul Schrader wrote and directed, which explored labour issues in a Detroit car factory. Nitzsche also worked with the Stones (he arranged 'Time Is On My Side' and 'You Can't Always Get What You Want', among others, and played piano on Marianne Faithfull's 'Sister Morphine', alongside Ry Cooder, Charlie Watts and Bill Wyman).

Jack Nitzsche told the *Los Angeles New Times* that *Performance* had been a good experience, partly because the filmmakers allowed him free rein, with no studio interference:

---

74 The René Magritte painting that Turner puts on the wall was real – Warners wanted the filmmakers to use a print (as usual in movies), but the filmmakers insisted on the real thing (which was rented from an art gallery).
75 Jack Nitzsche had got the job when Keith Richards suggested that Nitzsche would be good for *Performance* when he heard Nitzsche's soundtrack (unused) for the movie *Candy*.

I put all kinds of weird shit in that score. It was amazing. And Anita on the screen. Goddamn... To this day I'll be in a restaurant, or walking down a street or leaving a screening on a lot, somewhere like at Paramount, and someone will yell out *Performance*! Recently, Billy Friedkind saw me walking across the street and yelled, "*Performance*! The greatest use of music in a motion picture ever!" (B, 151)

Among the musicians on the soundtrack of *Performance* were Ry Cooder, Lowell George, the Merry Clayton Singers, Buffy Sainte-Marie, the Last Poets, Russell Titelman, Milt Holland, Bobby West, Gene Parsons, Amiya Dasgupta, Mick Jagger, and Randy Newman.

Mick Jagger had promised to provide a song for *Performance*, but Keef Richards decided not to co-operate. And if Richards didn't want to do something, the rest of the Rolling Stones usually followed suit. In the end, after it had dragged on and the song hadn't materialized, it was put together by Jagger, but without Richards (Richards would use this particular tactic many times in the Stones' career – particularly in his frequent fall-outs with Jagger. It was simple: the Rolling Stones could not be the Rolling Stones without Richards).

During Chas Devlin's magic mushroom trip, when he becomes enamoured of a candle and a shiny table (there are candles in every scene in Powis Square), the music is a jarring, repetitive piano.

When Pherber makes love with Chas, the zither music returns (in a different form). In this scene, Pherber is driving the drama, while Chas is more passive, lying back on the bed and allowing her to play around with him. Pherber is talking and talking and talking, but God knows what she's going on about.

In the sequence intercutting the court and mini-cab scenes, there's a strange Moog synthesizer sound.[76] It sounds like a zither used for the love-making scene (but it's probably a dulcimer – also used on 'The Hashishim').

Mick Jagger delivers a number of musical performances in *Performance* – the Robert Johnson blues number 'Come On In My Kitchen', which Mick plays and sings on his own (that's pure Jagger – performing a blues classic – his guitar playing is in the rhythmic, Keith Richards style),[77] the rap, and the 'Memo To Turner' video-within-the-movie.

When Chas and Lucy make love, the music is lyrical acoustic guitar. It's meant to be a loving act of love, rather than the more self-consciously 'kinky' or power-gaming kind of sex in much of the rest of the movie. [78]

---

76 The synthesizer was played by Bernie Krause (Mick Brown said that Jack Nitzsche played it); he had also performed on the soundtrack of *Point Blank*.
77 Mick Jagger was well-known for his passion for the blues and r 'n' b – like so many British rock stars of the period (such as Jimmy Page and Eric Clapton), Jagger had an extensive blues record collection, and knew literally 100s of blues classics.
78 The 'kinkiness' or 'perversion' of the sex scenes sets the free love of the hippy era (Turner and his *ménage-à-trois*) against the S/M of the straight world (Chas and Dana in the opening scene).

❋

I picked up a used copy of the soundtrack album for *Performance* in Notting Hill, near where the movie was filmed, hoping for more than it delivered: released on Warner Bros' record label (of course), it is typical of film soundtrack releases: some of it you recognize and enjoy, some of the pieces don't appear in the movie, and some don't work by themselves. The stand-out piece is definitely 'Memo To Turner', a rocky song very reminiscent of the Rolling Stones, and highlighting Our Mick.[79] 'Gone Dead Train', an upbeat blues number which opens the 1970 film, is sung by Randy Newman, now one of the biggest names in film music.

As for the rest, there's some bluesy slide guitar (by the excellent Ry Cooder),[80] some acoustic guitar augmented by sitar (very 1967), some gospel-style vocals – by Merry Clayton – she's the soulful woman's voice heard on the soundtrack at the end – and also on the Stones' 'Gimme Shelter'),[81] some mouth harp and singing from Buffy Sainte-Marie, the bizarre, pro-black rap by the Harlem band Last Poets, 'Wake Up, Niggers',[82] and some bland but pretty piano and strings pieces ('Harry Flowers'), reminiscent of John Barry in his 1960s mode (but nowhere near as good as the divine Barry). The instrumentation – acoustic guitar, slide guitar, sitar, jew's harp, dulcimer – is typical of the time.

On the whole, the *Performance* soundtrack isn't a classic, like *Hair* or the Beatles' movies from the same era. And though the pop music world fascinated Donald Cammell, music isn't one of Cammell's strongest points. No one would class Cammell among the great film directors who work with music.

---

[79] However, when it was released as a single, 'Memo To Turner' only reached 32 in the charts.
[80] Ry Cooder reprised this kind of guitar music for *Paris, Texas* (1984). Cooder had visited Redlands too, along with Jack Nitzsche, the band's arranger at the time.
[81] Merry Clayton also appeared in stage shows of *Tommy* as the Acid Queen.
[82] *Performance* consciously takes up black culture: it includes the Black Power-style rap by the Last Poets, over scenes of Turner and Chas in Turner's recording studio, and features cutaways to black people on the streets, and the Jimi Hendrix lookalike Noel at the railway station.

SEX IN *PERFORMANCE*

The opening of *Performance* is deliberately disorientating and skewed: the rapid images of jets and the sky, followed by the helicopter shots of a black Rolls Royce driving through the countryside intercut with images of two people fucking, plus the shifts in the soundtrack (from jet and engine noises which fade, to rock music, which's faded out quickly,[83] to the electronic sounds), all evoke a movie that is not your average Hollywood or British flick. Exposition is left out for a few minutes, and characters (or situations) are not introduced in the usual manner.

For instance, the audience has no idea who's in the Rolls Royce limo: it's just a vehicle driving along country lanes (and filmed with deliberately unruly helicopter shots).[84] The images could be decoded any which way. Similarly, the flash cuts of the two people tupping don't have any narrative weight or meaning, beyond being images of sex. Only as the intercutting between the images continues are faces glimpsed (concentrating more on James Fox's Chas Devlin); but as the characters haven't been introduced, the faces have little or no narrative value. (There are hints that the sex is a little 'kinky' or 'pervy', to use the slang of the time – there's Chas holding up a mirror while his girlfriend Dana (Ann Sidney)[85] appears to be giving him a blowjob, and there are suggestions of bondage or S/M, though of course it's the man who's performing bondage or S/M on the woman,[86] including slapping her face – audiences would have to wait until movies such as 1992's *Basic Instinct* to see the gender roles reversed, and a woman taking control of a man in a sex scene at the beginning of a mainstream movie).

Only when the love-making is over, are the characters revealed in a more conventional manner, and by the time it's next morning, the scene becomes positively pedestrian and everyday (with exchanges of dialogue out of a kitchen sink drama, along the lines of, 'want some tea, luv?', and 'what do you want for breakfast?').[87] And the Rolls Royce winds up at what appears to be a country hotel, and the chauffeur's (John Sterland) seen

---

[83] Randy Newman's song 'Gone Dead Train' (co-written with Russ Titelman).
[84] A black Rolls Royce at the beginning, and a white one at the end: you can read any symbolism you like in this, from 'good' and 'evil' to Zorasterian or Manichæan duality. And there's some social satire here, perhaps: you can get a Roller on both sides of the law.
At different times, *Performance* orchestrates a variety of principles in conflict, such as creation and destruction, art and chaos, sex and art, performance and inaction, life and death, etc. Chas and Turner and Pherber embody these principles in different ways. But all of the characters share common traits.
Narcissism is one of the strongest: all four principals in the Powis Square house are self-regarding types (always looking into mirrors, always taking baths, always changing their costumes, always manipulating how other people see them.
[85] Ann Sidney (b. 1944) won Miss World in 1964 (John Bindon's girlfriend Vicki Hodge was cast, but she wasn't a member of Equity). James Fox and Sidney had a brief affair.
[86] The sex that Chas enjoys with Dana – narcissistic with hints of S/M – is contrasted with the gentler lovemaking at Turner's place.
[87] However, there are some self-consciously arty moments – the close-up on Dana's ass in the mirror, for instance, as she gets dressed.

cleaning it (so presumably it's the lawyer's car, the car that gets doused with paint stripper later on).

The sex scene between Chas Devlin and his girlfriend Dana at the start of *Performance* is a deliberate tease for the audience, of course, because it has little narrative value, and Chas's girlfriend also doesn't feature in the rest of the movie. All the scene tells the audience is that Chas and his girlfriend fuck – well, *so what?* That's what all lovers do!, so there's no point showing it beyond titillation for the viewer.

The addition of suggestions of bondage (and mirrors) in the sex scene also add little to the 1970 Warners film at this point, except to inform the audience that these lovers like to use bondage and mirrors. It's the same with many other movies that open with a sex scene – as well as being teases for the audience, which movie producers, chomping on their cigars, are totally aware of, they are also 'fuck yous' to the film studio as well as the audience. (Some bad examples of putting the sex up front in the first minutes include *Betty Blue, Crash* and *Last Tango In Paris*, while *Basic Instinct* combines sex and death in an outrageous manner, as Catherine Trammell murders a guy as she rides him).

The sex scene in *Performance*, like the disorientating montage style of the opening, acts like the action-filled teaser in a *James Bond* film (which every action movie uses nowadays). It doesn't necessarily relate to the rest of the movie, it's there to grab the audience's attention, just like the crazy stunt work at the start of a *James Bond* picture. (Structurally, the sex scene could be inserted anywhere in the first 25 minutes of *Performance*).

❈

The sex in *Performance* is filmed in the manner of other films of the period: rapid cuts, for a start, which don't hang around too much. An emphasis on breasts and nipples,[88] and very little full body nudity (no cocks or cooches, for example, and no erections; Mick Jagger coyly covers his weiner). The film plays with that – there's a shot of James Fox's armpit (!), which's deliberately framed to appear like a vulva. Needless to say, by the standards of contemporary porn, the sex in *Performance* is pretty tame, and tamely filmed.

It's typical of *Performance* that the sex scene is also couched in a narcissistic and self-reflexive manner: Pherber films Lucy and Turner asleep before taking off her clothes and joining them in bed (she also glances in the mirror before going to the bed). So the handheld images of the threesome getting freaky are like a home porn movie. The sound of the camera whirrs, and the film takes up the viewfinder's point-of-view, as if the spectator is now watching Pherber's home movie. (The scene was shot

---
[88] There's a dissolve between a pyramid-like rock and a giant C.U. of a nipple.

with a wind-up Bolex camera on 16mm Ektachrome, deliberately pushed in the processing, to enhance the 'home movie' look. It's also scratchy film stock).

Other writers and artists who are contemporaries of Donald Cammell's who have foregrounded sex, sometimes in a similar manner to Cammell, include authors such as William Burroughs, J.G. Ballard and Marco Vassi, and filmmakers such as David Cronenberg, Bernardo Bertolucci, Pier Paolo Pasolini, Jess Franco and Walerian Borowczyk.

❂

Performance was one of many movies which explored more 'explicit' ways of depicting sexual acts on screen. It was the 1960s, the era of 'free love', the 'Summer of Love', the 'permissive society', the Pill, and a new liberalism in popular culture. *Performance* wouldn't be classed as one of the great erotic movies of the era – it's not in the same class, really, as *Immoral Tales* (1974), *Last Tango In Paris* (1972) or *Ai No Corrida* (1976). And the sex on screen is pretty tame and soft-core. But it does make fucking one of the major pursuits of the bohemian, artistic world, along with drugs, drink, tobacco, dancing and music (well, yeah, but fucking, drinking and smoking were in the 1960s – and still are today – primary activities for millions of people worldwide, with dance and music to a lesser extent).

But *Performance* was clearly a movie that was intended from the outset to push at the limits of what was acceptable in a mainstream, Hollywood movie, in the areas of the depiction of sex, violence and drug use. Although the filmmakers emphasized that they seemed to have been left alone during the shooting of *Performance*, they were also conscious that at some point they would have to submit their movie to the Hollywood studio.

The film lab (Humphry's) told the producers of *Performance* that the sex in the bedroom scene was too graphic, and broke the law (making the lab liable to the Obscene Publications Act). Humphry's wanted to destroy the film, but the producers got the negative back (and took their film processing to Technicolor).

❂

Penetration and holes are another recurring motif in *Performance* – mouths, eyes, genitals, bullet wounds, etc, in the familiar tropes of Sigmund Freud and Georges Bataille. Turner tells Chas Devlin about the fly agaric mushroom where 'the blood of this vegetable is boring a hole. This second hole is penetrating the hole of your face. The skull of your bone'. Whatever that means, it certainly points up the ending, when Chas shoots Turner, or vice versa. (There are also scenes where characters place a mirror or medallion on someone's head, foreshadowing the bullet at the end (and the third eye), as well as scenes where the camera zooms into an actor's head from the back).

There's plenty of female nudity on display in *Performance*, and some male nudity, too. But although *Performance* is stuffed with phallic allusions, from bullets to guns to penises to aeroplanes to cars to mushrooms, it steers clear of depicting the penis: instead, it uses, like 1000s of other movies, tropes such as guns and bullets. You don't need to know anything about Freudian psychoanalysis to understand what's really going on when Pherber's dismantling Chas's gun, for instance, or when Pherber and Lucy play with it. (Donald Cammell is no different from many another filmmaker in finding girls with guns sexy: Jean-Luc Godard, Howard Hawks, or Hayao Miyazaki. Yes, it was Godard who quipped that all you need to make a movie is a girl and a gun. Or, in Godard's case, two million girls and two million guns).

❂

There's a clever piece of parallel action which puts together via editing the jury in the courtroom and the punters who visit sex cinemas in Soho: in the courtroom, the jury are shown a film, a black-and-white porn flick about spanking (of course it's butt-slapping! what else could it be in a British movie but corporal punishment?!). The 1970 movie cuts to close-ups of the jury blankly watching the spanking; and when Chas Devlin and his boys visit the Cypriot guy in Soho who runs the porn cinema, there's the same (or a similar) film playing in the background.

Like so much in *Performance*, it's the *editing* that once again performs the magic here, deftly (and economically) putting together the law and pornography, the courts and the sleazy clubs (and suggesting that once out of the stuffy courtroom, the jury will become the punters who haunt the dens of iniquity in Soho. It's all about hypocrisy).

Performance elegantly evokes the emerging modern crime business and its links to porn and the sex industry. Porn is pure capitalism, as Jean-Luc Godard would say, just as crime is pure capitalism, and cinema is capitalism in one of its purest forms. A couple of years after *Performance*'s release in 1970, a giant, North American movie, *The Godfather*, explored the notion of organized crime (i.e., the mafia) as an equivalent for Western capitalism, and a stand-in for modern North America, and the whole Western way of life.

At the time of *Performance*, however, the sex industry was still branded as sleazy and degrading, and not only in Britain. Pornography wasn't as widely accepted as it is today. And *Performance* captures perfectly the shady underworld aspect of the sex industry, in London's Soho. And the way that the movie links the under-the-counter sex industry to the law and to lawyers, to the pillars of the community, vividly manifests the hypocrisy of the social system in Britain, which's still hypocritical and corrupt.

SEX AND VIOLENCE IN *PERFORMANCE*

The self-conscious and stylized kinkiness of *Performance* extends to the gangster scenes in another respect: when Joey Maddocks (Anthony Valentine) and his chums beat the shit out of Chas Devlin, they also hold him down on the bed, yank down his pants and Joey proceeds to whip him.[89] Only in a British gangster movie would a fight scene and a torture scene shift into spanking! How the Brits *love* their corporal punishment! [90]

That fight scene goes on and on, with rough and tumble stunt work; it's staged with a brutality that seems particular to certain British crime movies.[91] There's a kind of psychotic enjoyment in inflicting pain.[92] The feathers flying around and the slooshed red paint enhances the unreality. Needless to say, there's an undercurrent of gay sex to it, too: Harry Flowers had expressively ordered Chas not to get involved with Joey Maddocks, because it is too personal for him, which suggests that there is some relationship between the two that went sour.[93]

The fight is also intercut, bizarrely, with Turner in his house (but only very briefly). And all sorts of other material – such as the b/w photos of Chas Devlin in his boxing outfit. And it's also interlaced with flashbacks to

---

[89] Anthony Valentine was not happy with the way that Donald Cammell wanted to scene to be played with its obvious, oiled-up kinkiness: there was certainly tension between the director and the actor: 'Don and I always had an extremely uncomfortable relationship', Valentine admitted (B, 220). Valentine didn't like the idea, either, of appearing in what seemed to be one guy's 'rather black fantasy', which mixed in drugs, and sex, and violence (where the lines between reality and fantasy were deliberately blurred by Cammell). 'I think a lot of people on the movie got very disturbed by the violence, because there was a very heavy, very intense atmosphere of only barely suppressed violence, which occasionally would just break the surface' (B, 222).

[90] The Marlon Brando movie *One-Eyed Jacks* is another inter-text with *Performance* – Donald Cammell had apparently fainted when he watched the scene where Brando's hand's broken by Karl Malden (U, 35).

[91] Anthony Valentine has recounted at length how the scene was filmed: there wasn't a stunt co-ordinator; it was up to the actors to work it out for themselves. James Fox was so tough from his training at the Thomas a' Beckett pub, on the first take one of the guys got a broken nose and another had three broken ribs (B, 222).

[92] A detail has Chas adjusting the position of the objects on the coffee table before he leaves for work, emphasizing how neat his apartment is, which highlights the extent of the damage that Joey and his crew inflict on the place.

[93] Colin MacCabe is sure their relationship 'undoubtedly involves past homosexual experiences' (M, 29). Maybe. Maybe not. It doesn't really matter: much more pertinent to the film is that Joey is someone who can get under Chas's skin, and weaken his defences.

Chas and Dana tupping at the beginning of the picture (this is probably intended as part of Chas's mindscreen).[94] So the film makes those links between sex and violence that are beloved of Dead White Male Writers such as the Marquis de Sade, Georges Bataille and the Surrealists.

It's a commonplace of *avant garde* European art to put together sex and violence, or sexual violence and violent sex, and *Performance* goes along with that (you can bet that *Performance* is a favourite among the French *avant garde*). So the whipping of Chas Devlin by Joey Maddocks is directly equated with the S/M sex that Chas and Dana enjoyed (hell, Joey didn't even need to bring his own whip!).[95]

The fight closes with another modernist cinematic device: the screen washes out to red. That, like the red paint being thrown at the walls, may be another reference to Jean-Luc Godard, who has red paint and blood happily splashed around his movies ('it's not blood, it's red', as one of Godard's characters puts it).

Joey Maddocks' death is played with a pathetic fear on Joey's part – crawling backwards onto the bed and pleading with Chas Devlin. It's pitiful, and it's typical of this eccentric movie that it includes a shot from *behind* the sheets that Joey pulls up in front of him, as if he's a child trying to hide from the bogie man (the sound of dripping water, from the shower, is mixed high in the soundtrack, another of those analogies for the life literally running out of Joey, like after the murder of Marion in *Psycho*). Chas is pure, cold-blooded psychosis at this point: 'I am a bullet'.[96] This scene of gun-toting, shooting and death of course foreshadows the ending of *Performance*.

In a 1970 interview (in *The Guardian*), Donald Cammell remarked that *Performance* was about the significance of violence in artistic creativity, and in being an artist. The attempt in *Performance*, Cammell said, was

> to use a film for exploring the nature of violence as seen from the point of view of an artist. It says that this crook leads this fading pop star to realise that violence is a facet of creative art, that his energy is derived from the same sources as those of the crook. And that that energy is always dangerous, sometimes fatal.[97]

---

[94] There's also a brief insert of *Odd Man Out* (Carol Reed, 1947) in *Performance*, which acts as a kind of flashback for the childhoods of either Joey or Chas (R. and S. Umland call it a flashcut from the 'secret movie' inside *Performance*).
[95] There was even more to the dialogue where Maddocks tries to whip out the confession from Chas that he's gay: 'SAY IT!' he screams (Joey's lads have written 'POOF' on the wall). Joey also realizes that Chas may also be enjoying the whipping. This may also be a reference to *Lawrence of Arabia*.
[96] In *Performance*, Chas *is* violence itself, not someone being violent. It's the philosophy of Jean Genet, which Donald Cammell drew on; Chas is the 'loaded gun'.
[97] In D. Malcolm, 1970. It didn't have to be a rock star, Donald Cammell remarked, it could've been any artist at the end of the road. But Cammell was fascinated by the rock world, and also by Mick Jagger and the Stones, and their flirtations with satanic themes (which, of course, were only that – temporary flirtations).

The gangster wouldn't *use* violence, in Donald Cammell's conception (written at the time of *The Performers* script), he would *be* violence. As in Chas's announcement: 'I am a bullet': the gangster is a 'performer', he becomes violence itself (thus he has no need to use violence, though if he has to he will).

According to Mick Jagger, speaking a coupla years after making *Performance*, it was the lack of the ritualization of violence in contemporary society that Donald Cammell deplored. He wanted a situation where violence could be ritualized, Jagger said (well, there are sports games, football matches, festivals, live shows, and even movies, where violence is ritualized). That was a major theme in Cammell's work – that and the relations between the sexes, and what gender roles were and how they were performed (and how violence related to gender).

SEX IN DONALD CAMMELL'S MOVIES

As Marianne Faithfull explained, threesomes was Donald Cammell's preference when it came to kinkiness (well, *duh*, it's a standard fantasy of erotica, and probably a phantasie of millions of people). Apparently, it stemmed, according to Myriam Gibril, from finding his girlfriend and her sister in bed together when he returned to his studio in Chelsea.[98] Cammell was rumoured to have indulged in three-way sex with Anita Pallenberg and his girlfriend Deborah Dixon, and also with Michèle Breton, another of the actors in *Performance*. Fun rumours, but whatever the truth, multiple participants in fucking are a recurring ingredient in Cammell's cinema.

Characters who're unsure about their sexual preferences crop up in Donald Cammell's cinema – undercurrents of homosexuality occur in three of the four features that Cammell directed. Schizophrenic personalities too are a recurring element.

❉

Critics have drawn attention to the 'kinky' or non-conventional sex acts in Donald Cammell's movies, and for *British* movies, yes, they are fairly unusual. But not compared to European movies of the same period.[99] For

---

[98] Or it may have been when he found his girlfriend Rita in bed with her sister (U, 37). Whatever the legend or rumour, the notion of a threesome 'seemed to have a huge effect on his sexual imagination', according to his later girlfriend Myriam Gibril.

[99] One could point to the movies of Pier Paolo Pasolini, Dario Argento, Jess Franco and others, of the period, who are gorier, more sexually explicit, and more violent.

instance, in one single film, *Immoral Tales* (1974), Polish *auteur* Walerian Borowczyk and his team staged a blowjob in the surf on a stony beach while the guy recites the tide timetables (a sex scene unlike any other in cinema!); an extended masturbation scene in which God (no less!) commands a teenage woman to masturbate with a cucumber (depicted in close-up!); Countess Dracula (Countess Báthory, played by Pablo Picasso's daughter, Paloma Picasso, in her only film role) slaughtering twenty naked virgins and bathing in their blood (followed by some lesbian sex with her majordomo); and in the final episode, set in Renaissance Italy, the Borgias – father, daughter and brother – have an orgy while Girolamo Savonarola burns at the stake (the episode culminates with Lucrezia's brother Cesare fucking her from behind while she sucks off her father, the Pope).

PERFORMANCE AS GANGSTER MOVIE

What about *Performance* and the British gangster film tradition? Well, it's clear that *Performance* is a send-up and revision of the gangster flick. But it also wants to have it both ways: it wants to satirize criminals and the crime film, and it wants to exalt them.

By the time of *Performance* in 1968, the British crime movie had established numerous stereotypes, set-pieces, slang, motifs, etc. These were all pretty much the same as the North American crime film, though the British crime picture tended to be a little softer when it came to action and violence. The British gangster tended to be more of a Jack the Lad (as *Performance* puts it), at once playful and often with a sensitive side, a kind spot underneath.

The British gangster and crime film tradition extends back to the silent era. Highpoints included *Brighton Rock* (1947),[100] Alfred Hitchcock's British movies, and Ealing comedies (*The Ladykillers, Kind Hearts and Coronets* and *The Lavender Hill Mob*). In the 1960s, there was the comedy caper *The Italian Job* (1969), *The League of Gentlemen* (1960), *The Day They Robbed the Bank of England* (1960) and *Pink Panther* (1964). (Yes, some of these movies, and the others cited below were American-financed).

Following *Performance*, the British crime genre would continue to thrive (particularly on television – *Minder, The Sweeney*, etc), with films such as

---

[100] *Brighton Rock* is for me Britain's finest crime movie – terrific script, a fine cast, wonderful locations, and an extraordinarily bitter cynicism rarely found in *any* movie.

The Sweeney (1976 and 1978), *Get Carter* (1971), *The Long Good Friday* (1979), *McVicar* (1980), *The Hit* (1984), *Mona Lisa* (1986), up to the contemporary scene: *Lock, Stock and Two Smoking Barrels* (1998), *Gangster No. 1* (2000) and *Sexy Beast* (2000). The Krays even had their own movie, called, imaginatively, *The Krays* (1990).

By the 1990s, the British crime picture had become a cliché upon a cliché upon a cliché. It had been revamped a number of times – taking in the influence of European (French) cool (such as *Le Samourai*, 1967) and American epics (*Mean Streets, the Scarface* remake, *GoodFellas, Casino, Reservoir Dogs, Natural Born Killers, Boys N the Hood, Pulp Fiction*, etc).

The British crime picture has tried a number of ways of re-inventing itself: by using the flashy visuals and montage techniques of MTV and pop promos, for instance, or by depicting ever more graphic violence and gore. None of these extras can hide the fact that the gangster pic is running over the same ground it has always done. (The more recent British gangster movies for me are totally dull – Hong Kong cinema, for instance, is *infinitely* superior. But then, Hong Kong movies make almost *all* other movies seem tame and unimaginative!).

So over 100 or more years, the same character types, the same action scenes, the same settings, the same costumes, the same resolutions crop up time after time in the crime genre: the vicious hood, the woman who loves him despite his reputation, the good-hearted cop, the corrupt cop, the detective in a raincoat, the domineering police chief, the whore, the old lags, the gangster who repents, the crook trying to go straight, the mobster attempting to leave the organization, etc. And scenes such as: the interrogation scene, the chase around the streets of London (always with the white Jaguar car), planning the heist, the bank job, the getaway, doing time (and the prison break-out), R & R in a bar or strip joint, etc.

Performance is also part of a wave of movies produced in the 1960s which explored more graphic ways of depicting violence. Leaders in this field were filmmakers such as Arthur Penn, Sam Peckinpah, Dennis Hopper, Samuel Fuller and Robert Aldrich, and movies such as *Bonnie & Clyde, The Wild Bunch, The Dirty Dozen, Point Blank,* and *Vanishing Point* (in the West – but, again, Asian movies, especially Japanese and Chinese thrillers, were far ahead of Western products). And right after *Performance*, other movies pushed the envelope: *A Clockwork Orange, The Devils* and *Straw Dogs*.[101]

❂

---

[101] Donald Cammell admired *A Clockwork Orange* and *Straw Dogs*, which he saw in New York in 1971. David Bailey wanted to make an adaption of *A Clockwork Orange*, with Mick Jagger in the lead; Andrew Oldham was all for promoting the Stones as modern-day droogs from Anthony Burgess's novel (Oldham took up the 'nadsat' lingo that Burgess developed for the droogs and used it in his advertising copy for the Stones' PR. David Bowie created an image, with *Ziggy Stardust*, very much in the droog mold).

Harry Flowers is a crime boss who likes to lecture and declaim to his gang, presiding over them like a king with his courtiers. He holds court in his office, with his gangsters and heavies around him, and in the bar of a nightclub he runs. Everything about Flowers is a cliché of crime lords, right down to the seedy sides of Flowers' operation (such as the links to the tackier side of show biz in the nightclub).

Harry Flowers' 'chaps' include Rosebloom (Stanley Meadows), Moody (John Bindon),[102] and Dennis (Anthony Morton). Rosebloom is the most prominent, joining Chas Devlin on his missions to put the frighteners on people, and coming to collect Chas at the end. Moody is wonderfully dopey, and Dennis stays near the boss as a languid, world-weary, seen-it-all-before (and rather camp) adviser.

As well as the Cockney slang, the macho posturing, the cynical worldview and the undercurrent of violence in this brotherhood of minor London criminals, there is also a homosexual subtext (there are references to bodybuilding magazines, for instance, and sports such as boxing).

The first time I saw *Performance* I hadn't noticed the half-naked youth in the bathroom of Harry Flowers' hotel suite, which suggests that Flowers is spending the night with the boy. If you think of Flowers as a Roman emperor, with a penchant for acting grandiose and liking young trade, it all fits. At the close of the scene, Flowers enters the bathroom, turning to the camera with a smile – he's just about to have his bath with the kid.

That scene in Harry Flower's bedroom has all sorts of odd elements, including other homosexual signifiers (such as one of the henchmen looking at a photo of boys). Flowers looks particularly dishevelled, like Keef Richards after a night on the town. It's another mark of the clever twists in the gangster genre that the filmmakers don't have Flowers exploding over Chas Devlin killing Joey Maddocks (one expected response), but instead he's curled up in his bed, talking very low on the telephone, and continually pulling the covers over his head, as if to block it all out (and as if unconsciously mimicking Joey's last moments).

❂

The first part of *Performance* runs through some of the clichés of the gangster and crime genre, including showing Chas Devlin and his pals

---

[102] John Bindon (1943-93) was something of a legend himself – he dated Angie Bowie and Christine Keeler, was often in trouble with the law. His party trick, according to Mick Brown, was balancing 6 half-pint beer glasses on his wiener (B, 26).
As an actor, Bindon had appeared in *Poor Cow*, the adaption of Nell Dunn's book (Ken Loach, 1967), and went on to TV appearances in *The Sweeney*, *Z Cars*, and *Hazell*, as well as *Quadrophenia*. Bindon provided security for Led Zeppelin in the 1970s: he was arrested, along with manager Peter Grant, drummer John Bonham and tour manager Richard Cole, for beating the shit out of an employee of rock promoter Bill Graham in San Francisco.
Bindon had the credentials to play a criminal – he had been in prison before and after appearing in *Performance* (including being charged with murder in 1979). Actor Bob Hoskins testified in court for him: as Bindon put it, 'when Bob walked in, the jury knew I was OK'.

'putting the frighteners on' some people who haven't paid up for their protection (including a car hire business, and a guy, presumably in Soho or the West End, who sells porn and runs a porn cinema). The clichés come thick and fast: the white Jaguar, the English criminal slang ('grass', 'slag', 'ponce', 'frighteners'), the sleazy pubs and clubs, the macho bravado, the fist fights, the intimidation. And, yes, even the cliché phrase 'business is business' is trotted out.

All of this is very, very familiar to a British audience, to people who have seen *The Sweeney* and *Minder* and *Z Cars* and all the other cop, detective, thriller and crime TV shows and films. It's absolutely essential for a British crime movie to have a white Jag slewing round the corners of a back street in the East End or riding over Chelsea Bridge; there must be old, red, telephone kiosks; red double-decker buses; a sleazy nightclub scene; countless scenes in pubs; a crime lord who smokes cigars and sheds pearls of wisdom to his lads; a couple of ageing whores; and a wife or girlfriend who stands by her gangster through thick and thin (women are scarce on the ground among the minor criminals – only Chas seems to have a woman in his life).

There's a lengthy scene in a court in *Performance* where the lawyer Harley-Brown (Allan Cuthbertson) declaims about society;[103] at first, it's not clear how the lawyer and the court scene intersects with the scenes of Chas, Dana, Flowers *et al*, until a little later on, when Chas confronts the lawyer and his client Mr Fraser on the street at night (altho' there are thematic and social links, of course). The scene shows Chas Devlin at his menacing best, intimidating Mr Fraser and the lawyer (deliberately ignoring the lawyer), and persuading them that they won't name his boss Harry Flowers in their proceedings (it's the lawyer's Roller that Chas and his boys wreck).

The inter-cutting of the lawyer Harley-Brown and court scenes with Chas Devlin and his boys doing the rounds of intimidating businesses that should be paying protection money encourages both narratives to comment upon each other. Now the 1970 Warners film presents two sides of the law, the smug, self-righteous capitalists in court, and the criminal capitalists out on the street. In the script (in the two scripts of *Performance*), these scenes would have followed on from each other. So Chas encountering the lawyer and his client Mr Fraser would have been part of the series of scenes which would depict Chas doing his job.

The criminal underworld plot is not forgotten about entirely in the

---

[103] The lawyer's pontifications are deliberately over-blown (even for a grandstanding courtroom scene), and come across like the self-justification of out-and-out capitalists. Something about 'progress', about the people on the right side of the law being justified in their rightness and righteousness.

second half of *Performance*; in fact, there are numerous reminders of Chas Devlin's earlier existence: he calls up Tony Farrell a few times; Chas dreams of Turner as Harry Flowers in the 'Memo to Turner' episode; Turner and Pherber find his gun, and see the whip marks on his back; and they also discuss Chas often.

After seeing the wounds on Chas Devlin's back, Pherber kindly tends them, straddling him on the bed in pink pants and taping cotton wool across them (so another of James Fox's costumes is a wad of cotton wool and tape, like a shield).

✺

GANGSTER NARCISSISM.

The narcissism of gangsters has often been remarked upon, and it has always been a part of the gangster movie. Gangsters have always been well-dressed, and have often admired themselves in mirrors.[104] Chas Devlin in *Performance* is supremely narcissistic,[105] and confronts himself in mirrors more than most movie characters (he begins in the bathroom the morning after the opening lovemaking scene, and continues throughout the 1970 movie). He also wears a suit and a tie. He is meticulous in dying his hair for his disguise. He brushes his hair in the mirror in Harry Flowers' office (caught in the same frame as Flowers looking into the mirror).

His apartment (in the minimal, Scandinavian style) is impeccably clean and tidy (tickets to a show are placed squarely side-by-side, for instance). There's a drawer full of gold cufflinks. In Chas Devlin's apartment, the pop culture references are to the brash, showy, Las Vegas kind of entertainment: *Playboy*, the Talk of the Town, and also the Rat Pack: Frank Sinatra and Sammy Davis, Jnr.

---

[104] Masculine narcissism was a fetishized spectacle in 1995's *Casino*, most obviously in Robert de Niro's character, who had 52 costume changes. Part of Martin Scorsese's ritual each morning was choosing the suit, shirt, tie and jewellery with the costume designers (Rita Ryack and John Dunn) for each day's shoot ("Interview", *Sight & Sound*, 6, 1, Jan, 1996, 10).

[105] Narcissism and dressing properly (conservatively, in a suit), was part of Ronnie Kray's regime. The gangsters also address each other formally – 'Mr Brownjohn'.

MORE ON GANGSTERISM

Donald Cammell mixed with people in the bohemian, art, pop music, theatrical and aristocratic worlds (realms of society which were reflected in *Performance*). As Cammell explained, beneath each cultural scene was an undercurrent of crime,[106] and *Performance* is partly about the meeting of the two worlds, the aristocrats, artists, actors, pop stars and æsthetes encountering the gangsters, mobs and 'performers' in the criminal underworld.[107] It was about the Beatles and the Stones intersecting with the Krays and the Richardsons (two of the most famous London criminal families of the period).[108] As the ad in the *Village Voice* for the premiere in Gotham put it, 'somewhere in your head there's a wild electric dream. Come see it in *Performance*, where underground meets underworld'.

For Donald Cammell, the criminals in Britain of the period had a glamour and fascination (which many others have felt). They were powerful people, but they were also well-dressed and charismatic (or they mixed with glamourous people, so the aura of celebrity rubbed off on them).

The fascination with gangsters interacting with the worlds of fashion, music, show business and aristocracy ain't nuttin' new in cinema, of course: the Warner Brothers movies and *film noirs* of the 1930s and 1940s had already explored this fusion. The fascination continued into the contemporary era of North American movies, with films such as the *Godfather* films, *Casino, Pulp Fiction* and *GoodFellas*. It was the familiar world of guns, girls, cars, money, drugs, Las Vegas, action, and the mafia. (Meanwhile, in Asian cinema, gangsters intersect with glitz, casinos, gambling and showbiz all the time, and in real life, too).

So *Performance* was adding nothing new in this respect: in the American gangster movies of the Thirties and Forties, it would be Jimmy Cagney or Humphrey Bogart mixing backstage with the dancers in a Broadway musical; in *The Godfather*, director Francis Coppola, producer Robert Evans and co-author Mario Puzo depicted a singer based partly on Frank Sinatra having trouble with a film studio boss (loosely based on the fearsome Harry Cohn at Columbia). And Coppola's and Evans' troubled, unsatisfying but impressive follow-up to *The Godfather*, *The Cotton Club* (1984), mixed black show biz with New York gangsterism.

But in *Performance*, Donald Cammell, Nic Roeg, Sandy Lieberson and

---

[106] A flourishing pop culture and entertainment scene had to have its counterpart in the criminal underworld, Donald Cammell reckoned.

[107] In the 1960s, the criminal underworld in Britain was glamourized, as outfits such as the Krays forged links with the entertainment worlds. The Krays became minor celebrities, and hung out with celebs.

[108] In the 1960s, police corruption was rife, with Scotland Yard helping to allow organized crime to flourish. The corruption led to East End gangs moving their gambling empires into the West End, according to Barry Miles (98).

the team were also exploring the homosexual[109] aspects of the criminal underworld (which had links to the real-life criminals, such as the Kray brothers).[110] Gangster movies had often explored the *narcissism* of criminals, as they strutted around in expensive suits with a pretty girl on their arm. But not the gay subtexts: the American movies of the 1930s and 1940s up to the films helmed by Martin Scorsese, Paul Thomas Anderson, Abel Ferrara and Quentin Tarantino portrayed groups of men living intimately together, without ever acknowledging that any of 'em could be gay (similarly, American buddy movies and action movies typically depict bands of brothers in close proximity, but never drawing attention to the homoerotic aspects. Meanwhile, Chinese filmmaker John Woo has always denied any homoeroticism in his many famous movies of brotherhoods and male bonding, of men acting like modern-day samurai (but with guns instead of swords), of men suffering and agonizing in highly-charged, grandiose and operatic concoctions – *The Killer, A Better Tomorrow, Hard Boiled*, etc. For Woo, his gangsters are pursuing goals like honour, loyalty, friendship and integrity).

Gay sexuality and bisexuality and other non-heterosexualities were expected to be found in the worlds of show biz and pop music in cinema, but not in the gangster realm. So bringing gay sexuality out into the open was a new element in *Performance* (homosexuality had only been legalized in Britain not long before – in 1967). Pherber tells Chas that 'it's a man's, man's, man's world' (in *The Performers* script), and Chas insists that he's normal (B, 66).

So it's not the individual fusions in *Performance* that are innovative: gangsters and show biz, or gangsters and music, or gangsters and drugs, or music and drugs, or music and sex, or gangsters and sex. That had all been done before (and not just in North American A-movies like *The Godfather, The Big Sleep, Point Blank, Bonnie & Clyde, Double Indemnity, Out of the Past*, etc, but in thousands of B-movies and drive-in movies and exploitation movies). It was the idiosyncratic blend of all those elements that was new. And Donald Cammell, Nic Roeg and their team also added a gay subtext to gangsterism, which hadn't really been explored before.

And finally they added one element which was very unusual, and very

---

[109] Boxing, sport, body-building, the gym – *Performance* celebrates the homoerotic aspects of male grooming.
[110] Although known to be straight, Donald Cammell had made sexual advances towards Vartkes Cholakian (in 1979), and his editor Frank Mazzola, among others (U, 267).

particular to Donald Cammell – and that was occultism and paganism.[111] Cinema might have fused crime, sex, drugs, music, and show business, but not with arcane religions or occultism. You hadn't seen a pop music film or a gangster flick which included Aleister Crowley before (no, and you haven't seen one since).

The occult undercurrent in *Performance* takes in the Nizari Hashashim or assassins, and the links between drugs and violence (hash – cannabis). It was a favoured topic of writers such as William Burroughs[112] and Arthur Rimbaud. It was something that was in the air around this time – you find it also in bands such as Hawkwind and the Rolling Stones. As Turner quotes, 'nothing is true, everything is permitted', one of the mantras of the 1960s era (it's a more nihilistic expression of the concept of 'free love'). Aleister Crowley had famously announced 'do what thou wilt shall be the whole of the law', in his book *The Book of the Law* (and in graffiti), which many subsequent followers took to mean: 'anything goes'.

CHAS AND TURNER

The scene where Chas Devlin finally encounters Turner is vital, dramatically and thematically. It brings together the two main characters in the film, and has to do a number of things. One is to suggest their similarities as well as differences (the use of the notion of being a 'performer' is prominent here). When Mick Jagger leaps towards Chas, now suddenly switched from his orange dressing gown to funky stage gear of close-fitting black, wielding a microphone, he becomes the instantly recognizable Jagger, lead singer of the Rolling Stones.

It's absolutely typical of *Performance* that Chas Devlin should first see Turner in a mirror (the ceiling mirror). The staging of parts of the scene are highly idiosyncratic: Turner lurks in the shadows behind a screen, and Chas talks to him by looking up into the mirror. (Chas realizes that he has to tread carefully here).

Chas Devlin's primary objective in this scene is simple: he asks 'can I

---

111 Camille Paglia in *Sexual Personae* calls Hollywood the modern Rome, with its depictions of 'pagan sex and violence that have flowered so vividly in our mass media. The camera has unbound daemonic western imagination. Cinema is a *sexual showing*, a pagan flaunting. Plot and dialogue are obsolete word-baggage. Cinema, the most eye-intense of genres, has restored pagan antiquity's cultic exhibitionism. Spectacle is a pagan cult of the eye' (33).

112 William Burroughs and fellow avant gardist Brion Gysin had taken up the cult of the Assassins or Hashishim. An early bohemian group which included Alexander Dumas, Gérard de Nerval, Alfred de Musset, Honoré de Balzac, Théophile Gautier and Charles Baudelaire had called themselves Club des Haschischins.

stay?' And Turner's objective is to deflect him from that goal. The scene plays like an acting exercise: it's a regular kind of drama school task to have one actor want something, and the other actor has to refuse it. One has a goal; the other's the obstacle. So Chas repeatedly asks Turner: 'can I stay here?' And Turner responds that, no, he wouldn't like it, no, he wouldn't fit in, no, he doesn't want Chas to stay.

This goes on and on, and Turner only agrees after the conversation has reached one of the primary themes of *Performance*: *who are you?* It's when Turner asks Chas Devlin, 'do you know who you are?', and Chas doesn't really answer, that Turner assents (as if Turner recognizes that only people with fluid identities would fit in or would be welcome here. Nothing static, nothing fixed – everything in flux, everything is being negotiated. The house – Turner's world – is a space for discovery, of the self, of multiple selves. Someone who turned up *chez* Turner and announced: 'I know who I am, what I am doing, and where I am going', would automatically be refused entry).

One of the enjoyable aspects of the acting and characterizations in *Performance* is how Chas Devlin has to completely reverse his natural (or usual or traditional) personality when he goes to the Powis Square house: the audience has seen Chas acting very confident and heavy in scenes at the mini-cab firm, with the lawyer and his client Mr Fraser, with the sex club owner, and with the chauffeur.

This is a guy who can look after himself, who can 'put the frighteners' on all sorts of people. This is someone who can't be pushed around that easily. But when he encounters an ambiguous figure like Turner, he's suddenly out of his depth, and quite unsure of how to act. And Turner's Mephistopheles – Pherber – is another ambiguous figure that Chas Devlin can't control by his usual means. Chas perceives, rightly, that force isn't going to work here – and neither is money (which Turner returns to him).

One of the ironies of *Performance* is how a street-tough guy like Chas Devlin can be manipulated by two people, Pherber and Turner, who haven't got the strength to hurt a fly. Pherber and Turner don't imprison Chas, don't tie him up or shut him in the basement, don't threaten him physically, but they might as well have done.

It's as if, in killing Joey Maddocks, Chas Devlin has crossed a threshold, maybe into another world, into Hell – maybe he's stepped across the barrier between life and death. Because as soon as he kills Joey, in the real world, he's a man on the run.[113] But the film enhances that: now it seems as if

---

[113] A hunted animal gone to earth, as Donald Cammell described Chas in *The Performers* script, although Chas reckons the Turner's pad is the last place his firm (or the fuzz) will look for him, it's still a silly place to hide.

everything is conspiring against Chas (as if the world is now conspiring to punish him, in a Gnostic fashion, for his breaking of an ultimate taboo, murder).

Notice, for instance, how he can't even get into the house at Powis Square: Pherber teases Chas Devlin at length on the intercom (Pherber's teasing of Chas, which continues throughout the movie, starts right here: simply put, Chas has never encountered a person like Pherber before). That scene goes on and on, with numerous cutaways to other people in the square, including some guys watching him from a nearby house, who might be Harry Flowers' heavies. The Warners movie emphasizes that though this looks like an ordinary house, it might be Dracula's Castle or the Gateway to Hell (there's a shot looking up at the building, for example, making it look imposing).

So it makes dramatic sense that it can't be easy for Chas Devlin to get in – because once he's in, he can't come out (and maybe he'll wish he'd never gone in). Indeed, he never comes out, unless you count the fusion of Chas and Turner at the end. (Notice, too, when *Performance* cuts to a long shot of Chas in the hallway, there's an ominous chord on the soundtrack).

When Chas Devlin is on the run the film employs numerous cutaways – to people looking at Chas (i.e., towards the camera), or going about their daily business. The cutaways to ordinary people emphasize the paranoia and desperation of the man on the run (Alfred Hitchcock used them all the time). They are a very effective way of putting the audience into the mindset of the main character. (And also how a city can suddenly become very unfriendly, depending on your mental state).

Both Chas and Turner are fascinated by each other, and on one level the 1970 film is a love story that is never consummated. Chas learns to dress in a funky, cross-dressing manner, to become, as a New Age therapy session might put it, 'in touch with his 'feminine' side' (and, yes, critics still trot out that line of reasoning in discussions of Donald Cammell's cinema).[114] Turner, meanwhile, gets to perform, in a manner of speaking, for Chas alone, and plays with violence (he also takes a starring part in Chas's dream, in the 'Memo To Turner' sequence). (It might have been tempting to have Chas and Turner get freaky: maybe if *Performance* had been made thirty years later, a sex scene between the two might have been more accepted by audiences. But the film doesn't need it, because the attraction between Turner and Chas is plain to see. There is the fantasy of a love scene, however).

---

[114] For Mick Brown, Chas and Turner see in the other what they themselves lack or need: Chas possesses the masculinity (and violence) that Turner misses, and Turner is the feminized male that Chas denies (B, 165).

Mick Jagger reckoned that the character of Turner was Donald Cammell's fantasy of what Jagger was like:

> I think Turner is a projection of Donald's fantasy or idea of what I imagine how I am. The thing is that it's very easy for people to believe that's what I'm like. (1975, 169)

Of course: people always prefer the dream to the reality. They want the jet-setting, glitzy, wealthy rock star or movie celebrity, not a real person. Who wants reality? You're *in* reality (all the time!).

Turner was pretentious, Mick Jagger reckoned, and that was part of his downfall. Turner's 'intellectual posturing' Jagger found 'very ridiculous – that's what sort of fucked him up' (1975, 169).

It's often Turner who takes up the role of the film's schoolmaster or pedant: he's the one who reads aloud from books, for instance, or quotes Antonin Artaud[115] on the madness of performance, or explains to Chas Devlin (and the audience) about the assassins or Hashashim (and kind of identifies himself with the Old Man of the Mountain, Hassan-i-Sabbah).[116] These are moments when actors are simply used as the mouthpiece for a filmmaker, but in *Performance* it never comes across as lecturing or tiresome (partly because the scenes are kept short, partly because the material is fascinating, and partly due to the way it's staged).

There are curious elements to some of these scenes, too: for instance, when Turner reads aloud from a book, his reading is cut short by a fly. As Turner freaks out, there's a giant close-up of a fly on its back (a classic William Burroughs image).

❂

There are many optical superimpositions – of Chas Devlin and Turner, of Chas and Pherber, etc. There are freeze frames, too, sometimes at the end of shots. Full slow motion and step motion. There's an optical burn-in on the mirror in the bedroom, where Chas sees Joey Maddocks before he killed him. It does stretch credibility a little that Chas, a worldly-wise guy of the streets, wouldn't know what magic mushrooms are (there's even a scene where he watches Pherber picking them in the sunlit garden).[117] That scene is idyllic – it's filmed in warm sunshine. In a way, it's a curious scene in which not much happens, and maybe could be left out easily, without affecting any of the rest of the narrative. But it has an ironic function, because Chas is watching Pherber pick the mushrooms that will help to bring on what is close to a breakdown for Chas. (It also points up the

---

115 When he quotes from Antonin Artaud on the most authentic performance being the one that leads to madness, Turner is dressed up as a teddy boy, with a leather jacket and a quiff.
116 The Old Man of the Mountain and the Hashashim fascinated William Burroughs (B, 35).
117 Or maybe that scene's more about Chas becoming fascinated by Pherber.

eccentricity of these hippy folk: while your typical middle class people in the suburbs go into their gardens to pick vegetables for the kitchen, or flowers for the table, these bohemians grow plants specifically to take them on crazeeee head trips).

Despite the emphasis on drugs in *Performance*, Donald Cammell was not a partaker. He'd tried drugs like hash and acid, but Myriam Gibril said he was way too sensitive, and they affected him too much (B, 75).[118] Similarly, Mick Jagger, as is well-known, rarely indulged, and always retained his all-important self-control. Mick would get drunk occasionally, but wasn't into ruining his beloved body with drugs. I can't imagine the rather strait-laced and prim co-director Nic Roeg being heavily into drugs, either: but the production has some first class advisers in drug culture, with Anita Pallenberg at the top of the list (hanging out with Pallenberg, as Jagger later commented, nearly killed him).

---

[118] There were drugs around the set of *Performance* – inevitably, with Anita Pallenberg in the cast! A crew member quipped: 'you want to get a fuckin' joint, they're coming out of your ear 'oles. You want a cup of tea, you got no fuckin' chance' (P. Norman, 312).

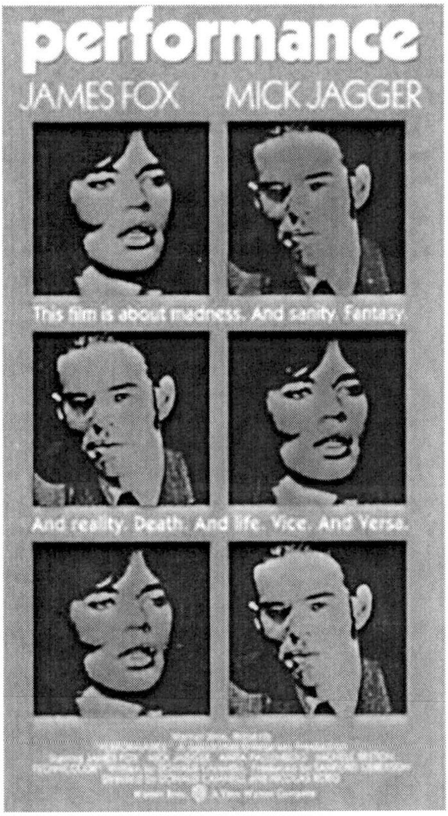
performance
JAMES FOX
MICK JAGGER
This film is about madness. And sanity. Fantasy.
And reality. Death. And life. Vice. And Versa.

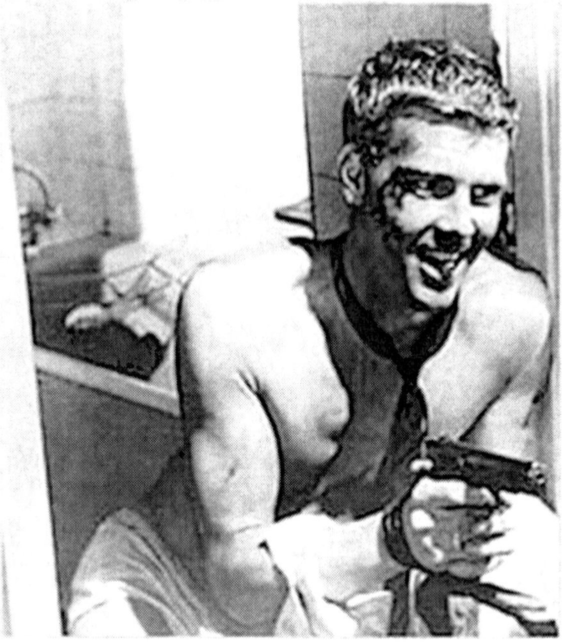

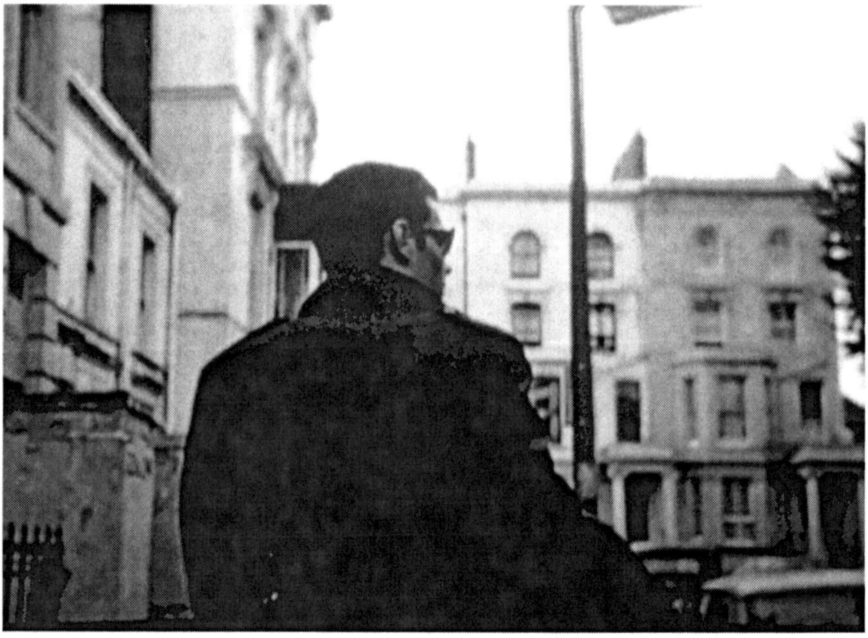

'I am a bullet'
James Fox in the performance of a lifetime.

'Vice. And versa', as the poster for Performance put it: Fox and Jagger, both remarkable in an extraordinary movie.

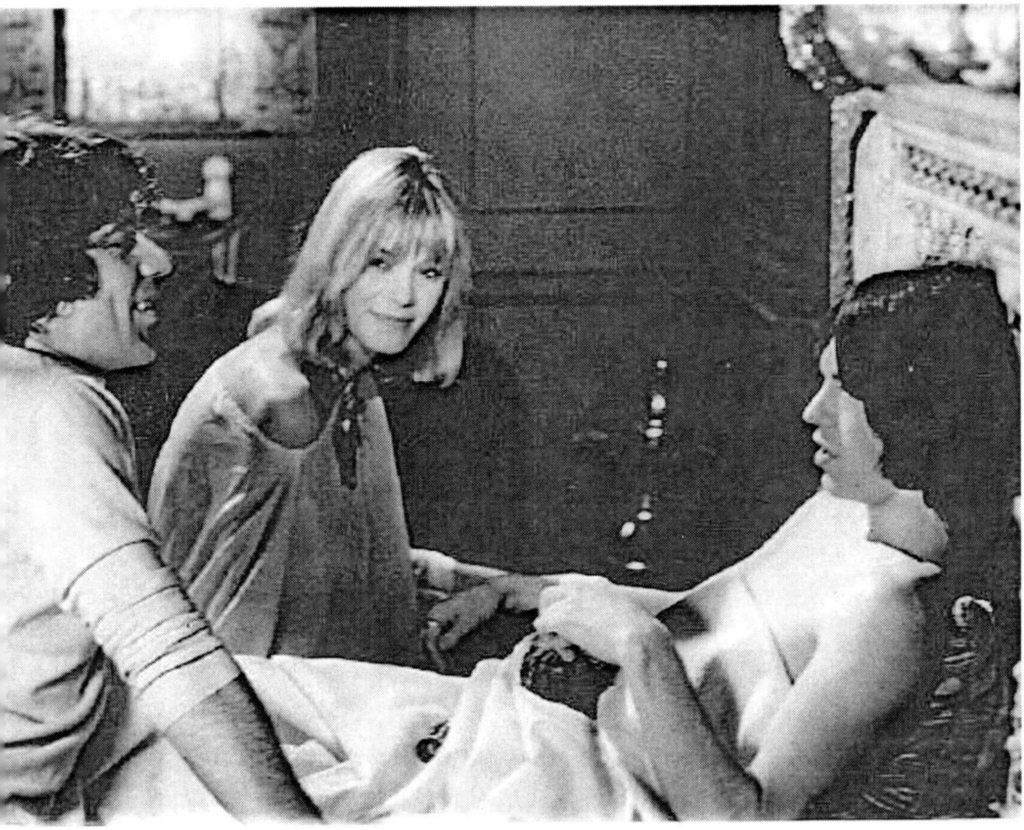

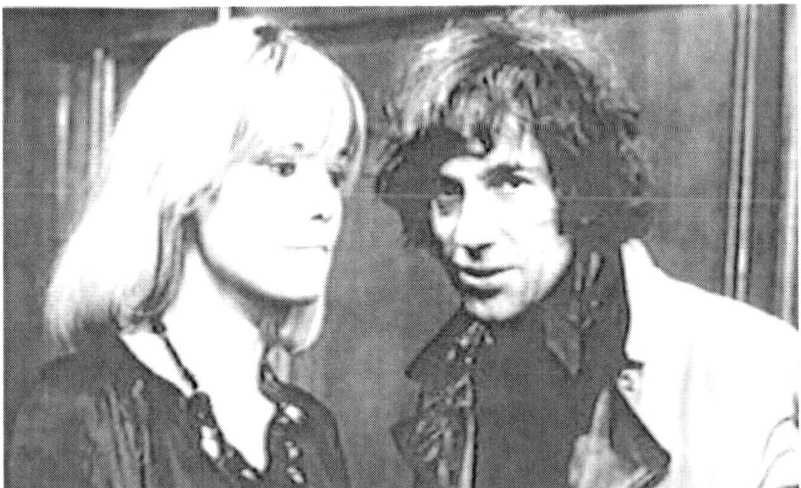

Very Sixties: a gangster on the run in a classic Godardian setting
(note the posters on the wall): James Fox in Performance.

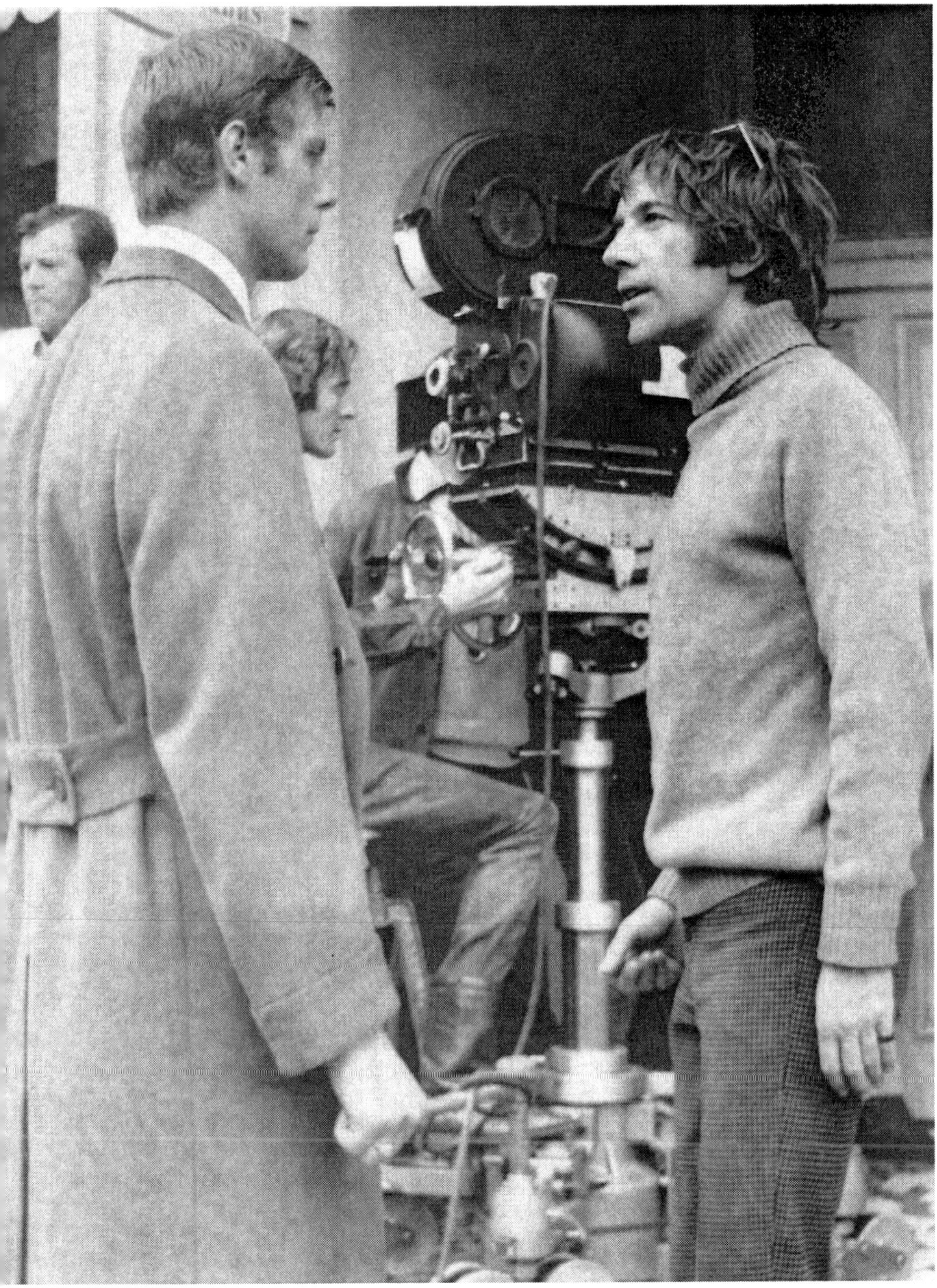

Anita Pallenberg

Pallenberg and Jagger photographed by Cecil Beaton
on the Performance set

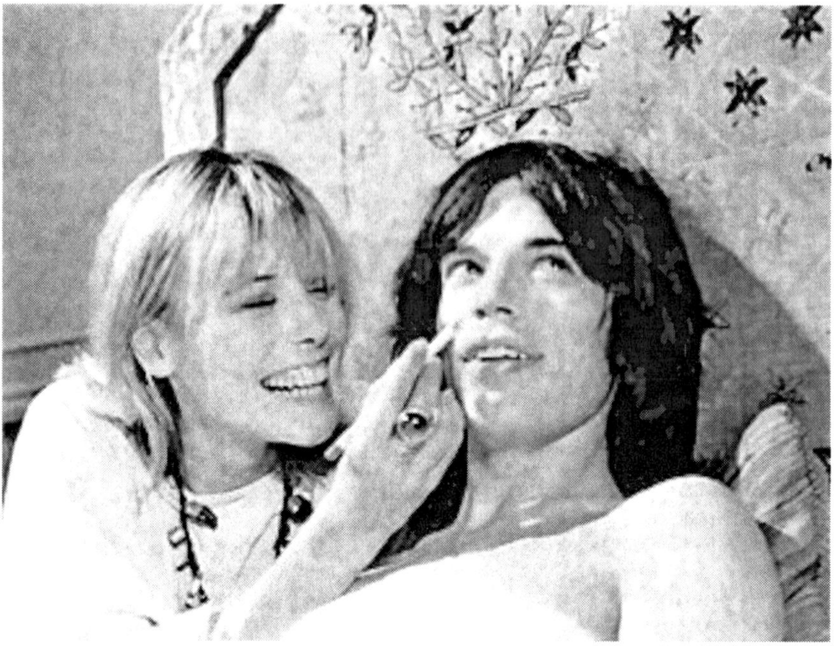

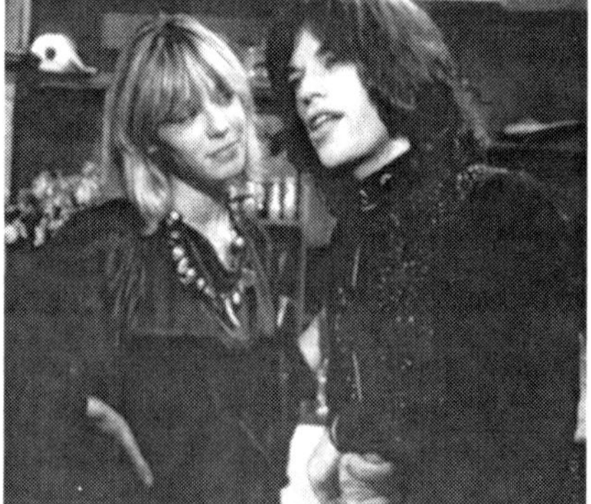

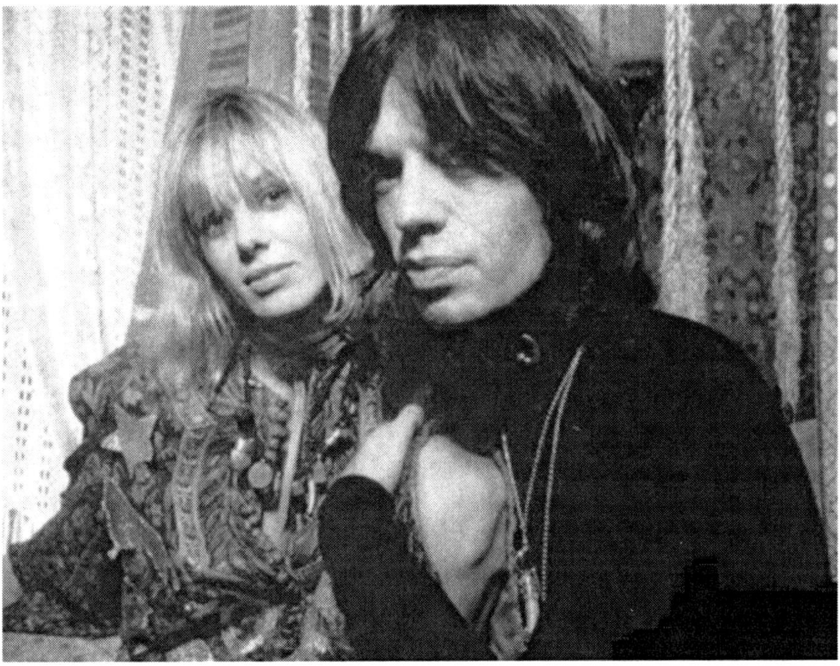

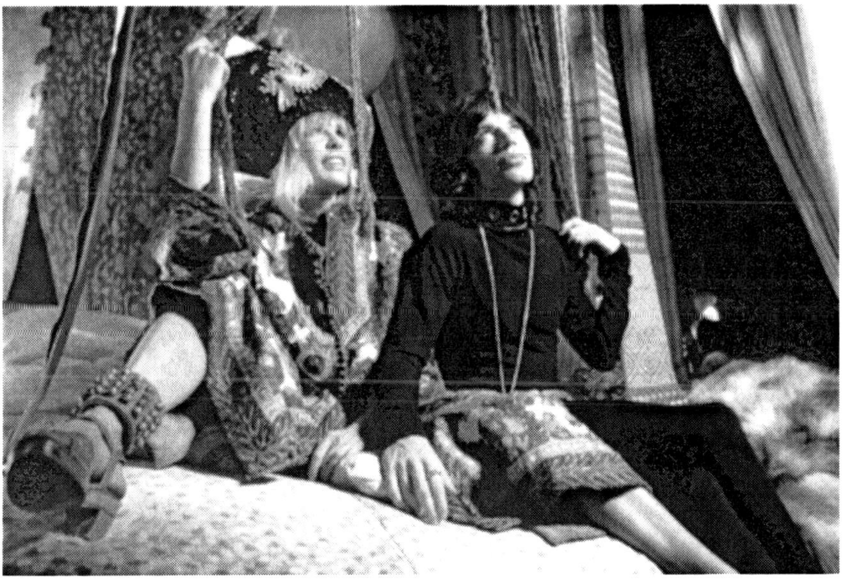

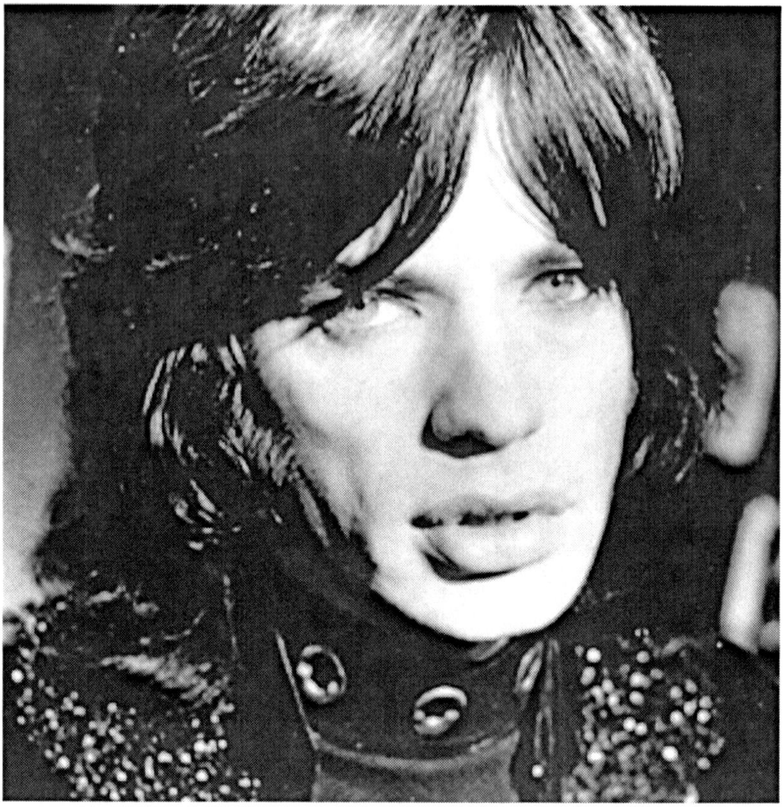

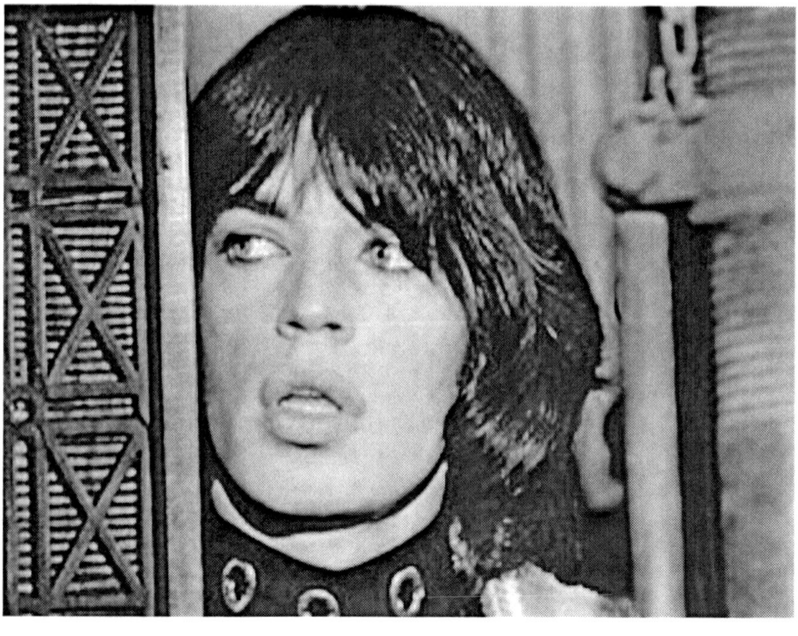

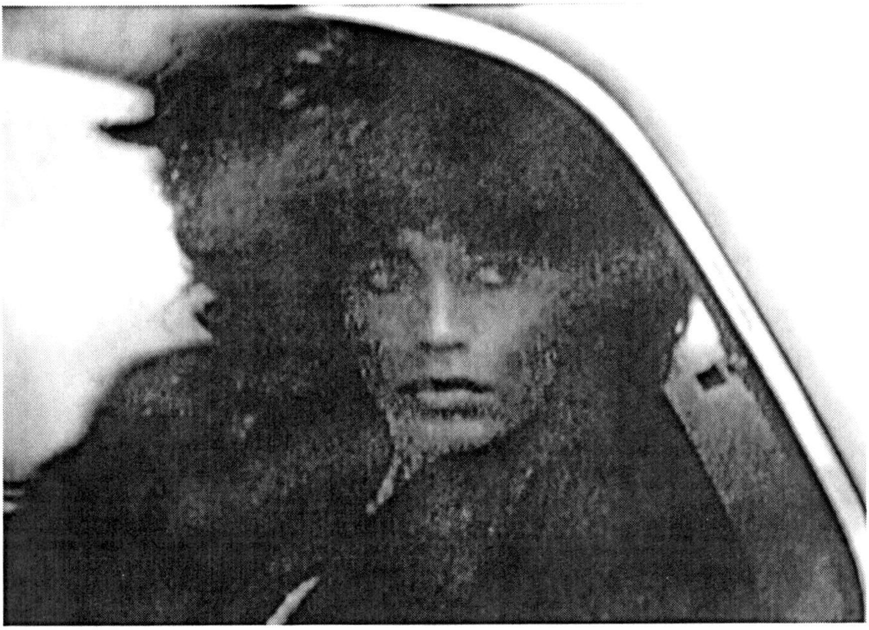

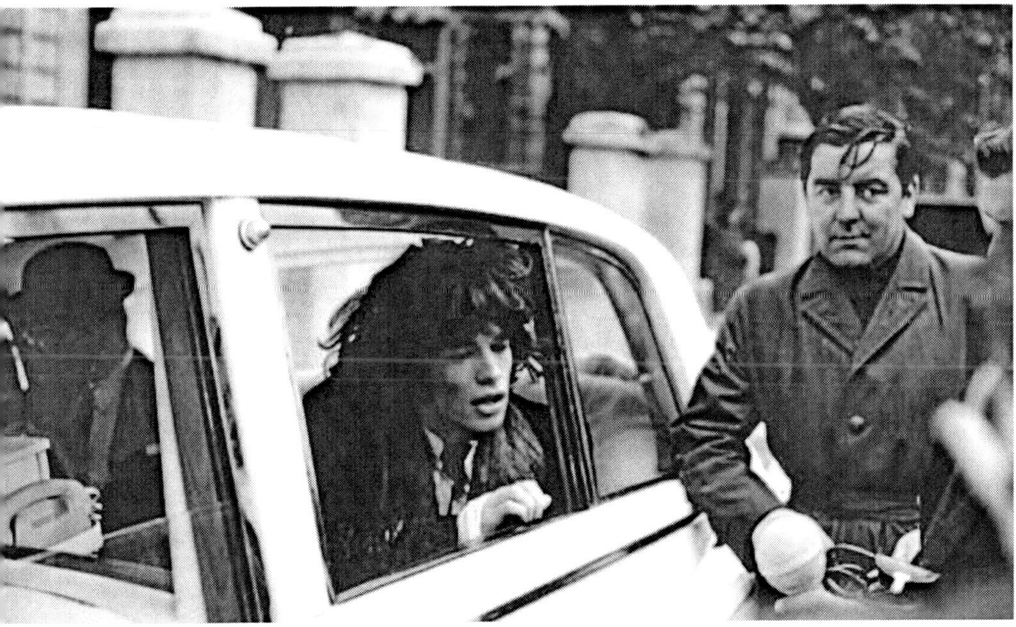

Mick Jagger with Donald Cammell (above).
And in the 'Memo To Turner' sequence in
Performance (below).

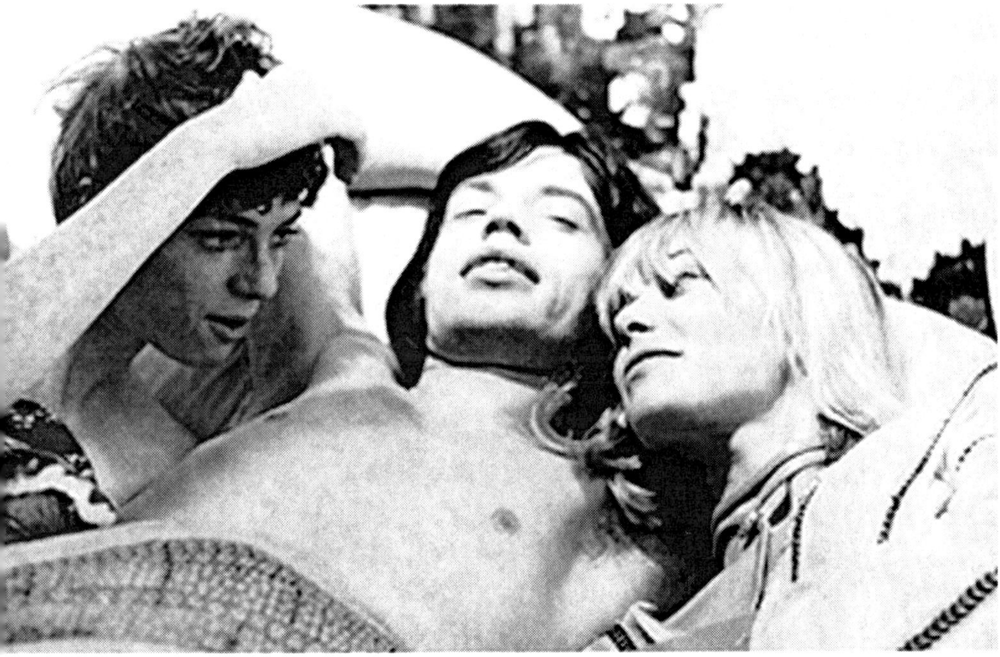

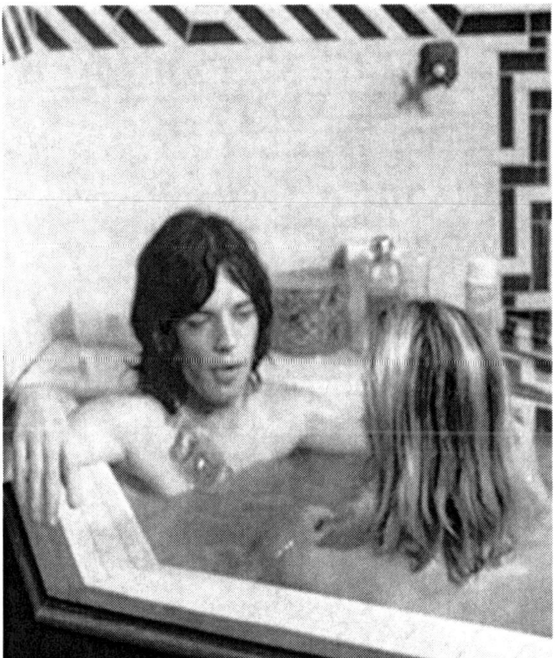

Two of James Fox's earlier movies: The Servant (1963), below, and Duffy (1968), above, which Donald Cammell co-wrote.

(© Columbia, above. Landau/ Elstree Film, below)

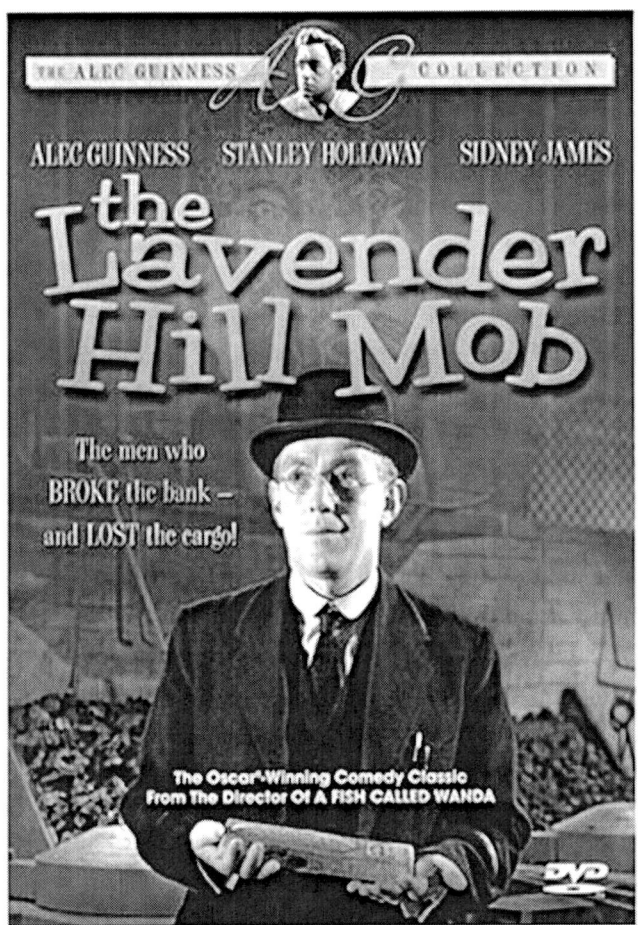

Earlier examples of British crime movies: The Lavender Hill Mob (1951), left.
And The Ladykillers (1955), below.
Two Ealing comedies starring Alec Guinness.

(© GFD/ Universal, left.)

THE ENDING OF *PERFORMANCE*

The ending of *Performance* of course has to be both apocalyptic and ambiguous. Nothing else would do after the barrage of bizarre imagery. Also, the ending has to be combine the two halves of the 1970 British-American movie: the gangster genre and the mind fuck. (In the two scripts, Turner watches Chas being taken away to his death from the window of the house).

So, Chas Devlin emerges from the basement (after tupping Lucy and offering to fetch the shampoo for her from upstairs when she's in the bath – what a nice, sweet guy!), and encounters Harry Flowers' henchmen, come to take him and kill him. The meeting brings together the two worlds in a piquant and ironic manner, because Chas is sporting hippy clothes and wearing the ginger wig. It's a great touch in the scriptwriting that Harry Flowers' boys don't draw attention to this at all (many other filmmakers wouldn't have been able to resist some quip or giggle at this point; Rosey looks him up and down just once – casual, non-committal). Maybe the hoods think this's Chas's disguise. It's a nicely under-played scene, too: Chas doesn't lunge at the heavies and make a run for it, he acts in a calm, cold manner, clearly thinking furiously.

The 1970 film goes from something very domestic and ordinary – Chas Devlin going to fetch the shampoo for Lucy in the bath (now playing the role of the caring boyfriend) – to something that's life or death: one man facing a bunch of men armed with guns. At this point, the hippy idyll is all over, brought to a sudden and complete end. It's reality time, the Freudian death principle.

When Chas Devlin reaches Turner's lair upstairs, for their final scene together,[120] the dialogue is pared down to short, vague but potentially meaningful phrases, like two lovers or killers sizing each other up, before one of them strikes. The scene is blocked very statically – Chas stands near the bed, and moves behind the hangings, and Turner[121] is in bed with Pherber – yet it is full of unspoken feelings and suggestions (Pherber's asleep again, but wakes up).

Note how both Turner and Pherber pull the covers up to their chins in the bed, like frightened children: the game is over, the play-acting is ended: now the roles are reversed, the teasing with the drugs by Turner and Pherber has ended, and Chas is back in charge (and also leading the scene, dramatically).

Note also how Pherber, Lucy and Turner begin discussing Chas Devlin

---

[120] We have to suspend disbelief that the hoods would let Chas outta their sight.
[121] Turner is introduced with a giant close-up, as if he's thinking about Chas.

in affectionate terms in the last reel of *Performance* – he's become their friend, part of their household (Lucy, for instance, who really disliked Chas at first, winds up doing him). In short, they don't want him to go.

- I might come with you, then.
- You don't know where I'm gong, pal.
- I do... I don't know.
- Yeah, you do.

Forget the dialogue, what is the subtext of this scene? You could argue many different ways, as you can with this whole movie.

It's a great touch, for instance, that Turner reverses his position completely, and tells Chas Devlin that he'll go with him, when Chas says he's got to go (now he's not going to America, but to his death). The statement of Turner's comes from a guy who's a total recluse, a guy who looks out of the window in the morning (just before Chas enters the bedroom), says it's a horrible day outside, and climbs back into bed with his lover. In his den he pulls the drapes: he doesn't want the outside world at all. The impression is that Turner hasn't been out of his house for months, perhaps years (only Pherber is depicted out of doors, when she goes to pick the fly agaric mushrooms). As if Turner recognizes that Chas has shaken his life up enough for him to feel able to leave the building.

And then the gun.

Well, that gun is another of the hyper-situated objects in *Performance*: characters pick it up, play with it, dismantle it. In one scene, Pherber shows it to Lucy; in another, she takes Chas Devlin's gun to pieces. This looks like one of those scenes where an actor will say: 'what do I do here?', and the director replies: 'oh, play with that gun for a bit. Take it apart'. Meanwhile, an actor in a Jean-Luc Godard movie will be told, time after time: 'take out a cigarette and light it', or: 'look in the mirror and play with your hair', or: 'play with the gun'.

Donald Cammell's gun fetishism is well-known, and in *Performance* it plays out to the max, when Chas shoots Turner. By this time, however, the 1970 movie has been toying with doubles and switching identities so much, the ending can play on any level you want:

(1) Chas kills Turner but becomes Turner by the end;

(2) Chas kills himself rather than be taken by Harry Flowers' hoods;

(3) if it really is Turner who's led outside and into Flower's Roller, he'll be killed anyway, in the countryside (which's what Flowers' chaps tell Chas they're going to do to him);

or – Chas and Turner become one. And so on and on.

In other words, however you play with the ending of *Performance*, most of the possibilities wind up in death. D-E-A-T-H. Even the fusion of Chas and Turner in some super-being or dual-in-one personality, will end in death. Or maybe death is the moment of fusion, so that the guy led out to the white Rolls Royce is already a corpse. (There are hints that Turner, without his demon, is already a shell of his former self: the blank stare and the all-black outfit suggest that he's already dead, or one of the living dead: a zombie).

It doesn't matter.

What matters is that *Performance* closes with a suitably apocalyptic and unreal ending, bringing together some but not all of the themes. One is the theme of death and suicide and murder, which's given a religious edge when it's linked to the assassins or Hashashim of the Nizari branch of the Ismali Shia Muslims in the Middle Ages.

Mediæval Persia and drugs and death – the note left behind by Rosebloom reads, 'Gone to Persia, Chas' (though how Rosebloom could know about the fascination with Persia, which actually comes from Pherber and Turner, not Chas, isn't explained. But it does suggest the fusion between the two worlds).[122]

There's a direct comparison made, too, between the modern-day gangsters and the bandits that might still live in the hills of Persia (the film cuts to a photograph of 'bandits' in somewhere like Iraq or Iran; they are both pirates, guys with guns). And the Hashashim are also compared, through implication, to modern-day 'performers' like rock stars (like comedians talk about 'killing' an audience: 'I was so good, I slew them tonight'. Conversely, if a comic does really badly on stage, s/he talks about 'dying' in front of the audience. And if you've performed comedy before an audience, it does feeling dying!).

But as soon as guns enter the frame, the party's over – the play-acting, the dressing-up and the circus show are over, gone, done, *dead*. Life might be a performance – whether you're a gangster, a juggler, a rock star or a drug addict – but guns mean *reality*, they mean *death*.

The end of childhood. Of innocence. Of pleasure.

Although Chas Devlin might have been discovering sides to himself that he never knew existed, and Turner has found someone that he can relate to and talk to (after a fashion, though they're from quite different worlds), those few days or weeks in the house in Powis Square were only ever an *interlude*. An idyll, but an idyll or utopia with a limited life span.

And when the mob boys turn up, the worlds are brought together in a

---

[122] The ending of *Performance* also brings together the two narrative strands, the crime genre/ gangster-on-the-run plot, and the hippy/ pop music/ bohemian/ drug plot.

cataclysmic manner. The music of the ending is also a hint at how the filmmakers want the audience to interpret or feel it: there is a woman singing (Merry Clayton backed by her singers), gospel-style, over consciously plangent and weird strings, producing a sound that's both soulful and melancholy (the woman singing) and slightly jarring or unreal (the strings).

❊

There are shots and scenes which have been taken out of the storytelling in the ending, which enhances the ambiguity: you expect to see certain elements, but they are not included. We've all watched the endings of stories where a character dies or is shot, and there are shots which are part of the storytelling: *Performance* decides, no, we're not going to include those.

There's a shot of Pherber with blood on her clothes in the elevator, that suggests that she's taken the body of Turner down to the basement, to hide it in the closet. If you think about that for a moment, it's an odd thing to do. Pherber acts more like the murderer than the girlfriend of Turner, who might be fairly freaked-out when he's just been shot right beside her in bed. No calls to the police (which might help Chas) for Pherber: instead she takes the body to the basement. Hm-mmm. Uh-huh.

But the ending of *Performance* is not about 'why?' Or questions like 'how?' or 'what?' or 'where?' The film *ends* – that's what counts. Other movies have tried for self-consciously 'ambiguous' endings', or multiple endings, but often come a cropper. The ending of *Performance* works because it is multiplitic, it is ambiguous, but it is also apocalyptic and unreal and psychedelic, which suits the movie perfectly.

♣

The ending of *Performance* is a kind of Do It Yourself kit, in which the filmmakers provide the viewer with a range of tools and motifs and incidents which they can piece together to create their own ending: Turner dies/ Turner doesn't die/ Chas shoots Turner / Turner kills Chas/ Chas kills himself/ Pherber kills Turner / Chas and Turner merge/ the Chas-Turner amalgam goes to his death in Harry Flowers' car/ Turner-Chas makes it to North America, and so on and on.

❊

Performance ends with the Rolls Royce car driving along a country road; Donald Cammell wanted the film to close in New York City. Cammell wrote to Sandy Lieberson about the final shot, which he wanted to shoot in New York:

> The final shot of *Performance* is of the greatest importance. It 'generalizes' the whole story; in other words, it indicates that the film has moved, during

its course, from a purely realistic level to a purely allegorical level. We see Chas, from the back, get into Harry Flowers' white Rolls-Royce, Harry says, genially, 'Hullo, Chas!' The Rolls moves off. As it passes close to camera, the figure inside in the red wig looks out of the window. The face is Turner's. Cut to a close high-angle shot, looking down on a street from a building. The white Rolls-Royce comes into close shot (angle down on its roof). As it rolls up the street, we zoom out to show Central Park West. We continue to pull up and back as the Rolls turns into Central Park. It recedes across the park – a greyish, misty shot. As the camera angles up to follow the car, the New York skyline (of Fifth Avenue in the distance) comes into frame.

✺

Performance closes with still photographs of deserts – these images might be the Iranian or Middle Eastern deserts (Persia being where Chas Devlin has 'gone to'). But they also point towards the American West, I think, and the deserts of California, Nevada and Arizona, which Donald Cammell was fond of (as his wife China Kong relates).[123] The American desert would of course feature strongly in *White of the Eye* and the unfinished *The Argument*.

✺

'GONE TO PERSIA': MORE ON THE ENDING.

There are two destinations evoked continually throughout *Performance*, particularly in the second half: one is 'realistic': the United States of America, the land of opportunity (all criminals go to America, quips Turner. Of course, because North America is the land of movie gangsters, and also the land of capitalism at its most advanced and unbridled). That's where Chas Devlin can realistically escape to, if his friend Tony Farrell comes up with the goods, and provides him with a passport and papers. (Chas is already mythologizing the U.S.A., as millions of Brits did in the 1960s (and since!) – note the references to the Rat Pack, Las Vegas lifestyle, etc, in his apartment).

The other destination is Persia (which Lucy introduces, when she's looking at photos of the Pyramids and the desert: 'he should go here', she tells Turner). Persia is a dream world, a world of magic and mythology. Persia is part of the Burroughs-Crowley-Anger-magickal elements of *Performance* (and the link with Jorge Luis Borges and Omar Khayyám's *Rubaiyat*).

Persia doesn't exist anymore (modern Persia is actually Iran: it's where North America and the West goes to war to protect their oil interests in the Middle East). But Persia, as Pherber imagines it, never did exist. Instead of Persia you could say 'the land of Oz', or 'beyond the rainbow', or 'heaven', or 'Shangri-La', or the 'planet Mars', or 'Koo-Koo-Fluffy-Pink Land'.

So when Rosebloom leaves the note that says, 'GONE TO PERSIA,

---

[123] The deserts of Spain were also part of Donald Cammell's life.

CHAS', on the bed, for Lucy to find, it further merges the gangster/ criminal narrative and the hippy/ druggy narrative. (There's no way Rosebloom could know this, but it does fit that he leaves the note for Lucy to find, not Pherber or Turner or Lorraine).

There are numerous little touches in the ending of *Performance*, too, which further complicate matters. For instance, after Chas Devlin has foolishly told Tony Farrell on the phone where he's staying, Rosebloom stands up, and moves around Tony's bedroom: he peeks behind a picture propped against the wall. It's like a flashforward to Turner's dead body hidden in the closet next to the empty picture frames.

'MEMO TO TURNER'

An indulgent movie, certainly: *Performance* is a movie about a pop star after all. You can imagine Hollywood film producers demanding that Mick Jagger sing and perform in the movie: you've got Jagger, one of the most famous singers of the era, so he's *got* to sing. And he does, a number of times. He performs a rap for Chas Devlin in his recording studio; he dances with a fluorescent lamp (while Lucy freaks out nearby); he performs a self-contained pop promo, the 'Memo To Turner', Turner-crime-boss scene; and he sings a blues song while playing an acoustic guitar (this last song is allowed to run on and on, far longer than necessary).

The 'Memo to Turner' sequence was hailed by some critics as the first pop promo in a movie. Of course it wasn't (there were the Beatles' films, the Elvis Presley films and others before that). It's justified within the film as a dream or fantasy (partly drug-induced) of Chas Devlin's: Turner appears in it, yes, but this is *Chas's* dream, and Chas's inner world is the motivation for it (the only characters usually given dream sequences of flashbacks or memory scenes in a movie are the main characters). But it would've been fascinating to see a dream sequence from *Turner's* point-of-view (especially one that included flashbacks to his earlier years).

The 'Memo to Turner' sequence also replays many moments from the earlier office scene, though with Turner taking Harry Flowers' place as the crime boss (which offers comments on the balance of power at Powis Square – so that now Chas Devlin is regarded Turner as his boss). For instance, there's a painting by the mirror (though now it's the René

Magritte canvas which Turner rejected). Moody appears at the door. Chas enters. The underlings offer comments. All of which are call-backs to the earlier office scene.

In the second half of the 'Memo to Turner' episode, Turner changes into his regular, black stage gear, as he grooves around the office. The lamp swings, justifying the shifting lighting. Chas sits in the middle of the room, impassive. The gangsters undress.[124] Harry Flowers appears towards the end. Turner tips out a drawer of bullets onto the desk (on top of wrestling magazines). 'Memo to Turner' closes with with the *hommage* to Francis Bacon, and the lights fading.

Martin Scorsese said he liked *Performance*, 'loved the music and I love Jagger and James Fox – terrific'. He was inspired to use 'Memo To Turner' in *GoodFellas* partly because of *Performance*. (And Scorsese went on to direct the *Shine the Light* concert show of the Stones).

PERFORMANCE AND OTHER MOVIES

Aside from *Performance*, there were only a few really good movies made about 'Swinging London' at the time. *Candy, Alfie, Duffy, What's New, Pussycat?* (and even films such as *Casino Royale* and *Our Man Flint* tried to cash in on the groovy scene).[125]

But few pictures manage to do it (many of those movies're just terrible – have you seen *Casino Royale* or *The Magic Christian* recently? *Soo* bad!). *Blow Up* and *Performance* are classics, of course, and *Barbarella* is a wonderfully over-the-top piece of European kitsch, but the film that really nailed how Swinging London/ Britain has been perceived over thirty or forty years is *Austin Powers* (1997; – the first film, not the far less satisfying, cruder and occasionally grotesquely mis-judged sequels). In *Austin Powers*, comedian Mike Myers and director Jay Roach lovingly send-up the late 1960s London scene (as well as *James Bond* and every spy thriller); like Michael McKean, Harry Shearer and Christopher Guest with the heavy metal *milieu* in *This Is Spinal Tap*, Myers and Roach know their targets intimately, and satirize them wittily and energetically.

---

124 Some of the actors were not happy about undressing for the camera in the naked gangsters scene, Stanley Meadows told *Neon* magazine: 'Donald wanted me to take my clothes off – one of his last-minute inspirations! I said no. He said, "What if Fellini asked you to do it?" I said, "You're not Fellini."' (B, 149)
125 Other movies related to the 'free love' and pop culture period would included *Yellow Submarine, Hair, Godspell, Stardust, Monterey Pop, Woodstock, Tommy,* and *Jesus Christ Superstar.*

⊛

Another movie that has some link to the themes in *Performance* is *The Final Programme* (1973), based on Michael Moorcock's *Jerry Cornelius* books (it was co-produced by Sandy Lieberson and Goodtimes Enterprises, one of the groups behind *Performance*).

Well, it's Jerry Cornelius and the hippy, fashionable set he hangs out with that have affinities with the *milieu* depicted in *Performance*, because the film version of *The Final Programme* is dreadful. Michael Moorcock bemoaned how bad it was in a letter to me, and unfortunately there have been no other movies of Moorcock's work (as there have been of his contemporary, J.G. Ballard, who's had movies made from *Empire of the Sun* and *Crash*).

Absolute Beginners (1986) is yet another movie which consciously references *Performance* – not only for its Notting Hill *milieu*, its pop music soundtrack, and its Pop Art æsthetic, but also in the casting of James Fox. Based on Colin MacInnes' 1959 novel, *Absolute Beginners*, a brave but misjudged attempt to revive the Vincente Minnelli-style Hollywood musical, was a flop at the box office. *Absolute Beginners* simply wasn't as impressive or cool as it so desperately tried to be.

⊛

The criminal aspects of *Performance*, in particular the psychological exploration of crime and violence, have been linked to *Point Blank* (John Boorman, 1967), a movie that Donald Cammell admired (he attended screenings of *Point Blank* with his production team).

Persona (1966), Ingmar Berman's *tour-de-force* psychological exploration of split personality and two people feeding off each other, is another intertext with *Performance*, for obvious reasons. *Persona* is a classic Ingmar Bergman film: the setting on the Swedish coast; the Expressionist lighting; the modernist techniques; the long passages of inaction and silence; alienation and isolation; strong female characters; the angst and neurosis; the psychology and interiority; and the Existential confrontations with the void. *Persona* is a dense, difficult work, of big close-ups of blank faces, sudden eruptions of anger, and figures moving silently against white walls. It's one of Bergman's more ambiguous, mysterious pieces.

The Servant (1963) is another movie that critics have linked with *Performance*, in particular how both movies force characters into an intense and claustrophobic relationship in a house (in London, too. And James Fox was of course in the Pinteresque *Servant*).

⊛

In relation to *Performance* I also think of *Altered States*, a troubled

1980 production which was many years in the making (really, it should've been released around 1970-71). It eventually reached the screen with Ken Russell directing (after numerous other directors had been approached, and after Arthur Penn had walked), with William Hurt and Blair Brown starring (author Paddy Chayefsky, to put it politely, was difficult to work with). But the exploration of alternative states of consciousness (particularly using drugs like mescalin) chimes with *Performance* (as well as the religious and mystical elements, and the formation of a new kind of human being).

Drug movies of the period of *Performance* included *Easy Rider*, of course, *Yellow Submarine*, *The Love-Ins*, *Chappaqua* and *2001: A Space Odyssey* (where punters would, according to legend, smoke pot during the Stargate sequence). Why bother? As Jean-Luc Godard said, instead of L.S.D. we have colour television.

And the immaculate *Withnail & I*.

PERFORMANCE AND WITHNAIL & I

A movie that bears comparison with *Performance* is *Withnail & I* (1987), produced by George Harrison, Paul Heller, Denis O'Brien, David Winbury and Lawrence Kirstein, and written and directed by Bruce Robinson. *Withnail & I* has become, like *Performance* and *Blow Up*, a cult classic movie, and rightly so. It has a very intelligent and witty script, a beautiful shape and structure, some great one-liners, some eccentric characters, and four outstanding performances (Richard E. Grant, Paul McGann, Richard Griffiths and Ralph Brown).

Richard E. Grant's Withnail is by turns flamboyant, neurotic, paranoid, childlike, sly, stuck-up, arrogant, morose, phenomenally lazy and doggedly alcoholic; Grant's over-the-top performance helped turn *Withnail & I* into one of the greatest British films. Withnail is simply one of the classic comic creations in British cinema. 'In expressing the sheer agony of the alcoholic waiting for the pubs to open, he was painful to watch. I have never felt more anguish for a human being in my life', remarked Ken Russell in *Fire Over England* (1993, 141).

Withnail & I shares with *Performance* a late 1960s, London setting, a bohemian lifestyle, hippies, drugs and alcohol, and rock music (a brilliant use of Jimi Hendrix).

Aside from Monty and the 'I' character of the title, it's *Withnail & I*'s fourth meticulously crafted character that chimes with the world of *Performance*: Danny (Ralph Brown), a dishevelled hippy, creator of the 'Camberwell carrot' (a gigantic joint), procurer of any drug, prone to making wild, philosophical statements (about rats, politics, drugs, etc).[126]

Like every cult movie, *Withnail & I* has its quotable one-liners: 'cool your boots, man'; 'even a stopped clock keeps the right time twice a day'; 'get in the back of the van!'; 'fork it!'; 'Monty, you terrible cunt!'; and 'you can shove it up your arse and fuck off while you're doing it!'.

The plot of *Withnail & I* was simple: two out-of-work actors escape from London for a weekend in the country, a cottage near Penrith in Cumbria (like Chas Devlin might escape to Devon in *Performance*). Camden in North London at the end of the 1960s was evoked primarily via music (the low budget filmmaker's cheap *mise-en-scène*), in this case, Jimi Hendrix and the Beatles, and Withnail and I's messy, cluttered apartment: no TV, no telephone, rats, freezing cold, a sink piled high with unwashed plates and cups, and friends who drop by and hang out for days (Danny and Presuming Ed). It's reminiscent of the Powis Square house, particularly the basement (and every student house).

The Cumbrian hideout seems just as cold, dilapidated and unwelcoming at first, until, in the morning, the 'I' character has a romantic awakening amid the beauty of the natural world (right out of D.H. Lawrence or British Romantic poets like William Wordsworth or Percy Bysshe Shelley. The scene might also be a reference to Ken Russell, who adored the Lake District).[127] Among *Withnail & I*'s memorable moments were the drives North to Lakeland and back; the surreal conversations with Danny; the drunken actors stumbling into the Penrith tea-shop and demanding cakes and wine; the pub scenes; Withnail loudly bemoaning his shabby life in the Camden apartment, and, later, standing on a Cumbrian hill at night and yelling that he was going to be a star.

---

[126] Danny the drug dealer would be perfectly at home in Powis Square, for instance (and might easily be Pherber's connection).
[127] In *A British Picture*, Ken Russell described his first sight of the mountain Skiddaw: 'I jumped out of bed, pulled the curtains and froze. My heart pounded, my blood raced, I caught my breath, my eyes widened, my hair stood on end, an unseen orchestra played a tremendous chord. Only clichés can describe what no one has ever been able to portray – a vision of God.' (130-1)

PERFORMANCE AND POP MUSIC FILMS

One way of looking at *Performance* is to see it as a rock music movie, part of a bunch of films of the time which explored the world of pop music. Among British movies ('British' tho' made with U.S. backing and some U.S. personnel), these would include the Beatles' films, the Cliff Richard films, and movies such as *Blow-Up* and *That'll Be the Day*.

In the United States of America, the obvious candidates for rock 'n' roll movies of the era include *Easy Rider, Woodstock, Monterey Pop, Gimme Shelter, Cocksucker Blues, Head*, the beach party movies, and the Elvis Presley flicks.

Following *Performance*, films that explored some of the same territory in the rock music world as *Performance* – among movies with a significant British music content – included: *Stardust* (1974), *The Isle of Wight Festival* (1970), *Let It Be* (1970), *Ziggy Stardust* (1972), *Tommy* (1975), *The Song Remains the Same* (1976), *The Rocky Horror Picture Show* (1975), *Quadrophenia* (1979), *The Rutles* (1978), *The Kids Are Alright* (1979), *Flame* (1974), *Pink Floyd Live At Pompeii* (1972), and *The Wall* (1982).

Without a doubt the brilliant comedy *This Is Spinal Tap* is the last word in sending up the whole megalomaniacal, over-the-top, debauched and idiotic aspects of the rock world. As Bono (U2) remarked of *Spinal Tap*, it was difficult to watch because it was so close to the truth. There's no doubt that marvellous as *Performance* is, it does also take itself a little seriously, and can come across as pompous and self-obsessed, rather like the narcissistic characters, Chas and Turner, that it depicts.

❈

As well as a 'Swinging London' film, or a film of the late 1960s, *Performance* can also be classed as a movie aimed at the youth market (15-24 year-olds). This is partly what Warner Brothers were after: a youth-oriented pic starring one of pop music's pin-ups of the era, Mick Jagger. In British cinema, youth-oriented films of the 1970s onwards included (ignoring for the moment that some of these were made with American or international finance): *That'll Be the Day, Stardust, Backbeat, Trainspotting, Shooting Fish, Bean, Up 'N Under, Shallow Grave, The Acid House, Human Traffic, 24/7, Four Weddings and a Funeral, London Kills Me, Shopping, Young Americans, Twin Town, Absolute Beginners, The Great Rock 'n' Roll Swindle, Withnail & I, Lock, Stock and Two Smoking Barrels, Snatch, Supergrass, The Pope Must Die, Eat the Rich, Rita, Sue and Bob Too, Letter To Brezhnev, Notting Hill, The Committments, Jubilee, Blue*

Juice, Tommy, Quadrophenia, Breaking Glass, Sid & Nancy, Spice World, Gregory's Girl, My Beautiful Laundrette, Young Soul Rebels, Rude Boy, Funny Bones, Babylon, Wish You Were Here, The Full Monty, Scum, Empire State, Naked, Coast to Coast and *Joyriders*. At least six of those movies consciously allude to *Performance*.[128]

And it's striking how many of these films used pop music in their soundtracks, or had a pop music theme song, or cast pop stars as actors, very much like *Performance*. Other key elements of these youth-oriented, British-set movies include: young, trendy actors; London as the main location; glamour and conspicuous consumption; 'streetwise' and 'bad' language; drugs and violence.

These pictures flatter their audience, offering often idealized, glitzy, astonishingly romantic images of Britain. Certain genres clearly recommend themselves: comedies (*The Full Monty, Withnail & I*, the *Comic Strip* films), romantic comedies (*Four Weddings, Notting Hill, Gregory's Girl*), musicals and biopics (*Stardust, Backbeat, Breaking Glass*), melodramas (*Rita, Sue & Bob Too, Wish You Were Here, Blue Juice*), and crime or gangster thrillers (*Performance, Lock, Stock and Two Smoking Barrels* and *Shopping*). When genres used pop music and its worlds directly (and not merely as part of the soundtrack), they tend to be (1) musicals, (2) biopics, or (3) melodramas. Thrillers, for instance (*Performance*'s genre), are much rarer.

POP MUSIC AS SHAMANIC RITUAL

There's certainly an element in Donald Cammell's personality of someone infatuated with the bohemian, artistic and pop music worlds, with gangsters and the underworld, and with show business and celebrities. That fascination inevitably has a superficial aspect to it, the schmoozing, being seen at the right parties and out with the bright, young things (in London, Paris or L.A.). Some of that can be found in *Performance*, before the film veers off into stranger areas.

Friends recalled that Donald Cammell would be thrilled by pop concerts (but we all are!),[129] and by pop stars such as Brian Jones and Mick Jagger.

---

[128] If you add American movies, there are numerous rock an' pop musicals with links to *Performance* – such as *The Decline of Western Civilization, Head, The Rose, Velvet Goldmine, Purple Rain, Saturday Night Fever, The Doors, Dreamgirls, Almost Famous, Ray, Jesus Christ Superstar* and *Under the Cherry Moon*.
[129] After seeing the Rolling Stones, Barbara Steele remembered, Donald Cammell would be excited. Shit, who wouldn't be – the Stones're one of the major rock acts!

James Fox said that Cammell was something of a performer himself, a charismatic and attractive individual; and Cammell was similarly drawn to sexy, young pop stars, criminals, movie stars and celebrities.

In contemporary North American cinema, filmmakers who have a similar fascination with the world of rock 'n' roll and show business (as well as the criminal underworld), would include Oliver Stone, Bob Rafelson, David Lynch, Cameron Crowe and Martin Scorsese. Both Stone and Scorsese have produced movies which are like brasher, American versions of *Performance*: *The Doors* (1991) and *GoodFellas* (1990). Scorsese has long been lauded for the way he's used pop music in his movies (though I would say that Jean-Luc Godard is *infinitely* more significant), and Scorsese has more recently directed a documentary on the Rolling Stones.[130]

Meanwhile, in *The Doors* (produced by Mario Kassar (Carolco), Bill Graham, Nick Glainos, Sasha Harari, Brian Glazer (Imagine), Alex Ho, and associate producers Clayton Townsend and Joseph Reddy), there were sequences which developed the religious, pagan elements in *Performance* and some of Donald Cammell's scripts: in *The Doors*, director Oliver Stone and his team conjured up rock concerts as ecstatic, shamanic events. This was the rock show as religious ritual, a bacchanale; *The Doors* forged links between dancing to music and mystical trances, Dionysian frenzies or witches' rites; between rock musicians and gods or demons or shaman; between the worship of divinities and the adulation of rock stars; between pilgrims and fans, groupies and mænads.

To illustrate these literary-critical interpretations of rock music, the filmmakers had a Native American shaman (Floyd Red Crow Westerman) dancing alongside Jim Morrison on stage. These ghostly dances culminated with a striking scene where Morrison was joined on stage by a few shamen, in traditional costumes and headdresses, his flailing movements following theirs (or vice versa), and the audience below dancing naked around a large bonfire.

Performance includes explorations of the same territory, as Turner talks about the wilder, shamanic aspects of rock music and performing (including the notion of the rock star as a demon as well as an angel). It's a pity, perhaps, that there isn't a giant, spectacular, orgiastic scene set at a rock concert in *Performance*, like the San Francisco scene in *The Doors*. After all, *Performance* has one of the icons of the live rock music scene of the era, Mick Jagger. *Performance* does feature Jagger singing and dancing, but those scenes don't have the high energy, shamanic impact of a concert in front of thousands of screaming, grooving fans.

---

[130] *Shine a Light* (2008).

SELLING *PERFORMANCE*

The editing process of *Performance* was troubled, but plenty of movies have a problematic editing period. It's the time in the making of a movie when the movie is rediscovered. Some filmmakers are well-known for preferring extended editing schedules – Francis Coppola, Tsui Hark, Martin Scorsese, and most famously Orson Welles.[131] They will keep working on the film, trying different cuts. They will re-arrange scenes again and again, as well as adding scenes left out of earlier cuts, and even slashing whole expensive sequences.[132] The real troubles begin when the studio starts to demand versions to show preview audiences: as soon as the preview process kicks in, the film starts to get out of the filmmakers' control (and most filmmakers absolutely detest the preview process).

Performance of course had disastrous previews (it's a very difficult movie to preview), and Warners wanted re-cuts. Again, that is not uncommon, and sometimes this process can go on and on, until everyone or no one is satisfied. Rudy Fehr, head of post-production at Warners, put a Warners editor on the picture which didn't work out with the filmmakers at all. Frank Mazzola joined the production soon after that.

❁

One of the key executives at Warners-Seven Arts for *Performance* was Ken Hyman (Sandy Lieberson in London would liaise with Hyman in L.A. about the film). John Calley was one of the more enlightened studio executives of the 'New Hollywood' period, who backed many important movies: it was Calley who helped to get *Performance* released (out-going executive Hyman wanted to forget all about the movie. Certainly Calley was a key in getting *Performance* into theatres).[133]

But Warner Bros' president, Ted Ashley, hated *Performance*. Ashley ordered more cuts to be made.[134] A year later, the young George Lucas had a run-in with Ashley and Rudy Fehr over his first feature, *THX 1138* (Fehr had told Frank Mazzola that he would not be allowed to re-cut *Performance* on the Warners' lot). Lucas (and Francis Coppola) was so angry with Warners he would not do business with them for years afterwards. Lucas loathed the way Warner Bros. treated his film. When four

---

131 When Orson Welles had enough time to edit his movies, such as *F For Fake*, he was able to establish and maintain his very individual and personal editing style. And it took a long time; Welles said he edited slowly, and films such as *F For Fake* took far longer to cut than to shoot. (That would be another factor that might put off potential backers of an Orson Welles film project – that the editing could drag on, as they would see it, for many months, with no end in sight.)
132 There was a costly sequence in *The Godfather 2* which didn't make into the final film (or the extended TV version).
133 At Warners, Fred Weintraub had supported *Performance*, and had, according to Sandy Lieberson, persuaded John Calley and Ted Ashley that *Performance* should be completed so it could be previewed.
134 Donald Cammell tried to drum up support for his movie during the post-production/ preview period, eliciting help from Mick Jagger, David Maysles and Kenneth anger.

minutes were cut from *THX 1138* by Warners' editor Rudy Fehr, on Ashley's orders, Lucas said it was 'like watching someone cutting the fingers off of his child'. The awful experience of *THX-1138* was one of the reasons that Lucas moved to the Bay Area, and remained suspicious of La-La Land for the rest of his career. 'L.A. is where they make deals, do business in the classic corporate way, which is screw everybody and do whatever you can to turn the biggest profit... I don't want anything to do with them', asserted Lucas.[135]

There was a changeover at Warners during the production of *Performance*, with Steve Ross and Kinney[136] stepping in. Ross had been a key figure at Warners, where he had pursued a policy of vertical integration – selling films and television back to itself, reducing costs but increasing profit. Ross was one of Steven Spielberg's mentors.[137]

❉

Performance runs at 106 minutes. There are slight differences between versions prepared for the British and the North American markets (it's quite common in movies for versions to differ). But the differences are fairly minor. The cuts ordered by Warners, for instance, amounted to 2-3 minutes. (Among the cuts was a shot of a naked guy in the bathroom in the Harry Flowers bedroom scene, and Joey Maddocks slashing Chas's foot with a razor).

One of the recurring fables about movies is that censors and studios often take out vital elements when they order cuts. Yes, obviously, in the case of movies such as *The Magnificent Ambersons*. But when the cuts are for violence, sex, sexual violence, drug use and the like, the cuts don't necessarily *ruin the entire movie*! A movie is much more two or three minutes long, and if it's any good it will survive having a few short shots or scenes deleted. The cult of the 'director's cut', too, is ambiguous: most filmmakers, even really successful ones, *do not* have final cut on their productions. The *studio* or the *producers* own the movie, *not* the filmmakers. And they can and do cut it anyway they like. It's about *money*. It's about getting a return on an investment.[138] (Thus, even many 'director's cuts' are produced in response to the market: they are created to squeeze some more revenue out of a movie).

Yes, it is a pity that the filmmakers couldn't retain this or that shot, this or that line of dialogue, but a film such as *Performance* is still incredible, disturbing and lyrical with its deletions.

---

135 George Lucas, in D. Thomson, *Overexposures*, New York, 1981, 40.
136 Kinney National Services had bought Warners in 1969. Their businesses included parking lots and the National Cleaning Co.
137 Steven Spielberg dedicated *Schindler's List* to the movie mogul. Spielberg greatly admired Ross, and even showed Liam Neeson home movies of Ross to inspire him in his role as Oskar Schindler.
138 And ego. And power-gaming.

❋

Performance would always be a tough movie to preview, to market and to distribute. If you know anything about previewing, you know that *Performance* would be a difficult picture to show to audiences who knew nothing about it. Aside from Mick Jagger, it would be tricky for the marketing team to focus on the right elements, in the right mix, to appeal to a mass audience. It has many of the juicy ingredients that appeal to a young audience, but not portrayed in this manner. Although Jagger was in it, it wasn't a rock musical. It wasn't a straight gangster movie or thriller, it wasn't a melodrama, and it wasn't a romantic date movie either.

In sum, *Performance* was a challenging movie to sell to an audience. That was apparent from the first previews, which as Sandy Lieberson recalled, were absolutely terrible, with some of the audience walking out (the first preview was at the Granada Theater in Santa Monica in July, 1969. Many head honchos of Warners were present, including John Calley and Ted Ashley, the Warners' publicity team, and Aaron Stern from the Motion Picture Producers' Association. The audience loudly complained during the violent scenes, some walked out, the movie was stopped, then started again after a break. It was a disaster).[139]

And, as far as Warner Bros. was concerned, *Performance* wasn't the sort of movie that could be saved by having one of their trusted veteran editors come in and re-cut it (but that's exactly what happened with *Demon Seed* and *Wild Side*). The key here is the *final cut* clause in the contract, and only a few of the most successful film directors get it (despite what they might say. The real power in Hollywood has *always* been with the *producers*, and *not* the *directors*. Even the filmmaker who was given that incredible contract by RKO, Orson Welles, did *not* have final cut, as many people think he did. RKO had final cut – and they proved it by completing *The Magnificent Ambersons* against Welles' wishes).

Indeed, the most crushing example of a director not having final cut in his contract and being fucked over by the studio is undoubtedly Orson Welles and the miserable case of *The Magnificent Ambersons* (a 1942 movie which can rightly be called the greatest American picture ever made, even including *Citizen Kane*, and even in *Ambersons'* hacked-about and re-shot state).

Orson Welles was famously in South America making *It's All True* when RKO ordered Robert Wise, Mark Robson and Jack Moss to re-cut *The Magnificent Ambersons*, and to shoot (with others, including Joseph

---

[139] When *Performance* was screened in Santa Monica in March of 1970, a wife of a Warners' executive was sick, apparently (not long after that, *The Exorcist* made vomiting in theaters *de rigeur*).
Performance should have been previewed on a college campus – UCLA or USC, for example – on a Saturday night to a young audience high on whatever substances were available.

Cotten and Agnes Moorhead), scenes which would smooth over the deletions. In the *Ambersons* fiasco, everyone has blamed everyone else over the years.

And it happened to Orson Welles again and again: *Mr Arkadin* (a.k.a. *Confidential Report*) was re-cut, as was *Macbeth*, and *The Lady From Shanghai*, and *Touch of Evil*. Soooo depressing.

Donald Cammell can't have had final cut over *Demon Seed* or *Wild Side*, and, with Nic Roeg, not over *Performance* either. A film director wouldn't receive it from a major Hollywood studio for a first-time movie, and in subsequent years Cammell didn't have the track record at the box office to be able to obtain it. It's amazing how many filmmakers you'd think were successful or well-respected enough to have final cut don't have it.

Even Jean-Luc Godard, for my money about the most significant filmmaker of recent times, had producers dick around with his films. The producer of 1968's *One Plus One* (Iain Quarrier), which starred the Rolling Stones, tacked on a segment to Godard's movie, which upset Godard so much he apparently laid into Quarrier at the London Film Festival.

Can you imagine someone thinking, *no, I just don't think Jean-Luc Godard can make good movies, so I'm going to re-cut his film!* Forgetting that by the time of *One Plus One*, Godard had directed *Contempt, Vivre Sa Vie, Bande à Part, Le Petit Soldat, Alphaville, Pierrot le Fou, Masculine Féminin, Made In U.S.A., Two of Three Things I Know About Her, La Chinoise, Weekend* and *Une Femme Est Une Femme*!!!! At least *five* of those movies – *Contempt, Vivre Sa Vie, Pierrot le Fou, Masculine Féminin*, and *Weekend* – are masterpieces, true, unqualified masterpieces.

I'm not suggesting that Donald Cammell is in the same class as Orson Welles or Jean-Luc Godard, and I'm sure he wouldn't have thought of himself like that either, but even the great filmmakers can be stuffed by the system.

❋

Performance was one of 16 films that Warners released in 1970: in the late 1960s, Warner Bros' hit movies included *Bonnie & Clyde* (1967), *Bullitt* (1968), *Woodstock* (1970), and *The Green Berets* (1968). Most of the other Hollywood studios released about the same number of movies in 1970, but Columbia and United Artists put out twice as many (J. Finler, 2003).

Bonnie & Clyde was Warners' biggest hit of the Sixties (the link between Warners and crime movies, and the recent success of *Bonnie & Clyde* and *Bullitt*, might have been factors in encouraging Warners to back

Performance). However, the budgets of both those movies ($3m and $5.5m respectively), were higher than *Performance*'s $2.08 million (£1.3m). Indeed, it wasn't until 1973 that Warners had a mega-hit movie – *The Exorcist* ($88.5 million in U.S. rentals alone).

Maybe Warners were hoping for another *Bonnie & Clyde* from *Performance* – the mix must've seemed appealing going in: gangsters + Mick Jagger + pop music. I think they got something just as fascinating and entertaining. But if you compare *Bonnie & Clyde* with *Performance*, you can see that there are many elements in *Performance* which might put off a mainstream audience (though not the violence – *Bonnie & Clyde* is famously violent, and more so, one could argue, than *Performance* – for instance, the Sam Peckinpahish, slo-mo apocalypse).

The *New York Times* lambasted *Performance* for being 'shocks piled on shocks', forming a new genre 'called the Loathsome Film'. For John Simon, 'you do not have to be a drug addict, pederast, sado-masochist or nitwit to enjoy *Performance*, but being one or more of these things would help'.

For David Thomson, *Performance* 'looks like a film self-consciously attempting to use the gangster genre as the basis for existentalist riddle'. Thomson complained that *Performance* 'howls with ideas', and that Donald Cammell 'seems intent on drawing in every possible comment on the mysteries of identity, shuffling the spurious in with the portentous and the eclectic' (644).

The counter-culture magazine *International Times* loved *Performance*:

> Probably the heaviest movie ever made: a kaleidoscope of transvestism, sado-masochism, death, bad fly-trips etc... It's a totally illogical movie, a series of seemingly unrelated incidents and complex inter-relationships flashed across the screen at almost subliminal speed: Jagger-Fox; Jagger-chicks; Fox-chicks; chicks-chicks. Chilling and very effective with superb editing and camerawork.

❈

The poster for *Performance* became famous: it depicted Mick Jagger and James Fox in their different guises in the film (there were also variations on this). The square portraits recalled Andy Warhol's art. The tag line was terrific: 'THIS FILM IS ABOUT MADNESS. AND SANITY. FANTASY. AND REALITY. DEATH. AND LIFE. VICE. AND VERSA.'

THE BITS THAT DON'T WORK

Noel (Noel Swabey),[140] the black musician that Chas Devlin overhears while waiting for his train to Devon, at Paddington station, is clearly a reference to Jimi Hendrix.[141] The London music scene had adopted the greatest rock guitarist of them all as one of their own in the mid-to-late Sixties.

This part of the 1970 film creaks, plot-wise, as this sort of scene does in other movies. It's a pity that Donald Cammell and the team couldn't come up with a more convincing way of getting Chas to Turner's place. The dialogue is once again way too on the nose, maybe deliberately so, as if the filmmakers *know* they're being dull and obvious. (However, the scene is staged in an interesting fashion, with the camera lingering on Chas sitting near Noel and his mom (played by Helen Booth, who's white). There are also numerous off-kilter details which help the scene to play – like the slow motion used for the waitress bringing Chas some food, and the odd zoom from Noel towards Chas, with his ear prominent in the frame.)

And it's typical of *Performance*'s wilful eccentricity that Paddington train station is introduced via a high helicopter shot – quite bizarre: no establishing shot of Chas Devlin entering the building, but a view of the station and railway tracks from way up high. Similarly, when Chas exits the station and takes a taxi, that's filmed in another high angle (as if the gods or the fates are watching or controlling Chas).

It also stretches belief that Chas Devlin, having killed a guy and knowing that the firm is probably going to wipe him out, would elect to stay in London, and in Notting Hill too, only a mile or two from the stamping ground of Harry Flowers' criminal empire.[142] There are 100s of non-descript places in Britain to hole up for a while: Basingstoke, Croydon, Hull, Leeds, Reading, Birmingham, Coventry, Doncaster... But the movie would be different had it been filmed in somewhere utterly dull and suburban (*Performance* in Crawley isn't quite the same!). *Performance* really does benefit greatly from its London settings.

---

[140] Ian McShane provided the voice.

[141] Noel is a guitarist, and his guitar case is decorated with topless models. Noel also sports a groovy, frilly, green, velvet jacket.

[142] In this respect, *Performance* recalls *Breathless:* David Bordwell and Kristin Thompson have analyzed *Breathless* in terms of *film noir* and classical Hollywood movies in their brilliant book *Film Art* and found that the motivations, goals and behaviour of the two lead characters are confusing, enigmatic, and at odds with the conventions of the crime genre and Hollywood models. Michel, for instance, spends the whole central third of the movie fooling around in an apartment with Patricia, not bothered about escaping: he seems 'more like a wandering, easily distracted delinquent than the desperate, driven hero of a *film noir*' (368). *Breathless* depicts a story that's 'quirky, uncertain, and deglamorized' (367).

Truth is, *Breathless* is *not* a deconstruction, a commentary or an exploration on *film noir* or Hollywood cinema of the 1940s, as David Bordwell and Kristin Thompson attest (tho' it is partly an *hommage*). Rather, *Breathless* takes up *some* elements from *film noir* and Hollywood cinema, but then forgets all about them in favour of exploring other things. That is, Jean-Luc Godard's movies *start out* with those sorts of intentions, but they can't sustain them, they lose interest, they get side-tracked, they wander off into other areas of cinema and film essay.

There's a nod towards Chas Devlin's background, when he telephones his mom and says he's going to stay with his aunt in Devon.[143] But Chas depends more on his colleagues in the criminal underworld – calling on Tony Farrell (played by the always wonderful Ken Colley), who has a job in the vegetable trade (and works out in a gym at the Thomas a'Beckett pub in the Old Kent Road in London, where James Fox went to train).[144]

The joke about Chas Devlin being a juggler is maintained to a silly degree, particularly by Turner (who, like Pherber,[145] doesn't believe it for a second, and proves it when he throws some balls at Chas). Maybe being a juggler was chosen because of its links to the circus: the Umlands have noted an enduring love of the circus in Donald Cammell, as in the cinema of Federico Fellini and Woody Allen (the circus as 'a sort of artistic utopia' [U, 53]). Cammell wrote a piece on the Bertram Mills' Circus in 1959, for *Lilliput* magazine:

> Efficiency, fractional timing, perfect teamwork, exceptional talent, the artistic flair, loyalty and damned hard work... these are the bases of circus existence.[146]

One of the elements that doesn't convince for me in *Performance* is the young girl, Lorraine (Laraine Wickens),[147] who acts as a motherly figure, helping out, bringing drinks (and providing background on Turner).[148] Apart from the fact that Wickens' Lorraine is badly dubbed in some prints[149] (by one of those weird English voices, which seems to be an older actor trying to sound younger, that you find in many movies which feature British kids, particularly in the 1960s and 1970s),[150] it's just not believable that a Dickensian street urchin like that would hang around with those hippies. (Li'l Lorraine is seen arriving at Powis Square with an older woman, presumably her mom, who was presumably the occasional cleaner and cook, Mrs Gibbs (but Turner's place obviously hasn't been cleaned for months! Or Mrs Gibbs is the worst cleaner in the world). Maybe there were more scenes involving her which were dropped; a housekeeper in this *milieu*

---

[143] Devon's probably a reference to Donald Cammell's younger days.
[144] As well training in the gym at the Thomas a'Beckett, Fox also stayed in Brixton (South London), hung out with the 'chaps' in the evening, cut his hair, and bought his suits from The Cut. It was Method acting preparation for the role (rarer in British movies than in American movies), and boy did it pay off. In fact, Fox later said (in *Comeback*) that, 'I became almost completely taken over by the role. I spoke, thought and ate like Chas.'
[145] Pherber can see that Chas isn't one of Noel's friends, but something about Chas fascinates her. The idea of this sort of personality, a rough man of the streets, coming to a bohemian/ hippy enclave intrigues her.
[146] Quoted in U, 56.
[147] Cammell had found Laraine Wickens in Chelsea. She had been collecting bottles for the deposits from stores when they were returned (B, 123).
[148] Lorraine's mom, Mrs Gibbs, is the housekeeper, but barely makes an impression (she's heard off-screen in a basement scene).
[149] The British DVD release uses more of Wicken's real voice.
[150] Think of *The Village of the Damned* or *Oliver!* or *Chitty Chitty Bang Bang*.

just isn'ts interesting. In the script, Mrs Gibbs is more prominent, and in earlier drafts).

'WHO ARE YOU?': IDENTITY IN *PERFORMANCE* OR, THE MIRROR MOVIE

Questions: w*ho are you? Do you know who you are?* These are aimed at Chas Devlin (in the nightclub scene) by Harry Flowers, and later by Turner. Chas's response to the questions reveals his journey: in the nightclub, he insists that he knows who he is (at that point, Chas, a man of action, *is* what he *does*. He's a 'performer', a doer, someone who puts the frighteners on people, works out in a gym, drinks, tups his girlfriend, etc. For him, action is character.

But when the 'who are you?' question arises later, Chas Devlin isn't so sure about the answer. What is identity? How is it constructed, and maintained? And what happens, the film asks, when it's attacked and questioned and disrupted? If you *are* what you *do*, but you're not *doing* the same stuff you usually do, what are you now?

✸

Characters employ mirrors during sex in *Performance*, like Chas in the opening scene, or Pherber when she's fooling around with Chas. Pherber puts the mirror beside Chas's face, to evoke split personalities, twins, doubles and all the rest of it, and also to superimpose her breast over his chest (bodies become interchangeable, and genitals too). Later, the 1970 film employed optical superimpositions in editing to evoke the same theme.

And if gender and identity are interchangeable, is there difference any more? Does everything become one? And does that make any difference? Or, to put it another, what does difference *mean*, or what *value* does difference have?

The answers that *Performance* comes up with are deliberately ambiguous. It's going to ask the questions and raise the issues, but it isn't going to tick off all the answers. Also, the notion of the dual-sex being is evoked: it's androgynous sex, maybe, or hermaphroditic sex, maybe. Once again, these themes of androgyny and hermaphroditism were in the air at this time in North America and Europe. I'm reminded of the androgynous creatures in Michael Moorcock's *Jerry Cornelius* books, or the movies of Andy Warhol and Federico Fellini (such as 1969's *Satyricon*), or *Barbarella*, and the rock stars like David Bowie, Lou Reed, Marc Bolan, the New York Dolls and others who messed about with blurring gender a few years later in the glam rock, early 1970s period.

❀

Pherber talks about Turner and mirrors, how he studied himself in the mirror, and one day discovered that something was wrong, that his demon had left him.

In this lengthy piece of exposition (i.e., a long monologue for Anita Pallenberg as she plays around on the bed with James Fox), Pherber tells Chas Devlin that Turner has lost his demon, his creative spark.[151] He's dried up. But he used to be amazing, as the young girl Lorraine explains to Chas, with a string of hit singles (while Chas is shaving in the bath, a scene that years later has creepy connotations). At this point, the film might have benefitted from a flashback to a concert or TV show depicting Mick Jagger in action. The film depicts Turner performing in the 'Memo to Turner' and in his workroom, yes, but not with an audience, at the height of his stardom.

As well as the countless images of mirrors, and uses of mirrors (a staple of any film exploring psychology – especially in the psychoanalytical thrillers of the Forties), the picture also makes much of the passport photo that Chas Devlin needs so he can get a fake passport in order to leave the country. The evocations of crossing borders, going beyond thresholds, of travelling to other worlds (such as the desert), needs no explication. Similarly, the passport photo scenes tie in with the theme of scopophilia and seeing in *Performance*.[152]

There's a further layer to the passport issue,[153] because Lucy needs to obtain a visa in order to stay in the country (the first time that Lucy talks at length – in the three-in-a-bath scene[154] – she's complaining about official red tape). The photos and the red tape are MacGuffins, clearly –

---

[151] 'Demon' might normally mean creativity in the way that Friedrich Nietzsche said: do not cast out your demons, lest you cast out the best part of yourself. But in a Donald Cammell film, 'demon' might have occult connotations.

[152] There's also a hint that Chas's friend Tony Farrell, in setting up the passport and airline ticket for Chas to escape to New York City, is deliberately dragging his heels, maybe on Harry Flowers' or Rosebloom's insistence, so the firm can have more time to track Chas down. And that turns out to be the case, because when Chas makes the phone call that seals his fate, Rosebloom is at Tony's (they're all drinking tea, *of course* – that's all the British ever do! Drink friggin' tea!). And even in this brief exposition scene, there's a moment where Moody is staring lewdly at Tony's wife, which Tony notices. It's the creepiest moment with Moody, especially if you know that actor John Bindon was often in trouble with the law, and was involved in a murder in 1979.

[153] As Chas makes love with Lucy in *Performance*'s last act, the theme of escape and travel and borders is evoked: both Chas and Lucy need to obtain government-issued papers (Lucy needs a visa to stay in the U.K., while Chas needs a passport to leave Blighty). Images of jets in the sky emphasize travel and journeys (and call back to the opening images – imagery of escape and transcendence).

[154] There are many scenes involving bathrooms and people in the bath in *Performance*: all of the four people in Powis Square take baths, sometimes together (a bath scene is also an excuse for more nudity, of course. That may be another Godardism – there are many bath scenes in Godard's movies). Group sex or one guy with two women was one of Donald Cammell's fetishes, according to Anita Pallenberg: certainly erotic triangles and groups crop up in most of his movies, from *The Touchables* and *Duffy* to *Wild Side*. (Mick Jagger, ever the professional, didn't want to use real joints in the bath scene).

obstacles for the characters. But as obstacles they tie in to the theme of identity (i.e., it's better if the obstacles for your characters in a story have some relation to the bigger themes of the movie).

As well as mirrors, there other many other devices of seeing and optics in *Performance*, as there are in other films about voyeurism, seeing, and the dangers of looking (such as *Vertigo, Blade Runner, Rear Window* and *Peeping Tom*): the still camera, the movie camera, the photo viewer, etc (and, true to modernist form, the film's camera often looked through the viewfinders of these cameras, so the action became a film-within-a-film; *Performance* is thus one of those movies which is continually commenting on itself, and on the act of making movies. Like *Vertigo, Psycho, Ghost In the Shell* or *Blade Runner*, it is supremely self-reflexive). And, like *Blade Runner, Ghost In the Shell* and *Peeping Tom*, there are the requisite close-ups of eyes in *Performance* (and of characters watching other characters unobserved). And there was a surprising number of to-camera shots (often of characters looking into the lens which took Chas's point-of-view in a scene).

MORE ON IDENTITY

On another level, *Performance* is not about the worlds of entertainment and crime and how they collide: it's about *identity*, how identity is constructed, and, more importantly, how it can be deconstructed. It's a movie called 'performance', and is partly about the way that identity has to be performed, how it has to be routinely re-inforced. It isn't just a given, it doesn't just exist, it has to be performed, rehearsed, expressed. Mick Jagger or Jimi Hendrix or Janis Joplin aren't like they are on stage all the time: in concert, it's a *performance*, a construct, a *fiction*. It only exists as a performance, in that moment (though it can be recorded – but there is a huge gulf between the portrayal of a rock show or a play on video or film and actually being there).

Feminist writer Judith Butler and her notion of 'performativity' (explored in *Gender Trouble*) is one of the obvious reference points here. Some feminists regard sexuality as being expressed through performances and gestures, rather than being some essence, a given, something 'natural'. Thus heterosexuality itself is not an unchanging 'institution', but may already be a 'constant parody of itself', as Judith Butler suggests (1990, 122). Heterosexuality, Butler reckons, is continually imitating itself, always miming its own performances in order to appear 'natural'. Catherine MacKinnon wrote (in "Feminism, Marxism, Method, and the State"): '[s]exuality is that social process which creates, organizes, expresses, and directs desire, creating the social beings we know as women and men, and their relations create society.'[155]

The American poet Adrienne Rich, in her influential essay "Compulsory heterosexuality and lesbian existence", says that heterosexuality is not 'preferred' or chosen, but has to be 'imposed, managed, organized, propagandized, and maintained by force'; for Rich, 'violent structures' are required by patriarchal society in order to 'enforce women's total emotional, erotic loyalty and subservience to men' (1980).

Performance, and some of Donald Cammell's other films to a lesser extent, consciously explores fluid sexual identities, eschewing heterosexuality for a 'pan-sexuality' which takes in homosexual and lesbian sexuality. Lesbian, gay and queer cultural theory has continually addressed the problem of identity and gender. There are certain sexual and social 'positions' or 'categories' which are seen as 'outside' the (patriarchal) norms, which have affinities with the female 'outsider' figures of Julia Kristeva and Luce Irigaray. The lesbian, for instance, is sometimes seen as an 'outsider', like the black woman, or the feminist. (The characters are outsiders – but often thru preference rather than fate, accident or external pressure).

Gender and sexual identity categories are becoming increasingly blurred. For example, there are 'physical' lesbians, 'natural' lesbians, 'cultural' or 'social' lesbians, and 'male' lesbians (men who position themselves as lesbians). There are men with vaginas and women with penises; there are queer butches and aggressive femmes, there are F2Ms and lesbians who love men, queer queens and drag kings, daddy boys and dyke mummies, transsexual Asians, butch bottoms, femme tops, women and lesbians who fuck men, women and lesbians who fuck *like* men, bull daggers, porno afro homos, lesbians who dress up as men impersonating women, lesbians who dress up as straight men in order to pick up gay men, butches who dress in fem clothing to feel like a gay man dressing as a woman, femmes butched-out in male drag and butches femmed-out in drag.

Performance doesn't go as far as most of the above, but it does feature notions of fucking with gender: Turner is a self-consciously

---

[155] Catherine MacKinnon: "Feminism, Marxism, Method, and the State: An Agenda for Theory", in N.O. Keohane, *et al*, eds. *Feminist Theory: A Critique of Ideology*, Harvester, 1982.

'feminine' or 'effeminate' or maybe bisexual guy, Pherber holds up a mirror, twinning herself with Chas Devlin (who's dressed as a woman in make-up and a wig), while Lucy is a boyish woman. (Chas draws attention to the fact that she has small tits and looks like a boy, when he tups her towards the end of the movie).

In this scene, there's another suggestion of playing with gender, when Lucy is filmed in bed wearing Turner's blue-and-white dressing gown, so it appears that Turner might be beside with Chas Devlin. Only when the characters start to make love is Lucy revealed. Prior to that, Turner was depicted sitting in the basement, watching Chas asleep. In the shot just before Lucy and Chas make out, it is clearly Turner who's lying on the bed next to Chas.

If there are any two people out of the four who really should make love, in terms of the Warner Brothers' movie's themes and narrative, it should be Chas Devlin and Turner. It must have been tempting, and I bet the filmmakers considered it, having Turner make out with Chas – and it would been a suitable twist if Chas had come on to Turner, rather than the expected other way around. But although *Performance* depicts lesbian sexuality – Lucy and Pherber often embrace – it pulls short of showing guys in a clinch (despite the gay sexuality being suggested amongst Harry Flowers' firm). Instead, it shows gay sex in a teasing manner. It's the idea of sex.

Thus, the sexual configurations include Chas Devlin and Lucy, Chas and Pherber, Turner and Pherber, Pherber and Lucy (and Turner with both), but not the final coupling, Chas and Turner. Instead, the union of Chas and Turner is in the time-honoured manner of male bonding – through violence, through the phallic penetration of a bullet.

Sexual/ social identities are continually being blurred, redefined, performed, questioned, and this is what one level of *Performance* is about. Terms such as 'straight' and 'gay', hetero and homo/ hommo, are no longer adequate for these multi-layered, postmodern sexual identities.

Fucking with gender, at least at a mild, fashion-conscious level, was in the air at the time of *Performance* – and even more so in the two or three years following *Performance*'s release in 1970. Marc Bolan, David Bowie, Iggy Pop, Sweet, and the New York Dolls messed about with bisexuality and homosexuality (lesbian sexuality was nowhere to be seen at this time in North American and European pop music culture – this was all about boys. Yeah, and it still is very much all about the boys).

SEX, POP MUSIC AND IDENTITY

From the beginning, pop music was sexist (does this really need stating?). Groups such as the Rolling Stones, the Who and the Kinks were portrayed as macho yet feminized heterosexual lads. The Stones were 'bad boys', as stage-managed by Andrew Loog Oldham: they got thrown out of hotels and restaurants, made 'offensive' LP covers, had a scruffy appearance,[156] and so on. The Stones were offered to fans much as Elvis Presley had been in the previous decade – as rebels but nice boys underneath.[157] Oldham created headlines such as 'WOULD YOU LET YOUR DAUGHTER GO WITH A ROLLING STONE?', and press releases such as

> They look like boys any self-respecting mum would lock in the bathroom. But the Rolling Stones – five tough young London-based music makers with doorstep mouths, pallid cheeks, and unkempt hair – are not worried what mums think.[158]

The press release neatly throws the Stones as a bomb simultaneously at the frumpy, older generation (the moms) and the sexually active younger generation (the screaming, female fans). The Rolling Stones were dressed in jeans and casual clothes, to look like street kids. But as George Tremlett pointed out in *Rock Gold*, in 'real life there were about as rebellious as a bunch of City bank clerks, and came from similar backgrounds' (84). Mick Jagger, for instance, had a quiet, middle-class background in suburban Dartford, Kent.

It suited Andrew Oldham to build up the Rolling Stones as the rough, rebellious counter-parts to the clean-living image of the Beatles. Record labels and PR companies used similar marketing strategies in the Seventies, with punk rock, in which teenage delinquents slouched around sneering and swearing.[159] These were marketing and hype strategies designed to offer stories to the media, which thrives on conflict. (Critics have noted that Mick Jagger drew on Oldham's manipulative svengali persona in *Performance* – Nik Cohn called Jagger 'almost Oldham's disciple'; it was a role that Oldham (he was younger than Jagger) might've played himself).

The Rolling Stones' songs ironically explored notions of 'rough', pseudo-working class desire and economy: 'Satisfaction', 'Under My Thumb', 'Jumping Jack Flash', 'Stupid Girl', and 'Get Off My Cloud'. The Who too cultivated an alienated, disaffected, crazed (white, male,

---

[156] 'Scruffy'? Not really – but *very* studied, *very* self-conscious, yes!
[157] Philip Norman, 1972.
[158] In S. Reynolds, 1995, 19.
[159] In the mid-1990s, the marketing departments of record companies created artificial battles between bands: pitting Blur against Oasis (and later, Oasis against the Spice Girls).

bourgeois) stance in songs such as 'My Generation', 'I Can't Explain' and 'Anyway, Anyhow, Anywhere'.

❊

After the 1960s, the revitalized 1950s pop music of the early Seventies took the form of glitter and glam rock. The teen mags – *Fabulous 208, Jackie, Mirabelle, Rave* – enshrined the teen idols of the 1970s (glam) era: David Cassidy, Marc Bolan, the Osmonds, the Bay City Rollers, Gary Glitter, Sweet, and David Soul.

For girls, it has been suggested, an escape could be made into the world of pop idols, as found in young 'women's magazines' such as *Jackie* and *Mirabelle*, in the pin-ups and posters, the TV appearances. This teen pop world was an extra-domestic space, a place beyond the home, beyond school and work. In the glittering world of teen pop stars there was a release from household chores, young motherhood, difficult parents and home problems. Thus, although *Performance* features women in key roles – Pherber and Lucy, primarily – it is also very much a masculinist movie, a narrative seen from the point-of-view of two men (Chas and Turner), and the worlds they come from – rock music and organized crime – are very masculinist, patriarchal worlds. In short, *Performance* is a film made by and about men (and, I would add: for men).

Boys, on the other hand, could identify with the self-conscious 'androgyny' of the art rock side of the 1970s glam rock era – Roxy Music, David Bowie, Iggy Pop, Sweet, Mott the Hoople, the New York Dolls, and so on. Glam rock 'dissolved the star/ fan division not by the stars becoming one of the lads, but by the lads becoming their own stars'.[160] (Most 'gender-bending' or 'androgynous' pop stars are male – Michael Jackson, Boy George, Prince, Billy Idol, Motley Crue, etc. Gender-benders have a long history: Elizabethan courtiers, beaux, dandies, Regency fops, the *fin-de-siècle*, Decadent æsthete, and so on).[161]

Boys could have their hair cut *à la* David Bowie Aladdin Sane style, they could follow each of Bowie's incarnations, as Ziggy Stardust, Aladdin Sane, the Diamond Dog, the Cracked Actor, the Thin White Duke, the alienated alien in *The Man Who Fell to Earth*, the Berlin/ Weimar/ *Cabaret* mannequin, and so on. In 'serious' rock criticism terms, the teenybopper acts of the 1970s – the Osmonds, Mud, the Bay City Rollers, David Cassidy *et al* – never produced 'serious', lasting work, while Roxy Music, David Bowie and Lou Reed are continually held up as examples of important art (as are the Rolling Stones). Lou Reed, Iggy Pop, Bowie and Bryan Ferry were for art students and musos, while Cassidy, the Osmonds and Gary Glitter

---

160 Simon Frith, "Only Dancing: David Bowie Flirts with the Issues", *Mother Jones*, 1983.
161 J. Still, 1993, 45.

were fluffy pap, definitely 'for girls'.

Lou Reed, David Bowie and Roxy Music cultivated a 'androgynous'/transvestite/ gender-bending look, a reinvention of the *fin-de-siècle* dandy or fop, that seemed to rewrite notions of gender, but didn't really. From the harsh, hip streets of New York to the doomed decadence of Weimar Berlin, the pop dandies were distinctly products of patriarchal, masculinist culture. These glammed-up rock stars may have flirted with bi-sexuality, but they remained (like Mick Jagger, and like Turner in *Performance*) heterosexual icons.

The playing with sexual roles turned out to be superficial, 'a matter of style'.[162] *Performance* and the depiction of the rock world in it is very concerned with style and fashion – it's very much about the *look* of the whole thing (and that was something that Donald Cammell, as a painter, was keen to get just right).

The Rolling Stones' album *Some Girls* had the band montaged into women's hair and clothes, but Mick Jagger's songs were (as always – and always since then) about doing women all night, or being let down by women, or desiring unattainable women, or complaining about women.[163] Earlier, for the cover of 'Have You Seen Your Mother, Baby, Standing in the Shadow', the Stones cross-dressed and cruelly mocked female stereotypes (Keith Richards as an air stewardess, Charlie Watts as a bourgeois madam in a fur, Bill Wyman and Jagger as wrinkled, old women). The suggestions of misogyny in 'Have You Seen Your Mother' was also very much to the fore in 'Mother's Little Helper', about housewives who needed drugs to stay afloat.

---

[162] R. Dyer, 1979, 67.
[163] Roxy Music's record covers, for instance, (in)famously featured soft-core pornography shots of women. (Brian Eno of Roxy Music was a collector of pornography).

CULTURAL ECHOES OF *PERFORMANCE*

3

CULTURAL ECHOES OF *PERFORMANCE*
☆

ANITA PALLENBERG

Before researching further into *Performance* and Donald Cammell's films, I hadn't realized just how important Anita Pallenberg (b. April 6, 1944) was to *Performance* and to the Rolling Stones. She is a force of nature, a formidable personality as everybody who knows her attests (but was sometimes self-destructive). Pallenberg has been described as a skilled manipulator of people, as well as a temptress and a witch.[1] She had a poisonous wit, by most accounts, which would denigrate people ruthlessly (with her ability to size people up instantly and to put them down, Pallenberg would've made a fearsome politician!).

> Anita in those days was absolutely electrifying. Whenever she came into a room, every head would turn to look at her. There was something kittenish about her, a sense of mischief – of naughtiness. (Christopher Gibbs)[2]

> I've often thought to myself that if you go out for the evening with Anita, you stand a very good chance of being killed. (Marianne Faithfull)

Anita Pallenberg was another of the charismatic figures in *Performance*'s *milieu*: she had relationships with the Italian photographer/painter Mario Schifano,[3] Brian Jones, and later Keith Richards (from 1967 to 1979). A former fashion model, Pallenberg had been an assistant to Jasper Johns in New York City, and hung out with Andy Warhol and Larry Rivers. So Pallenberg was a scenester, a woman on the scene, at parties, hanging out with artists and celebrities (before she met the Stones, Pallenberg was already a veteran of the *dolce vita* scene in Rome and the Factory scene in Gotham).

Anita Pallenberg was already a worldy-wise woman by the time of appearing in *Performance* (more than most in the cast, including Mick Jagger and James Fox); she spoke five languages,[4] and was of German, Swiss and Italian descent[5] (and came from a wealthy family: her mother Paula Wiederhold was German, her father Arnaldo Pallenberg was an Italian travel agent and artist.[6] She was born in Roma). Her childhood was spent in France, Germany and Spain; she hitchhiked around Europe; she

---

[1] According to Donald Cammell, Anita Pallenberg 'could be very mischievous, very smart – very witchlike, as she used to think' (B, 199).
[2] In P. Norman, 1984, 165.
[3] Mario Schifano later had an affair with Marianne Faithfull, adding further layers to what Philip Norman dubbed 'the 'Mick-Keith sexual labyrinth' (373). Pallenberg stood in for models for Schifano when they were indisposed or late.
[4] Her father sent her to a German school (partly to learn German), which she resented. But later she appreciated being able to speak five languages.
[5] Her ancestors included the Symbolist artist Arnold Böcklin – her great-great-grandfather. Anita Pallenberg's father and grandfather were also painters (based in Rome).
[6] Aristocratic, but not rich.

studied[7] in New York and Rome (she went by boat to Gotham from Rome in 1963);[8] and she settled in London.

Prior to *Performance*, Anita Pallenberg had appeared in *A Degree of Murder* (Volker Schlöndorff, 1966),[9] *Candy* (1968), and one of the key cult movies of the time, *Barbarella* (Roger Vadim, 1967).[10] After *Performance*, Pallenberg acted in only a few films, including *Michael Kohlhaas – Der Rebell* (1969), *Dillinger Is Dead* (Marco Ferreri, 1969), *Umano non umano* (1972), *Berceau de cristal* (1976), *Hideous Man* (2002), *Go Go Tales* (Abel Ferrara, 2007), *Mister Lonely* (2008), in which James Fox also appeared, *Cheri* (2009), and the dreary, too-earnest Francis Bacon biog *Love Is the Devil* (1998).

One of the reasons that Anita Pallenberg didn't act much after films like *Performance* and *Barbarella* was because of her drug habit, according to Victor Bockris.[11] Possibly – but Pallenberg clearly also felt impatient with filmmaking (and acting); she is a personality that likes more control. Also, I would imagine that the roles offered to Pallenberg were not ones she wanted to play: she is not an actress to play the girlfriend of the hero, for example (even tho' that is what she was cast as in *Performance*). The wife, the mother, the secretary, the assistant – no, Pallenberg is much more suited to *femme fatale* and seductress roles. *Basic Instinct*, perhaps, or playing a super-villain in one of the recent spate of superhero flicks. (There's also the feeling that Pallenberg found it difficult to find things to do that could sustain her interest, would be challenging enough, would satisfy her creativity and high intelligence, and would offer enough income. So that, apart from being a soul-mate to Keith Richards and a mom of two kids, Pallenberg's main preoccupation in the 1970s seemed to be being a drug addict).

Many people found Anita Pallenberg an awe-inspiring person, clever, together, confident, and a little scary. Keith Richards famously said that when he first met her: 'She knew everything and she could say it in five languages. She scared the pants off me!' Pallenberg was 'so very powerful' for Chrissie Shrimpton (Mick Jagger's girlfriend), but she didn't use her powers in an evil way, Shrimpton said: 'she was very weird and freaky and strong, but her feelings were genuine.' (ib., 91) Plenty of folk didn't like her at all (such as Mick's wife Bianca Pérez-Mora Macias,[12] and Jagger was

---

7 Anita Pallenberg was expelled from school at 16. She studied medicine, graphic design and picture restoration as a teenager.
8 Anita Pallenberg has recounted that she hung out with some of the *dolce vita* set – Federico Fellini, Pier Paolo Pasolini, Luchino Visconti, Alberto Moravia *et al*.
9 Incidentally, Brian Jones provided the soundtrack for the little-known *A Degree of Murder*. Jones had accompanied Anita Pallenberg to Munich to make the movie, and had been jealous of Volker Schlöndörff.
10 Unfortunately, Anita Pallenberg was dubbed – by Joan Greenwood – in *Barbarella*.
11 V. Bockris, 2002, 159.
12 'An Inca princes dressed like a Dior mannequin', as Philip Norman put it (1984, 345).

wary of Pallenberg at first, and suspected that she might be a disruptive influence on the Rolling Stones: 'Mick, especially, was very hostile,' Pallenberg acknowledged. 'Even today, I can squash him with just one word. But he was the one most against my seeing Brian and being around the Stones').[13]

For photographer Gered Mankowitz, Anita Pallenberg was 'the epitome of the incredibly beautiful, incredibly stylish Sixties woman,' but he also regarded her as 'evil and manipulative and wicked' (ib., 91). Linda Keith (Keith Richard's girlfriend) admired Pallenberg: 'she was the most wonderful and powerful person. I have huge respect and admiration and love for her' (ib., 91).

Philip Norman described Anita Pallenberg in his superb biography of Mick Jagger thus:

> Anita was stunningly beautiful in the crop-haired, snub-nosed, long-legged way that perfectly suited sixties fashion, but with an extra, almost feral quality, 'like a cheetah', John Dunbar recalls. She was formidably intelligent, fluent in four languages, and knowledgable about art and the obscurer ways of German and European literature. She also had a recklessness and appetite for devilment that would cause more than one of her new rock 'n' roll friends to suspect her of being a witch. (193-4)

For cult writer Terry Southern, Anita Pallenberg was a much more complicated personality than Keith Richards: she would play games; she 'has a mischievous deviousness' (ib., 161). When Richards first encountered Pallenberg, he wondered 'what the fuck is a chick like that doing with Brian?', because Pallenberg seemed to Richards altogether too strong and confident to be with Jones.

❈

Anita Pallenberg's influence on the Rolling Stones has been attested by many commentators – on the whole band, not just on Keith Richards or Brian Jones or Mick Jagger.

According to observers (such as Christopher Gibbs), the relationship between Anita Pallenberg and Brian Jones was full of arguments and yelling – they couldn't agree on anything, they brought out the worst in each other, and Jones could never win an argument with Pallenberg.

Brian Jones does strike me at times as a bit of jerk – not the self-destructiveness, the thievery, and the chronic self-absorption – but the occasional pompous behaviour, the misguided views, the moronic baiting of audiences, and the childish attention-seeking.

Brian Jones was also a woman-beater – he beat up Anita Pallenberg! What a twat! Plus a girl who stayed with Jones in an American motel,

---
[13] Quoted in P. Norman, 1984, 166.

Anna Wohlin,[14] and Suki Potier, among others, were also hit by Jones. Girlfriends would receive black eyes and bruises (including even Pallenberg, a powerful woman). There is also a creepy aspect to Jones, a pathetic, self-pitying attitude.

That Brian Jones could be abusive with women has been attested by a number of observers. As Philip Norman put it, behind the golden-haired, charming exterior of Jones, 'lay complex sexual hang-ups and a strain of sadomasochism which booze and drug-fuelled insecurity and paranoia could bring out in highly unpleasant ways' (2012,165). Once Anita Pallenberg threw Jones over for Keith Richards, during the infamous Moroccan trip,[15] he became very jealous; Jones replaced Pallenberg with several girlfriends who were her clones (including Suzi Potier and Anna Wohlin).

It seems odd that someone as talented as Brian Jones felt powerless to do anything about the attention that Mick Jagger was generating in 'his' band, and taking the attention away from him. I mean, he was the lead guitarist, it was deemed 'his' group, he could've done a little more than just stand there on stage, peering at the audience and smiling occasionally. Anything was up for grabs at that time! (Maybe that ridiculous hair style didn't help, with Jones seeming to hide behind the golden fringe).

Certainly in the realm of songwriting, Brian Jones didn't pull his weight, and found himself being eclipsed by the creative partnership of the Glimmer Twins (however, Jones made sure he pocketed more dough than the rest of the band from their live shows). Despite his amazing musical facility, his multi-instrumentalist abilities, Jones couldn't come up with songs as strong or as commercial as those written by Richards and Jagger. Andrew Oldham tried locking him in a room (as he had done with Mick and Keith), but that didn't work either.

Anita Pallenberg and Brian Jones indulged in some S/M during the first weeks of their romance (when things were going well, before the beatings) – Pallenberg was altogether more sophisticated and skilful sexually than Jones's previous girlfriends: she would dress up Jones in drag (as Françoise Hardy), or whip him, and at one time they put on Nazi SS costumes.[16] Well, that's how popular legend has it. But soon the magic has dissipated into some violent altercations, arguments in which Pallenberg would emerge black and blue. And in public, Pallenberg wouldn't denounce Jones. (Marianne Faithfull found it difficult to take that Pallenberg could

---

[14] Swedish wannabe dancer, Anna Wohlin, 19, was among Jones's last girlfriends.

[15] That trip to North Africa – the car journey across Spain (which included Donald Cammell's girlfriend Deborah Dixon and the chauffeur Tom Keylock), the arguments between Anita Pallenberg and Brian Jones, the abuse, etc – is well-known. It was during the Moroccan jaunt that Pallenberg left Jones, and departed with Keith Richards after a particularly violent bust-up with Jones.

[16] Playful Pallenberg persuaded Jones to put on a Nazi SS uniform for a photo shoot for the cover of *Stern* magazine (which they of course rejected, and there were complaints in the British press). Pallenberg admitted that it was her idea – 'it *was* naughty'.

appear as the dominatrix in Jones's sexual fantasies one moment and a victim of his physical abuse the next ('he would pick up anything – a tray of sandwiches, a whole table – and just throw it', Pallenberg said). That a very powerful woman like Pallenberg – a highly intelligent and independent woman – would put up with that kinda of shit is scary, creepy and disturbing).

Anita Pallenberg eventually ended dating Brian Jones during a visit to Tangiers (one of the key destinations of the time, along with Paris and New York – *Duffy*, scripted by Donald Cammell, Harry Joe Brown and Pierre de la Salle, was set in Tangiers). Jones made his way back to Paris, to stay with Cammell. Keith Richards took Pallenberg with him.

✳

In 1971 the Stones moved to the South o' France, for tax reasons. That didn't go so well after a while: everybody converged on Nellcôte, where Keith Richards, Anita Pallenberg and the family lived on the Riviera.[17] By this time, both Richards and Pallenberg were heavily into drug-taking, and had an entourage of druggy hangers-on which some in the band (like Mick Jagger and Bill Wyman) didn't find especially conducive to working on music sessions. (Meanwhile, the French authorities were staking out the Richards house, and raiding it. Around this time, too, Richards seems to have particularly accident prone, with hotel rooms regularly setting on fire, and Redlands burning down).

The Richardses were beset with troubles – they lost a baby[18] (due to cot death, but there are hints that Anita Pallenberg might have been negligent), and the teenager Scott Cantrell killed himself on Pallenberg's bed in 1979. Pallenberg was linked to a man shot dead by police in West London in 1983 (in the same year, Pallenberg's room in the Grosvenor House Hotel was raided by police for drugs).

One of the reasons that Anita Pallenberg eventually broke up with Keith Richards was because of sex: Pallenberg wanted it, and Richards wouldn't give it (Richards was known for having a far less screaming libido than fellow Stoneses like Brian Jones and the Mouth. Bill Wyman, however, insisted that *he* had far more women than all of the Stones put together). As a friend quipped, 'Anita was always running Keith down for not having fucked her properly'.[19] Barbara Charone remembered that Pallenberg would scream at Richards: 'I haven't been fucked in months! Is television more important than me?'[20]

---

[17] Keith Richards' pettiness came to the fore here, when he charged his fellow band members £100 ($150) for staying at his home.
[18] Named Tara JoJo Gunne (after Tara Browne and a Chuck Berry song character).
[19] Quoted in V. Bockris, 2002, 160.
[20] Quoted in ib., 217.

For quite a bit of their time together, Anita Pallenberg and Keith Richards were heavily into drugs[21] – including heroin[22] (which Pallenberg was taking when she was pregnant).[23] That didn't help the situation sometimes – they'd be so out of it they'd set their bed on fire (fires seemed to flare up regularly in Richards' life at this time). And they wouldn't talk to each other much, Pallenberg recalled, except to ask each other 'have you got anything?' (i.e., druuuuugs). They were arrested in Toronto in 1977, on charges of possessing heroin (one of their lowest times). [24]

And Anita Pallenberg deeply resented the hangers-on that Keith Richards seemed to attract (like Brian Jones did). These were the creeps who would stay for weeks on end.

> When our relationship started to deteriorate it was because of all these people [Pallenberg remarked]. We could never be alone. I couldn't stand it, because I was aware of them, but he was completely unaware of it. He was living in this other world.[25]

Mick Jagger also disliked the Keith Richards entourage, partly because he wasn't into smoking and drug-taking in the same quantity, and it also affected their working relationship (Jagger stumbling into dark, messy rooms full of druggy hangers-on and scorning the scene is a recurring theme in the Rolling Stones legend). In Switzerland, Anita Pallenberg complained that Richards' entourage of yes-men meant there was 'no private life, no time to talk', just a bunch of drug suppliers. Pallenberg and Richards were soon both seeing other people.[26]

Anita Pallenberg and Keith Richards have two children – Marlon (b. August 10, 1969) and Dandelion (re-named Angela) (b. April 17, 1972). Pallenberg was rumoured to have had an affair with the 17 year-old Scott Cantrell, the gardener who killed himself on Pallenberg's bed in South Salem with a 0.38 handgun owned (stolen) by Richards on July 20, 1979 (it may have been a game of Russian roulette inspired by the 1978 Oscar-winning movie *The Deer Hunter* – and it wasn't the only copycat incident. See the

---

21 During a drugs raid at Cheyne Walk in the early 1970s, the cops found heroin, methadone, grass, Mandrax, pipes, weighing scales, and Keith Richards' collection of weaponry: 2 shotguns, a French blunderbuss, a .38 Special, knives and boxes of bullets. (Richards was fond of collecting guns as well as guitars – like the guitar that Scotty Moore played with Elvis Presley. Dogs and cars were also favoured as part of the Richards menagerie).
22 Of heroin, Keith Richards said: 'while I was a junkie, I still learned to ski and I made *Exile On Main Street*' (P. Norman, 1984, 359).
23 Anita Pallenberg rejoiced in her heroin addiction, according to Philip Norman, relishing inducting other people into it (such as Mick Taylor's wife), and calling heroin 'Henry' (she also scorned Richards' apparent inability to really handle heroin addiction.
24 Keith Richards faced legal proceedings for drug arrests in, among others, Chichester, Aylesbury, London, Fordyce, Nice and Toronto.
25 V. Bockris, 2002, 175.
26 The Richards-Pallenberg relationship did come to blows occasionally: according to Tony Sanchez, Richards and Pallenberg laid into one another on a car trip following an album launch at Blenheim Palace.

Wild Side chapter for more info).[27] Their son Marlon was in the house in New England at the time, and Pallenberg was in the room, 'tidying up' (she was later cleared of being involved with Cantrell's death, which was deemed to be suicide).[28] This notorious incident was another factor in the break-up between Richards and Pallenberg (Richards taking up with the Swedish woman Lil Wergilis was another).

Anita Pallenberg said she was never Mick Jagger's girlfriend, and hadn't had an affair with him, including during the making of *Performance*.[29] Yes: altho' wives such as Bianca Pérez-Mora Macias feared that Pallenberg was working her way thru the Rolling Stones (Jones then Richards), and had her eye fixed on Jagger,[30] Pallenberg wasn't interested. Besides, Pallenberg was deeply involved with Richards at the time, and it's unlikely that Jagger (despite his well-known promiscuity) would've jeopardized the all-important relationship he had with Richards and the band.[31]

Like Donald Cammell, Anita Pallenberg was into the occult and magic,[32] even, according to rumour, to the point of taking garlic with her to bed to ward off vampires! But, according to Keith Richards, neither he or Pallenberg were particularly into the occult (although Kenneth Anger thought they were);[33] it was an image, for him (as for many rock stars), and a way for her 'to mess with people's heads' (V. Bockris, 130). Mick Jagger, meanwhile, was interested in occultism for a while, was flattered by the allusions to Lucifer (and took to wearing a wooden crucifix).

CANDY.

If you haven't seen *Candy* (Christian Marquand, 1968),[34] I'd recommend it as one of the more bizarre, so-bad-it's-*bad* movies of the 1960s: a host of big name actors (including Marlon Brando, John Huston, James Coburn, Walter Matthau, Charles Aznavour, Ringo Starr and Richard Burton) wander aimlessly through a completely pointless film.[35] Best of all is Brando's truly weird religious guru (a satire on the hippy gurudom of the

---

[27] The Russian roulette scene in *The Deer Hunter* was associated with 31 incidents involving Russian roulette with handguns between 1979 and 1982, according to Steven Prince in *Screening Violence* (2000).
[28] However, Anita Pallenberg was fined $1,000 for possessing a stolen gun.
[29] V. Bockris, 127.
[30] Bianca Macias 'was tormented by rumors that Mick was having an affair with her' (P. Norman, 1984, 358).
[31] Actually, that's not true – Jagger happily screwed some of the bands' girlfriends.
[32] Donald Cammell later said: 'I wish I'd never got involved in magic. It fucked everything up.' (M, 82).
[33] Kenneth Anger visited Redlands in 1967, Keith Richards' home in Sussex; Anger suggested that Richards and Pallenberg have a pagan wedding ceremony, with him presiding as the priest; Pallenberg was keen, but Richards declined.
[34] There's a connection with *Performance*: Jack Nitzche was commissioned to compose the score for *Candy*, but the producers didn't like the music he wrote. By the way, director Christian Marquand, a friend of Marlon Brando's, plays the French plantation guy in *Apocalypse Now*.
[35] Mick Jagger and Keef Richards were asked to do the music for *Candy*, but, as Jagger recalled, the film people didn't want to pay them much (£2,000/ $3,000), and no royalties (1975, 171).

era, and the Beatles with the Maharishi), who tups Candy in the back of a truck rumbling through the North American desert. Anita Pallenberg has many scenes with Coburn's mad doctor as a wicked, sexy nurse (with some echoes of her role in *Performance* as a sidekick who supports her boss in his barmy exploits).

The book *Candy* (1958) by Terry Southern[36] and Mason Hoffenberg is a terrific satire on contemporary North America and pop culture, containing some self-consciously over-the-top scenes of fucking and debauchery. The 1968 movie of *Candy*, needless to say, captures absolutely bugger all of the novel. (Buck Henry adapted the novel – parts of which, you have to admit, are unfilmable).

Why didn't they cast Anita Pallenberg in the lead role in *Candy?* – because the actress they chose as Candy – Ewa Aulin – has the charisma, the comic timing, and the sex appeal of a stale cheese sandwich (Swedish Aulin has the long, blonde hair, the pouty, all-American look, but she sinks the movie). *Candy* is one of those all-star co-productions of the 1960s[37] which tried to fuse European and American actors and sensibilities but failed miserably (other flops would include *Casino Royale* and *The Magic Christian*). At least movies such as *Those Magnificent Men In Their Flying Machines, Those Darling Young Men In Their Jaunty Jalopies* or (a.k.a. *Monte Carlo or Bust*) or *It's a Mad, Mad, Mad, Mad World* had some half-decent scripts and witty moments. [38]

---

[36] *Blue Movie* was a crude send-up of the sex film industry; at one point it was going to be made by Stanley Kubrick, complete with explicit penetration and come shots (it would be another twenty-five years before Kubrick finally tackled graphic sex on screen, in *Eyes Wide Shut*, with Hollywood movie star couple Nicole Kidman and Tom Cruise). Terry Southern's *Blue Movie* hugely exaggerated the porn world, in the style of his earlier book *Candy*, and his work with Kubrick on *Dr Strangelove*. Apparently, when Kubrick showed *Blue Movie* to his wife, she reportedly told him 'Stanley, if you do this I'll never speak to you again' (LB, 329-330). At one point, Warners was going to do *Blue Movie* with Mike Nichols directing Julie Andrews (David Lean has also apparently considered it, although it's difficult to imagine Lean, or Julie Andrews, tackling a story on the porn industry!). And it's hard, too, to imagine Kubrick directing such a movie: the comedy in *Blue Movie* derives from some graphic portrayals of sex acts, which Kubrick and co. did eventually illustrate in *Eyes Wide Shut*, but that was a detached, abstract and surreal take on sexuality. *Eyes Wide Shut* was really about marriage, fidelity and monogamy.
[37] *Candy* was an American-Italian-French co-production.
[38] But *Candy* is far more enjoyable in its craziness than a later movie adapted from a Terry Southern book, *The Magic Christian* (1970), a truly abysmal outing starring Peter Sellers, Ringo Starr, Christopher Lee, Lawrence Harvey, Yul Brynner, Raquel Welch, etc.

ANITA PALLENBERG, THE ROLLING STONES AND THE CHELSEA SET

One of the centres of the Rolling Stones/ Chelsea scene was 1, Courtfield Road, off Gloucester Road in Londinium, where Brian Jones lived with Anita Pallenberg (other hang-outs included Paul McCartney's places in 29, Lennox Gardens and Cavendish Avenue,[39] the Indica gallery & bookstore, John Dunbar's place, Barry Miles's house, and Robert Fraser's art gallery).[40] For Pallenberg, her den with Jones was 'the Grand Central of rock' (Marianne Faithfull described Pallenberg as 'a phoenix on her nest of flames' at the centre of this 'veritable witches' coven of decadent illuminati, rock princelings and hip aristos').

The Chelsea set which the Rolling Stones moved in included the art dealer Robert Fraser,[41] antique dealer Christopher Gibbs, drug dealer Tony Sanchez, photographer Michael Cooper,[42] UFOlogist John Michel, Stash Klossowski (son of the painter), Tara Browne (the Guinness heir), and visitors such as William Burroughs, Terry Southern, Kenneth Anger, Brion Gysin, Paul McCartney, George Harrison, Eric Burdon, the Spencer Davis Group and Peter Noone.

Chelsea continued to be a hub for music and art in the 1970s – the punk rock movement had one of its centres there, with Vivienne Westwood and Malcolm McLaren and their Sex/ Seditionaries shop[43] (Anita Pallenberg later worked with Westwood, after studying fashion on a course).

❂

Anita Pallenberg battled with alcoholism (and went regularly to Alcoholics Anonymous). Pallenberg struggled with heroin addiction in the 1970s, and went to rehab (which worked for Keith Richards). She put on weight – these were her worst times. Richards' family (and his lawyers) reckoned that Pallenberg was a bad influence and wasn't a fit mother to Marlon (a bad influence on Richards! What a laugh!).

---

39 Visitors to Macca's bachelor pad in Cavendish Avenue included Mick Jagger, Marianne Faithfull, Tara Browne, Stash de Rollo, John Lennon, Ivan Vaughan, John Dunbar, Robert Fraser, the Monkees, Brian Jones and Barry Miles (B. Miles, 341).
40 Anita Pallenberg had met Brian Jones in 1965 – maybe in Paris, at one of the Stones' Olympia shows, or in Germany, at another show (U, 66). Pallenberg said it was in Munich. At the time, Jones's girlfriend was Zou Zou. Pallenberg said: 'I fell in love with Brian – all the way. He was a great guy, you know.' (P. Norman, 1984, 166).
41 Robert Fraser was an art dealer in his late twenties from a well-to-do Scottish background. Barry Miles portrayed Fraser as 'a nervous Old Etonian homosexual with a fantastic eye for art' who was also a heroin addict (243). Christopher Sanford described him as a gay '27 year-old Old Etonian army officer turned art-dealer-cum-junkie' (73).
42 Michael Cooper photographed the covers of *Sgt Pepper* and *Their Satanic Majesties*. He died from an overdose in the early 1970s.
43 It is significant that Malcolm McLaren's and Vivienne Westwood's shop at 430, King's Road in London, cited so often as one of the creative cauldrons of punk fashion, went through a number of changes. First it was called *Let It Rock*, and sold Teddy Boy and Fifties clothes. Then it was called *Too Fast to Live, Too Young to Die*, and sold biker clothes (Westwood said the only 'true example of Street Fashion' was the rocker). Finally, it became *Sex* and sold S/M & fetish clothing. Underground sex gear became one of the taboos which the punks brought out into the open.

In later years, Anita Pallenberg lived alone in a mansion in Chelsea. She enjoyed gardening. Pallenberg studied fashion (graduating from Central St Martin's in 1994), and wanted to work in textiles. She went to India (Jaipur) for 6 months, but found the fashion industry too cutthroat.

THE LATE SIXTIES

The late Sixties in Britain was the time of 'happenings', psychedelia, bands like Soft Machine, Cream and Henry Cow, the UFO, Middle Earth and Speakeasy clubs, Arts Labs, the Notting Hill Free School, the London School of Economics, and magazines such as *IT, INK, Friends, Spare Rib* and *Oz*. Posters for the gigs advertized them thus: 'bring your own happenings and ecstatogenic substances'.

The 1960s in Britain were a time of clubs and dance halls such as the Cromwellian, Scotch of St James, Ad Lib, Club a Go Go in Newcastle, Dis-a-Gogo in Cardiff, Lindella Club in Glasgow, the Cavern and Mardi Gras in Liverpool, the 100 Club, Hammersmith Palais and the Scene in London, and dance hall networks such as Mecca, Top Rank and Locarno, and fashionable figures such as Mary Quant, Vidal Sassoon, Ossie Clark, John Lennon, Jean Shrimpton, Twiggy, Dusty Springfield, Mick Jagger, David Frost, Kenneth Tynan and Joe Orton.

The Roundhouse events were some of the most famous of 'Swinging London': two bands played simultaneously at either end of a huge space; four movies were projected on white sheets hung on the walls (with a foreign movie in another room); there were light shows; people dancing; people making out; and everybody seemed to be taking drugs. *Performance* doesn't show a rock concert – it has its own happenings inside the house at 81, Powis Square (where, for instance, Lucy dances while Turner flails a strip light around).

Other early gigs of this late 1960s era included the 'All-Night Rave Pop Op Costume Masque Drag Ball Et Al' which opened London's Roundhouse in October, 1966, the 'Spontaneous Underground' Sunday afternoons at London's Marquee (the Rolling Stones debuted as a band on July 12, 1962 at the Marquee), the '14-Hour Technicolour Dream' at Alexandra Palace, the 'Barbeque '67' bash at the Tulip Bulb Auction Hall in Spalding (Jimi Hendrix, the Move, Cream and Geno Washington were on the bill), and the 'More

Furious Madness From the Massed Gadgets of Auximenes' at the Royal Festival Hall in 1969.

Some of the members of the British counter-culture/ underground/ psychedelic scene of the 1960s included John 'Hoppy' Hopkins (*IT, Oz, UFO*, etc), Richard Neville (*Oz, Play Power*), Jeff Nuttall (*Bomb Culture*), June Bolan, Heathcote Williams, Jim Anderson, Christopher Logue, Caroline Coon, Joe Boyd, Mark Boyle, Duncan Campbell, Martin Cropper, Stash de Rola, Felix Dennis, Tony Elliot (*Time Out, i-D*), Mick Farren (*IT*), Michael Horovitz, David Jenkins, Sam Hutt, David May, Jonathan Meades, Barry Miles, Keith Morris, David Offenbach, John Dunbar, Jonathan Park, John Peel, Marsha Rowe, Chris Rowley, Nicholas Saunders (*Alternative London*), Su Small, Doug Smith, Derek Taylor, Ed Victor, Cassandra Wedd, David Widgery, John Wilcock and Robert Wyatt.

✻

1968 was of course a year of political unrest, riots, assassinations, etc; it was the year of May, 1968 in Paris, of anti-Vietnam War protests, of civil unrest, and the assassination of Bobby Kennedy – and *Performance* is part of that cultural and social shift. It's partly a film about the end of the Sixties, for some critics. Anita Pallenberg remarked that Chas's character represented some of the forces that were threatening to bring about the end of the decade of free love, music, decadence and hippy ideals.

But *Performance* is also ambiguously reluctant to confront global politics head on. Compared to a filmmaker such as Jean-Luc Godard, who was on fire creatively around this period, with movies such as *Weekend* (1967), *Le Chinoise* and *One Plus One* (both 1968), Donald Cammell and Nic Roeg seem to prefer to block out the world outside, and focus on the mind and drug games inside Turner's digs at 81, Powis Square. No references to the Vietnam War, to Communism, to the battles between left and rightwing politics. The last thing Chas Devlin or Pherber or Turner are going to do is join a bunch of radicals and anarchists on the barricades in Paris (similarly, altho' the Rolling Stones have been linked to the political upheavals and the radical politics of the late 1960s, they simply weren't interested).

What comes through in *Performance*, thick and strong, though, is the atmosphere of nihilism and violence of 1968. The idealism of the mid-1960s, of hippies and druggies and pop musicians and *avant garde* artists, is rapidly evaporating in a haze of hash-induced madness and violence and confused identities.

THE ROLLING STONES

The Rolling Stones,[44] with their self-conscious, contrived 'tough', sneering image (entirely manufactured), were often trumpeted, like many other bands, as 'the greatest rock 'n' roll band ever' (every band has been lauded thus: Led Zeppelin, the Who, the Beatles, Nirvana, etc). The Stones toured every three years or so through the 1970s, 1980s and 1990s tours (such as the *Steel Wheels, Licks, A Bigger Bang* and *Voodoo Lounge* tours), which celebrated the ageing rockers who reckoned they could still cut it live (and audiences thought they could).

The Rolling Stones tours,[45] including a 50th anniversary bash which had a revisit to Hyde Park, were enormously lucrative, putting the Stones among the highest paid performers in the rock and pop world.[46] Many acts from the 1960s era have reformed and toured, but the Stones have remained one of the most successful.[47] The 1975 U.S.A. tour grossed 409,317 dollars after tax for the Stones, from a 27-city, 68-day schedule. 2.9 million heard the Stones live on the early 1980s tour. For the 1989 tour, the Stones augmented the band with three backing singers, two keyboardists, and a five-piece horn section. A good seat on the *Bridges To Babylon* tour (1997) cost $300. The Stones made $289 million from the tour.[48]

The *Licks Tour* was a biggie, in support of the Rolling Stones' *Forty Licks* album (yet another greatest hits package). The 2005-2007 tour, *A Bigger Bang*, generated $558 million gross (from 147 concerts). Around $2 billion has been earned by the Rolling Stones since 1989. Their fee is now $6 million for a performance.[49] The songs of Jagger and Richards have made about $56 million (including $4m (or $5m) alone from Microsoft for 'Start Me Up'. Pepsi paid $2m for 'Brown Sugar' in 1997). By 2013, over their 50-year career, the Stones had written and performed about 400 songs. The Glimmer Twins were asked to compose a song for a *James Bond* movie but a million or two couldn't entice them. The Stones received $4 million from the Verve when the British indie act used part of 'The Last Time' (from *Today's Pop Symphony*), put together by Andrew Loog Oldham

---
[44] The name comes from a Muddy Water's song, and it was Brian Jones who named the band.
[45] Christopher Sanford summed up the Rolling Stones tours thus: 'egos run amok in one-night stands hazed over by trashed rooms, dope, strange faces in packed halls, sex, and enough hero-worship for anyone' (2013, 379).
[46] Merchandizing was a big deal, with a huge proportion of income being generated from tat. Merchandizing for the Rolling Stones included belt buckles, knickers, shoes, socks, lighters, glasses, patches, badges, dolls, wallets, and of course Tee shirts, posters and jackets.
[47] Not least because their ticket prices are some of the highest in pop history! And, following the split with Allen Klein in 1971, they've had a much tighter control of the business side of the band.
[48] *Bridges To Babylon* (1997) sold 6 million copies, restoring some of the Stones' musical credibility. The tour was a hi-tech extravaganza that Christopher Sanford characterized as drawing on Siegfried and Roy, *Arabian Nights*, Liberace, Andy Warhol, Albert Speer, U2 and Cecil B. DeMille.
[49] C. Sanford, 439.

in 1966, on their single 'Bitter Sweet Symphony' (1997).

Somehow, the Rolling Stones roll on, outlasting all of the their contemporaries:[50] as Philip Norman remarked in his Mick Jagger biography:

> Only the Stones, once seemingly the most unstable of all, have kept rolling continuously from decade to decade, then century to century, weathering the sensational death of one member and the embittered resignation of two others (plus ongoing internal politics that would impress the Medicis); leaving behind generations of wives and lovers; outlasting two managers, nine British prime ministers and the same number of American presidents; impervious to changing musical fads, gender politics and social mores; as sexagenarians still somehow retaining the same sulphurous whiff of sin and rebellation they had in their twenties. (4)

References to Mick Jagger and the Rolling Stones have cropped up in thousands of places in popular culture, such in the Carly Simon song 'You're So Vain' (Jagger sang b.vox, but Simon insisted it wasn't about Jagger), and in 'American Pie' by Don McLean. One of their funniest appearances was in *The Simpsons*, as the leaders of a rock Summer camp.

Mick Jagger strutted around[51] in his aggressive, eccentric way, spindly in tight leggings, spending hours on his body, slimming and keeping in trim.[52] Jagger's stage presence is genuinely remarkable – you can't take your eyes off him (altho' Keith Richards is many fans' favourite; and in the early days it was Brian Jones who often stole the limelight). Jagger delivers a highly stylized, super-charged sort of performance, an amalgam of many forerunners (including James Brown, Little Richard and Elvis Presley, plus of course all of the bluesmen that Jagger absolutely revered). [53]

Keith Richards (b. December 18, 1943) – 'Keef' – the 'Human Riff' – looked, meanwhile, like death warmed up, with a monkey-face, a haggard drugs casualty who's somehow made it through (the Richards persona is as studied and affected in its own way as the Mouth's persona, and observers (such as William Burroughs in 1989) have noted how Richards can turn on the laid-back rock star persona when necessary). Richards, an easy target for satirists, is actually a witty philosopher with his own brand of wicked humour (his autobiography (*Life*) is very amusing, as are his biographies). He's always been the Stones' most prominent axeman since the departure of Brian Jones. It might have been Jones's band originally,

---

[50] They had survived 8 American Presidents and 7 British Prime Ministers.
[51] When Mick Jagger saw James Brown performing live, he studied all of the moves that the godfather of soul delivered, and copied them shamelessly. The head tossing, the eyes staring wildly, the feet paddling the floor, and the flailing arms.
[52] Keith Richards regarded many of Mick Jagger's escapades and preferences with bemusement or (when they were getting along) scorn. You'd never get Richards running around a freakin' track before a show! The idea of Richards *jogging* is utterly preposterous!
[53] Meeting his blues idols in Chicago was for Mick Jagger, according to Philip Norman, 'the most thrilling experience of his life thus far' (151). Jagger absolutely revered Muddy Waters, Chuck Berry, Howlin' Wolf, Buddy Guy *et al*.

but after his death in July, 1969, it was Mick Jagger's and Richards' band. There's no Rolling Stones without Jagger, sure, but there's also no Rolling Stones without Richards). Richards is also the musical leader of the band.

Keith Richards' autobiography generated sales of apparently $12 million in the U.S.A. (making him one of the most successful authors of recent times). In 2012 Richards' financial worth was estimated at $290 million (Mick Jagger was worth about $360 million).

Keith Richards has his own style, too – scruffy jeans, cowboy boots and leather jackets in the 1970s, and later augmented by a skull ring, fish hooks, and amulets in his hair (which he later dyed blue). A rock gypsy look, you might call it. A Batik scarf is placed over hotel lamps to create a mood. The Richards *milieu* also includes Moroccan furniture, sheepskins, beanbags, ashtrays, classic guitars, and bottles everywhere.[54]

Keith Richards famously disliked Mick Jagger's penchant for ridiculous stage costumes and OTT theatricality. For Richards, all those lights and special effects were the preserve of pantomime, and Mick's stage clothes looked like 'fucking Danny La Rue'. It was the *music* that should come first, Richards insisted, and for live shows Richards would be happy with a few lights just so he could stumble his way across the stage to his amps (and the cocaine secreted in the special compartments inside them).

Keith Richards had fierce and old-fashioned ethics when it came to the band: loyalty was paramount ('no one leaves this band except in a pine box', Richards snarled, *à propos* Mick Taylor's defection in 1974) • the band should never leave a man behind (when the group fled following Richards' Toronto drug bust) • nobody was allowed to mess about with the band on stage (like Pete Townshend, Richards was very protective over his stage) • photographers and the press were fair game for a punch or two • and arguments were often settled with a fight (Richards is by far the most violent of the Stones. He is also the Stone with the collection of weaponry, and doesn't waste an opportunity to use it).

Keith Richards, tho', is *not* a lead guitarist: no, Richards is a *rhythm* guitar player, and that sense of rhythm and timing is absolutely fundamental to the Stones phenomenon musically. The classic Rolling Stones song begins not with Mick Jagger's vocals or Charlie Watts' drums, but a Richards riff (and in concert it's Richards who typically starts the show, running on to bang out the famous riffs to 'Start Me Up', or 'Street Fighting Man', or 'Jumping Jack Flash').

Brian Jones was increasingly off in his own world – it was 'his' band (originally), and Mick Jagger and Keith Richards had come to *him* (after

---

[54] Philip Norman described the Queen Anne house in Cheyne Walk which Anita Pallenberg transformed into a replica of a Moroccan hashish den: giant candles, beaten metal lamps, and a mirror ball (1984, 309).

seeing him at Alexis Korner's place); but altho' Jones was a formidable musical talent (one of those guys who can pick up any musical instrument and get a good sound out of it, according to many observers), he lost control of the direction and momentum of the band, with Jagger and Richards taking up centre stage.[55] Jagger in particular was simply too ambitious and too focussed (and too much of a control freak) to allow anything to upset the artistic or professional equilibrium (and the money-making machine that the band became).

Brian Jones's drug and drink addictions contributed towards his declining influence over the Rolling Stones from the mid-1960s onwards, but he was also a manic depressive personality, succumbing to fits of bitter jealousy, sudden furies, and suicidal tendencies.

Brian Jones was something of a Jekyll and Hyde type, with part of him 'permanently wound up, spending his time gobbling acid and shagging', while the other part was 'a sentimental and endearingly shy man who loved his mum', according to Christopher Sanford (153).

Brian Jones was the key dandy in the Rolling Stones – it was Jones who had the late 1960s rock star look down pat, with his Afghan coat, his pink shirts, purple suits, black boots, floaty scarves, and blond locks. He was 'a Botticelli angel, Beau Brummel and a likely recruit for the SS all rolled in to one', as Christopher Sanford put it (100).

What's striking about Brian Jones's role in the Rolling Stones is just how long the rest of the band tolerated him for. For months, and even years, it seems that Jones was in a psychological freefall: apart from taking plenty of drugs and drink, he was messing about on stage, hardly playing anything, and baiting the audience. In the recording studio, he contributed little, being out of his head or simply not bothered. At band meetings, he would be asleep on the table.

The Rolling Stones took to leaving Brian Jones behind, and getting on with shows and recording sessions without him. When he was focussed and relatively sober, Jones could be amazing, with his natural talent for musicality, but he was increasingly unable to contribute much. Mick Jagger especially was very concerned about touring in the U.S.A., and not being able to get the necessary travel documents due to Jones's health. For Jagger, always the professional performer and the switched-on businessman, it must've rankled no end that Jones could be so out of his tree for much of the time. (When Jones died in July, 1969, a U.S.A. tour was organized only a few days later; it was the first American tour for over three years, so that Jones's condition was probably a cause for the delays).

---

55 For Andrew Oldham, Jones lost his influence over the Stones when he resigned himself to playing rhythm guitar, rather than playing all sorts of instruments (P. Norman, 1984, 119).

At the back of the band, Charlie Watts (b. June 2, 1941), the jazz aficionado, laid down a solid backbeat with the air of a grim, craggy undertaker (or a stony-faced Harpo Marx).[56] Watts was a quiet, reserved personality, happiest when he was ensconced in his Sussex home with his wife Shirley, his dogs, his collection of American Civil War memorabilia, his classic cars (which he couldn't drive), and his jazz music side projects. Watts would take the craziness surrounding the Rolling Stones with a tired, seen-it-all-before weariness – he was no prima donna control freak like the Flapping Tongue, and no fierce surviving-against-the-odds rock star like Keith Richards (who would defend the Stones and their music to the death).[57]

Bill Wyman (b. October 24, 1936) could come over as smug and aloof on bass (a classic 'quiet one' bassist). Wyman was older than the others, and when he joined was more the professional musician than the wannabe blues fan. (Wyman was the diarist of the Rolling Stones outfit, recording all sorts of details for posterity, including his apparent success with groupies and hangers-on. It was Wyman (he reckons) who had the most women on tour – and anywhere).

Joining the Rolling Stones organization later (in 1975), Ronnie Wood (b. June 1, 1947) was Keef Richards Lite, an unassuming but important musical presence in the Stones' sound. Wood had played with the Faces, the Birds and the Jeff Beck Group. Wood wasn't cut into the main action financially until quite late in his time with Stones (like some of the other Stones, Woods also struggled with addictions, checking himself into rehab for alcoholism so many times it became a joke (tho' not to Mick Jagger, of course)).

Ron Wood eventually got the job of replacing Mick Taylor (almost by default), tho' the band had also considered and auditioned Jeff Beck (top choice), Mick Ronson, Harvey Mandel, Rory Gallagher, Geoff Bradford, Steve Marriott, Chris Spedding, Peter Frampton, and Wayne Perkins.

The truth was that a musician joining the Rolling Stones had to fit in socially, had to be able to undertake the gruelling tours, was partial to a tipple or a line, and had to be able to withstand working with Mick Jagger and Keith Richards. Musical ability was almost not important. As Richards put it:

> We're looking for a Brit who looks cool, with a fucking good sense of humour, who's slightly shorter than you, plays OK, likes a pint, won't freak out on the

---

[56] You could say that Charlie Watts was a reliable drummer who kept a steady beat. You could also say that he was, like Ringo Starr, a rather boring drummer, and that the rhythm section of the Rolling Stones was actually fairly routine.
[57] However, Watts did battle with addictions (including to heroin).

road, isn't going to jump ship and can get on with Jagger.[58]

Ron Wood, who looked like Keith Richards' twin, with the shock of black hair and sunken cheeks, wasn't the greatest guitar player technically, but, much more importantly, he fitted in socially with the band.

Ian Stewart ('Stu'), Nicky Hopkins, Bobby Keys and Mick Taylor[59] were also part of the Stones' musical circle. Keyboard player Stewart (1938-85) was with the Stones from the early days, but was demoted to the position of roadie and road manager (which he continued to do for many years). Taylor (b. January 17, 1949) was young (20) when he was invited to audition for the Stones in 1969 following the death of Brian Jones (Eric Clapton had been asked, too, and Woody was considered). Jagger and Richards had been very impressed by Taylor's guitar playing at the audition.[60]

Toppermost in the Rolling Stones sound was Mick Jagger's voice: very early on, Jagger rejected 'English' or 'British' vocal stylings, and went completely American. To the point where Jagger has one of the silliest voices in the history of pop music, resulting in some extreme twangs an' drawls that sound ridiculous even when presented to a funk 'n' soul-lovin' audience in Alabama and Louisiana or a bunch-a hillbillies in Texas. (Listen to His Jaggness on 'Street Fighting Man' – it's 'street fightin' maaiihhnnn' in the chorus! It's completely preposterous!).

That was the trend in British pop in the 1960s, a'course – performers like David Bowie and Roger Daltrey who hung onto an 'English' vocal style were in the minority. It was like someone being offered a big, shiny Cadillac for free but opting to keep driving a cramped, rusty Morris Minor. *Don'cha wanna be ridin' a Harley D. down Main Street with a groovy chick behind ya headin' ter the beach for some surfin'? Or would ya rather be eatin' fish 'n' chips in a dingy café in rainy, cold Bethnall Green?*

America or England?

Dreary, foggy, suburban Britain or glitzy, out-size America?

The Rolling Stones opted for the Great American Dream.[61]

As Paul McCartney put it, Route 66 and the American South in the blues music that he and John Lennon loved sounded so much more

---

[58] Quoted in C. Sanford, 273.
[59] Mick Taylor left in 1974.
[60] But Mick Taylor became disenchanted with life in the Stones, resenting being in the second tier in the hierarchy, and finding the lack of royalties from songs which he was certain he had contributed to irritating. Taylor also became another casualty of addiction, which seemed to afflict anyone who joined the Stones empire. So that, by the end of his time in the band, and for years afterwards, he was skint and an addict.
[61] Indeed, how 'British' are the Rolling Stones? The boys from Dartford, Kent and the Home Counties of dear Old Englande are in fact very 'American': their music is wholly American in form and in its inspirations; their image as rock and rollers is American; they have made most of their $$$$ from touring in the U.S.A.; some of their sidemen are America; and some of 'em, including Keef Richards, live there

glamourous than dear, old England:

> We know about the Cast-Iron Shore and the East Lancs Motorway but they never sounded as good to us, because we were in awe of the Americans. Even their Birmingham, Alabama, sounded better than our Birmingham. (B. Miles, 201)

The Rolling Stones in the Sixties cultivated a 'street tough' image, which, they claim, bands have copied many times since, even though they themselves took up North American blues and r 'n' b imagery (and young social rebels had been done ten years earlier, in the U.S. of A.). The music and the culture of rock and pop music is American, and black, as numerous commentators have noted: the Stones took pretty much everything musically from North America. Altho' some Brits argue otherwise, pop music, like jazz, and blues, and rhythm & blues, is an *American* cultural form (with roots going back to African American culture, and Africa itself).

As with other British acts such as the Animals, the Kinks, the Small Faces, Georgie Fame & the Blue Flames, the Yardbirds, John Mayall, Eric Clapton and Jeff Beck, the Rolling Stones' work drew[62] on North American rhythm & blues and black music (Chuck Berry, Bo Diddley, Slim Harpo, John Lee Hooker, Elmore James and Willie Dixon – these were composers and performers that Jagger, Richard, Jimmy Page, Eric Clapton and everybody else in Britain exalted).

The Rolling Stones were not radical or revolutionary,[63] tho' they might've been perceived that way.[64] In fact, they were careful *not* to make 'controversial' or unpalatable statements, in the press or their songs or at their concerts. Actually, as Philip Norman put it, 'the Stones were about nothing but being the Stones' (2012, 206). It was what they were best at: they were, above all, musicians (and entertainers). Like many pop acts of the period (such as the Who and Led Zeppelin), they were actually professional about putting on a decent show, about not missing a show, about pleasing their audiences (which's partly why Brian Jones's wayward behaviour on stage rankled so much with Mick Jagger and Keith Richards).

In the early days, the Stones were touring small blues clubs and gigs, making only £25-50 ($38-75) a night (in 1963, this meant Victorian town halls, pubs, theatres, cinemas, corn exchanges and even kids' parties, where the band was pelted with cream buns, according to Philip Norman [2012,

---

[62] Alexis Korner's Blues Incorporated was a key influence in Britain.
[63] Mick Jagger's appearance at the British Vietnam Solidarity Campaign march in March, 1968, was partly cosmetic: the Lapping Tongue might've spoken out against the Vietnam War, but his politics were fundamentally conservative and liberal. Jagger is a man who discusses money and investments and business to an obsessive, detailed degree, who has homes in Mustique, New York, London, etc, and who hobnobs with the British gentry.
[64] The Rolling Stones were conservative, land-owning Englishmen rather than radical activists, as C. Sanford pointed out (2013, 206).

109]). Like every other band in Britain, the Stones did the familiar touring in the back of a van, schlepping up and down the highways of dear, old Blighty, playing in ABC cinemas and the back rooms of pubs, sometimes to tiny audiences. Touring in Britain meant sleeping on the way back to London, or staying in grubby B & Bs and cheap hotels; making small amounts of money (with Brian Jones pocketing more than the rest of the band); and often receiving apathetic responses from the crowd (and sometimes violent reactions – the Stones had plenty of missiles thrown at them on stage over the years, apart from panties and bras).

❋

The Rolling Stones messed about with gender in the 1960s in their public image, though their gender-fucking was mild by today's standards (and even by 1970-72, David Bowie would go far beyond them). Even at their most foppish, with Brian Jones, Keef and Mick looking lovely in frilly cuffs and flower power collars, they were still heterosexual men, as Patti Smith insisted:

> Ya never think of the Stones as fags. In full make-up and frills. They still get it across. They know just how to ram a woman.[65]

The Stones mixed fey, foppish ('feminine') dandyism with hard-edged, strutting ('masculine') rebellion. Brian Jones in particular cultivated a camp character with his dandyish fashion (Jones was clearly a fashion pioneer in the late 1960s, and had sufficient quantities of narcissism and arrogance to back it up). In his 'real' life, though, Jones could be sexist, even misogynist, as could Mick Jagger and Keith Richards.

It was a cliché in fashionable circles that the really 'cool' people preferred the Stones to the Beatles. The Stones were regarded as the Beatles with sex added. Patti Smith gives her reaction here to seeing the Rolling Stones on television in the 1960s. For her the Rolling Stones were

> five white boys sexy as any spade. their nerves were wired and their third leg was rising. in six minutes five lusty images gave me my first glob of gooie in my virgin panties.... I was doing all my thinking between my legs. I got shook. light broke. they were gone and I was cliff-hanging. like jerking off without coming... on that silver screen they were bigger than my bed. my head spun. my pussy dripped. my pants were wet and the Rolling Stones redeemed the white man forever. (ib., 211)

In the late 1960s and early 1970s, the Rolling Stones, their managers, their PR people, their record company and their advertizing companies, carefully cultivated their bad boy image. They wore dresses (tho' some

---

[65] Patti Smith, "The Rise of the Sacred Monsters", *Creem*, 1975, in C. Heylin, 211-2.

would have preferred never to see Charlie Watts crossdressing!).[66] On the cover of a rare edition of 1971's *Sticky Fingers* the Stones' sexism was alive and well: a woman's fingers were shown poking out of a can of Fowler's Treacle.

Then there were the Rolling Stones' links to the Devil, as they cultivated a vaguely 'occult' image (which of course didn't last very long, and was dropped once it had served its purpose). During the era of *Their Satanic Majesties* and 'Sympathy For the Devil',[67] the apocalyptic spectacle of the notorious Altamont gig took place in the U.S.A..[68] The Altamont Speedway concert is often referred to as 'the day the Sixties died': 'America At Altamont could only muster one common response. Everybody grooved on fear. One communal terror of fascist repression.'[69] Altamont is seen by critics as the end of the era of free love and hippy-dippy ideals.

The Rolling Stones, at a concert relying on the Hells Angels for security (tho' the Stones were not directly involved with including the Hells Angels),[70] saw it going horribly wrong when an audience member died. This is the ultimate authentification of a rock act. Hendrix died, Joplin died, Presley died, Holly died, Cobain died, Bolan died, Morrison died. Rock critics always seem to cite the fact that Meredith Hunter[71] was murdered during the Stones' song 'Sympathy For the Devil', as if this is a terribly poignant, ironic event. Like *wow*, the youth died while Mick Jagger sang about having 'sympathy for the Devil'. *Cray-zee*. It's another form of simplistic (and offensive and insensitive) rock music (criticism) self-validation. (Actually, it was during the song 'Under Your Thumb', as the documentary *Gimme Shelter* shows).

The *Their Satanic Majesties* album[72] had taken a *long* time to complete (10 months), and in the middle of immense pressure (including the arrest, jailing and trial of the songwriters in the band, and the departure of their manager and producer, the Loog). It is this era of the Rolling Stones that *Performance* draws on.

✱

---

66 Jones was fond of dressing up in women' clothes.
67 The notion of including the Devil in 'Sympathy For the Devil' came not from Robert Johnson's pact, or the blues as the 'devil's music', or Aleister Crowley, but from the Russian novel *The Master and Margarita* by Mikhail Bulgakov (which Mick Jagger had been introduced to by Kenneth Anger).
68 Another 1960s star who played Monterey and Woodstock, Country Joe McDonald, became famous for the cry 'F-U-C-K' which was chanted before his song 'Feel-Like-I'm-Fixin'-to-Die Rag'.
69 George Paul Csicsery, "Altamont, California", *The New York Daily News*, December 8, 1969.
70 When Mick Jagger criticized the Hells Angels, they were furious. There was apparently an attempt made on Jagger's life in 1975 by the Angels, according to the FBI (using a boat to approach a Long Island house where the Stones had convened, but a storm prevented the act).
71 The guy who was accused of knifing Meredith Hunter, Alan Passaro (but found not guilty by a jury in Alameda County, CA), was found 14 years later floating in a lake.
72 The title, thought up by Mick Jagger, was derived from the British passport, which said, 'Her Britannic Majesty's Principal Secretary of State for Foreign Affairs Requests and Requires'. Jagger changed that to *Her Satanic Majesty Requests and Requires*. Decca insisted that this anti-royalist title was altered to: *Their Satanic Majesties Request*.

The Redlands drug bust (on February 12, 1967) was among the most notorious of events involving the Rolling Stones – when the authorities in Blighty decided to make an example of the band as representatives of druggy, hippy, rebellious counter-culture. The heavy-handed clampdown led to tough sentences and a public outcry against the law. [73]

Among the party-goers at the Redlands bust were Christopher Gibbs, Nicky Cramer, a friend of Keith Richards', Robert Fraser, his friend Ali, Michael Cooper, David Schneidermann[74] (the 'Acid King' drug supplier), George and Patti Harrison,[75] Marianne Faithfull and Mick Jagger. (The incident was referenced in *Performance*, and some of the participants – Jagger, Pallenberg, Gibbs, Fraser, etc – were part of the film's production).

The events of the Redlands bust have been recounted numerous times – how the group had taken a short walk on a pleasant afternoon, before the police raided the building; how at first Richards & co. thought it might be fans outside; how Marianne Faithfull had been wearing nothing but a rug (which she let slip upstairs when a female officer examined her);[76] and how the group had reacted to the whole raid. (Not long after Redlands, the authorities went after Brian Jones with a vengeance). All of this was pure gold for the media, which had a feeding frenzy with the sexy combination of drugs, cops, pop music, celebrities and nudity.

❋

The Rolling Stones had a number of managers, but the two most famous were Andrew Loog Oldham and Allen Klein. Oldham[77] was a 19 year-old tyke on the make in London's music business scene when he met the Stones. A larger-than-life personality, arrogant, a social climber, Oldham was more like a rock star than the Stones themselves, as Philip Norman noted: 'in his egotism, arrogance, grandiosity, self-indulgence and lack of self-control he was far more like a rock star than any of them, Mick especially' (179).

Andrew Oldham was self-consciously camp (at a time when many of the notable pop music managers were gay),[78] yet heterosexual. (There were rumours that Oldham and Mick Jagger had a relationship[79] – they were

---

[73] There were public demonstrations against the heavy sentences outside the *News of the World* offices in London, and in Piccadilly Circus.
[74] Altho' David Schneidermann is usually regarded as the one who snitched to the authorities during the Redlands bust (he left the country very rapidly), Tom Keylock is sure it was David Litvinoff.
[75] The Beatle was regarded by some as the lucky charm – when Harrison and Patti left early, the police moved in. It seemed as if the authorities would not touch the Beatles, but anyone else was fair game. In fact, the police did go after the Beatles later.
[76] When Anita Pallenberg wears a fur coat in *Performance*, that might be a reference to the Redlands bust (but Brian Jones also wore similar clothes).
[77] Christopher Sanford reckoned that Brian Jones and Andrew Oldham were very similar types (which may be why they fell out): 'both were maddening, touching, intermittently sadistic, very nearly very great, self-created and self-destroyed' (50).
[78] Oldham probably enjoyed the shock value of appearing gay, altho' he insisted he was straight (P. Norman, 180).
[79] Chrissie Shrimpton was among those who suspected it.

very close, and some observers reckoned they were in love with each other. They would share a bed from time to time, but in the manner of guys kipping, not having sex. It was common for bands to sleep anywhere on tour, and it meant nothing to be sleeping in or on the same bed.) Oldham was fascinated by Jagger, and vice versa. It was Oldham, for example, who talked up Jagger as one of the key selling-points of the band, rather than their 'leader', Brian Jones.

Andrew Oldham was fiercely ambitious, with his sights set on the top act of the 1960s, the Beatles (he wasn't the only manager who ultimately wanted to manage the Beatles – Allen Klein did too). During a crucial period, Oldham was not only the band's manager, but also its record producer (making him a hugely important figure in the history of British pop).[80] He was also the band's best mate – the 'sixth Rolling Stone', as he was sometimes dubbed. Yet for Oldham, the Rolling Stones were only one of a number of projects he was developing.

Eventually, the band and Andrew Loog Oldham went their separate ways. A critical factor was that Mick Jagger and Keef Richards thought that Oldham had deserted them during the Redlands bust. Oldham simply went off to California (to help supervise the Monterey Festival). In their hour of direst need, Jagger and Richards felt really let down. By this time, tho', Oldham had already helped to broker the deal with Allen Klein,[81] lessening his input into the Stones' affairs.

Andrew Oldham had been firmly opposed to the direction the Rolling Stones (and Mick Jagger in particular) wanted to take on their album *Their Satanic Majesties*. Noodling around with electronics, Mellotrons, sound effects and voices off (very much inspired by *Sgt Pepper's*) was not what Oldham had in mind for the Stones (later Jagger admitted that they had been a little out to lunch with *Their Satanic Majesties*. It's not the Stones' finest work, and many regard it as an experiment that didn't quite succeed).[82]

Sgt Pepper's had made everybody sit up and take notice: it was impossible to ignore, and for good reason it still tops polls for the Best Album Ever. *Sgt Pepper's* led directly to a bunch of concept albums.[83] The

---

[80] 'The Loog' negotiated a tape-lease deal for the Stones (with Decca), which hadn't been done before (in which master tapes of the Stones' recordings would be leased to the record company).
[81] The band split with Allen Klein (acrimoniously) in 1971. They sued Klein for around $30 million in the New York Supreme Court (but settled for $2 million).
[82] *Satanic Majesties* was 'a retro, Beatles-lite confession that sounded closer to a pot party than an album', remarked Christopher Sanford (156). The affinities with *Sgt Pepper* were numerous, from the cover photo taken by Michael Cooper, to the recurring songs at the opening and close, the use of sound fx and talk, and technical jiggery-pokery in the recording studio.
[83] Concept albums (as they were called) were fashionable in the late 1960s/ early 1970s for pop acts with intellectual, spiritual or artistic aspirations. They included *Days of Future* by the Moody Blues, *Ogden's Nut Gone Flake* by the Small Faces, *S.F. Sorrow* by the Pretty Things, Keith West's *Excerpt From a Teenage Opera*, *Tommy* and *Quadrophenia* by the Who, and *The Village Green Preservation Society* by the Kinks

Stones delivered quite a few flower-power, 'free love' sort of hippy songs, including 'She's a Rainbow', 'We Love You', 'Lady Jane' and 'Dandelion' (the era when the Stones hired a string orchestra, or the London Bach Choir (for 'You Can't Always Get What You Want'), or used unusual instrumentation such as clarinets, or a Mellotron.[84] Unusual for a blues-soaked act, that is – there's not a lotta Mellotron in the blues output of Howlin' Wolf or Muddy Waters!).

As with the Beatles, the Rolling Stones became completely disenchanted with Allen Klein, who had promised them, as he had the Beatles, fame and riches. Only later did it become known that Klein had invested some of the Stones' money (around $1 million) in an off-shore account. For years in the late Sixties, altho' the Rolling Stones were very successful, with their albums, singles, tours and TV appearances, they had to beg for money from Klein in New York.[85] (The Stones were under pressure to keep coming up with hits: every 8 weeks, Keith Richards said, they had 'to come up with a red-hot song that said it all in two minutes, thirty seconds'.[86])

Born in Noo Joisey in December, 1931, Allen Klein was a major hustler who promised his acts he could nose around in their finances to find their unpaid monies (which he did). Klein's tactics were clever, sly, and manipulative (and occasionally violent). He was a formidable manager, and a feared opponent.

Later the Stones dubbed Allen Klein 'Fatso', and deeply resented having to beg his New York office for dough (meanwhile, the Stones' empire found it very difficult to run a business when the people holding the purse strings were on another continent and ignored telex after phone call after telex). [87]

Allen Klein was keen on promoting the Rolling Stones in the movie world: he promised no less than five Stones movies at one time in the mid-1960s (intending to emulate the Beatles). One project was to be based on Dave Wallis' novel *Only Lovers Left Alive*.

Following the departure of Allen Klein, the Rolling Stones took up with Prince Rupert Lowenstein, who looked after their finances for the next 40 or so years. Using Dutch off-shore accounts,[88] the Stones, up to 2007, had paid only $7.2 million in tax on an income of $500 million.

✳

The Rolling Stones' repertoire, like the Beatles' *œuvre*, is full of what are now regarded as 'classics': the r 'n' b 'Little Red Rooster', 'I Wanna Be Your Man' and 'Satisfaction' (with its iconic opening guitar lick), the hymns of a

---

[84] It was Brian Jones who often introduced the unusual instruments to a Stones session, and played them.
[85] For their first U.S.A. tour, the Stones received earnings of just ten shillings (one dollar) each, according to Philip Norman (1984, 127).
[86] P. Norman, 1984, 162.
[87] Sometimes minders in the Stones empire would fly over to Gotham to physically demand money.
[88] Based in Amsterdam, as well as the Netherlands Antilles.

generation ('Get Off of My Cloud', 'Under My Thumb', 'Gimme Shelter'), the 'raunchy' numbers such as 'Let's Spend the Night Together', 'I Just Wanna Make Love to You' and 'Some Girls', the wistful, hippy anthems like 'She's a Rainbow', 'Dandelion' and 'Ruby Tuesday', the pseudo-occult pieces, such as 'Paint It Black' and 'Sympathy For the Devil' (which became notorious after Altamont), and the attempts at political relevance in songs such as 'Street Fighting Man'[89] and 'Undercover'.[90]

It took quite a while for the Jagger-Richards songwriting partnership to get up to speed, and to achieve the self-confidence and genius of the most famous and celebrated partnership in 1960s music, Lennon and McCartney. For years the Rolling Stones delivered cover versions, often of their idols in the blues world. Their first albums, too, were full of rocked-up covers of blues classics. (Indeed, it was some time – 1966 – before the Rolling Stones released an album that was written entirely by themselves. Of course, it was expected in that era for all pop acts to cover existing songs, or to have songwriters who wrote for them. And some rock performers started out as songwriters before moving to the other side of the footlights). 'The Last Time' (1963) was the first hit written by Mick and Keef (their third number one, it was based on a 1955 gospel spiritual song by the Staple Singers).

'In 'Brown Sugar' (originally titled 'Black Pussy'), Mick and the boys concocted one of their finest assimilations of North American blues and British, jangly guitar pop, with a fervid evocation of sexual desire, as also found in 'Let's Spend the Night Together'. In 'Let It Bleed', the psychosexual dramatics of the American blues is given a crude, rubber lips make-over: 'everybody needs someone to cream on, baby you can cream on me'. In 'Under My Thumb' the band conjured yet another paean to *femme fatales*, and also in 'Honky Tonk Women' and 'Lady Jane'. (Bitter break-up songs are also part of the repertoire, with the personas in the songs ranting about women who've left them. You're too late, you're out of time, you're yesterday's news, the songs' narrators insist of the women who've spurned them, nursing their bruised egos. In this masculinist, pussy-hungry world,[91] it's the guy who ditches the woman, not vice versa). [92]

'Jumping Jack Flash' was the story of a wild boy who managed to escape his abused upbringing where he was beaten with a strap by a hag. 'Ruby Tuesday' out-Kinks the Kinks. 'Get Off of My Cloud' is a terrific piece of Jagger-led cockiness: forget the lyrics (delivered in a *faux* Memphis

---
89 Inspired by Jagger's involvement with anti-Vietnam War protests at the American Embassy in London in 1968.
90 This had a trendy promo shot by Julian Temple in a Latin American setting.
91 Black women are the horniest, the Jagger-persona insisted on 'Some Girls': they really do just want 'to get fucked all night', Jagger sang (altho' French, English, Italian, Chinese and American girls were cool, too).
92 These are the Rolling Stones songs, like 'Under My Thumb', that drive feminists nuts.

accent), 'Get Off of My Cloud' is all about the feel, the drive, the groove (like a *lot* of the finest Stones songs, including the slowies and the ballads). 1965's 'Satisfaction' was also about escape and fulfilment – about materialism as much as sexual gratification. 'Satisfaction' was a pop landmark, Philip Norman asserted, as important as 'Heartbreak Hotel' by Elvis Presley. And altho' it seemed to be a pæan to masturbation ('vocalised by the one among [the Stones] seemingly least in need of it'), it was all really about Mick Jagger.

Pills an' drugs crop up as references in the lyrics of a few late 1960s songs by the Rolling Stones. Pills that help busy moms get thru the day ('Mother's Little Helper'), pills that bohemians get from the doctor or the Chelsea Drugstore, and the 'brown sugar' that's better'n sex. Women that get their kicks in Stepney instead of Knightsbridge. People on the edge of nervous breakdowns ('19th Nervous Breakdown').

In 'Midnight Rambler' (on the album *Let It Bleed*), a male outsider becomes a predator, invading homes as a sex-murderer. In 'Gimme Shelter', the male vagabonds become victims themselves, wanting shelter. In 'You Can't Always Get What You Want', the Jagger-persona admitted that there are social limits, that 'satisfaction' cannot always be achieved. '2000 Light Years From Home' (written in prison during the drug arrest, and boosted by Brian Jones's Mellotron noodlings), is an attempt (not entirely successful) at space rock.

The nomadic hobo theme continued with the albums *Sticky Fingers* and *Exile On Main Street*, although by this time the Rolling Stones' personas were not alienated teenagers but burnt-out desperadoes ('Soul Survivors'). On *Black and Blue*, the Stones revived their misogyny, with an ad campaign that included a tied-up woman saying: 'I'm Black and Blue from the Rolling Stones and I love it'.[93]

Getting your rocks off • getting high • getting with it • getting groovy • getting laid – much of the Rolling Stones' output is purely hedonistic. A lot of their material was about nothing more profound or original than women, sex, romance and partying (in the typical Stones song, the Jagger-persona complains about being mistreated by some dollybird or other – very different from the reality of the Stones' lives!).[94]

Orgies, orgasms, cocaine, wine, drink, parties, etc. *Got a coupla Puerto Rican hookers and a case o' wine, so how about we mess an' fool around*

---

[93] The Velvets incorporated 'dangerous' topics into their music: drugs in 'Heroin' and their key song 'I'm Waiting For the Man', the S/M scene (out of Sacher-Masoch's bland novel) in 'Venus in Furs', decadent (Germanic) Europeanism (in 'Femme Fatale', 'Black Angel' and 'European Son'). They sang about gender-benders, homosexuals and transvestites, social outsiders living in the heroin hell of pre-AIDS America. And baked beans in 'Heroin an' Beans'. Just kidding!

[94] But for hippies *circa* 1967, what is more profound than love?

like we used to? Satan-Jagger sings on the *Some Girls* album.[95] Sure Mick, come on up, we too can live a fantasy, jet-set, coke-addled lifestyle where every night's like bein' back at Studio 54 in 1978!

And the hits keep comin' – taken together, the Rolling Stones' output is gigantic: 'Wild Horses', 'As Tears Go By', 'Have You Seen Your Mother, Baby, Standing In the Shadow?', 'Out of Time', 'Stray Cat Blues', 'Can You Hear Me Knocking?', 'It's Only Rock 'n' Roll' and 'It's All Over Now' (and a'course the hits have been collected in 2,076,501 'greatest hits', 'platinum collections' and anthologies).

What's striking about the Rolling Stones' output is that many of their songs are *not* hard-rockin' pieces, or cock-walkin', struttin' numbers. Rather, they are fluffy, throwaway pop, with nary a hint of 'edge' or 'violence'. The 'world's greatest rock and roll band' on record is actually a great pop act, churning out the sort of chart pop that serious musos and rock critics despise among lesser bands. But because it's the Rolling Stones (as with the Beatles), they are indulged.

It's also worth pointing out that many of the Rolling Stones' famous songs are actually mid-tempo, or slow tempo numbers, with quite a light instrumentation. (The mid-1960s recordings are hampered by some indifferent or weedy technical production: in the recording studio, the Rolling Stones weren't at the forefront.[96] Not only because the recordings are in mono or early stereo, but because the overall production doesn't do the songs justice. And there's often a feeling of separation between Mick Jagger's vocals and the rest of the band, that's more'n just the distance of putting the lead vocals on later. But the compositions, of course, and the performances, have always come through. And besides, when the records are played very loud, it doesn't matter).

✳

Keith Richards employs acoustic guitars to a striking degree in the Rolling Stones sound, even tho' the image of Richards on stage is a rock star with his Fender Telecaster or Gibson (Richards has a collection of some 3,000 guitars!).[97] Richards is a devotee of the acoustic guitar, and you can hear it on many of the Rolling Stones' famous pieces.

Keef Richards often plays down his role musically in the Rolling Stones, claiming that he's not a lead guitar player, that he's more of a mediator between musicians, or a conduit, and he's happy to play rhythm guitar and let others take over the solos and lead roles (altho' of course Richards is

---

95 *Some Girls* sold some 8 million copies.
96 The Glimmer Twins were often credited with co-production. Later, when expert producers such as Glyn Johns got involved, the sound of the Stones became closer to doing the songs justice.
97 Quite a few have been stolen over the years – 11 or so were nicked from his Nellcôte house in the Riviera, and the replacement axes were also filched.

perfectly capable of doing all of that – this is a guy who as a youth copied all of Chuck Berry's solos in his house in Dartford, Kent until he knew them by heart). Besides, Richards may not the 'lead' guitarist in the Stones, but he is certainly, since the death of Brian Jones, the premier Stones guitar player.

What Keith Richards is a master of, for musos, is the riff (he's dubbed the 'Human Riff'). Often it's the guitar riff that begins a Rolling Stones song, a three or four note musical motif that relies as much on *rhythm* and *timing* as on melody (and on the spaces between the notes and the chords – Richards doesn't play everything as a stream of notes).

MICK JAGGER

> Mick likes knowing what he's going to do tomorrow. Me, I'm happy to wake up and see who's hanging around. Mick's rock, I'm roll.
>
> Keith Richards

Mick Jagger (born Michael Philip Jagger, Dartford, England, July 26, 1943), had a genteel, middle-class upbringing (not rock 'n' roll *at all*), with a father, Joe Jagger (1913-2006), who was a physical education teacher at a local school, and a mother (Eva Ensley Mary, 1913-2000), a hairdresser.[98] This was a household which had a chores rota planned by Jaggers' parents: he (and his brother Chris) were expected to do chores around the house according to the timetable (which included physical training in the garden).[99]

Like Keith Richards, Mick Jagger grew up in Dartford in Kent,[100] a small, unremarkable town that's situated in the North-West corner of Kent, on the River Thames, not far from London (thus, it's really one of countless satellite towns around the capital, filled with people who commute into the city). For many, Dartford is simply a place you pass thru, on one of the nearby motorways, on your way somewhere else.[101] It's not a famous destination

---
[98] Jagger's mom was born in Oz, of English stock – so there's an Australian connection to *Ned Kelly*.
[99] Friends visiting Jagger's house remembered how Joe Jagger would call his son back in to do his chores or training before leaving.
[100] Jagger and Richards had met at Wentworth Primary School in 1950, when the 7 year-old Richards had impressed Jagger by talking about his guitar. Later, they famously encountered each other at Dartford railroad station (in 1961), and got talking. It was one of those fateful meetings which changed the course of their lives, and of British pop music.
[101] Dartford was once a market town, but was ruined in WW2, like many towns in South-East England. And ruined again when the town planners demonstrated their lack of imagination and flair by building horrible flats and offices.

in the South-East of England like, say, Canterbury or Brighton.

Encouraged by his dad Joe, the young Mike Jagger was a keen sportsman, playing cricket, rugby, soccer and basketball. With pa, he would go canoeing and camping (the physical training would be kept up by Jagger throughout his life – on the big world tours he'd have a training area set up backstage. It was typical for Mick to run a few laps before going on stage – which is about as *un*-rock 'n' roll as you can get! Running laps would be the *last* thing Keith Richards would do before a show – he'd be having his shepherd's pie[102] washed down with vodka!).

A very smart child, Mick Jagger turned out to be an unexceptional student (he gained the 11-plus exam to enter Dartford Grammar School, was good at French and English, but didn't do so well for his O-levels (GCSEs) or his A-levels.)

At an early age, Mick Jagger became enchanted by music, and like so many of his peers (such as the members of the Beatles, the Who, Led Zeppelin and everybody else), he was impressed by the arrival of North American music in the form of rock 'n' roll in the mid-1950s (and also jazz and skiffle). He saw Buddy Holly live in 1958, at a concert in nearby Woolwich, and admired all the usual suspects (such as Little Richard, and of course Elvis Presley). But it was *blues*, far more than pop, rock 'n' roll, jazz, show tunes or skiffle, that really touched the young Jagger, turning him on to blues music for life. [103]

At this time, getting access to the blues in austere, post-WW2 Britain, was difficult: it wasn't in the charts, it wasn't played on the radio (except occasionally on Radio Luxembourg), it wasn't on TV (ever), and it wasn't in the stores. Thus, blues music fans tended to send away to American stores and record labels (such as Chess),[104] in an era way before E-bay, Amazon and the internet.

There was another way in which music fans could consume (American) rock 'n' roll: in movies. Many British rock musicians have noted how significant it was when they first saw *The Girl Can't Help It* (Frank Tashlin, 1956) or *Blackboard Jungle*, *Don't Knock the Rock*, *Rebel Without a Cause* and *East of Eden* (both blues and rock 'n' roll, like the movies, and the fashions, were *American*: whether it was jazz, blues, rock 'n' roll or r 'n' b, it was all North American. In the 1950s, British youth was Americanized to a profound degree, and it hasn't recovered since: from the 1950s

---

[102] At one concert, in Toronto in 1989, Richards kept 53,000 punters waiting (and the band) while a replacement shepherd's pie was cooked (because some roadies had eaten it).

[103] At school, Mick Jagger had started a record club, for chums to listen to records during lunch hour. He was also part of a makeshift band, though it was nothing like as committed or as skilful as the teen bands of many of his contemporaries.

[104] Marshall Chess of Chess Records sent vinyl to Mick Jagger from the U.S.A.; later, Chess would work with the Rolling Stones.

onwards, British culture (and society) has been thoroughly Americanized).

Friends and observers have all noted that Mike Jagger was a friendly, laid-back, sporty, middle-class sort of youth, with few indicators of his later superstardom beyond his passion for blues music and rock 'n' roll, and his love of showing off in front of a few people when it came to singing (Jagger was too cool to be bothered to play a guitar). He was skinny, short, and only occasionally went for fashionable clothing (tho' he was clouted at school for wearing a jacket with gold trimming). Jagger has noted, tho', that he seemed to have admirers among girls without seeming to try (despite not being the most handsome of the boys in school), and the famous rubber lips would occasionally draw taunts of 'nigger'.

Dartford Grammar School was a typically stuffy, repressive, traditionalist, royalist, conservative, macho and boysy institution, where corporal punishment was casual and widespread. Rugby, school hymns, national anthems, rigid rules, and strict discipline. Mick Jagger was wholly part of the regime (and his father also taught at the school part-time). Indeed, at one point, Jagger was considering becoming a school teacher.

After Dartford Grammar School, Mick Jagger went up to London to study for a degree at the London School of Economics, a school with a reputation for radical, left-wing thinking (Bertrand Russell and John Maynard Keynes had lectured there). At the time, only a small percentage of school leavers went to university – most worked. In this period (early 1960s), at 18 and 19, Jagger still hadn't really exhibited the traits that would see him become a superstar by the end of the decade (not least, the aspects of being driven and ambitious – because Jagger wasn't that keen on going to university, or even on his chosen subject of economics. He was, like so many people at the same age, still searching for (or waiting to find out) what he *really* wanted to do).

From accounts of their first meetings and the friendship that developed between them, Keith Richards and Mick Jagger were fascinated by each other. To a degree, Jagger took Richards under his wing: Richards was from the wrong side of the tracks, seen from the viewpoint of the middle-class denizens of Jagger's Dartford in Kent (Richards lived on a working class housing estate). Richards' father Bert was absent, and his mother was very different from Jaggers' folks. But Richards had the guitar, and the ability to play, which Jagger didn't have: Richards was a natural when it came to music.

Like many another music fan of the era, Mick Jagger and Keith Richards would listen to records for hours on end, discussing every detail (you can see them doing this in the *CocksuckerBlues* documentary – you see them sit still, quiet and intent as music plays). And they would copy the records, getting the chords down, the phrasing, the lyrics and the vocalizations (Richards had already spent a *long* time at home copying Chuck Berry, Scotty Moore and Muddy Waters, often playing on the landing because it had good acoustics).

Mick Jagger and Keith Richards were thus utterly typical of rock musicians from the 1950s to the present day in terms of hanging out in their bedrooms, listening to music, copying it, and making the first moves towards emulating their idols (who at the time were very much of the North American blues tradition). This was months and years before they even performed in front of a paying audience (however, one of their number had an open reel tape recorder – a Phillips Joystick – so they began to record their musical efforts. And in those days, if someone had a piece of machinery or an instrument, like an amp, a guitar, a mixing desk or a truck, they were automatically in the band; Bill Wyman, for instance, had impressed the band with his battery of amplifiers). [105]

❋

Mick Jagger is one of those rock 'n' roll heroes who is often lampooned, a caricature of himself, with his spindly legs, huge lips and Mockney, mid-Atlantic drawl (he has a number of accents or voices). He's known on first-name terms, as 'Mick' (like Eric (Clapton), David (Bowie), Marc (Bolan), Jimi (Hendrix), Bob (Dylan) and so on).[106] While Keef Richards and Ronnie Wood were the party animals, hanging out all night after the gig, taking drugs, drinking and carousing, Jagger looked after himself. A keep-fit fanatic, Jagger was still strutting around the stage doing the cockwalk in coloured tights in his 60s.

Mick Jagger's chameleon social qualities are quite something to behold. Look at the filmed press conference following the Redlands drugs bust in 1967, for instance, when Jagger speaks in controlled, English, Received Pronunciation tones about 'responsibility' to the assembled hacks.

By 1993, Mick Jagger had 7 children with 3 mothers, homes in New York, Texas, Mustique and the Loire, and was worth over $100 million (in 2010, Jagger was estimated to be worth $298 million). Jagger was sometimes portrayed (in the broadsheets, in *Rolling Stone, Q, Mojo*, etc) as a rock star who understood the rock business, knew about fandom and fame, and knew what aspects of the Stones to emphasize. Jagger

---

[105] In the early days, Brian Jones, Mick Jagger and Keef Richards used to share an apartment in London Town (in Edith Grove in Chelsea) – a bunch of boys living in squalor (yeah – and now the Rolling Stones charge $150 for the cheapest tickets to their shows!). As well as the squalid flat at 102, Edith Grove, World's End, Richards and Jones also lived in a Notting Hill squat, and a shared room in Brackley Road, Beckenham.
[106] Mick Jagger was well-known for moving in a variety of social circles, from rock and roll to art, fashion, film and high society.

understood that rock music critics carried a lot of personal baggage with them when they approached the Stones:

> with people who write about the Stones and myself: they want everything again. It's like saying, "I want to feel the same way I did when I made love for the first time." They want to feel like they did the very first time they heard the first eight bars of 'Gimme Shelter'. But it's never going to be like that again!

Mick Jagger, as rock star, was always 'on', according to some observers – it was as if he always on stage, always thought he was in the spotlight, even when he appeared downstairs at home in his pyjamas. Jagger was famously a control freak, the top dog in the Rolling Stones enterprise, who oversaw the important aspects of the operation. In the pecking order of the band, Keith Richards and Jagger were at the top, with Bill Wyman, Charlie Watts, Ron Wood, Ian Stewart and others (such as Mick Taylor) in the second tier.[107] The entourage bloated to include hairdressers, trainers, managers, secretaries, roadies, engineers, drivers, PR people, etc (and there were plenty of more dubious hangers-on, such as drug dealers and groupies).

Marianne Faithfull recalled that living with Mick Jagger meant living with someone who was acutely conscious of being a rock star, someone who thought he was 'starring in an endless film', that he 'had to look good all the time for the great director in the sky'.[108]

Mick Jagger and Marianne Faithfull[109] were an item at the time of filming *Performance*. Philip Norman described Marianne Faithfull as

> a stunning combination of beauty and innocence, mistily innocent-looking, yet with a voluptuous figure; shyly and refinedly spoken, yet with an inquiring intellect and a rich mezzo-soprano singing voice. (2012, 118-9)

When Marianne Faithfull swanned into a lunch party for Adrienne Posta, Tony Calder recalled: 'it was like someone turned the sound down. It like seeing the Virgin Mary with an amazing pair of tits'. And both Mick Jagger and Andrew Loog Oldham muttered: 'I want to fuck her'.[110]

One of the striking aspects of the Rolling Stones operation was how much it centred around Mick Jagger – to the point where the band's logo

---

[107] For 19 or so years Ron Wood was on a salary, and not cut into the more lucrative deals in the Rolling Stones empire (so he was earning far less from touring and recording than the others). Mick Taylor complained that during his time with the Stones he hadn't been financially compensated for his contribution to songwriting.
[108] P. Norman, 2012, 307.
[109] Marianne Faithfull's mom was Erisso von Sacher-Masoch, whose great-uncle was the Leopold von Sacher-Masoch who penned *Venus In Furs*. Her father was psychologist Dr Glynn Faithfull, who lived in an Oxfordshire experimental commune.
[110] P. Norman, 2012, 109.

was the famous lapping tongue, and the rubber lips.[111] It's crude, and sexist, as Philip Norman points out, but it also reminds everyone just who is running the show (6). But it doesn't fully reflect the band.

Someone as talented as Mick Jagger could've had alternative careers – in politics, for instance.[112] He could've developed himself as a writer or poet.[113] He could've had a career as a solo artist, in the Elvis Presley or Frank Sinatra mold; but he always preferred to be fronting a band.

Mick Jagger took up a solo career, beginning with his first album *She's the Boss* (1985). It featured Pete Townshend, Herbie Hancock, Jan Hammer and Jeff Beck. (Subsequent solo outings included *Primitive Cool*, *Wandering Spirit* and *Goddess in the Doorway*). Keith Richards, meanwhile, has released far less solo material, but he has been involved with numerous musical collaborations (he resented Jagger's pursuit of solo music projects, tho', because they took time and energy away from his beloved band).

Mick Jagger was knighted in 2003 (much to Keith Richards' disgust! Richards was absolutely furious[114] that 'Brenda' (as Richards liked to call Jagger), had accepted an accolade from the British establishment which had put them in prison in the 1960s (and which had pursued him and his 'old lady', Anita Pallenberg, in the 1970s with further drug busts).)

Mick Jagger wasn't averse to throwing his weight around literally, from time to time: at a party at the Skindles Hotel in Maidenhead in the early 1970s (when the Stones were about to flee to France in tax exile), Jagger's response to a noise curfew at 2.00 a.m. was to pick up a table and hurl it thru a plate-glass window (which Kenneth Anger reckoned must've cost £20,000/ $30,000). And Jagger, tho' eclipsed in the Wild Man of Rock stakes by Keith Moon or Ozzy Osbourne, has been known to trash hotel rooms.

The Rolling Stones wasn't a one-man show, but everybody knew who they had to please first, and if he wasn't pleased, the displeasure would percolate down thru the band's hierarchy. Any decision involving the Rolling Stones would have to have Mick Jagger's OK. Like many dictators, Jagger liked to have things done *his way* or not at all.[115]

Mick Jagger was, like other rock stars of the era (such as David Bowie, Marc Bolan, and Elton John), fiercely competitive, keeping a close eye on what everyone else was doing. He was also supremely narcissistic, devoted to the Cult of Jagger, maintaining the legendary status as the king of cool,

---

111 Rolling Stones Records had its own logo – the lips and tongue of Mick Jagger (the idea was Marshall Chess's); a reminder, as Philip Norman put it, of just who was the star and the boss of the Stones.
112 When Mick Jagger became friends with Tom Driberg, a famous left-winger, there were suggestions of him running for office. Jagger just laughed.
113 At one time, Jagger was considering writing his autobiography. But he didn't like going back over the past (unlike Bill Wyman, who liked to record everything), and lost interest.
114 'I went berserk and bananas at his blind stupidity', Keith Richards told *Mojo*.
115 In later years, Keith Richards took to calling Jagger 'Brenda', or 'His Royal Fucking Highness'.

the rock star as rock god.[116] (And he was devoted to his body – Jagger was never gonna be a victim of rock 'n' roll excess, like Brian Jones or – very nearly so many times – his fellow Glimmer Twin. No – Jagger valued the body beautiful too highly, and maintained his skinny frame with a training regime that would kill many rockers way before barbiturates, heroin, cognac or Mandrax. In this respect, Jagger was the polar opposite of Richards[117] – and Anita Pallenberg – who would indulge in whatever was going, and for many years were committed heroin addicts).

The love life of Mick Jagger has been the subject of tabloid gossip for half a century. As with Warren Beatty and Charlie Sheen, the number of women that Jagger is reckoned to have dated is legendary, and includes model Chrissie Shrimpton[118] (sister of Jean); Marianne Faithfull;[119] Bianca Pérez-Mora Macias[120] (they married in 1971 and separated in 1977; they have one child, Jade Sheena Jezebel);[121] model Apollonia von Ravenstein; 18 year-old starlet Mia Farrow; Patti Boyd (who also dated George Harrison, Eric Clapton and Ron Wood); Mackenzie Phillips; model Jerry Hall (they dated in 1977; married in 1990; the marriage was annulled in 1999; they have four children);[122] singer Linda Ronstadt; Luciana Gimenez, a 29 year-old thong model from Rio (they have one child, Lucas Maurice Morad);[123] Carinthia West (a 25 year-old model and photographer); Valerie Perrine, a Texan actress; Victoria Vicuna, a Venezuelan model (both in the early 1980s); Bebe Buell (mother of actress Liv Tyler); actress Angelina Jolie; heiress Sabrina Guinness; Dana Gillespie; L'Wren Scott, a 34 year-old American stylist (1967-2014); 19 year-old model Sophie Dahl (granddaughter of Roald Dahl); TV star Amanda de Cadenet; Irish singer Andrea Corr, 22; Carla Bruni (at the time Eric Clapton's squeeze); actress Marsha Hunt (they had one child, Karis); 'the Pisces Apple lady' (Chris O'Dell), who had liaisons with George Harrison and Ringo Starr as well as Jagger; Pat Andrews and Suki Potier (Brian Jones's girlfriends); Tina Turner (backstage

---

[116] Andrew Loog Oldham had taught Mick the value of *image* above all in the pop business, and Jagger has carefully maintained that icon status, to the point of elbowing aside people who got in his way, or dropping people he didn't think were helping his career any more.

[117] When Keef Richards takes his solo spot during every Rolling Stone show, he begins by saying, 'nice to be here. Hey, it's nice to be *anywhere*, you know' (or: 'nice to see you, hey, it's nice to see *anyone*, you know').

[118] Chrissie Shrimpton was an early love of Jagger's, and he was utterly devoted to her. Unfortunately, they also used to have incredibly violent fights, with Shrimpton giving as good as she got (including hitting and scratching Jagger). Shrimpton was 'strong-minded and extremely hot-tempered', according to Philip Norman (1984, 115). As usual, it was Jagger's roving eye that precipitated the end of the relationship. (At one time, Shrimpton tried to commit suicide by taking pills).

[119] Mick Jagger apparently had a threesome with Marianne Faithfull and one of the local women in a Tangiers brothel.

[120] She had been engaged to Michael Caine.

[121] Mick Jagger rented (with Bianca) the famous mansion at 414, St Pierre Road in Bel Air, which William Randolph Hearst had built for Marion Davies. It had later been used by Howard Hughes (as a hideaway) and John and Jackie Kennedy for their honeymoon. (It was also the house used for the studio mogul scene in *The Godfather* with the horse's head).

[122] Jagger wooed Jerry Hall away from singer Bryan Ferry.

[123] The settlement with Morad was $4 million.

at a 1960s gig in Bristol's Colston Hall, apparently); one of the Ikettes, Pat Arnold; another Ikette, Clauda Linnear; Uschi Obermaier (Keith Richards' girlfriend); Linda McCartney (according to Bill Wyman), before she met Paul; Cecilia Nixon; plus a host of groupies (often these were young American (Californian) women who were happy to spend a night (or just a few hours) at Cheyne Walk or a Parisian hotel; they had names like Susie Suck, Miss Mercy, Suzie Creamcheese, Kathy Kleevage, and of course the Plaster Casters).

Indeed, it might be easier to say who in the Western world *hasn't* slept with Mick Jagger! ('In the oversexed world of rock, in the whole annals of show business, Jagger's reputation as a modern Casanova is unequalled,' noted Philip Norman [7]).

The Rolling Stones members shared lovers: both Mick Jagger and Keith Richards had affairs with Marianne Faithfull; Richards and Brian Jones shared Anita Pallenberg; Jagger slept with Pat Andrews and Suki Potier (two of Jones's girlfriends), one of Bill Wyman's (Astrid Lundström), and another of Keith's (Uschi Obermaier); and photographer Mario Schifano dated both Faithfull and Pallenberg.

Among Keith Richards' liaisons were Emeretta Marks (an actress in *Hair*), Uschi Obermaier, Marianne Faithfull, Lil Wergilis, and Patti Hansen. Ron Wood, meanwhile, went out with Patti Boyd, George Harrison's missus (later with Eric Clapton, and also Jagger, of course).[124] Wood dated a succession of (much) younger women, including Krissy Findlay, Sally Humphreys and Ekaterina Ivanova.

That 'old rubber lips' has his boorish, sexist side is well-known – the paternity suits, the slew of failed relationships and disappointed women left behind in his wake are numerous. (By the 1970s, women who got involved with Michael Philip Jagger knew the score – marriage wasn't on the cards, a baby would not be welcome (or provided for), and paternity suits would be denied (as with Marsha Hunt and their daughter Karis).)

Like David Bowie, Jimmy Page and a host of rock stars, Mick Jagger couldn't keep it zipped up. For him sex didn't seem to mean much beyond pleasure, and altho' some of the women he dated tried to be open-minded about his promiscuity (such as Marianne Faithfull), others found it hurtful (such as Angie Barnett, who tried an 'open marriage' with Bowie, but found it hurt when it went the other way).

MICK JAGGER IN MOVIES.

In movies, undoubtedly the key year for Mick Jagger was 1970 – it saw the release of his follow-up to *Performance*, *Ned Kelly*, and the

---

[124] Mick Jagger snatched Eric Clapton's new girlfriend Carla Bruni away from him.

important concert movie *Gimme Shelter*, with its evocations of Altamont; and in 1970 *Performance* finally received its premiere, in Gotham, in July. A number of possible film projects were discussed following *Performance* for Jagger. One was *The Sermons of Jean Harlow and the Curses of Billy the Kid*, based on Michael McClure's play.

That Mick Jagger's film career stalled after *Performance* and *Ned Kelly* has perplexed some observers – because Jagger could have had a prominent career in movies. Certainly he looked for suitable roles, and was offered many parts. Usually, he got cold feet as the start date approached, and would bail out. It took *a lot* to maintain Jagger's interest in a film role.

You'd have to agree that it would require a particular kind of character for Mick Jagger to play – but he also didn't give himself enough of a chance to develop himself as an actor, so that he could've gone on to play all sorts of roles, from, say, a *James Bond* villain to an *Austin Powers* postmodern comedian (after all, in *Performance* many reckoned he was playing himself. He wasn't – he is actually nothing like Turner except in a few minor ways – but he was playing a role that had been tailor-made for him).

Some of the film projects considered by Old Rubber Lips but rejected (and negotiated by his film agent Maggie Abbott) included *Zardoz* (John Boorman, 1974), a bonkers futuristic fantasy; *Time After Time* (1979), an H.G. Wells versus Jack the Ripper yarn starring Malcolm McDowell; *Blame It On the Night*, about a rock star and his estranged son; he was considered for the role of the Acid Queen in *Tommy* (1975), which was taken by Tina Turner; *Stranger In a Strange Land*; a sci-fi story set on Mars; Gore Vidal's *Kalki*; he auditioned for the lead role in *The Rocky Horror Picture Show*; *A Star Is Born* might've been a terrific vehicle for Jagger (the ageing rocker was played (very well) by Kris Kristofferson in the 1976 flick); *Dirty Rotten Scoundrels* and *Ishtar* (in which Jagger would've been paired with David Bowie); *I Never Promised You a Rose Garden* (1977), from Joanne Greenberg's novel; Anthony Burgess's *Nothing Like the Sun*, about the Immortal Bard; *The Moderns* (1988), a wonderful melodrama set in the Parisian artistic circle of the 1920s; *The Vatican Caves* from André Gide's novel, was considered for Jagger and Bianca (to be directed by Paul Morrissey); *Inside Moves* (1980), with Jon Savage and David Morse; *Annie* (1982), playing the Rooster; and *The Man Who Fell To Earth* (1975) would've reunited Jagger with director Nic Roeg, but the part went to Jagger's friend (and professional rival), David Bowie. Movies by Steven

Spielberg,[125] Andy Warhol and Franco Zeffirelli were also proposed. Meanwhile, Donald Cammell offered projects to Jagger from time to time, none of which came to anything.

Why didn't Mick Jagger take up any of these film offers, some of which turned out to be wonderful movies? The pattern was repeated many times: his British agent Maggie Abbott (who worked with Sandy Lieberson, one of the producers of *Performance*, at Creative Management Associates), would send scripts or treatments to Jagger, which the superstar would consider. Jagger would sometimes be enthusiastic, sometimes indecisive, or he'd have commitments with 'the greatest rock 'n' roll band in the world' which would clash with the film schedules. But, as biographer Philip Norman pointed out, most often it was simply a case of Jagger getting cold feet (2012, 474). (But Jagger appeared in *Fitzcarraldo*, of course, before that troubled production had to be re-scheduled. And he did appear in other people's movies from time to time – such as the utterly amazing, hugely enjoyable 1977 comedy *The Rutles/ All You Need Is Cash*).[126] Jagger was involved as one of the people behind the movie *Enigma* (2001),[127] based on Robert Harris's novel of WW2 (altho' I'm sure most people would prefer to see Jagger in front of the camera). Jagger has been committed to acting as a film producer, but his track record so far is lacklustre.

Among Mick Jagger's later movies were *Freejack* (1992), *Bent* (1997), and *The Man From Elysian Fields* (2002). Jagger's biggest film performance would've been in *Pirates of the Caribbean*: Keef Richards had tried to persuade Jagger to appear in *Pirates 4* (2011), but of course Jagger declined. Johnny Depp,[128] a friend of Richards', had been instrumental in encouraging the rock star to appear in *On Stranger Tides* as Captain Teague, a crusty, old pirate and his screen father (Depp had based his comic *tour-de-force* Captain Jack Sparrow partly on Richards, and hoped that Richards would enjoy it. Of course he did!).

---

125 A rock concert movie featuring a galaxy of stars including the Beatles was touted in the late 1970s, with Steven Spielberg as director. This project would've been co-produced by Mick Jagger, giving him a greater stake in the project, and perhaps encouraging him to commit more.

126 One of the very best films about the Beatles, and one of the great pop music films of recent times, was *The Rutles* (a.k.a. *All You Need Is Cash*, 1978), largely the work of Eric Idle and Neil Innes (it was co-directed by Gary Weiss, who also operated the camera). *The Rutles* contains an outstanding soundtrack by Neil Innes; it is very funny, beautifully written and edited, and brilliantly conceived. *The Rutles* is so good it comes across as the real thing, the real story of the Beatles. George Harrison said when asked what it was like being in the Beatles that it was like *The Rutles* film. *The Rutles* blends (1) the real history of the Beatles with the received or perceived story of the Beatles in popular culture; (2) it adds a layer of Pythonesque and alternative Brit comedy and silliness; (3) it blurs fact and fiction energetically, and uses real people reminiscing about events very close to history; (4) and the music (by Innes) is simply remarkable: the pastiches of the Beatles' music are pure genius.

127 It was produced by Jagged Films, which Mick Jagger created in 1995 with Victoria Pearman. However, *Enigma* also boasted a dozen or so other producers! And no one went to see it anyway.

128 The affinities between Johnny Depp and Keith Richards are numerous: both were rock guitarists; both were rebels and disliked authority; both have trashed hotel rooms and thumped photographers; both partook of pharmaceutical substances; both liked to smoke and carouse; both lived in France and L.A.; both were highly individual (even eccentric); both were survivors in showbiz; both had their own idiosyncratic dress sense; and both hated dentists.

Needless to say, Keith Richards looked like he had walked on the set of *Pirates of the Caribbean 4*[129] straight from the limo, and didn't need any make-up,[130] wigs, jewellery or costumes to play a hearty, old sea-dog.[131] It was an absolute delight to see a rock legend like Richards in a giant Hollywood movie; it should've happened years ago! After all, his Glimmer Twin, Mick Jagger, had been starring in movies way back to *Performance* in 1970 (to have both Jagger *and* Richards in *Pirates* – that would have been a coup!).

Unfortunately, Keith Richards is on screen for all too short a time – in *Pirates of the Caribbean: On Stranger Tides*, Jack Sparrow[132] looks round then back in an early scene and Richards' Captain Teague has vanished (tho' he has more to do in *Pirates of the Caribbean 3: At World's End*). Because Richards certainly has the quirky sense of humour that the *Pirates* flicks coulda exploited more).

NED KELLY.

Ned Kelly (1970)[133] is interesting now chiefly because it stars Mick Jagger[134] (that it was directed by Tony Richardson is of passing interest I guess, for students of British cinema – not many of them are still around!). As with *Performance*, Jagger's star power far overwhelms everything else in *Ned Kelly*, whether it's the characters, the story, the settings, the themes or the photography. Because you're always thinking: 'that's Mick Jagger!' Well, that feeling only enhanced *Performance*, of course, but in a historical piece like *Ned Kelly*, is hampers the proceedings.

Ned Kelly is a sort of British-plus-Irish-plus-Australian Western – a British Western about horse thieves set in Australia. As directed by, at the time, one of the great producers of Westerns, Sam Peckinpah, it might've been much more successful (the Peck was a master at this sort of story about outlaws – particularly at giving 19th century cowboy movies a real contemporary relevance and political zing, tying movies like *The Wild Bunch* and *Pat Garrett and Billy the Kid* to the anxious times in the U.S.A. of the

---

129 A featurette on the DVD of *Pirates 4* reveals that people from all over the studio came to the set to see the rock legend do his cameo.
130 Keith Richards enjoyed the dressing up part of the role, as one might expect. Costume designer Penny Rose had given him an extravagant, embroidered red frock coat, and plenty of jewellery. Here, the concept of pirates as rock stars paid off, with a genuine (and genuinely cool) rock star.
131 Our Keef was supposed to appear in *Dead Man's Chest*, but had apparently fallen out of a palm tree (!) and injured his head (while he was in New Zealand, during the Rolling Stones' tour in 2006). If you know anything about Keith Richards, and if only half (a tenth!) of the stories are true, then that guy should really be dead by now! (Incidentally, the gag with Captains Barbossa and Sparrow tied to palm trees in a later movie may be a nod to Richards' antics.
132 I would imagine that Johnny Depp (a huge music fan, and musician) was buzzed to have Keef Richards as his on-screen father. It's so cool!
133 Co-written by Tony Richardson and Ian Jones, and produced by Neil Hartley.
134 Keef Richards confessed that he and Marianne Faithfull had had an affair while Jagger was filming *Performance* (Richards said he had to make a hasty exit from the Cheyne Walk house when Jagger returned from the set early one night.

late 1960s, and issues such as the Vietnam War and political activism. Unfortunately, *Ned Kelly* is 10 million miles from *The Wild Bunch* or *Pat Garrett and Billy the Kid*!).[135]

Mick Jagger lost interest in it soon after making it (a recurring tendency for Jagger), and the 1970 movie seems unsure of what it wants to be (I guess the idea of playing an outlaw appealed to the Lapping Tongue, with a thematic/ social crossover from rebellious rock star with Ozzie outlaw).[136] The *form* of *Ned Kelly* seems so American, to me – reminiscent also of *MacCabe and Mrs Miller*, *Pat Garrett and Billy the Kid* and *Heaven's Gate* – that scuzzy, grungey, unwashed, hairy-beard kind of tough Western, where it's all about texture and mood and feeling. (However, set-pieces such as the hold-up, where Kelly and his lads stick up some guys to steal their horses, are wilfully subverted by playing the nondescript folkie music by Shel Silverstein over the top.[137] Here we see Jagger killing someone on screen, tho' he's no Steve McQueen or John Wayne).

All was not well behind the scenes, tho' – Marianne Faithfull attempted suicide in Oz, while Mick Jagger was filming *Ned Kelly* (she might've appeared in the movie – instead her part was played by Diane Craig at the last minute). There had been protests at the airport (Australians objected to a limey playing an Aussie anti-hero), Jagger complained about the script to Tony Richardson, and Jagger was injured during production (when a prop gun exploded, hurting his hand).

While some of the technical aspects of *Ned Kelly* are impressive, and Clarissa Kaye-Mason as the mom of the household delivers a spirited performance, you do get a little tired of yet another shot of horses or the boys against a sunset on a hill. In *Ned Kelly*, the texture and atmosphere aren't striking enough, and the story just doesn't grip the viewer. It's not *The Wild Bunch*, *Badlands* or *Bonnie & Clyde*. And, as outlaws on the run, it's over-shadowed by all of the North American counterparts of the time (not only the movies I've cited, but also an enormous hit of 1969: *Butch Cassidy and the Sundance Kid*).

Well, the finale of *Ned Kelly* with its siege is exciting, and there's the preposterous image of Edward Kelly staggering along a railroad track in his homemade armour while 20,000 cops try to bring him down (again, as an evocation of the End of Mythical Individuality and Heroism, *The Wild Bunch* or *Bonnie & Clyde*, to name two obvious contenders just prior to *Ned Kelly*,

---

[135] *Ned Kelly* had a limited release in June, 1970, and 'would go on to grace all the 'Worst Movies in History' lists', as C. Sanford put it (2013, 200).
[136] It doesn't help that Mick Jagger's vocal track is pretty much all looped (and that Jagger's Oirish accent doesn't convince a jot).
[137] Why oh why didn't the filmmakers ask Mick Jagger to score the movie? You quickly get fed up with the music, and there's *way* too much of it!

are infinitely superior).[138] The critical reception of *Ned Kelly* was predictably negative, and tho' Mick Jagger took much of the brunt of the bile, it's the concept, the script and the direction that contributes more towards its poor quality. According to Donald Cammell, Jagger burst into tears after seeing *Ned Kelly;* Jagger called it, 'that load of shit! I only made it because I had nothing else to do'.[139]

GIMME SHELTER.

Gimme Shelter (the Maysles Brothers, and Charlotte Zwerin, 1970) is one of the classic, rock concert movies, featuring the Rolling Stones at their peak on tour in the Land of the Free (yet again). Famous for its footage of the infamous Altamont Speedway gig,[140] *Gimme Shelter* also includes many scenes backstage, in recording studios, in dressing rooms, at press conferences, doing press interviews, managers and lawyers arranging the Altamont gig (minus the band), the band fooling about (tho' they're pretty sedate, and far from being heavy duty party animals), plus live turns from Ike and Tina Turner and Jefferson Airplane.

Although the Rolling Stones became linked in legend to Altamont, the event was in fact originally planned by the Grateful Dead. It wasn't the Stones who put on the show, or invited the Hell's Angels to do the security (some have questioned the notion of 'security'). Mick Jagger was keen to do a concert in the U.S.A. as big as Woodstock, and to recreate the Hyde Park[141] experience on the other side of the pond (and to do a free gig – the Stones were already famous at this point for over-charging for tickets).

The concert footage in *Gimme Shelter* is of course incendiary – even when the photography is as abysmal, under-lit, out of focus and shaky as in *Cocksucker Blues*, and the sound's grainy mono. You can't fail with a band this white-hot, and music this good (even the most cack-handed film crew could come up with summat interesting – and a lot of crews were technically incompetent in this era. Compared to the albums, recorded on 4, 8, 16 and 24-track machines, the film sound for the concert movies in the 1960s and 1970s is appalling).

On the downside, the cameramen in *Gimme Shelter* (led by David and Albert Maysles)[142] concentrate too much on Mick Jagger, so that the rest of the Rolling Stones are only glimpsed around the edges. Of course, you can't

---

138 *Ned Kelly* was remade in 2003, with Heath Ledger in the title role (Lynda House and Nelson Wooss produced, Gregor Jordan directed, and John McDonagh adapted Robert Drewe's book).
139 P. Norman, 1984, 343.
140 When they were cutting *Performance*, Altamont happened, and Donald Cammell felt as if his movie had been a 'little bit prophetic', in its evocation of the ritualistic aspect of violence and the relation of violence to rock 'n' roll.
141 Hyde Park was the biggest concert of its kind, with around 250,000 punters turning out to see Rolling Stones (150,000 had attended not long before, to see Blind Faith).
142 George Lucas was a cameraman at Altamont.

take your eyes off Jagger (but in *Gimme Shelter* you don't have any choice!), with his cock-walk, his elbows flailing like a chicken, his head nodding, his perpetual pouting and posing and his hand-clapping (Jagger claps his hands *a lot* on stage, as if he's a teacher trying to encourage a bunch of bored, jaded school kids to join in and sing along). The grinning rubber lips are on form in *Gimme Shelter*, so they threaten to swallow everything else (for many, Jagger would be the premier frontman of any rock band in history).

Meanwhile, the concert footage in *Gimme Shelter* cuts to grooving, swooning, singing, and dancing audience members, as is customary, and the odd brave girl who makes it onto the stage, only to be dragged off (roughly) by burly roadies (there were many more stage invasions in the Stones' career, and many much nastier than the ones shown here). Meanwhile, Bill Wyman stands there, impassive, doleful, an undertaker playing his bass in the upright position, Mick Taylor recedes into the shadows on lead guitar,[143] Charlie Watts turns his sad, turtle face to the camera from time to time, and Keef Richards attempts to steal some of the limelight from the Flapping, Lapping Tongue (no chance! Brian Jones couldn't do it, and Richards can't do it! Imagine a Rolling Stones concert movie from *Richards*' point-of-view – unthinkable! But many fans would love to see that!).

An unusual device in *Gimme Shelter* (still rare today) has the Rolling Stones viewing rough cuts of the footage (which was assembled by Charlotte Zwerin): they were filmed watching themselves on the Steenbeck editing table, providing a film-within-a-film commentary (tho' not especially enlightening – off-stage, at this time, they weren't particularly pithy or entertaining. The Stones are, off-stage, just a bunch of guys from suburban England).

Altamont Speedway has become a legendary concert, of course: in *Gimme Shelter*, you can see just how cack-handed the organization of it all was.[144] You see the Hell's Angels acting like bullies, everyone's drinkin' and smokin', and some folk're out of their heads (the 1970 movie captures what appear to be some bad drug trips). The stage's only three feet high,[145] there's no security between the stage and the audience (the road crew're constantly trying – and failing – to clear the area), and performances're fraught with anxiety and interruptions. Altamont is how *not* to organize a big rock show.

---

[143] At times Taylor looks awed, uncomfortable, and unsure.
[144] Altamont also had some overdoses, 300+ injuries, and four deaths (two youths were run over by a car in their sleeping bags, and another drowned in an irrigation ditch).
[145] The stage had originally been built (by Chris Monck) for the first venue, at Sears Point (a far better venue, with more facilities and access).

Altamont Speedway had no facilities set up for a big concert, was miles from anywhere, had no adequate parking, and was on level ground, requiring a much higher stage than three feet for sightlines. It didn't help either that the gig was in the middle of Winter (it looked more like a mobile hippy camp than a rock show with facilities for visitors).

Meanwhile, *Gimme Shelter* cuts back to the caravan backstage where the Rolling Stones are holed up, surrounded by groupies and the press, having no idea what's going on (they had helicoptered in from Frisco). But, away from the stage area, plenty of punters're having a great time, dancing, stripping off, drinking, and partying (some concert-goers still maintain they had a good time at Altamont, despite what happened). *Gimme Shelter* demonstrates that, even at their most disastrous, rock shows are still entirely about the *audience*, – *not* the band, *not* the performance, *not* the lighting and effects, *not* the critics and the press, and *not* even the music or the songs. It's the *audience*, in the end, that makes music fly, that makes music their own.

Thus, away from the pandemonium around the stage at Altamont Speedway, thousands of people were partying. We've all been at big events where something crazy has occurred (including deaths), but we only found out afterwards. Altho' Altamont was a badly planned and badly produced show, its mythical status as the End Of The Sixties has only occurred afterwards – and only in the press, in the media.

As the evening escalated into violence and craziness in California, performers came and went (including Santana, Jefferson Airplane, and Crosby, Stills, Nash and Young – amazing line-up! But the Grateful Dead opted not to appear – they took one look and climbed right back in their chopper). While some commentators have glowered at the Stones for leaving rapidly for Frisco in a helicopter right after the gig, and not offering any word about Meredith Hunter (or his girlfriend), others, such as Mick Jagger's biographer Philip Norman and Sam Cutler, have praised Jagger for his bravery in continuing with the show. Jagger faced 'distractions that few other star vocalists can ever have faced', as Norman put it (383).

Gimme Shelter shows the concert stopping and starting, as fresh scuffles occur in the audience. The Hell's Angels appear to be everywhere (at least from the vantage point behind the band), and the ones who aren't wasted give the Rolling Stones murderous looks. Mick Jagger tries a number of times to get everybody to cool down (and others grab the mike too, and Keith Richards yells at the audience). But nobody could really see what was happening. The aggression is palpable even in a technically inept documentary decades after the event. To stand in the middle of that turmoil, with the Angels wielding billiard cues, wouldn't be everyone's cup of tea. Yet even after many brawls have broken out, the band continued to play, and many in the audience appeared to be enjoying themselves.

THE ROLLING STONES ROCK AND ROLL CIRCUS.

The Rolling Stones Rock and Roll Circus (1968, prod. Sandy Lieberson, dir. Michael Lindsay-Hogg) was conceived partly to give the Stones something substantial to do performance-wise, and to heal rifts within the band and its entourage (Mick Jagger was travelling to Australia for *Ned Kelly*, which meant the band couldn't tour). It was Jagger who conceived the idea (but the legal ramifications of the TV show were still being debated by lawyers into the mid-1990s).[146]

The accounts of the recording of that ill-fated TV show have become legendary – how, for instance, everything was running late, there were technical problems, and the audience was getting tired, and Mick Jagger rallied everybody in the early hours to get the recording (in his excellent biography of Jagger, Philip Norman reckons it was one of Jagger's finer moments, rallying the troops, and whipping up the energy when everyone was flagging).

The line-up was very impressive for *The Rolling Stones Rock and Roll Circus* (the band by this time had plenty of people they could call on, including the Who, Eric Clapton, Mitch Mitchell, John Lennon,[147] Yoko Ono, Jethro Tull and Taj Mahal), but somehow the show doesn't work. It's a bit like one of those all-star movies of the 1960s which, given the quality and the number of the stars assembled, should at least provide some entertainment, but don't. Many fans reckon that the Who blew the Rolling Stones away in the awkward *Rock and Roll Circus* show.[148]

Getting the tone right was vital for *The Rolling Stones Rock and Roll Circus*, but the concept of a cheesy, seedy circus with His Jaggedness as the ringmaster wasn't fully explored. In trying to send up putting on a 'bad show', it just became bad. (For this and other reasons, the show was withheld for over 20 years).

COCKSUCKER BLUES.

Cocksucker Blues (1972) was a tour documentary directed by Robert Frank, at the invitation of the Rolling Stones[149] (during their *Exile On Main*

---

[146] The 66-minute show was released in 1996.
[147] Mick Jagger was a friend of John Lennon's, visiting him in Gotham, and was one of the participants in Lennon's 'lost weekend'; others included Ringo Starr, David Bowie, and Harry Nilsson.
[148] Jagger and Richards were not happy with going on so late, as the top-billed act, and that the Who had eclipsed them.
[149] It was Charlie Watts who asked Robert Frank to photograph the Stones' next album cover, and to shoot the documentary.

Street tour of North America of 1972).[150] *Cocksucker Blues* (great title!)[151] became a notorious movie when it was withheld from release, due, apparently, to some of the scenes in it.[152] The movie became the subject of conflict between Robert Frank and the filmmakers and the Rolling Stones (to the point where Frank wasn't allowed to release it, and could only screen it if there was a topless groupie with big tits, lines of cocaine, a bottle of Remy, and an irate road manager in the room at the same time).

The Stones themselves were apparently in shock when they saw the completed cocksucking movie. Mick Jagger told Robert Frank he wouldn't be able to work in the U.S.A. again if it were released. Well, yeah - but any movie studio (Warners had first look) could've set their editor dogs on it, and slashed out all the incriminating bits with drugs, and some of the nudity (tho' leaving in some skin to titillate the punters - this was 1972, after all!). Thus, it wasn't just the sex 'n' drugs aspect of *Cocksucker Blues* that probably upset the Dartford lads, but the overall portrait of them as... as scorchingly legendary pop stars *on stage*, yes, but *off-stage* as... as, well, a bunch of rather dull people in their late twenties, slogging through a tour (pop music is just *work*, after all), and getting bored out of their minds along the way, packing and unpacking their clothes, snoozing, chatting, drinking, smoking, and dragging behind them an over-size entourage (and their giant, black bodyguards).[153]

The 1972 tour featured Stevie Wonder as the warm-up act. The set opened with 'Brown Sugar', featured many songs from *Exile On Main Street*, a scary version of 'Midnight Rambler', and the closing sequence of 'Honky Tonk Women', 'Bye Bye Johnny' and 'Jumpin' Jack Flash'. 'Street Fighting Man' ended the evening, with the Lapping Tongue throwing 20,000 roses into the crowd.

The tour immortalized in *Cocksucker Blues* was a lucrative one for the Rolling Stones: they grossed $3 million from 462,000 punters (at a ticket price of $6.50) over 8 weeks (their holding company Promo Tours took $2 million after 30% tax).

Cocksucker Blues is a terrific document of a rock band on tour in the

---

150 Among the authors covering the U.S.A. tour for magazines like *Saturday Review* and *Rolling Stone* were Terry Southern and Truman Capote. But their 'combined literary talents would contrive not one sensible or original word about the tour in print', according to Philip Norman (1984, 361).
151 You hear a bit of Mick Jagger's crude cocksucker blues song on the soundtrack: 'where can I get my cock sucked?| Where can I get my ass fucked?' Written with Keith Richards, it was intended as a 'fuck you' to record label Decca, which the Rolling Stones had recently left for Atlantic (they owed Decca a final song, and this was their parting gesture).
152 *Ladies and Gentlemen: The Rolling Stones* was released instead (filmed by Butterfly, John Lennon's company).
153 Garry Mulholland noted that 'it's some achievement to be handed full access to the greatest rock 'n' roll band in the world at their peak, naked babes who will do anything they're told, tons of smack and coke, the landscape of America... and still end up making something boring' (123-4).

1970s, partly because it features many unguarded moments[154] (tho' some are staged), partly because it's Mick, Keef and the boys (a legendary ensemble in rock music), and partly because it has some classic incidents which you associate with Seventies rock excess (groupies, drugs, silly pranks, and of course some highly combustible rock music).[155] *Cocksucker Blues* does have so many ingredients of the rock 'n' roll tour – the jet hired for the tour, the limos, the scenes by the swimming pool in L.A., some fooling around with naked groupies, and of course some drug use.

But much of the controversial material in *Cocksucker Blues* actually occurs within the entourage – the roadies, the hangers-on, the groupies and the fans (the entourage that Bianca Pérez-Mora Macias dubbed 'the Nazi state'; Bianca famously loathed touring, and all of its rock music, boysy goings-on). But *not* the band themselves (altho' there are scenes where Keith Richards and Michael Jagger are apparently snorting or going to snort some coke, and scenes where Richards seems to be nodding out on heroin). But the infamous 'orgy' on the tour jet, for instance, was a staged event (when director Robert Frank complained that nothing was really happening. That a director asks for summat racy to be staged 'cos nothing seems to be happening *says it all*. And this is the Rolling Stones we're talking about!). In the fake 'orgy' some groupies're undressed and fool around with what appear to be burly, teamster-size roadies (one of 'em undresses a 19 year-old groupie), while some of the Rolling Stones (including the two Micks – Jagger and Taylor), accompany the antics with impromptu music (when they were coaxed out of their lairs).[156] And in a post-coital scene in a hotel bedroom, one of the entourage plays with the come splattered on her naked body (the sex, by today's full-on porn standards, is relatively tame, altho' this was the era when X-rated movies were going mainstream).[157]

But what also comes over in *Cocksucker Blues* is the exhausting slog of going on tour – the schlepping from the plane to the limo, from the limo to the hotel, from the hotel to the gig, from the venue to the after-party, from the party to the hotel. And so on. And on. *And on.*

Non-descript American hotels and motels (I've stayed in many), scruffy backstage rooms and locker rooms, echoey, concrete service halls, crappy

---

[154] Certainly few major rock acts have allowed such access or such scenes to be included in the final cut. Most acts would veto much of the material.
[155] After some concerts, the band were already on their way from the venue after the encores, and with a radio mic Mick Jagger was able to talk to the audience.
[156] The 'tour doctor' schtupped one of the groupies, according to Truman Capote, while wearing his safety belt. When he deplaned, he was carrying his pants.
[157] But if there's a naked or partially nude woman in the vicinity, Robert Frank and co. make darn sure their cameras are there to capture every skin-tingling second (cameramen everywhere, faced with the opportunity of pointing the lens at a crusty, old roadie or a pair of jiggling boobs, will always choose the groupie).

backstage areas, people wandering in and out aimlessly, airports, climbing in and out of cars...

It becomes a treadmill. Shit, in the end even entertainment is simply *work*. It's boring, it's repetitive, it's going thru the motions. You get to the stage, you jump and shout for two hours (well, Mick J. does), then you're off. Oh, yeah, it *is* the legendary *Rolling Stones*, and the *music* is fantastic, but the drudgery of working on a tour is also captured in *Cocksucker Blues*.[158] Quite rightly. (Stones watchers and fans prefer to see Keef Richards as dozing off because of his heroin habit – they want the glamour of drug-taking – but in fact Keef might simply be sleeping. Yeah, just that: catching some sleep. Because touring is exhausting – shit, some pop stars have heart attacks on tour (David Bowie), some people can't bear to tour and vow never again (Kate Bush), and plenty either go nuts or return exhausted).

According to one of the Stones' organization, Jo Bergman, the tour was *not* fun: 'it wasn't fun. And it wasn't supposed to be'. It was, rather, all about making money thru showbiz.

Cocksucker Blues certainly benefits from the celebrity-spotting moments – Andy Warhol, Truman Capote, and Tina Turner – and Stevie Wonder, their warm-up act, joins the boys on stage for a reggae version of 'Eyesight To the Blind' (just kidding).

There is plenty-a music in *Cocksucker Blues*, but it isn't a classic music documentary in this regard. Partly because the filmmaking is so shoddy, and the quality of the recording and over-dubbing is terrible. You can say the *visual* crudity of *Cocksucker Blues* – the handheld camera, the outta focus shots, the flashed film stock, the grainy, under-lit photography – all adds to the piece.[159] Visually, yes. But sound-wise, *Cocksucker Blues* is a mess. It needs a Walter Murch or a Randy Thom (Bay Area movie sound specialists) to go in there and clean it up, and to re-present those famous songs with the punch and clarity they deserve.

So *Cocksucker Blues* is great because it captures the excess and hot-house atmosphere of a rock music tour, with its pranks and drug-taking and groupies, but it also gets the day-to-day routine of it, the hard work of it all. And the bullshit – *Cocksucker Blues* is full of inane conversations, where people talk utter drivel. That's also cool, because it reminds you that, when they're on stage performing their classic numbers, the Rolling Stones (or any rock band, or any bunch of performers) can be white-hot and electric. But off-stage, in everyday life, they could also be really boring

---

158 A typical pop music documentary might focus on stage performances, with off-stage scenes kept to silly antics or sound-bite interviews. But *Cocksucker Blues* switches it the other way around, so the stage shows are short interludes in an account of a circus of travelling musicians.
159 Robert Frank is without doubt one of the worst, technically inept cameramen ever to shoot a movie.

people. Given the opportunity to speak, to really say something, they come over as innocuous.

There're scenes in *Suckingcock Blues* in the suite of Bianca and Mick Jagger in New York (at the posh Sherry-Netherland Hotel) which have a glacial calm, like something out of a Carl-Theodor Dreyer movie (or maybe a seven-hour Andy Warhol movie), in which *nothing happens*. What might've been an insight into the married life of the Jaggers – Bianca Jagger[160] is there, Mick Jagger is there (on his birthday) – but Robert Frank might as well have filmed a blank, white wall or a vase of flowers.

And there are surprisingly few arguments in *Cocksucker Blues,* as if by now the Rolling Stones circus was a well-oiled machine, running on autopilot. In a documentary which purports to show 'everything', you'd expect to see moments where this large band of musicians and roadies and make-up artists and managers blow up in each other's faces (we all know some of the antagonisms and resentments that seethed under the surface!). And we know, too, that some of the concerts on the Stones' 1972 U.S.A. tour had some hairy moments.

The tour included four bomb scares, an explosion, a party on a rooftop in Gotham, Keith Richards smashing his hotel room windows, a run-in between Richards and a female process server on the jet (and a photographer), riots on the street, and stage invasions.

BLACK MAGIC IN LONDON

...AND ALEISTER CROWLEY AND KENNETH ANGER

> All absolute sensation is religious.
>
> Novalis

Pagan London. Occult London. Black Magic London.

It's important to remember that *Performance* was filmed in 1968, but was released in 1970 – it was closer in spirit to 1967, then, but also drew on the post-Summer of Love culture, and on the increasing nihilism of the late 1960s (such as the disillusionment in North America over the Vietnam

---

[160] You can't help noticing that Bianca Jagger, with her perpetual frown, is hardly the life and soul of the party (she said she looked stupid when she smiled),

War).[161] (For a good indication of the disillusionment with all things establishment, the movies of Jean-Luc Godard of the period – particularly the self-hatred and unbridled rage in *Weekend* – are perfect).

The cultural allusions in *Performance* are typical of the cultish aspects of the post-Summer of Love era: Satanism, demonic magicke, Aleister Crowley, Kenneth Anger, William Burroughs, Timothy Leary, the Islamic assassins ('nothing is true, everything is permitted') and so on, the sort of stuff pop musicians like Led Zeppelin's Jimmy Page and the Rolling Stones themselves were into (*viz*, 'Their Satanic Majesties', etc).

The mantra 'nothing is true, everything is permitted', derives from the Hashishin (although Donald Cammell thought it came from Friedrich Nietzsche). It links to Aleister Crowley's philosophy, to Oscar Wilde and André Gide, and of course to the drug culture of the 1960s. (Crowley's 'do what thou wilt' came by way of François Rabelais and William Blake).

Like later black leather/ Goth bands such as Killing Joke and Psychic TV, Led Zeppelin (and Jimmy Page in particular) were devotees of half-sham mage, half-genuine occultist Aleister Crowley (1875-1947).[162] Guitarist Page collected Crowleyania (indeed, Page had the biggest collection in the world), and visited the usual Crowleyan sites (Scotland, the abbey of Thelema in Sicily). He bought Crowley's Scottish retreat, Boleskine House in 1970, on the shores of Loch Ness. Here Crowley named himself Lord Boleskine or the Laird of Boleskine. The lodgekeeper supposedly went mad and tried to murder his family, due to Crowley's satanic influence (there are a multitude of rumours and legends surrounding Crowley, which only adds to his appeal to rock stars like Jimmy Page).

Aleister Crowley's life was a mixture of sadism, sex magic with men and women, failed marriages and disastrous relationships, several attempts at creating cults or religions, god awful poetry, summoning up demons, a lot of posing in outrageous costumes, trying to raise money for crazy schemes, and idiotic behaviour. (His life is crying out for a major movie to be made, because it contains so many completely bonkers incidents. Incredibly, by the 2010s a picture still hadn't been produced (see below), although Crowley had of course influenced a number of film characters).[163]

Some other incidents in Aleister Crowley's life include: in Mexico, after the Scottish period, Crowley tried to make his reflection disappear in a

---

[161] Donald Cammell was not much interested in politics, or at least not in the events in Paris in May, 1968, according to his girlfriend Deborah Dixon (M, 78).
[162] Aleister Crowley is one of the gurus of the late 1960s, along with Arthur Rimbaud, Che Guevara, Martin Luther King, and Malcolm X. Crowley seemed perfect for the mystique that coalesced around the Rolling Stones (and Led Zeppelin), with his drug use, bisexuality, his 'do what thou wilt' motto and his bevy of groupies (the 'Scarlet Women').
[163] There hasn't been a movie directly made about Aleister Crowley, but he has been the subject of documentaries. It doesn't matter, though – because Crowleyan mythologies have been explored in the cinema of Kenneth Anger. Indeed, Anger has been the perfect interpreter of Crowleyania on screen.

mirror (and apparently nearly succeeded). Mirrors often crop up in magic, and in Donald Cammell (and Jean Cocteau's) movies. Crowley had been associated with the Golden Dawn (but it had been a troubled association – Crowley was described by W.B. Yeats as 'an unspeakable mad person').

According to Aleister Crowley, his *Book of the Law* was dictated to him by a mysterious voice – by the Ancient Egyptian god Horus, no less. Or was it Crowley's Guardian Angel? (Or another irate landlady?). It doesn't matter: 'do what thou wilt shall be the whole of the Law' was the key dictum of *The Book of the Law*. And the magician took to putting it on all his letters, and graffitting it on walls.

Another of Aleister Crowley's rituals was to use sex magic – in Paris, Crowley buggered Victor Neuberg as part of a sexual magic rite. Sadism was an ingredient of the Crowleyan magicke, as well as the 'serpent's kiss', which meant biting the wrist or throat (Crowley had his teeth filed down to perform this vampiric act!). Crowley's devotees around this time – when he opened a Satanic Temple on Fulham Road in Londinium – included many women (including rich women, and the Ragged Ragtime girls – chorus girls from Moscow). Later, Crowley got into drugs big time (heroin). Colin Wilson defined Crowley's chief defect in *Mysteries*: he 'had almost no capacity for natural affection' (1979, 468).

As well as Aleister Crowley, other popular occult figures that fascinated so many bourgeois artists and writers in the West in the second half of the 20th century included Madame Blavatsky, A.E. Waite, the Golden Dawn, MacGregor Mathers, Dion Fortune, Eliphas Levi, Paracelsus, etc.[164]

As well as Aleister Crowley's form of magicke, the occultism favoured by Sixties artists and writers included the *Qabbalah*, Black Masses, ancient Egyptian religion, the Tarot, reincarnation,[165] clairvoyance,[166] the Knights Templar, and so on and on and on and on. Then there was Eastern mysticism, including Taoism, the *Tibetan Book of the Dead*, *I Ching*, Zen Buddhism, Confucianism, Shintoism, Hinduism, etc.

The novelist John Cowper Powys was among those who met Aleister Crowley. In a 1958 letter Powys recalled that he had met Crowley once, at a literary dinner at Foyles' bookshop, where Powys was speaking. He bought Crowley a bottle of wine, 'which he had finished before my speech was over!'[167] Another connection between Powys and Crowley was Louis Wilkinson, Powys's friend, who edited a book of his letters: Wilkinson read

---

[164] About the best introduction to this kind of occultism is Colin Wilson and his two books *The Occult* and *Mysteries*.
[165] Aleister Crowley said he had been a Pope (Alexander VI) and Cagliostro in earlier lives.
[166] It's amazing that there isn't a seance or Black Mass or some arcane ritual in *Performance* – many horror films of the period, including the famous Hammer horror movies and Italian gorefests, featured this sort of occult goings-on.
[167] In *The Letters of John Cowper Powys to Nicholas Ross*, Bertram Rota, London, 1971, 149.

some of Crowley's poetry at the magician's funeral at the Brighton crematorium. People were surprised to hear Wilkinson's voice intoning Crowley's invocation 'Io Pan! Io, Pan!',[168] which's part of the 'Hymn To Pan' (the recitation of course outraged the local authorities. But local authorities are quite easy to outrage).

So it's not difficult to see why Aleister Crowley should appeal to so many rock stars. Jimmy Page's passion for Crowley led to Crowley devotee and 'underground' filmmaker Kenneth Anger commissioning Page to write a soundtrack for his 1981 film *Lucifer Rising*,[169] inspired by Crowley's poem 'Hymn To Lucifer', which featured Donald Cammell and his then partner, Myriam Gibril, as the Ancient Egyptian gods Osiris and Isis (a famous sequence has Cammell and Gibril, in Ancient Egyptian costume, lifting staffs and signalling to each other across a valley in the desert). 'It was typecasting. Donald was in love with death, and Myriam was a life-force that would balance out his gloomy side', according to Anger (B, 44). Anger regarded Cammell as Crowley's 'magickal son'. As well as Cammell and Gibril, *LuciferRising* featured Marianne Faithfull, Hayden Couts, and Anger himself. (*LuciferRising* was filmed in Gizeh, Luxor and Karnak in Egypt, London and Avebury in England, and in Externsteine). 'My approach to art is the Egyptian one,' Anger said in 1971, 'and I am building for eternity. You might as well make it in steel or carve it in the hardest granite'.

The Crowley dimension also led to rumours of Jimmy Page dabbling in black magicke. There was talk of a Led Zeppelin 'curse', which supposedly caused some of the misfortunes that dogged the band, such as Robert Plant's car accident in Rhodes, John Bonham's death, and later Plant's son's death. Page was also the target of death threats, and for a time had to have bodyguards posted outside his hotel rooms.

Jimmy Page didn't particularly discourage the Aleister Crowley/ black magic accusations. He seemed to live something like the kind of life-style that Crowley lived: rock star debauchery, dressing up in black, lighting lots of candles, taking cocaine and heroin, and living in eccentric houses. He would stay awake for days and nights on end, in darkened rooms, virtually isolated from the outside world. Observers did not know what to make of Page's pursuits of magic – especially in white, Anglo-Saxom, Protestant Middle America. It no doubt enhanced Led Zeppelin's charisma to have black magic leanings, though – as with the Rolling Stones or Black Sabath

---

168 In L. Wilkinson, *Letters to Louis Wilkinson, 1935-56*, Macdonald, London, 1958.
169 As well as Jimmy Page, Bobby Beausoleil and the Freedom Orchestra provided music. Kenneth Anger said that because Page was too busy with Led Zeppelin, he used Beausoleil's score instead. At one time, Anger said he had planned to have the Rolling Stones in *Lucifer Rising*, with Richards as Beelzebub, and Jagger as Lucifer (V. Bockris, 130). Jagger, inevitably, declined. Anger described the magical component in the Stones' music as 'its strong sexual connotations. It's basically music to fuck to'.
Mick Jagger had provided the score for *Invocation of My Demon Brother* (1969), Kenneth Anger's film about Aleister Crowley.

and numerous other acts.

At one time Kenneth Anger was working in the basement of Jimmy Page's Kensington mansion, Tower House, editing the movie. Anger called Tower House Page's 'evil fantasy house':[170] it had themed rooms (painted butterflies in the bedroom, a mermaid in the 'ocean room', a zodiac in the 'astrology hall'. It sounds like the Powis Square house in *Performance*. This area of Londinium (Holland Park Road and Melbury Road)[171] is known for its unusual attributes: Lord Leighton's house[172] is nearby, and film director Michael Powell also lived here (in Melbury Road). It's an area of the capital that makes writers such as Iain Sinclair and Peter Ackroyd, who lerv Londonium, go gooey with excitement.

✺

Eventually, a movie about Aleister Crowley did appear – *Chemical Wedding* (Julian Doyle, 2009). It promised much – a movie about the Beast himself! – but delivered so little. How can you miss, when you've got someone like Crowley as the subject of your movie? Well, *Chemical Wedding* did miss. If you know anything about Crowley, you'll know that it's the kind of sensational material that writes itself. Even if Crowley did less than 10% of what he was supposed to have done, it doesn't matter, because the legend is simply incredible. But, despite casting an impressive actor like Simon Callow as Crowley, *Chemical Wedding* was another reason why British cinema in the 1990s-2000s was in very dire straits. The script (by Bruce Dickinson and Doyle) was crudely crafted, with so-obvious exposition and predictable plotting, and a dumb-ass sci-fi device for bringing Crowley back from the dead and into the present day, to save on the budget (so that *Chemical Wedding* came across like a crappy episode of *Dr Who* or *The Outer Limits*). Oh, if only Ken Russell had directed a Crowley biopic! Or Dario Argento. Or Donald Cammell, in, say, 1982, after *Demon Seed* and b4 *White of the Eye*.

✺

The Aleister Crowley associations are over-done by critics (in regard to *Performance* and rock music), especially by those who don't understand Crowley's philosophies. The sensationalism of Satanism and sex magicke take over. But Jimmy Page, Kenneth Anger, Donald Cammell and thousands of others responded to Crowley not only at the tabloid level: 'do what thou wilt' was not only about following your own will (and to hell with everybody else), it was about freedom and transcendence (including self-transcendence). Of course it chimed with the late 1960s concept of 'free

---

170 S. Davis, 1985, 161.
171 In an early version of *The Performers*, the rock star would've lived in Melbury Place.
172 You can visit Leighton House, which gives you an idea of the decadence and exotic stylization of the late Victorian period.

love' (as did the sex magicke). But it was also a plea for fulfilling your potential, and not being constrained by authority or laws.

As to the sex magicke advocated by Aleister Crowley and his acolytes, well, that's easy to relate to at the level of enjoying a Good Fuck. It's just a Good Fuck, and everyone likes a Good Fuck, right? Of course, adherents of sex magicke (and associated erotic pathways of the Orient, such as Tantrism and Taoist sex magic, popularized in the late 20th century, so they became part of the New Age and mind/ body/ spirit movement), would say there is more to it than that. Yes. There is. But sex magicke in the Crowleyan manner (and in the Western sex magic arena) is also very much about that simple thing of enjoying a Good Fuck.

The Aleister Crowley and magical ingredients in the cinema of Donald Cammell have been over-done by critics, as Cammell himself admitted, as well as his brother David and his wife China Kong. There's infinitely more Crowleyania and magicke in the cinema of Kenneth Anger than Cammell, for instance. Music, money, movies, literature, painting, fashion, celebrity, relationships and sex were *far* more important to Cammell than magicke and Crowley.

But the Crowley connection keeps cropping up – why? – because the old codger is fun to write about!

KENNETH ANGER.

Kenneth Anger (born 1927, Santa Monica, CA) is known as one of the chief American *avant garde* filmmakers, alongside Stan Brakhage, Jordan Belson, Maya Deren, Hollis Frampton and Michael Snow. Anger is a film legend and, like Orson Welles, Werner Herzog – and Donald Cammell – he liked to embellish and mythologize his own life.[173] As well as *Lucifer Rising*, Anger is known for films such as *Fireworks* (1947), *Eaux d'Artifice* (1950/ 1953), *Rabbit's Moon*[174] (1950/ 1972), and many others. His most famous piece is *Scorpio Rising* (1963).[175]

I remember seeing *Scorpio Rising* at Bournemouth film school in the early 1980s: it makes an instant impression with its combination of bikers, leather, homosexuality, hints of S/M, and the outrageous fusion of 1960s pop songs with religious movies – specifically, images of Christ lifted from a cheesy, Sunday school movie. James Dean and Marlon Brando (from *The Wild One*) are in there too. And Adolf Hitler.

Scorpio Rising is a classic cult movie in every sense: it displays anti-

---

[173] 'Anger's cultivated image is as important as the films he makes', opines Raymond Murray (9).
[174] *Rabbit's Moon* was an *hommage* to Géorges Méliès, the forerunner of *all* fantasy and magical cinema. It was made during Kenneth Anger's sojourn in France, and including French olde worlde motifs such as Pierrot the clown and Columbine.
[175] *Scorpio Rising* was a short that featured Bruce Byron, Johnny Sapienza, Frank Carifi, Bill Dorfman and Steve Crandell.

establishment and rebellious attitudes, acute fashion-consciousness, an exploration of subcultures (Hell's Angels and biker culture, boots, belts, chains, jeans, leather jackets), has a brilliant title, and a terrific soundtrack (which includes Elvis Presley, the Randells, the Angels, Bobby Vinton, Ray Charles, the Crystals, Kris Jensen, Claudine Clark, Gene McDaniels, the Surfans and Little Peggy March).[176] *Scorpio Rising* also tested the U.S.A.'s censorship regime, when it was seized and later cleared of charges of obscenity by the State of New York (contributing to the collapse of that particular censorship board).[177]

If you made a list of the elements that a cult movie should have, *Scorpio Rising* has them in spades. (Certainly the mix of pop music and visuals was influential: Martin Scorsese and David Lynch have been influenced by *Scorpio Rising*, for Andy Medhurst, in pictures such as *GoodFellas, Mean Streets* and *Blue Velvet*).[178] And, like a proper cult movie, *Scorpio Rising* was controversial, and confiscated by the Los Angeles police, and, incredibly, the American Nazi Party sued Kenneth Anger over the use of the swastika!

Made when he was 19,[179] *Fireworks* is a cult, underground movie *par excellence*: it stars Kenneth Anger himself, and depicts in a dreamy manner gay sex and violence (it was seized by police in San Francisco in 1960). Bruce Kawin and Gerald Mast describe *Fireworks* in *A Short History of the Movies* as

> clearly his own adolescent and masochistic fantasy, the symbolic dream journey of a lonely, horny boy... who is picked up, beaten, and raped to satiety by sailors, climaxing (literally and figuratively) with the image of a penis metamorphosizing into a Roman candle. (in G. Mast, 469)

Meanwhile, Raymond Murray noted in *Images In the Dark: An Encyclopedia of Gay and Lesbian Film and Video* that, 'coupled with its euphoric montage', *Fireworks* 'seems too aware, too sophisticated to come from someone in their late teens' (10).

Invocation of My Demon Brother (1969) is a key intertext with *Performance*: it features Mick Jagger and the Stones in concert, Anita Pallenberg, Jimmy Page, Robert Fraser's house, and of course Aleister Crowley throughout (Jagger provided the soundtrack, which was due to have been supplied by Anger's lover, Bobby Beausoleil, who later joined the

---

176 As Gerald Mast and Bruce Kawin point out, the use of pop music on the soundtrack of *Scorpio Rising* clearly influenced *Easy Rider* and *American Graffiti* as well as *Performance* (in G. Mast, 470). There were lawsuits, however, because Anger had not gained permission to use the music.
177 In G. Mast, 470.
178 A. Medhurst, in J. Romney, 1995, 75. 'Blue Velvet' is one of the songs in *Scorpio Rising*, taken up as the theme song of David Lynch's 1986 movie, but, as Anger pointed out, he used it first.
179 One of Kenneth Anger's first films was made with film stock left over from a family vacation (it was called *Who's Rocking My Dreamboat*).

Manson Family). Anaïs Nin appears as the Goddess Astarte (in fragments not used in 1948's *Puce Moments*.[180] Anger often recycled or reworked older material).

Invocation of My Demon Brother is a classic mix of Angerian elements: wild visual effects, opticals and superimpositions, vivid colours, flash cuts, magickal rituals (with Kenneth Anger himself as a magus conducting an 'Equinox of the Gods' rite), numerous symbols and talismans, nudity, and a Moog synthesizer score performed by Mick Jagger live to the picture (which wasn't used). You could intercut *Invocation of My Demon Brother* (and many of Anger's movies) with *Performance* and it would fit in seamlessly. Donald Cammell said that Anger[181] was 'the major influence at the time I made *Performance*' (B, 96).[182]

Kenneth Anger is probably *the* major Aleister Crowley aficionado of modern times (he had 'Lucifer' tattooed on his chest, and thought himself to be a recinarnation of Crowley). 'Anger considers himself a magician: his camera is his conjuring tool, editing is his incantations', as Raymond Murray put it in *Images In the Dark* (9).

Kenneth Anger was also known for his books exposing the gossipy, lurid underbelly of Hollywood (as in *Hollywood Babylon*). Published in 1959 (with editions in 1965 and 1971),[183] *Hollywood Babylon* was one of those tabloid-style, coffee-table books aimed at a youth and bourgeois market – it would sit nicely beside books on the paranormal or horror movies, yes, but also recipe books and gardening books. (Many of the stories have since been debunked).

Kenneth Anger spent some time in Europe: as he put it after hearing from Jean Cocteau, who admired *Fireworks*, he was off: 'one fan letter from Cocteau and I hightailed it to Paris' (he left for France in 1950).[184] He worked with Cocteau and also apparently attempted suicide. Anger returned to North America (to Brooklyn) in 1962. He also lived in London. In later years he was the guest of fantasy film legend Forrest J. Ackerman in his monster museum in Hollywood.

---

180 *Puce Moments* was an abandoned project about a fading Hollywood star dressing up to go out.
181 Derek Jarman was also influenced by Kenneth Anger: it's easy to detect the influence of Anger on Jarman: the mix of sadomasochism, homoeroticism, ritual, masquerade, Aleister Crowley, and religious imagery. Jarman's cinema is virtually a rehash of Anger's cinema, as well as Pier Paolo Pasolini's and Ken Russell's, tho' not nearly as good, as inventive, or as enjoyable.
As well as Kenneth Anger, Derek Jarman also cited William Burroughs, Allen Ginsberg and Robert Rauschenberg as influences (1991, 137). William Shakespeare, Christopher Marlowe, John Dee and the Elizabethan era (such as alchemists, magicians, herbalists) were recurring influences on Jarman, and also C.G. Jung, Percy Shelley and William Blake, the Apocalyptists, the late Victorians, and Powell and Pressburger. All of those artists and writers would influence hundreds of others in the 1960s and 1970s, including Donald Cammell.
182 M. Brown, 1999, 96.
183 *Hollywood Babylon* wasn't published in the U.S.A. until 1975 (and a later edition in 1985).
184 In Paris, Kenneth Anger had a go at adapting *The Story of O*, a famous piece of French erotica.

Anita Pallenberg in Peformance (top),
and modelling (bottom)

Anita Pallenberg with two of the Rolling Stones:
Keith Richards (above), and Brian Jones (below).

Images from Cocksucker Blues (1972)

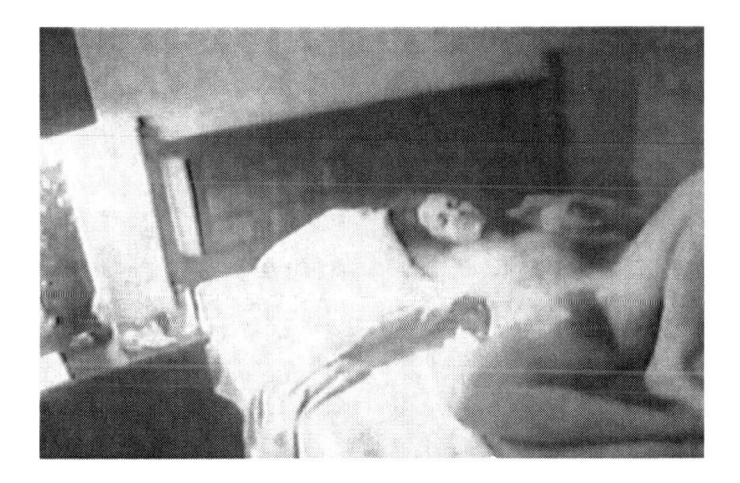

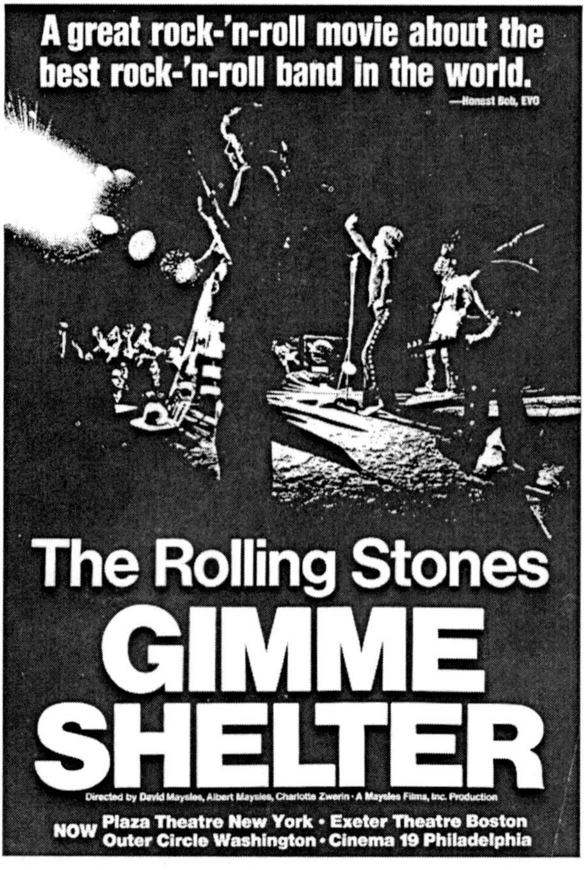

A great rock-'n-roll movie about the best rock-'n-roll band in the world.
—Honest Bob, EYO
The Rolling Stones
GIMME SHELTER
Directed by David Maysles, Albert Maysles, Charlotte Zwerin · A Maysles Films, Inc. Production
NOW
Plaza Theatre New York · Exeter Theatre Boston
Outer Circle Washington · Cinema 19 Philadelphia

The Rolling Stones in Hyde Park, 1969 (above).
And still going strong: on the 50 years tour (below).

MICK JAGGER
AS "NED KELLY"
WOODFALL presents A TONY RICHARDSON FILM
Screenplay by TONY RICHARDSON and IAN JONES · Produced by NEIL HARTLEY
Directed by TONY RICHARDSON
Music and Lyrics by SHEL SILVERSTEIN Songs sung by WAYLON JENNINGS
TECHNICOLOR®
United Artists
GP

Two late 1960s films with links to Performance: the camp classic Barbarella (1967, Marianne/ Dino de Laurentiis), above.

And Candy (1968, Selmur/ Dear/ Corona), a bizarrely dreadful French-Italian-US co-production, right.

Another film with links to Performance, MGM's Blow-Up (1966).

(© MGM)

DEMON SEED

4

DEMON SEED
☆

Demon Seed (1977) is an example of what most of the Hollywood film industry produces: a producer-led project based on a book by a well-known author (Dean Koontz).[1] Most Hollywood movies are based on existing properties, whether they are stage plays, TV shows, sitcoms, cartoons, novels or, more recently, computer games, theme park rides and comic-books.

So one of the most important facts about *Demon Seed*, as far as this study of Donald Cammell's cinema is concerned, is that Cammell *did not originate the project*. I can't stress this enough, because it impacts on so many aspects of the production and the final film. It meant, for instance, that Cammell hadn't come up with the basic idea, with the storyline, with the characters, with the situations, with the script, with the themes, with the ending, and so on.

It also meant that Donald Cammell didn't have any of his own feelings or creativity invested in the project, initially. It wasn't a film he was burning to make; it wasn't a project he had been nursing for years, like Francis Coppola with *Tucker*, for instance, or Orson Welles with *Julius Caesar* and *Don Quixote*. It wasn't a project that Cammell had hawked around the Hollywood studios and production companies for eons, trying to get off the ground. It wasn't a project that an actor had invited him to write. It wasn't a book that Cammell had optioned and scripted.

Robert Jaffe and Roger A. Hirson have the screenplay credits for *Demon Seed*. Jaffe had already written twelve drafts of the screenplay before Cammell came aboard the production. There were further rewrites before Hirson was commissioned to rewrite it again, delivering a first draft on April 8, 1976 (U, 174). Elia Katz rewrote the script a number of times, but was uncredited. Yet more rewrites, of the dialogue, were done by Stanley Elkin.

So on *Demon Seed*, Donald Cammell was a director for hire. Nothing wrong with that: but it meant that the relationship between the filmmaker and the project was different from, say, *Performance* or *Wild Side*, which Cammell had originated (*Wild Side* with China Kong). *Performance* for example clearly came out of Cammell's experiences with the Chelsea set and the London scene, was clearly partly inspired by his encounters with people like Brian Jones, Mick Jagger and the Rolling Stones, and the wonderful Anita Pallenberg. But the film he directed after *Performance* that made it into theatres, *Demon Seed*, wasn't like that at all.

Donald Cammell realized that *Demon Seed* was someone else's story, and that he'd tried 'to make it into something different'. But it hadn't worked. Cammell was bemused why he'd been approached in the first

---

[1] Many movies and TV movies have been adapted from Koontz's books; *Demon Seed* was one of the first.

place to helm *Demon Seed*. He later said that two other directors had declined the project,[2] so he wasn't first choice by any means. Maybe it was because the adaptor, Robert Jaffe, knew his work (U, 169). And, not being a name, he would of course be cheaper. *Demon Seed* went over-schedule by two weeks and a day (U, 172).

Demon Seed was, as the opening credit announces, 'A HERB JAFFE PRODUCTION' (Jaffe's credit comes after the roaring MGM lion).[3] In no way could *Demon Seed* be classed as 'a Donald Cammell film', then. But very few movies actually deserve the director's propriety credit, in my humble opinion. Or, to put it another way, *very few* contemporary filmmakers (and not only in Hollywood) are justified in putting 'a film by' at the top of their movies. Ingmar Bergman could (but didn't). Orson Welles could (but didn't). But how can Paul S. Anderson or McG put 'a film by' at the start of their movies? It's bollocks.

So *Demon Seed* is very much a producer's movie: it's exactly the kind of movie where a film producer has bought the option on a book and commissioned someone to write the script, then started to make a deal to produce the movie (in this case, with Metro).

Demon Seed is the kind of movie that John Carpenter, Joe Dante or Dario Argento could probably have had fun with – it's got that B-movie, silly concept, and can take place at a Roger Corman-level budget, in two studio sets: the house and the Icon facility. *Demon Seed* certainly has that Cormanesque or low budget feel to it, and in some respects it's simply a monster movie: it's a girl and a monster (though the girl's played by a major actress, and the monster's a computer).

Why doesn't *Demon Seed* work? Primarily, the script, the script, the script (by Robert Jaffe and Roger Hirson). Technically, it's fine: *Demon Seed* was filmed by one of the stars of the 'New Hollywood' generation, Bill Butler, whose credits include *Jaws*, *The Conversation*, *The Rain People*, *One Flew Over the Cuckoo's Nest*, and *Grease* (four of those five movies are Hollywood classics, and brilliantly shot). Donald Cammell's regular editor, Frank Mazzola, cut the film. Music was by Jerry Fielding. Edward Carfagno was production designer. Barbara Krieger was set decorator. Jennifer Shull cast it. Don L. Cash and Lee Harman did the make-up. Dione Taylor was hair stylist. Sandy Cole, Joie Hutchinson and Bucky Rous were wardrobe. Edward Teets was A.D. Jerry Jost, John Riordan and William L. McCaughey did the sound. Harry V. Lojewski was music supervisor. Julie Christie, Fritz

---

[2] Brian de Palma was one of the directors who had passed up making *Demon Seed*.
[3] Herb Jaffe (1921-91) was not a big time film producer. Prior to *Demon Seed*, he produced the enjoyable John Milius desert romp *The Wind and the Lion* (which is a pretty big movie). But you probably not have heard of Jaffe's other movies, which included *Fright Night*, *Jinxed*, *Maid To Order*, *The Lord of Discipline*, *Dudes* and *Remote Control*. Incidentally, Jaffe's son, Robert, wrote the first script of *Blade Runner*, in 1975. Needless to say, Philip K. Dick didn't like it.

Weaver, Gerrit Graham, Barry Kroeger and Lisa Lu were among the cast.

So *Demon Seed* had some first-rate collaborators working on it, including DP Bill Butler, editor Frank Mazzola, and actress Julie Christie. The film does have a low budget look to it (well, low budget by Hollywood's standards), but that hasn't stopped many a filmmaker delivering a top quality movie. The budget is what it is, as Terry Gilliam put it, and you have to work with whatever you've got. No doubt the production could've benefited from a few thousand dollars here and there – no filmmaker working in the Hollywood system would turn down some extra cash. (The practical special effects, by Tony Fisher and co., of Proteus with the crappy wheelchair and polyhedra, could really do with more money).

But the budget isn't why *Demon Seed* doesn't work, and neither is it the technical aspects. No, it's mainly the script, the script, the script. And this is the case with 99% of Hollywood movies that tank. Because technically, Hollywood movies are amazing. And quite a few have some good actors in them. It's all down to the material (though in the case of *Demon Seed*, the post-production was troubled, with Herb Jaffe and MGM not seeing eye to eye with Donald Cammell and his team about how the movie should play).

Part of the trouble is that the Dean Koontz project is a little dodgy going in. Here's the pitch: a super-computer goes crazy, trapping a woman in a house, and deciding it wants to have a child with her. Well, uhh, okay. It's a horror movie, then, a chiller with futuristic elements? Yes: a girl and a mad machine.

The premise might be enough for a fifty-minute TV special, or an episode of *The Twilight Zone* or *The Outer Limits*, but when it's stretched to feature film length (95 minutes), it gets just a little thin. There's simply not enough going on to sustain the suspense. *Demon Seed* really needs more incident and more action (and also some *decent* action! Too much of *Demon Seed* is just lame). And perhaps some humour.

And you have to buy into the premise in the first place. The filmmakers make that a little difficult at times. For instance, one of super-computer Proteus's main weapons is a wheelchair with an electric arm attached to it (called Joshua). Very silly (that flippin' arm/ wheelchair combo even performs complex experiments on Susan Harris, as well as being able to tie her to a table).[4] And when Susan shuts out the robot wheelchair from the kitchen, all the super-computer can do in retaliation to Susan is turn up the heating.

And you have to believe that poor Julie Christie is completely incapable of getting out of her own house (and Christie is a tough woman on screen

---
4 There are only vague hints at the sexual probing in the novel.

if ever there was one – a few years earlier she'd been the tough-as-nails hooker in the wonderful *McCabe and Mrs Miller* (1971), opposite Warren Beatty, and before that a woman who runs her own farm in *Far From the Madding Crowd*, and of course Lara in *Doctor Zhivago*).

But there are plenty of horror films which have utterly bonkers premises, and you either buy them whole or don't bother watching the movie. There are things that a filmmaker can do, though, to persuade the audience that the nutty premise is possible (or at least, entertaining).

Julie Christie (b. April 4, 1941) was at the time one of the few genuine, British, female stars in international cinema. She was known as the romantic lead in films such as *Far From the Madding Crowd* and *Doctor Zhivago*, as well as playing feisty, independent women (in *McCabe and Mrs Miller*). One of her best known roles was in 1973's *Don't Look Now*, from Daphne de Maurier's story (and directed by Nic Roeg). [5]

However, *Demon Seed* would not be a highpoint in Julie Christie's film career, even though she's acting her socks off. Christie is always watchable, and she plays the victim of the super-computer's nefarious schemes very well. The problem is partly that a good performance in an average or sub-standard movie isn't as memorable as an ordinary turn in an excellent movie. If a film's fantastic, everyone benefits, and performances can seem far more impressive than they really are.

Demon Seed clearly wasn't a wholly satisfying experience for Donald Cammell, and the movie demonstrates that. Cammell didn't have final cut, needless to say (highly unlikely anyway for most directors, and certainly for a director-for-hire on this project), and the cut wasn't his. He acknowledged that the 'dumbest errors were mine'. Part of the problem is the script, which Cammell later said 'went through endless rewrites', and there were too many executives at MGM involved.[6] In a 1984 interview with Jon Savage, Donald Cammell said that although he rather liked *Demon Seed* now, he was 'very upset that I couldn't make it the way I wanted to. It was re-edited'.[7]

Demon Seed was previewed in Phoenix, AZ, in late January, 1977. After that, the studio took the picture away from the filmmakers (an all too familiar story), and edited it *their* way. Accounts differ as to how much the MGM editors took out (David Cammell said 20 minutes, Frank Mazzola reckoned about 11 minutes), but for the filmmakers it meant that the movie was not now the work they had intended.

---

5 *Don't Look Now* was famous for its sex scene between Julie Christie and Donald Sutherland which employed the parallel editing style of *Performance*.
6 Donald Cammell, in the PR material for *White of the Eye*, and quoted in U, 179f.
7 In J. Savage, *Vague*, 23, 1990-91.

THEORIZING *DEMON SEED*.

You could of course wheel in the cultural theory and sci-fi favourite theme of machines and computers and technology being problematic, that the Western world relies too heavily on technology. It's humans and machines again. And it's robots and computers who become more human, and start thinking and feeling like humans. Yeah, yeah, yeah.

Oh, and while you're at it, you could trot out the arguments about surveillance and the invasion of privacy. All of those cameras and eyes and screens. Yeah, and you could bring out Laura Mulvey and Jacques Lacan and Garrett Stewart and Scott Bukatman and all the other postmodernists and cultural theorists who have written about voyeurism and scopophilia, and talk about how *Demon Seed* is a film about looking and being looked at.[8] You could do all that, but I'm not going to bother.

You could theorize, but *Demon Seed* isn't good enough to really support it. There are other movies which are far superior in exploring the science fiction theme of humans and machines interacting: *2001: A Space Odyssey*, *Alien*, *A.I.*, *Blade Runner*, *Westworld*, *Solaris*, and the granddaddies of them all, *Frankenstein* (1931) and *Metropolis* (1926).

♣

Feminists would decimate *Demon Seed*: Andrea Dworkin, Catherine MacKinnon, Mary Daly, Susan Griffin, Susan Brownmiller, Xavière Gauthier. Absolutely tear it to pieces. There wouldn't be much left after the smoke had cleared.

So let's not even bother to do that.

Third wave or postmodern feminists, however, might enjoy some of the issues explored in *Demon Seed*, because they link up to similar issues in films which some postmodern and third wave feminists have exalted, such as the *Alien* series, the *Terminator* movies, *Frankenstein* and *Blade Runner*. It might be hard to see what feminists could applaud in big, loud (rightwing and reactionary) action movies and horror flicks such as *The Terminator* and *Alien*, but critics in books such as *Alien Zone* and *Alien Zone 2* (1990 and 1999) have applied Julia Kristeva's theory of abjection and the maternal realm to these movies, and explored the relation between monsters and the feminine, between monsters, otherness and the maternal (other favourite movies for such feminist and post-feminist analyses include *Dracula*, *The Thing*, and of course the over-rated *Matrix*).

---

[8] To make it perfectly clear, there's a gratuitous scene of Julie Christie naked in the shower, and looking at her butt in the mirror, while the house computer spies on her.

DEMON SEED AND HORROR CINEMA.

Cameras often perform phallic roles in films – sometimes quite obviously in horror films (think of Alfred Hitchcock's works). Cameras often bear down upon characters – typically the female 'victim' in horror scenarios. In the horror movie *Demon Seed*, Julie Christie is menaced by a computer system which uses her home security surveillance cameras to imprison and impregnate her. The computer wants a child, and uses a telescopic, artificial penis to rape the woman. This is perhaps the only rape in the cinema which's shot from the point of view of the penis (according to Carol Clover in *Men, Women and Chain Saws: Gender in the Modern Horror Film*). But not in Japanese *animé*! (such as in *The Legend of the Overfiend*).

In horror cinema, one of the most common kinds of shots is the first-person, handheld camera, typically used to depict the killer that stalks its victim (as at the beginning of *Hallowe'en*). In horror 'slasher' films, the camera is usually distinctly phallic and masculinist, while the 'victim' is often female. Tania Modleski said (in *The Women Who Knew Too Much: Hitchcock and Feminist Theory*) that slasher movies portray how 'men's fears become women's fate' (107). The woman is caught in the sights of the camera which then kills her, as in *Peeping Tom*. In *Demon Seed*, the camera is often aligned with Proteus, giving the computer's point-of-view of Susan.

The murderer in slasher horror films is often a sexually inadequate male, 'a male in gender distress' – 'men who kill precisely because they *cannot* fuck'.[9] The audience, Carol Clover suggests, identifies with the killer, cheering him on as he assaults his victims, and then cheering on the (female) self-rescuer. In some horror films, Panaglide or Steadicam technology is used for the first-person killer shot, giving the camera movements that strange, floating quality which's somewhere between a steady tracking shot and the wobble of the handheld camera.

VISUAL EFFECTS.

Demon Seed is also a visual effects movie. I guess many viewers wouldn't think of Donald Cammell as a special effects director – like, say, George Lucas,[10] James Cameron or Robert Zemeckis – but in *Demon Seed* he had to be. *Demon Seed* is as much a special effects movie, in its own way, as *Altered States* or *Frankenstein* or a Ray Harryhausen flick. On a more modest scale, perhaps, but still packed with visual effects.

---

[9] C. Clover, 1992.
[10] *Demon Seed* was released the same year as *Star Wars*, of course. Needles to say, *Star Wars* – and *Close Encounters of the Third Kind*, also released in 1977 – make *Demon Seed*, in terms of visual effects, look pretty ropey.

There are practical effects, for a start, all over *Demon Seed*: fire, smoke, lasers,[11] and explosions. Special make-up[12] (such as for Proteus's child). Numerous images for Proteus's screens (some are live, some are burn-ins). Live footage for the terminals (often a nightmare for the practical effects people to hook up and co-ordinate with the action). Practical manipulations for the robot arm and the mad polygons.

Aside from the different elements of animation, there's a ton of stock footage and second unit footage in *Demon Seed* (the first shot of Donald Cammell's first film was stock footage). There are moons, star fields, giant suns, skies, foetuses in the womb, animation of foetuses growing, cells, etc (*2001: A Space Odyssey* is one of the touchstones here).[13] The visuals for Proteus were by teams headed up by Ron Hays and Jordan Belson (Belson's formal experiments in film included *Mandala*, 1955, *Allures*, 1961, *Re-Entry*, 1964, *Phenomena*, 1965 and *Samadhi*, 1967).[14] Later, Belson's colourful blobs and liquids would appear in the wonderful *The Right Stuff* (Phil Kaufman, 1983), to evoke the visions the astronauts and pilots see).[15]

Animation in *Demon Seed* came from Bo Gehring, Wang Laboratories, and the Computer Science Dept at the University of Utah.[16] Moon photos came from Lick Observatory, with aerial footage from MacGillivray Freeman. (Donald Cammell's Goddess-oriented penchant is made explicit by the superimpositions of the moon over the foetus in the womb – the moon being *the* symbol of the Goddess).

In orchestrating all of this footage from numerous sources, much of the credit should go to Frank Mazzola and his editorial assistants Gary Bell and Freeman Davies, Jr. Using the customary Donald Cammell montage style of editing, Mazzola and his team layered stock footage on top of the principal photography to form a convincing blend of sci-fi.

THE MOVIE AND THE NOVEL.

I admit I only got halfway thru the novel of *Demon Seed* before giving up. It's a potboiler, not especially gripping, and rather predictable... and there are better things to do in life than read *Demon Seed*!

There's plenty more sex in Dean Koontz's 1973 novel than in the 1977 MGM movie. The super-computer Proteus is particularly interested in giving

---

[11] Lasers were *de rigeur* for rock concerts by Led Zeppelin, Genesis and Yes at the time of *Demon Seed*. And films such as *Alien* also used lasers.
[12] Frank Griffin and Burman Studios provided the special make-up.
[13] There was plenty of animation, *avant garde* experimentation and abstract forms of movie-making which preceded the Stargate sequence in *2001: A Space Odyssey*. For instance, James Whitney (*Yantra, Five Film Exercises, Catalogue*), Bruce Conner (*A Movie*), Oskar Fischinger, Robert Breer (*Fuji*), Harry Smith, Stan Vanderbeek (*Science Friction*), Len Lye (*A Colour Box, Kaleidoscope*), Norman McLaren (*Begone Dull Care, Neighbours*), and Stan Brakhage (*Mothlight, Dog Star Man, Flesh of Morning*).
[14] Donald Cammell had been impressed by Belson's film *Chakra*.
[15] G. Mast, 1992, 468.
[16] It included Synthavision, Tetralinks, Delta Wing, and Genigraphics.

Susan Harris orgasms: they share an erotic relationship like regular lovers. The film cut out most of that. The novel also relates some of this in the first person – from the computer's point-of-view, which the movie also dropped. For instance:

> The geometric configurations[17] of her passionate reactions were as phenomenally beautiful and perfect as everything else about her. She arched and twisted, squirmed against the couch, clutched her breasts, beat her fists on her lips, writhed and rose up, fell back and sighed, tossed her head back and forth to make a flag of her hair, raised her hips, gripped her own buttocks, all with a fluid grace that amazed me and excited me.
> I gave her another orgasm.
> And another. (86)

So Susan Harris and Proteus are engaged in this sadomasochistic, erotic relationship,[18] with the machine happy to make Susan come and come. Dean Koontz's novel is not quite pornography, but the amount of weird machine-woman sex is close to porn. But in the 1977 movie, the relationship is much more about power, and is exploited for its horror potential. There's certainly no scene where Susan has multiple orgasms and seems to be enjoying it.

It's a staple of a sub-set of sci-fi cinema – sex between people and machines, or people and robots/ cyborgs. Everyone's favourite dystopian futuristic movie set in 2019 in L.A., *Blade Runner*, explored this same territory. (Japanese cinema is far in advance of Western cinema in depicting the interaction of humans and machines, including in eroticism. For instance, *Ghost In the Shell, Appleseed, Metropolis, Akira, Macross Plus, Robot Carnival, Roujin Z*, etc).

But contemporary Hollywood cinema doesn't get much further than the sensational image of humans interacting with cyborgs at the most extreme levels: sex, violence and death. Even movies enshrined by the critical academy, such as *Blade Runner*, don't go much beyond the titillating question: 'what's it like to fuck an android?' (In fact, there was a scene scripted and shot in *Blade Runner*, but deleted, when Deckard visits his injured pal Holden, and Holden asks Deckard if he's fucked the replicant Rachel. Deckard doesn't answer, but Holden clearly thinks it would be sick to do so – it'd be like fucking your washing machine, he tells Deckard. And that's what Deckard chooses in the end: to fuck a robot. If Deckard *is* a robot, then *Blade Runner* depicts a romance between two robots. If Deckard *isn't* a replicant, it's even weirder: a guy who so desperate he'd prefer to live

---

[17] That phrase – 'geometric configurations' – is a total steal from J.G. Ballard (*circa Crash* and *The Atrocity Exhibition*).
[18] The elements of sexual abuse (by Susan's grandfather) were dropped from the novel. In the movie, Susan's retreat into her Howard Hughes' lifestyle is explained differently.

with a machine!).

The *Demon Seed* novel by Dean Koontz has a creepy quality to it – beyond the horror genre scenario of the computer and the woman. You find it in other novels of the 1960s through 1980s – there's a voyeuristic, titillating emphasis on sex and the body.

Dean Koontz, though, said he was

> more happy than not with that film. The book is a lot more frightening, I think, but overall they did a first-rate job on a surprisingly modest budget and got twice the number of effects on the screen they could've been expected to produce for the money they had.[19]

No doubt the filmmakers joked that having Julie Christie tied to the bed was some kind of S/M fantasy (maybe the kind of thing that Warren Beatty would dream about). Certainly the elements of bondage are foregrounded: poor Susan Harris is strapped to her bed or a table while a robot wields a variety of phallic devices around her, including an extendible metal arm for penetrating her. Susan is jabbed with injections, and drugged. It's actually a fairly gruesome, torture-by-machine film, except there are no Nazis conducting fiendish operations on her, or cackling witchfinder generals testing to see if she's a witch (*à la The Devils*).

If you take away the science fiction element, *Demon Seed* is the story of patriarchal violence and power: it's about men inflicting a series of experiments on a woman, in order to understand her secrets, or the mysteries of life, or whatever. Super-computer Proteus turns out to be another of those movie villains who hanker after immortality. That automatically dooms him from the start.

But in a truly perverse manner, Proteus also gives Susan the attention that's lacking from her husband Alex Harris. And in a twisted way, Proteus fulfils some of the functions of the stereotypical spouse: he spends time with Susan Harris, he cares for her, makes sure she's eating, and does the ultimate marital duty of conceiving a child with her.[20] Except that the computer is also a violent psychopath (and that was similar territory that Donald Cammell and China Kong would explore in their next movie, *White of the Eye*).

THE FLAWS IN *DEMON SEED*, AND HOW YOU MIGHT IMPROVE IT.

How would the 'master of suspense' direct *Demon Seed*? I mean Alfred Hitchcock.[21] With Susan Harris holed up in a confined space by a crazy presence, you could compare *Demon Seed* to *The Birds*, or *Psycho*

---
19 D. Koontz, quoted in B. Munster, *Sudden Fear*, in U, 182.
20 An unvoiced subtext of *Demon Seed* is that Susan might like another child, but Alex clearly doesn't.
21 The computerized system in Susan's house is called 'Alfred', possibly a nod to Hitchcock.

Hitchcock, I think, would have definitely made more of the difference in mood and suspense between Alex at the Icon facility and poor Susan trapped in her own house by Proteus. He would have cut from Susan in the house to Alex at Icon (which *Demon Seed* does do), but he would have made much more of it.

Hitch would I reckon have staged the crucial scene where Walter Gabler comes to the house at lunchtime to check on the system more suspenseful, because that was precisely the sort of scene that Hitchcock excelled at.

Had Joe Dante, Ivan Reitman or John Landis helmed *Demon Seed*, they might have introduced a cute family pet for the house, which Proteus would've dispatched in a funny-gory manner (maybe by capturing the cat in a blender, like one of the gremlins in *Gremlins*). No doubt Dario Argento or John Carpenter would've made the imprisonment of Susan bloodier and more vicious (later horror films wouldn't look away, as *Demon Seed* tends to – the slasher horror movies of the early 1980s were only a few years off, helped along by the mega-success of *Hallowe'en* in 1978. See the chapter on *White of the Eye*).

Another defect of *Demon Seed* is that the characters aren't particularly appealing, or interesting. This is a mistake that so many movies make: if it's the kind of movie where the viewer is supposed to be rooting for the characters, then the filmmakers need to do a bit of spadework and establish these characters for the audience, and persuade the audience to be fond of them (or at least to want to follow them). *Demon Seed* doesn't do that. (It doesn't help that there's zero chemistry between Julie Christie and Fritz Weaver, playing her husband).[22]

Susan and Alex Harris are separating in *Demon Seed*: that plot point is introduced *before* Proteus goes nuts, so it's clearly meant to be one of the issues that's at stake (i.e., it's the emotional subplot). But the faults or problems that Susan and Alex have in their relationship are too banal and too haphazardly circumscribed, so they don't carry any weight. It doesn't matter at all if Susan and Alex are going their separate ways, because the audience doesn't care a jot for these cardboard characters. Some tenderness or some empathy between the two would have enhanced the emotional heart of the movie.

Can anyone remember what *Demon Seed*'s couple argue about in that

---

[22] Fritz Weaver isn't the most charismatic of actors, and the casting does let the movie down somewhat (it doesn't help that Weaver's heart clearly isn't in it). How different the movie might have had MGM and the producers agreed to Marlon Brando taking the role of Alex Harris? According to Frank Mazzola, Donald Cammell had somehow talked Brando into appearing in *Demon Seed*. But Brando was known to be difficult to work with (and he was, at times), and following the success of *Last Tango In Paris* and *The Godfather*, his price had gone way up. Mazzola also reckoned that MGM and the producers didn't want to deal with two difficult personalities combined, Brando and Cammell (U, 171). *Demon Seed* would have fitted in with Brando's plans to travel to the Philippines, too, because Brando didn't arrive to shoot *Apocalypse Now* until the end of August, 1976, a couple of weeks after *Demon Seed* wrapped.

scene in the basement laboratory? I can, 'cos I've I've watched the movie again for this book! They've grown apart, and Alex realizes he's been too cold and too engrossed in his work. But what should be the establishment of some kind of rapport and some kind of loss doesn't occur in this flat, flat scene.

Only later, after an hour into the 1977 MGM film, is a piece of back-story inserted which makes clear the chief reason for the couple breaking up: their daughter has died from leukaemia the year before (well, in 1976, so presumably it's meant to be the year before *Demon Seed* was released). So that's why, when Proteus's child is revealed underneath its natty, metallic carapace, it looks like Susan and Alex Harris's daughter.

Yes, yes, we get it: Alex and Susan Harris lost a daughter, but now they've gained a new child, who's designed by a computer, so Alex'll love it, and was born from Susan's womb (though she would rather kill it).

But why oh why was that vital piece of back-story left so late in the 1977 film? The audience needed that much earlier. OK, yes, back-story typically unfolds in the middle or 3/4s through a conventional script, but without it, the dramatic juice it generates comes in too late. (Again, Alfred Hitchcock provides the model here: the audience must be given sufficient information, Hitchcock said. It was a key ingredient in Hitch's cinema of suspense).

♣

The introduction of a curious ingredient throws the 1977 MGM movie off course for a moment: the disturbed child, Amy (Dana Laurita), that a friend (or maybe it's the housekeeper [Georgie Paul]) brings to the house). Fatally, the relationship between Susan Harris and the girl isn't made clear: presumably Amy's Susan's adopted child, or maybe Susan's child from a previous marriage (Susan is much younger than Alex), or maybe a child that Susan looks after.[23] Or, what the hell, who knows?!!

At first, Amy doesn't want to get out of the car. Then, inside the house, Amy freaks out, apparently because Susan Harris is going away. We see Susan acting motherly and comforting the child, which links up with the theme of Proteus and children, of course. But the scene, with its primal therapy staging, seems to come from a different movie. [24]

It doesn't go anywhere, either. Maybe it's one of those subplots that get left on the cutting room floor (in which case, why leave it in in the first place?).

♣

Why would the designer of a super-computer give it a complex screen

---
[23] Apparently, Amy is one of the mentally ill patients that Susan as a psychiatrist treats.
[24] *One Flew Over the Cuckoo's Nest*, maybe, which DP Bill Butler also shot.

system which employs abstract, 1960s, lightshow patterns? Because, uhh, *Demon Seed* is a *movie*, and a blank computer screen just ain't that exciting (though much cheaper). Some of the abstract and geometric animations are fun (mainly based around the circle and concentric circles), and clearly derive from lightshows at rock concerts, laser shows, and the Stargate sequence in *2001: A Space Odyssey* (as well as being early forms of computer animation).[25] Sci-fi movies would be using similar devices for years.

Similarly, why would a computer engineer give the machine such a creepy voice? Complete with echo and reverb effects. (Robert Vaughn was the voice).[26] Because it's a movie, and computers have to have weirdo tones (any sci-fi flick), soft, women's voices (*Alien*), or blank, camp voices (*2001: A Space Odyssey*). [27]

One of the biggest holes in the plot of *Demon Seed* is that Fritz Weaver's Alex Harris doesn't make contact with Julie Christie's Susan Harris back at the house *even once*. Nope. He leaves for work, and that's the last time he's at the house, until one hour and eighteen minutes into the film, when we're in the last reel, with only 15 minutes to go.

No, Alex Harris *doesn't* call Susan to see how she is, *doesn't* go back to the house to pick up something he's forgotten, *doesn't* go back there to sleep, or whatever. So presumably Alex and Susan have already separated, but, if so, their separation slips past the viewer unnoticed. Alex simply never goes back to the house, allowing Proteus to have his wicked way with Alex's wife.

How very stupid.

A man does come to the house, though, twice: poor Walter Gabler (Gerrit Graham),[28] Alex Harris's fellow nerd[29] at the Icon facility, who's promised to check on the computer system at Susan's house.[30] Walter has one of the sillier deaths in science fiction movies: after dicing with death-by-laser (wielded by that bloody wheelchair-and-arm again), he's crushed

---

25 The conception of Proteus's child is conceived totally like the Stargate sequence in *2001: A Space Odyssey*, complete with the simulation of a forward motion through patterns of light, images of the moon, images of a foetus, and Jerry Fielding's orchestra aiming for Dimitri Shostakovitch-style, modernist weirdness. It's all meant to be 'cosmic', oh so cosmic. Proteus has even been aiming a telescope at distant stars near Orion.
26 Robert Vaughn recalled that they tried 'different voices, different ages, different accents', over a 12 day recording period (although Vaughan had been commissioned for two days). In the end, Donald Cammell and the team decided that what Vaughn had done on the first day would be used in the film (in *Outré: The World of Ultramedia*, 18, 1999).
27 The unlikeliest computer voice was probably 'Slave' in the BBC's TV show *Blake's 7*, which had a Brummie accent. That would never happen in a Hollywood movie.
28 Donald Cammell had known Gerrit Graham from *Simona*.
29 Yes, Walter plays chess on his terminal at work.
30 Walter's death is one of the elements of the film that suffered from MGM's re-cut of the movie. But missing bits of information – like why did nobody miss Gable, or what happened to his pick-up – are simply minor details, which wouldn't bother any viewer if the rest of the movie was really good. It isn't, so audiences pick up on all the errors.

to death by flailing polygons![31] (The polyhedrons are another of the many misguided elements in this crazy movie – not only can Proteus's polygons unfold and attack people, they can also conduct scientific experiments, including holding test tubes at the end of their triangular wedges!. The blocks the computer employed derived from 'Tetralinks', tetrahedrons which were children's paper toys, brought to the project by the technical adviser on the show, Caltech neurologist Bob Stewart.)

The concept of *Demon Seed* had potential, but not with this script, not with this cast, not with this filmmaking team, not with these producers, not with this budget, and not with these resources.

---

31 Complete with a dummy head that pops up. Oh dear.

Classic horror movie stuff in Demon Seed:
a woman (who just happens to be young and attractive),
trapped in a house by a crazy computer

(© MGM/ United Artists, 1977)

JULIE CHRISTIE
CARRIES THE
"DEMON SEED"
Never was a woman violated as profanely...
Never was a woman subject to inhuman love like this...
Never was a woman prepared for a more perverse destiny...
Fear for her.
METRO-GOLDWYN-MAYER presents A HERB JAFFE PRODUCTION
JULIE CHRISTIE in "DEMON SEED" FRITZ WEAVER
Screenplay by ROBERT JAFFE and ROGER O. HIRSON · Directed by DONALD CAMMELL · Produced by HERB JAFFE
Music JERRY FIELDING · Filmed in PANAVISION® METROCOLOR
MGM
United Artists

JULIE CHRISTIE
CARRIES THE
"DEMON SEED"
Fear for her.
JULIE CHRISTIE "DEMON SEED" FRITZ WEAVER
MGM
United Artists

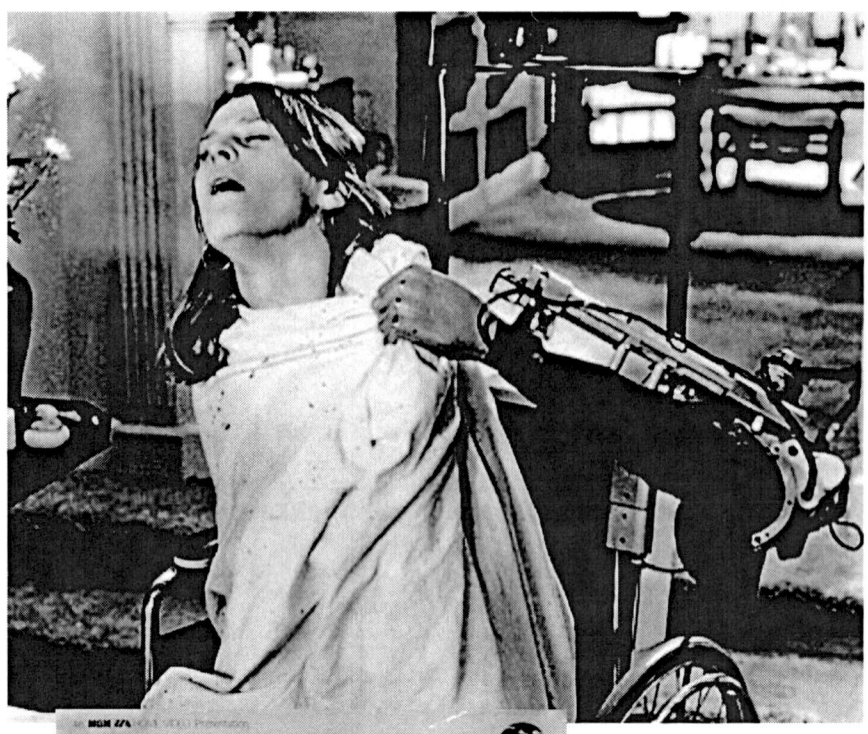

Scary stuff: a woman and, uhh, a robot arm fixed to a wheelchair.

Demon Seed (1977, MGM/ Herb Jaffe)

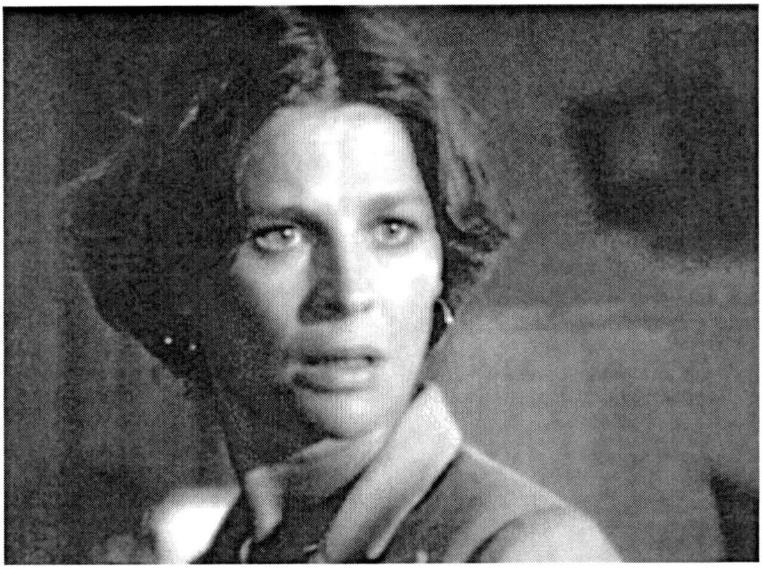

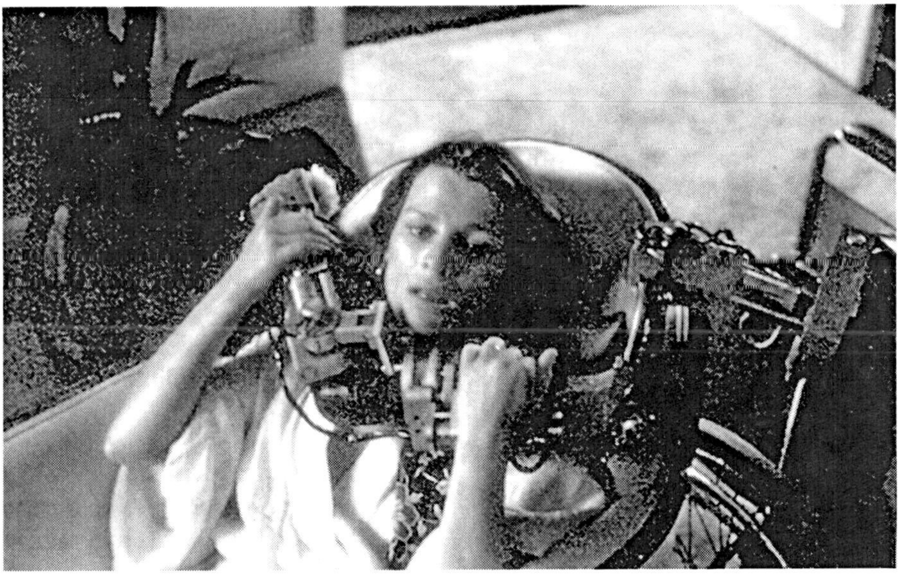

Some images of British superstar Julie Christie, and the films she appeared in before Demon Seed: two hits from the Sixties: Doctor Zhivago (1965, MGM/ David Lean/ Carlo Ponti), right. Far From the Madding Crowd (1967, EMI/ Vic/ Applia), below.

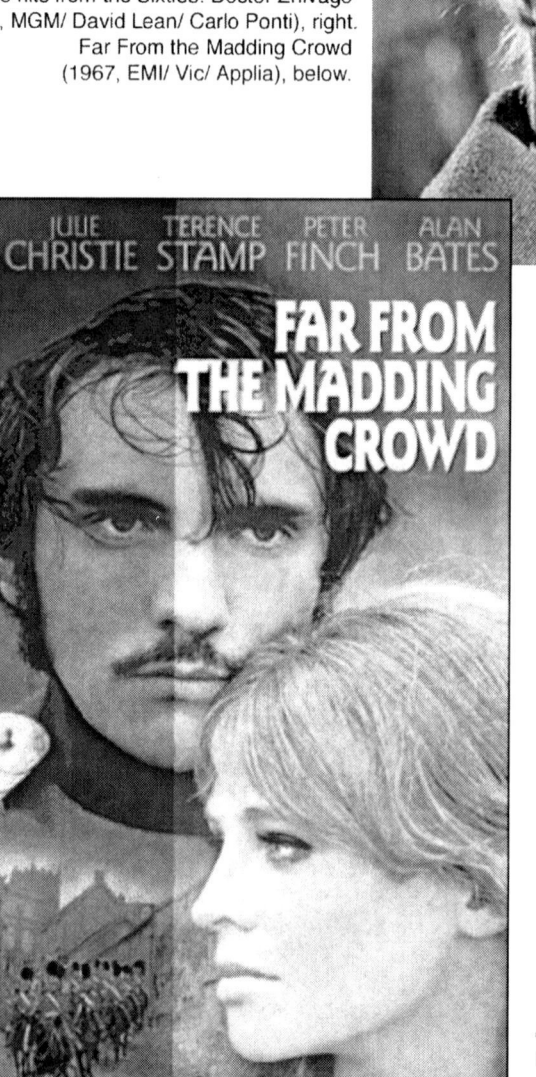

(© MGM, above.
MGM/ Warner-Pathé, left)

Two classic 1970s movies starring Julie Christie: the wonderful McCabe and Mrs Miller (1971), a Warners picture written by Robert Altman and Brian McKay (and shot by Vilmos Zsigmond, master of smoke and light, who shot Donald Cammell's The Argument), left & below.

And Don't Look Now (1973, BL/ Casey/ Eldorado), bottom.

(© Warner Bros, above. Casey/ Eldorado/ Paramount/ Warner, below)

WHITE OF THE EYE

5

WHITE OF THE EYE

★

All barriers are only there for the traversing.

Novalis (*Pollen*, 87)

White of the Eye (1987) was made for producer Elliott Kastner; it was produced by Cassian Elwes and Brad Wyman[1] and co-written by Donald Cammell and China Kong; Alan Jones was DP; it was edited by British veteran Terry Rawlings;[2] costume designer was Merril Greene; Jeanne van Phue was chief hair and make-up; Nick Mason and Rick Fenn composed the music; George Fenton was music supervisor; Andrew Z. Davis was first A.D.; Pamela Rack cast the film; Philip Thomas was production designer; and Bruce Litecky was sound mixer.

The budget of *White of the Eye* was $2.5 million. Shooting took place in Miami and Globe, Arizona, from the middle of January to March, 1986, over about 6 weeks (a very short schedule). Donald Cammell and China Kong had completed the first draft of the script in November, 1985, soon after being offered the project. (Originally, the production was going to be set in Virignia; when it shifted to Arizona, the script was adjusted [U, 213]). Cannon bought the movie for distribution (and they cut 6 minutes from it).[3]

White of the Eye was based on *Mrs White*, a novel by Margaret Tracy (a pen name for Andrew and Laurence Klavan). It starred David Keith, Cathy Moriarty, Ann Evans, Alan Rosenberg, Mark Hayashi, William Schilling and David Chow. Donald Cammell had met Cassian Elwes in 1985 in London, which led to the link with producer Elliott Kastner (Kastner was Elwes' step-father). At the time, Cammell had lost another project, *The Last Video* (set up with EMI), and Elwes came to him 'after God knows how many unrealized projects'.

David Keith (b. May 8, 1954) had appeared, prior to *White of the Eye*, in *Gulag, The Lord of Discipline, An Officer and a Gentleman, Brubaker* and *The Rose*. You'll see Keith crop up in many other movies. He's one of those American actors who, while not a big star, has appeared in all sorts of films. When you see his C.V., you're surprised by just how many projects he's been part of.

Cathy Moriarty (b. November 29, 1960) played White's wife, Joan; Art Evans was the police investigator, Charles Mendoza; Alan Rosenberg was Mike Desantos, Paul's buddy from way back; Alberta Watson was Anne Mason; Marc Hayashi was Stu; William Schilling was Harold Gideon; and the Whites' child Danielle was played by Danielle Smith.

On the crew, one of the stars of *White of the Eye* was undoubtedly the Steadicam operator Larry McConkey (Douglas Ryan was camera operator).

---

[1] Wyman was only 21 at the time.
[2] Terry Rawlings was a veteran editor of movies such as *Alien, Blade Runner, Legend, Yentl, Chariots of Fire*, and *Watership Down*. Following *White of the Eye*, Rawlings cut *Phantom of the Opera, The Core, The Musketeer, GoldenEye, Slipstream* and *Alien 3. White of the Eye* was edited at Pinewood Studios in England.
[3] The movie was passed uncut by the BBFC. Scenes that were cut out included Joan working in a thirft store.

Like many other filmmakers working in the Western film industry, Donald Cammell had become enamoured of the Steadicam apparatus, and the floaty movement of the Steadicam was the signature move in *White of the Eye*. (Some of the first horror films to showcase the Steadicam included *Hallowe'en* and *The Shining*. However, the Steadicam had already appeared in movies such as *Rocky* and *Saturday Night Fever*). But this created tension between the DP, Alan Jones, and Larry McConkey: Cammell wanted two cinematographers on the show. According to producers Brad Wyman and Cassian Elwes, Cammell hoped to film scenes two ways – once with Jones as DP, and once with McConkey operating the Steadicam. Not an ideal situation; but in the end, a large proportion of *White of the Eye* is shot with a Steadicam.

White of the Eye is not one of the great horror movies or thrillers, but it does carve out its own niche, adding a cosmic and religious slant to the intense psychological drama of your regular serial killer movie.

ASPECTS OF *WHITE OF THE EYE*

MUSIC.

Pink Floyd's drummer Nick Mason and guitarist Rick Fenn produced the music for *White of the Eye* (George Fenton was music supervisor). There's rock music and bluesy electric guitar (as in *Performance*), pulsing tablas, and also the loud drones and eerie effects favoured by slasher horror movies. (Sound-wise and visually, when *White of the Eye* depicts the murders, it plays very much like other stalk 'n' slash movies, or an American TV thriller).

Among the opera and classical music heard in *White of the Eye* was Ruggero Leoncavallo's *Pagliacci* (1892, *Vesti la giubba*), and Gustav Mahler's *Second Symphony*.

Hot Chocolate's 'You Sexy Thing' is a recurring song in *White of the Eye*, sung by the characters, and associated with Michael (it was apparently a reference to when Donald Cammell met China Kong). George Jones ('The Grand Tour'), Hank Williams ('A Country Boy Can Survive'), and Booker T. Jones are also featured. Music and sound is part of Paul White's profession – though there are far less references to music or examples of music than in some comparable movies.

THE AMERICAN DESERT.

White of the Eye is a hymn to the desert, and to rural and suburban life in Middle America. It's a pretty accurate portrait, I think, with its images of Interstates running across the desert, giant factories and quarries glimpsed from the road, people driving beat-up trucks, scruffy cafés, the expensive, big houses with their swimming pools and terraces, dusty, grimy garages and gas stations. (Helicopter shots are favoured once again – the first time that Paul White is introduced is in his van on the highway, seen from a helicopter. And, boy, do the filmmakers squeeze every ounce out of hiring the helicopters from Arizona Wing and Rotor for a few days: there are shots of Tuscon, of the quarries, of Paul's van on the road, of factories, and of the explosion at the end).

The desert is exalted in the opening sequence[4] of *White of the Eye* which resembles an Oliver Stone movie (recalling the beginnings of *Natural Born Killers* and *U-Turn*). Or is it that Stone is producing an *hommage* to Donald Cammell and *White of the Eye* in his own films? Eagles, cacti, lonely roads, blue skies, cars, sandstone bluffs – they recur in Stone's movies.

NATIVE AMERICA.

With its desert and run-down, small-town settings and its characters who live in isolated homes, *White of the Eye* resembles a laidback Western. The motifs of the cowboy movie are evoked a number of times (Mike Desantos, for instance, has Apache ancestors; there are guns; hunting, etc).

The Native American elements are woven into *White of the Eye* at a low level – the film deliberately doesn't make something big out of them.[5] But they are there, if you want to see them: how Mike talks about his forebears, for example, and also about 'the white of the eye' (an invention of the scriptwriters), which he uses to refer to the spell that Paul White has put on him and Joan: 'then he came along and he laid his eye on us – the Apaches call it the 'white of the eye''.

The objects symbolically placed by the killer in a crucifix are not meant to be related to Christianity (although many viewers will no doubt interpret them like that), but to ancient Native American crosses, and to the four cardinal points (there is also a compass, which's given by Paul White to Mike at the time when he's stolen Joan away from him; Mike throws it into the quarry pool at the end).

---

[4] The credits of *White of the Eye* bring in totemic animals, such as eagles (and the killing-and-eating cycle of life in the natural world). It's a familiar trope, used in many another movie.
[5] Filming in Arizona is perfect for the references to modern-day Native American societies and cultures. There are many Native American reservations there, for instance. These elements were added after the movie moved from Virginia (the novel was set in Connecticut).

However, Mike Desantos's ancestry doesn't help him much – at least not in the battle for Joan with Paul White. Turns out that Paul is much better at the things Mike's ancestors and Apache forebears were noted for in the cultural stereotype (such as hunting). Mike waves around the gun he's bought in front of Paul (the gun is a further phallic, homoerotic component in the Paul-Mike flashback scenes, as it is in numerous action movies). No need to point out the symbolism of the gun in relation to Mike's sexual inadequacy with Joan (and how Paul can satisfy Joan sexually).[6]

THE BLACK HOLE AT THE CENTRE OF THE UNIVERSE.

The key scene in *White of the Eye* is undoubtedly where Paul White confesses everything to his wife Joan. It's a great scene – Donald Cammell has Cathy Moriarty play it quietly hysterical, weeping all the time, while David Keith becomes increasingly crazy, to the point where he's lunging around the room, and he picks up a vase and hurls it out of the window.

Certainly China Kong and Donald Cammell can write a terrific monologue for a psychotic guy, and Paul White's diatribe in *White of the Eye* doesn't disappoint. He tells Joan he killed the women to put them out of their misery; he says it was as if someone else was perpetrating the crimes, while he watched, disembodied (he was 'chosen', he maintains: a voice tells him, 'Paul White, you are the One'); and finally, when Joan mentions God, Paul responds, no, this is light years beyond God – it's the great black hole at the centre of the universe, and that hole is female, of course ('I told you about that fucking black hole? It sucks everything into it. Believe you me, I know the difference between male and female, and it is definitely female', Paul yells at Joan).

Donald Cammell and China Kong have taken up the ancient association of women with death, the vagina as a black hole that eats everything up (the castrating mother), the woman or vagina as the gateway to hell, a hell hole, the womb of death. It's the familiar demonization of women found in the early Christian theologians, in Tertullian or Origen of Alexandria or St Augustine. (And the Gnostic aspects are obvious: in Gnosticism, God is elsewhere – 'God is the middle man', Paul White tells Joan), and the universe has been created and is being ruled by the demiurge, the Devil. And these Gnostic notions are linked to the feminine, and women's role in the Fall – the fall into matter, the move from Paradise to the material world. Paul makes the familiar connections between modern-day women and Eve

---

6 As well as some on-screen sex, there are many knowing looks between characters, and sexual innuendo in the dialogue.

in the *Bible*, that women are part of evil matter).[7]

If the sexual relations and psychotic views of Paul White are familiar stuff from numerous thrillers and horror movies – it's all about the mother! (as in *Psycho*) – Donald Cammell and China Kong and the team make it play because of the way they stage it, and the way that David Keith plays it, and how it's written.

It's quite right, for instance, that Paul White finally goes nuts in a two-hander scene at night with his wife, not, say, down at the police station in front of Charles Mendoza and his colleagues. *White of the Eye* is a film about a marriage falling apart, among other things, so it's correct that the revelation scene should occur only between husband and wife. If you take out the murder and the investigation, *White of the Eye* is a story about a marriage and life in contemporary North America in the suburbs.

FLASHBACKS.

White of the Eye is a flashback movie: the flashbacks are to ten years earlier, depicting how Joan and Mike Desantos met Paul White. The flashbacks are not filmed in the same way as the present day scenes – it's not simply the drained colour, but the use of the camera, of music, of sound, etc.

The shortcut of music from the period (Hot Chocolate's 'You Sexy Thing') is employed at the start of the flashbacks, as in countless other movies, as music is one of the quickest ways to put an audience into a particular time period. The flashbacks are inserted throughout the 1987 movie. Joan and Mike are depicted in a van heading West, for Los Angeles, across the Arizonan desert. The scenes are some of the less convincing aspects of *White of the Eye* – Joan and Mike arguing about music, and Joan deliberately sabotaging Mike's beloved 8-track cartridge player (it's this incident that prompts the bickering couple to stop off in Globe, Arizona, to get it fixed).

So it's not the most convincing of pretexts to get Joan together with Paul White, but it does use music, which's Paul's eventual job, of course. And one would imagine that Donald Cammell and China Kong, often cited by critics as great screenwriters, could've come up with a better scene than the one where Mike Desantos discovers Joan and Paul getting freaky. Maybe Kong and Cammell enjoyed the very triteness and predictableness of the scene (and there's the phallic gun again, and the impotent firing of the gun into the hi-fi machinery). But *Othello* this ain't.

The whole erotic triangle back-story in *White of the Eye* between Joan-Mike-Paul is terribly predictable; yes, there is texture and idiosyncratic

---
[7] The Biblical/ Christian affinities with the names Paul, Michael and Joan are obvious.

imagery, but dramatically and narratively it's still a join-the-dots story of betrayal.

The 1987 thriller enters far more intriguing territory when it puts Mike and Paul on a hunting trip: the filmmakers know this is going to pay off well, because they save the last flashback – of Paul threatening Mike with blood, a knife and a kiss – right to the end.

PAUL WHITE THE SERIAL KILLER.

Paul White's job is one of those occupations created for the movies: he sells and installs luxurious hi-fi. He's an artist! He builds elaborate wooden cases for the amplifiers. A different kind of fetishism (there are scenes of Paul at work in his garage, like an alchemist in her/ his laboratory, or a sculptor in her/ his studio).

Paul White's profession recalls those movie-movie jobs like Harry Caul's in *The Conversation* (1974), a sound recording specialist, or Thomas in *Blow-Up* (1966), a fashion photographer. In the novel *Mrs White*, Paul is a carpenter.

But the filmmakers don't go down the route of bugging and surveillance with Paul White's job; they do, however, make Paul an unusual kind of worker. For instance, he has a technique of humming in order to discern the best way to use the acoustics of a room with his arms outstretched (the allusions to religious chants like Hinduism's A-U-M or Native American songs are obvious).

Why does Paul White kill people? The movie does not offer clear-cut motives. Although *White of the Eye* is packed with psychoanalytical material, and evokes issues such as sex, marital breakdown, the problems of communication, Existential dissatisfaction, and of course insanity, it does not tie a pretty bow around the killer at the end. It's not 'cos of his mother (well, partly), or solitude, or child abuse, or sexual frustration, or a chip on the shoulder, or because everybody laughed at him in fourth grade when his swimwear slipped off in the pool. 'I did not try to diagnose or pass judgement on the reasons for serial murder', Donald Cammell said (U, 221). And the movie is better for it.

Paul White was a bad boy as a youth, in contrast to the novel *Mrs White*, and may have inherited the criminal tendencies from his father, just as his daughter Danielle seems to be 'anti-social' like her father Paul (U, 214f).

Cannibalism is hinted at in *White of the Eye* – that Paul White is one of those crazeee suckers who eats his victims. Once again, this sort of idea is not uncommon in horror movies.

THE MURDERS.

The murders're conducted in *White of the Eye* somewhat in the style of American TV cop shows. The identity of the killer is withheld: that's pointless in one way, because we know who the murderer is! In fact, in the Alfred Hitchcock model, it's so much juicier knowing who the criminal is from the start (as in *Shadow of a Doubt*, a masterpiece of a story about a murderer in small-town America). Hitchcock's movies were not whodunits or detective stories, in which someone investigates a crime and solves it.

> I've never used the whodunit technique, since it is concerned altogether with mystification, which diffuses and unfocusses suspense [explained Hitchcock]. It is possible to build an almost unbearable tension in a play or film in which the audience knows who the murderer is all the time, and from the very start they want to scream out to all the other characters in the plot, 'Watch for So-and-so! He's a killer!' There you have real tenseness and an irresistible desire to know what happens, instead of a group of characters deployed in a human chess problem.[8]

Anne Mason (Alberta Watson) appears for the first time in *White of the Eye* in a fur coat, recalling Pherber's first scene in *Performance*. And Anne plays the seductress, too, like Pherber; that scene is a riff on the 'bored housewife' theme of pornography: Paul is the TV repairman who's come round to fix Mrs Mason's satellite system. And, what a surprise, she comes onto him. Pure male fantasy stuff.

What lifts this above the mundane, though, is that the seduction's intercut with Joan running into Mike Desantos, now a car mechanic in a scruffy garage, and very down on his luck. So he never made it to L.A. By this time, Joan seems unhappy with Paul White, suspecting something is wrong. The encounter with Mike defies belief, script-wise, but it doesn't matter.

So what's clever about the writing in this middle section of the 1987 movie is how the erotic and adultery plot is entangled with the serial killer plot. When Joan drives out to Anne's place and discovers Paul's van parked down a dirt track, she slashes his tyres because she thinks he's in Anne's house having an affair (she'd be better off burying a knife in his neck!).

But when this comes out into the open, what does Paul White do? He returns to Mrs Mason's home and kills her! So when Joan is yelling at him in the police interview room, from her perspective it's all about emotional betrayal, and Paul having an affair, and lying about it through his teeth. As she tells him, she knows his act.

Paul White's victims (at least the ones on screen) are affluent, sexy

---

[8] C. Geduld, *Film Guide To 2001: A Space Odyssey*, Indiana University Press, Bloomington, IN, 1973, 128.

women (youngish or middle-aged).[9] That's part of the stereotype of the serial killer movie, of course: in the Hollywood rulebook, the stakes are higher if the victim is beautiful and sexy ('cos nobody gives a shit about fat, ugly girls). Yes, it's sexist and dumb, but that's Hollywood.

Paul White is an artist, too: he's the serial killer as would-be Pablo Picasso or Jackson Pollock. After he's done the deed, he arranges the murder scene artfully, including creating ancient, Native American crosses from household utensils. He obviously didn't know about CSI. (Donald Cammell remarked that he was after something like the abstraction of Piet Mondrian. In the movie, the cop Charles Mendoza refers to Pablo Picasso).[10]

The first murder in *White of the Eye* – of Joyce Patel – takes place in the kitchen of her home. In amongst the dramatic build-up to the killing (with the requisite point-of-view shots and images of eyes watching),[11] are numerous still-life arrangements, which wouldn't look out of place in a design magazine on contemporary American homes. Clean, neat lines – one can see Donald Cammell the painter (and production designer Philip Thomas, set decorator Richard Rutowski, and the prop master) arranging the objects *just so* on the tables and surfaces (as filmmakers such as Andrei Tarkovsky and Walerian Borowczyk liked to do. Somehow, that knife and that vase has to be placed *right there, like that* – and only the director can do it!).

There's a pay-off to all this somewhat obsessive arranging of still-lifes and vignettes of affluent living in suburban America: because when the murder occurs, Terry Rawlings and his editorial assistants go to town, cutting in numerous inserts of objects and small-scale actions: the vase tipping over, the flowers falling to the floor, the goldfish flipping on a piece of meat, etc. It's murder as a flashy montage.

Instead of depicting the knife going in – the meat shot of the pornography of killing[12] – the filmmakers cut to everything around the wrestling couple.[13] Glass breaking, water dripping, flowers falling, fish wriggling, liquid slopping around. Many another filmmaker uses tropes like a bottle or vase smashing to correspond to something a character's feeling, but in

---

[9] The first of Paul's victims is depicted shopping in Tuscon. The scenario of the affluent, attractive woman and the young guy carrying her boxes is employed, with the audience aligned with the guy's gaze at her body as he walks behind her to her car.
[10] And that's partly another clue – because Paul regards the way he designs hi-fi systems as something of an artform. In the novel, the identity of Paul as the killer is revealed in the first murder.
[11] *White of the Eye* is another movie that gets plenty of mileage out of its footage of giant eyes (usually it's Paul's eye, but sometimes it's Joan's eye).
[12] Alfred Hitchcock boasted that there is no shot of the knife penetrating Marion's skin in *Psycho*. Maybe not, but it's still one of the most violent and outrageous deaths in cinema history. Once seen, never forgotten.
[13] *White of the Eye* is another film that makes the age-old correspondences between death and sex, between one person murdering another person and sex.

White of the Eye there are multiple examples of such visual correspondences. In this respect, *White of the Eye* is not a gory picture, in the sense of showing graphic violence (no multiple squibs going off, as in a John Woo or Sam Peckinpah movie), but it is full of dread and the fear of violence. More of a Hitchcock than a Peckinpah approach.

BEAUTY, DEATH, MAGIC, TRAGEDY.

As Weston La Barre notes in his marvellous book of anthropology and psychology, *The Ghost Dance*,[14] there is not much difference between the artist, the genius, the criminal, the psychotic and the mad person, seen from one viewpoint. Donald Cammell's cinema explores the affinities between them all, which artists have long known about.

The German Romantic poet Novalis wrote:

> Madness and magic have many similarities. A magician is an artist of madnesses. (79)

Similarly, William Shakespeare wrote in *A Midsummer Night's Dream*: 'The lunatic, the lover and the poet,/ Are of imagination all compact.' (V.i.7) In the art of Shakespeare, there are deep connections between lovers, lunatics, poets – and fools. They are all caught up with some kind of 'madness', some kind of 'abnormal', 'extraordinary' subjectivity. Their goals may be different, but they are all connected psychologically. Similarly, for so many poets, love can be seen as a 'madness', and there is a narrow dividing line between the religious maniac and the fool ('love is essentially an illness; hence the miraculous significance of Christianity,' Novalis commented).[15] There is the 'holy fool' figure in Russian history, the 'trickster god' in ancient mythology, and King Lear's clown, the court jester who is allowed to transgress the boundaries that others are not allowed to cross. St Paul, after all, veered from madness to mysticism, and before his conversion and sainthood was an extremely unlikeable, morally dubious creature.

Novalis as a poet sees the unity of all things, so he writes: 'All barriers are only there for the traversing' (87). This is the Romantic poet talking here: this is a very Romantic notion, it seems, this perception that barriers are there to be transgressed. This is the poet as social rebel speaking, knowing that art must go to extremes. Thus, madness, poetry, idiocy, genius and love form a continuum which is life itself.

The dictum is perfect for an analysis of Donald Cammell's cinema: that once a barrier has been created, it has to be (it *demands* to be)

---
14 Weston La Barre: *The Ghost Dance*, Allen & Unwin, 1972.
15 *Works* (Tieck and Schlegel), 288

transgressed. Filmmaking as an eternal fairy tale, an eternal creation and breaking of prohibitions, leading to the breaking of all taboos.

Friedrich Nietzsche had a theory that the more tragic tragedy becomes, the more sensual it becomes. In other words, tragedy has a sensual dimension which increases as the sense of tragedy increases. William Shakespeare's tragedies are his most erotic works. Think of the erotic entanglements of love and death in *Macbeth*, or *King Lear*.

The German Romantic poet Novalis too spoke of the erotic quality of intensity and absolutism. Power is an aphrodisiac, it is said: the powerful people are those who can go to extremes. Tragic characters go to extremes – Macbeth, Oedipus, Othello – they push against their ontological boundaries. They practice a kind of absolutism or extremism that seems particularly Romantic. Novalis notes the sensuality of power and extremism in his fragments, as when he writes:

All absolute sensation is religious. (197)

Tragic power and political power is sexual and seductive, and so is magical power. Novalis asserts that:

Magic is like art – to wilfully use the sensual realm. (119)

Magicians throughout history have also been erotic figures: Aleister Crowley, Georg Gurdjieff, Merlin, Paracelsus. The eroticism of magic is obvious: witchcraft, for instance, was and is regarded in sexual terms. Witchcraft was a heresy, certainly, that disturbed the Church for religious reasons, but many of the accusations brought against witchcraft were of a sexual nature.

Donald Cammell's movies are partly about the sensual attraction of great power – the figures of the gangsters and rocks stars in *Performance*, for example, or the serial killer in *White of the Eye*.

THE FINALE

White of the Eye gets sillier and sillier towards the end. Poor Joan finds body parts hidden under her bath. But no, she doesn't freak out and grab her daughter and get the hell out of there. No! She doesn't make a simple phone call to the authorities (characters in these sorts of movies *never* do). No! She doesn't call up that mobster she knew from a crazee night in Vegas and ask him to shoot her husband in the head. No! She stays in the house, and listens to her husband's bonkers confession.

And after Paul White's confessed to multiple murders, Joan *still* doesn't run away with Danielle. Oh, no: she lets Paul fuck her! This is where *White of the Eye* is truly perverse: the filmmakers seem to be saying, well, this woman really *lerrrves* her man! So much so that she'll tup him after he's confessed to killing a bunch of women, going back years, and right after she's discovered bits of bodies in the bathroom. He smashes his way into the closet, and instead of running like hell, she lets him do her! Insanity! (I don't think it's meant to be interpreted as a rape, either: it is not depicted, in movie terms, like a rape. Joan is portrayed as a submissive personality. Critics Rebecca and Sam Umland mention that it's an 'anal invasion', as they call it, though I'm not sure why they think it makes any difference if it's anal or vaginal intercourse). *White of the Eye* is a portrait of a very creepy, sadomasochistic relationship – marriage as slavery.

But the filmmakers of *White of the Eye* don't want to end things there, either. They want to stage a big chase and a cat-and-mouse scene and a climactic face-off. Except here is where a really good stunt co-ordinator[16] and stunt team and an action director is really required. Because, let's face it, Donald Cammell and his associates were not the best action filmmakers in the world. Not as bad as Jean-Luc Godard, who wilfully and self-consciously throws away action scenes and shoots them in a deliberately naff manner (the gun battle in *Prénom: Carmen*, for example, or ones at the end of *Vivre Sa Vie* or *Bande à Part*). But *White of the Eye* is still fairly mediocre, action-wise.

OK, let's forget the fact that none of the actions of Joan make much sense in the final reel of *White of the Eye* – how she drives along a dirt track to a friggin' quarry, instead of right into town! Or how instead of getting the hell away from this psycho, she crawls into the clothes closet and weeps.

Oh dear. Oh deary dear.

OK, let's forget all that, and forget that Mike Desantos just happens to show up, fully armed! And let's forget that the filmmakers have Mike push

---
16 Dan Bradley was stunt co-ordinator.

Paul White along into a quarry pit, which just so happens to be the perfect place for the practical effects guys (led by Thomas Ford) to stage a big explosion.

But even if we forget all that, and accept too that movies often get increasingly nutty in the final minutes, the action in *White of the Eye* is *still feeble*. There are some cinematic flourishes – like the camera strapped to David Keith's chest, *à la Mean Streets* or Raul Ruiz (actually, that technique goes back to *The Last Laugh* in 1924),[17] or Keith hollering like a maniac ('I love you, Joanie!'). But it's not enough.

One piece of back-story is saved for this climactic face-off in *White of the Eye*: just what the hell did happen on that crazy hunting trip ten years ago? Up in the hills, Paul White went a little nuts, twisting a dead deer's head, smearing blood on his muzzle, and threatening poor Mikey with a giant hunting knife (and kissing him too). Macho power, obscure ritual, vampiric blood-drinking, gay sex, and downright weirdness – it doesn't really matter, because the dramatic point of the scene is clear, however you want to slice it up: Paul has threatened Mike, asserted his superiority over him, as well as taking his woman.

Like other veteran editors, Terry Rawlings knows every trick in the trade. But even Rawlings couldn't make the climax really work. Apparently, Donald Cammell had asked Rawlings to tighten up the final reel by slicing two frames off every cut, an unusual method (but not unknown) of punching up the climax. Rawlings said editing that whole reel in one day had been a nightmare.

For Donald Cammell, Joan is clearly a masochist: she stays with her man even after discovering that he is a murderer. While her response may stretch credibility, and might depart from so-called 'reality', Cammell has seldom been concerned with being 'realistic'. *White of the Eye* is a dramatic movie: *dramatic*, that is, it's a heightened story, playing more like a fairy tale than something conventional in the so-called 'real' world (the allusions to opera emphasize the exaggerated aspects of the piece). The movie asks the question: what would you do if you found out you were married to Bluebeard?

That Joan stays with her guy and doesn't turn him in Donald Cammell thought would be more interesting:

> I thought it would be more interesting to have her deeply in love and, when she realized he was a psychopath, forced to decide whether to abandon him, or hang on in there and confront him with it and continue to love him, even up to the point where it degenerates into bestiality. (U, 216)

---

[17] For *The Last Laugh*, to simulate the drunkenness of the hero (the hotel porter, played by Emil Jannings), the camera was tied to camera operator Karl Freund's chest (on a little, wooden board).

WHITE OF THE EYE AND PIERROT LE FOU

White of the Eye has some affinities with *Pierrot le Fou*, a 1965 movie written and directed by Jean-Luc Godard): most obviously when Donald Cammell consciously refers to *Pierrot le Fou* by having Paul White strap himself up with bombs and bullets, and paint his face red, which's what Jean-Paul Belmondo does at the end of *Pierrot le Fou*.

Pierrot le Fou was a major event for some critics, filmmakers and viewers, a very important movie which echoes down the decades. For many young people, *Pierrot le Fou* had a huge impact, and became one of Jean-Luc Godard's more influential and beloved pictures. Critic Michel Cournot was nuts about it, writing: 'I feel no embarrassment declaring that *Pierrot le Fou* is the most beautiful film I've seen in my life'. Godard's future wife, Anne Wiazemsky, was very impressed with *Pierrot le Fou*, and wrote to him to tell him so; it was a turning-point in the beginning of their relationship.

Another affinity with *Pierrot le Fou* and *White of the Eye* is the notion of *Pierrot le Fou* being 'the last movie', the end of something, of everything – of cinema. In *Pierrot le Fou*, one can see how Jean-Luc Godard and his team were thinking along the lines of making the Last Film, or the last film that could be made about a romantic couple, or a film about the 'last romantic couple'.[18]

It's worth looking at the very end of *Pierrot le Fou*, because *White of the Eye* mirrors it in many ways: there's a face-off between three people, an erotic triangle (with all the usual aspects of jealousy and betrayal), a rocky setting next to water,[19] guns, and a guy with explosives strapped to his body.[20]

The very last section of *Pierrot le Fou* has Ferdinand Griffon (Jean-Paul Belmondo) pursuing Marianne Renoir (the divine Anna Karina) in a fishing boat, ending up in the rocky, dry, dusty terrain of South France, on the cliffs above the sea, the setting for the twin deaths that close *Pierrot le Fou*. Marianne's death has the appearance of a chase and an accident – Ferdinand seems to want to kill Fred (Dirk Sanders, her lover), not Marianne. So the time-honoured configurations of melodrama are evoked here, as Ferdinand kills his lover, Marianne.[21]

The 1965 film is deliberately (and irritatingly) incoherent in the gun

---

[18] And this talk of being the 'last' film or 'last romantic couple' of course relates very much to Arthur Rimbaud and *Une Saison en Enfer* and to the theme of suicide

[19] The film's set in the South-West desert, so it's significant that the filmmakers opt to stage the climax next to water.

[20] Other elements that *White of the Eye* and *Pierrot le Fou* share are anger – there's a huge amount of rage in *Pierrot le Fou*. And suicide.

[21] *White of the Eye*, meanwhile, couldn't have Paul killing Joan – that would be too much. It's Paul who *has to die*, but although the film hints at the possibility that Joan might finish him off (she asks Mike for the gun), she's also concerned when Mike's shot up Paul's legs.

battle, as usual in a Jean-Luc Godard movie, but it's pretty clear that Ferdinand Griffon shoots Fred first *then* he shoots Marianne Renoir. He kills her, when there's no real need to, now that Fred is apparently out of the way.

It's all shot in a hurried, one take manner, deliberately fake. No squibs, just a bit of red on the clothes (it's as far away from a Hong Kong action movie as you can imagine!). When Ferdinand Griffon carries his lover to a house (which's conveniently empty and unlocked), the film continues with its heightened, unreal form. Marianne Renoir dies on a blue bed (she has a wound in her forehead, which would presumably mean instant death). She says, 'I'm sorry', and Ferdinand uses the Thomas Hardyan phrase: 'too late'.[22]

Does Ferdinand Griffon kill Marianne Renoir in the classic tragic manner, to kill the one he loves? Does he do it because he can't bear the thought of her with someone else? Has he already decided to kill himself after shooting her? Is it, then, a kind of suicide pact? It could be any of these, and more, of course: it's a multi-purpose, melodramatic ending. What's for sure, is that it's already 'too late' when she's dying on the bed, as he tells her. (And it's definitely 'too late' for Joan and Paul White in *White of the Eye*, after his confession, or maybe way before that. But good ol' girl Joan still stays with her man).

The following scene in *Pierrot le Fou*, where Ferdinand Griffon wraps red and yellow-coloured explosives around his head, is certainly memorable. He doesn't do it in the house, but walks outside, bellowing incoherently, onto a cliff overlooking the sea – a most appropriate spot for a suicide (*White of the Eye* picked up the idea of the guy hollering – when Paul yells that he loves Joanie, and it's all going to be all right).

As he's wrapping the explosives around his skull, Ferdinand Griffon says, 'what I wanted to say...' but he doesn't say it. Is it a Rimbaudian renunciation of poetry, of saying? It certainly continues the Rimbaudian theme of *Pierrot le Fou*. Maybe it does have autobiographical links here: what *were* Jean-Luc Godard and his team of filmmakers going to say? And, surely, by the end of the film, they've already said it, if they were going

---

[22] The last section of *Pierrot le Fou* recalls the idyll at the end of *Tess of the d'Urbervilles*, when Angel Clare and Tess Durbeyfield live together for a few hours, on the run from the authorities because Tess has murdered Alec d'Urberville. The end of *Pierrot le Fou* has that same air of fatality and tragedy, like the end of a William Shakespeare play, like *Romeo and Juliet*. You know it's got to end badly, and the lovers put off facing up to it. Even *White of the Eye* has a bizarre kind of erotic interlude, when Joan and Paul tup *after* she's found conclusive evidence that he's a serial killer.

to say it at all?[23]

What makes this suicide sting is having Ferdinand Griffon appear to relent at the last moment, trying to put out the fuse, muttering *merde, merde*. It's a touch of comedy and tragedy which saves the scene from being completely suffocating. And when the film cuts to the long shot of the explosion on the cliff and slowly pans to the right, it's an ending at once silly, irritating, a cheat, as well as pathetic, sad and hopoeless.

By contrast, Paul White in *White of the Eye*, desperate at the end, lights the fuse, but grabs onto Mike Desantos's leg, to take him down with him. Mike gets his own back, for a short moment, when he unloads the gun right into Paul's face (though the movie doesn't show that in detail).[24]

White of the Eye closes with 20 different second unit shots of the explosion in the quarry (from inside the quarry, from up on the cliffs, from a helicopter, etc). Hell, it *is* a Hollywood movie! (where big stunts are typically filmed with a bunch of cameras).

But in *Pierrot le Fou*, Jean-Luc Godard and Raoul Coutard opt for a single long shot of the explosion, with the camera drifting to the right, across the Mediterranean, with the sea low in the frame, until it reaches the sun. It's the final shot, an ecstatic shot.

A verse from Arthur Rimbaud's *A Season In Hell* is quoted after the deaths of Marianne and Ferdinand, at the end of the 1965 film. Both Marianne and Ferdinand whisper the lines in voiceover:

Elle est retrouvée!
– Quoi? – l'Eternité.
C'est la mer mêlée
   Au soleil.[25]

An angelic ending? Beyond death? Love conquering death? Maybe: it can be fulfilment, or heaven, or more despair and irony. It's one of those multi-purpose endings.[26]

No ecstatic, love-in-death ending for *White of the Eye*, though: Paul White has gone too far, is psychotic, and a multiple murderer. And Marianne in *Pierrot le Fou* wouldn't put up with Paul – she'd have left him

---

[23] That sudden inrush of a lack of confidence, which assails Godard's characters from time to time, is very understandable, and not just for artists, but it isn't something that Godard has to worry about. He is a major, major artist who is always saying something, always creative, always full of insights.

But even geniuses have nagging doubts now and again. It's just the rest of us who look at them and think, what are they worrying about? They are Michelangelo Buonarroti! They are Vincent van Gogh! They are Arthur Rimbaud!

[24] Few movies do – not only is it a difficult special effect to achieve, it's also summat that censors don't like.

[25] The translation by Andrew Jary of the first stanza which the film quotes runs thus: 'It is rediscovered! | – What? – Eternity. | It is the sea frayed | With the sun.' (A. Rimbaud, *A Season In Hell*, Crescent Moon, 2007).

[26] The poem itself is certainly intended by Rimbaud to be ecstatic; its position in *A Season In Hell* evokes former ecstatic states (and the poet's former life, when he quotes it).

ages ago (besides Paul is just too serious and self-absorbed for Marianne; but Marianne does leave Ferdinand, of course, when she tells him she wants more to life than bumming around in the same clothes by the sea in South France).

WHITE OF THE EYE AND OTHER MOVIES

The allusions to cinema in *White of the Eye* include *More* (Barbet Schroeder, 1969), in the opening image of the sun, *Psycho*, and *Love Is My Profession* (1958), where Brigitte Bardot reveals her body to Jean Gabin.

As well as *Pierrot le Fou*, *White of the Eye* also consciously evokes *Peeping Tom*, a 1959 thriller written by Leo Marks and directed by Michael Powell, in the scene where Paul White drowns Anne in the bath, and holds up a mirror, so she can witness her own death visually.[27] In *Peeping Tom*, Carl Boehm's serial killer had a mirror fixed to his tripod, so his victims could watch themselves screaming as they were stabbed and filmed.

Peeping Tom was lambasted by some critics on its release, but has since become a cult favourite for some viewers. *Peeping Tom* was bound to be appreciated by certain filmmakers and critics, especially the late modernists and postmodernists. Like *Psycho*, *Peeping Tom* lends itself well to a rigorous, filmic deconstruction with its dramatic exploration of the relation between desire and looking, desire and death, desire and women, desire and cinema, desire and art. *Peeping Tom* (like *Psycho*, and like *Performance*), is one of those films that becomes an endlessly discussed 'text' in critical cinema studies, a film almost tailor-made for critics to bring in Sigmund Freud, Jacques Lacan, Slavoj Zizek, voyeurism, scopophilia, the mirror image, narcissism and intertextuality.

With all those bathroom scenes in *White of the Eye*, a recurring location in Donald Cammell's cinema (and also in Jean-Luc Godard's cinema), it recalls *Psycho*, the granddaddy of all serial killer movies.[28] In *White of the Eye*, Anne is killed in the bathroom, and Paul White stashes his trophies away in the bathroom. *Psycho* of course brilliantly exploited the vulnerability of being naked in the shower, unarmed, and far from help.

Alfred Hitchcock is definitely a presence lurking behind *White of the*

---
[27] This foreshadows Donald Cammell's own death.
[28] Although *Psycho* and *Peeping Tom* were different films, it's interesting that Alfred Hitchcock could make his piece about a twisted killer and be lauded for it, while Michael Powell was vilified.

Eye (as with *Demon Seed*: the film reworks elements of *Shadow of a Doubt* (1943), for instance: the small American town where a murderer lurks, and only one person knows that kind, old uncle Charlie (Joseph Cotten) is really the Merry Widow killer. *White of the Eye* depicts exactly the kind of suburban American town that Hitch liked to explore – you can see it in *The Birds* and *The Trouble With Harry*.

And, exactly as Alfred Hitchcock would have done, *White of the Eye* lets the audience in on the identity of the killer early on, so the suspense derives from *when* and *how* the murderer will be revealed. Although *White of the Eye* employs the classic devices of the 1980s stalk 'n slash movie to stage the murders – the ominous music, the rapid montage, the point-of-view shots, the sneaky Steadicam movements – and it withholds a long shot of the murders, or a C.U. of the killer's face.

Alfred Hitchcock often described the basic premise of suspense: placing a bomb in a suitcase under a table while two people talk, and letting the audience know that there's a bomb in the suitcase. That's fundamental suspense (and as Hitch explained, the price is never paid – the bomb never explodes). In *White of the Eye*, there's a bomb ticking throughout the movie – Paul White, a serial killer who's trying harder to deflect suspicion. But the audience knows that Paul is going to go off at some point (and he does, literally!).

WHITE OF THE EYE AND HORROR MOVIES

The horror film genre has several celebrated epochs: the German Expressionist era, with masters such as Fritz Lang, F.W. Murnau and Paul Leni, and films like *The Cabinet of Dr Caligari*, *The Golem* and *Nosferatu*; the great Universal *Frankenstein* and *Dracula* movies, the era of James Whale, Todd Browning, Boris Karloff, Lon Chaney and Bela Lugosi; the B-movies and 'creature features' of the 1950s; Britain's Hammer Studio's colour remakes of the Universal films; Alfred Hitchcock's ground-breaking *Psycho* (and *The Birds*); the demon/ devils films of the 1960s and 1970s: *Rosemary's Baby*, *Repulsion*, *The Devils*, *The Omen* and *The Exorcist*, and directors like Roman Polanski and William Friedkin; the 'slasher', 'stalk 'n' slash' and 'video nasties' of the late 1970s and early 1980s, *Hallowe'en*, *Friday the 13th*, *Amityville Horror*, *Nightmare On Elm Street*, *The Texas Chainsaw Massacre*, and filmmakers such as John Carpenter, Brian de Palma, Wes Craven, Sam Raimi, David Cronenberg, Dario Argento, George Romero, Tobe Hooper, and Abel Ferrera; and the 'postmodern' horror films: the *Scream* series (1996 onwards), the *I Know What You Did Last Summer* series (1997 onwards), *Wes Craven's New Nightmare* (1994), the *Blair Witch Project* films (1999 onwards), the *Urban Legend* films (1998 onwards), and the *Scary Movie* series (2000 onwards), providing a very welcome and very funny debunking of horror movie clichés.

It's possible to see *White of the Eye* as part of the rise in horror film production following the massive success of movies such as *Hallowe'en*. The 'slasher' and 'video nasty' horror films of the late 1970s/ early 1980s were also called 'stalker' or 'stalk 'n' slash' films, 'slice 'n' dice' films, 'body count' films, and 'teenie-kill'.

These included: the *Friday the 13th* films (1980 onwards), the *Nightmare On Elm Street/* Freddy Kruger series (1984 onwards), the *Hallowe'en* series (1978 onwards), the *Psycho* sequels, the *Amityville Horror* films (1979 onwards), *The Exorcist* sequels (1977 onwards), *Final Exam* (1981), *My Bloody Valentine* (1981), *Deadly Blessing* (1981), *New Year's Evil* (1981), *The Burning* (1981), *Happy Birthday To Me* (1981), *Night School* (1981), *The Slumber Party Massacre* (1982), *Visiting Hours* (1982), *Driller Killer* (1979), *The Toolbox Murders* (1979), *Terror Train* (1980), *Prom Night* (1980), *Hell Night* (1981), *Graduation Day* (1981), *The Evil Dead* (1983), the *Hellraiser* films (1985 onwards), the *Lawnmower Man* series (1992 onwards), the *Candyman* films (1992 onwards), and the seminal slasher, *The Texas Chainsaw Massacre* (1974).

Some of these low budget horror flicks were made by directors who became celebrated: Wes Craven, Sam Raimi, David Cronenberg, George Romero, and Abel Ferrera (special effects and make-up technicians also became fetishized: Tom Saviani, Carlo Rambaldi, Dick Smith, Rob Bottin, Albert Whitlock, Stan Winston and Rick Baker).

Horror authors were also celebrated: Stephen King, Dennis Wheatley, Clive Barker, and James Herbert, among more recent authors, and 'classic' writers such as H.P. Lovecraft, Mary Shelley, Robert Louis Stevenson, Bram Stoker and Edgar Allan Poe. There were also bigger budget, A-list horror movies at the time, such as *The Shining* (1980), *The Hunger* (1983), *Dressed to Kill* (1980), *Poltergeist* (1982), *Fright Night* (1985), and *An American Werewolf in London* (1981).

Economics played a large part in the revival of the horror flick in the late 1970s: as soon as studios, executives and distributors saw that gorefests could be lucrative, they started to make their own, remade earlier films, or got into endless rounds of sequels, copies and spin-offs. Splatter movies could be made cheaply: they did not require A-list stars; they could use young and largely unknown (i.e., cheap) casts; they did not require expensive sets or costumes; they could be set in pre-existing locations; and they did not need extensive script work or rewrites. (Most of 'em follow the simple formula of a girl and a monster, or a group of kids and a monster).

The late 1970s and early 1980s saw a massive increase in horror film production: from 35 films in 1979 to 70 in 1980 and 93 in 1981 (there was another peak between 1986 and 1987, which was the time of *White of the Eye* of course). In the 1990s came the 'postmodern' or ironic horror film, still aimed at the same (largely female)[29] teenage audience: *Scream, I Know What You Did Last Summer, Blair Witch Project, Scary Movie*, etc. Though postmodern, self-reflexive, full of in-jokes and allusions to other movies, these were still primarily horror films, with the requisite buckets of blood, gory make-up effects, violence, the supernatural, stalking, repressed sexuality, and dæmonic father figures.

One of the offshoots of the resurgence in the horror genre from the late 1970s inwards was the elevation of the villains, the demons, psychos and murderers, to the status of hero and icon: Jason (*Friday the 13th*), Freddy Krueger (*Nightmare On Elm Street*), Michael (*Hallowe'en*), Norman Bates (*Psycho*), Leatherface (*Texas Chainsaw Massacre*), and Pinhead (*Hellraiser*). *White of the Eye* isn't one of those sorts of films, but it is a movie in which the protagonist is a mass murderer.

The ancestor of the 'slasher'/ 'teenie-kill'/ horror movies of the late 1970s and 1980s, the films that inaugurated the revival in splatter flicks, are sometimes taken to be *The Texas Chainsaw Massacre*, or *The Exorcist* (from 1974 and 1973 respectively).

Other critics go back further, to 1960's *Psycho*. Hitch's black comedy had many of the elements of the modern slasher/ horror film: the social outsider anti-hero/ killer, who is schizophrenic, voyeuristic, sexually repressed, painfully shy, and comes from a damaged family;[30] the sexually active (and beautiful) female victim; the murder weapon (a knife) and phallic slashing (most 'slasher' films contain images of stabbing, slashing, tearing, and rending); the Middle American setting; the 'castle' or haunted house of classic horror (with the basement being the forbidden room); the attacks are sudden, shocking, and shot from the victim's point-of-view;

---

[29] The audience for slasher/ 'teenie kill' horror films is 55% female, even though much of the violence is directed by men against women.
[30] The killer is not always fundamentally masculine and phallic – sometimes he is sexually repressed, or a virgin, or celibate, or a transvestite, or transsexual. In *White of the Eye*, Paul White certainly has hang-ups – it's all to do with the mother, the black hole at the heart of the universe. But the filmmakers also make him sexually attractive to women – the way he wins Joan away from Mike, for instance, in the flashbacks, or how Anne Mason seduces him.

and there are bravura camera angles, moves and tricks.

Another important predecessor was *Jaws* (director Steven Spielberg was, like most of the 'movie brats', an *aficionado* of Alfred Hitchcock, and *Jaws*, as well as Spielberg's other films as director, employed not a few Hitchcockian effects, including the track-and-zoom from *Vertigo*).

Jaws presaged the 'slasher'/ 'body count' films in many ways: it revived the B-movie format, the simple structure of a girl and a monster (in the opening sequence); the monster which has supernatural powers; the monster that will never go away, can never be defeated, until right at the end; the subjective viewpoint of the shark; the pranks and false alarms that increase suspense; the holiday setting (July 4th weekend) which was popular in subsequent horror flicks. (And was sequelized and cloned).

The typical setting for the modern 'slasher' film is suburban America and Middle America, which *White of the Eye* employs down to the tiniest detail – a small town, a college campus, summer camp, allowing for isolation and vulnerability (the Whites handily live some ways from other houses).

The typical narrative structure has a gory murder at the beginning of the picture, with subsequent deaths throughout the film, as the victims are picked off one by one, until the monster is revealed and killed at the end (the series of victims may arise from the simple Hollywood formula of 'more is better' – having six victims instead of one). *White of the Eye* follows that basic narrative structure.

Some horror movies use the detective or murder mystery format, with the identity and motives of the killer being revealed and explained at the end of the film, as in the traditional whodunit. Others, like *White of the Eye*, show the killer early on (though not in the very first murder scene).

Stalkers and monsters favour masks – hockey masks, ski masks, gas masks, cartoon masks, etc (Paul White in *White of the Eye* has his own 'killer' outfit', which includes a pair of gloves). Many horror monsters are apparently unkillable, relentlessly inventive, emotionally dead, vicious loners. They often have a supernatural aspect to them, linking them to earlier murderers, or demons, or the Devil.

The archetypal shot of the modern horror movie is the subjective shot, the killer's point-of-view, filmed with a handheld camera, or a Steadicam glide (which *White of the Eye* employs fully). Other typical shots include low angles and high angles, or the tilted camera; the camerawork in horror films is often self-conscious, making the viewer aware of framing, movement and space. The camera often teases the audience, playing games with their expectations, cueing false alarms, jokes and pranks, and surprise appearances. The music is often very busy in horror films, guiding the viewer and their reactions; offscreen noises are often employed (such as creaking doors or heavy breathing).

White of the Eye also employs editing techniques such as washes out to white, giant C.U.s of an eye, reversed (negative) colour film stock, freeze frames, step-motion, Donald Cammell's signature rapid montage, and bleached-out stock for the flashbacks to the 1970s.

White of the Eye exploits subjective camera to the full, particularly, as one would expect, in the murder scenes. These are scenes which filmmakers love to shoot – no, not because they are crazy murderers! (well, not all of them!) – but because these scenes are perfect for exploring the possibilities of making cinema to the max. You've got everything in a murder scene: all of the experimentation with the camera, with viewpoints, with eyes and the lens, with manipulating time and space, and with the motifs of the looker and the looked-at, the hunter and the hunted.

In short, you'd have to be a really bad filmmaker if you couldn't deliver a compelling murder sequence. That sounds morbid, but horror films and murder mysteries are morbid! If you want to see it like that.

The use of first-person camerawork in horror movies not only aligns the viewer as a sadistic spectator, it also preserves the murderer's identity. Thus, the killer is kept as an unidentified, menacing, perhaps supernatural presence. As the camera can appear to 'control' the action in a film, because all scenes and shots are staged specifically for the camera's benefit, the first-person camera in horror cinema can appear as if the killer is controlling events. If a successful murder is only ever seen from the perspective of the killer, it seems as if the psychotic personality is controlling everything in front of the camera.

Among the ingredients in the formulaic stalk 'n' slash, slasher, or 'teenie kill' horror flick (many of which you can see in *White of the Eye*) were: a psychopath or monster attacking a mixed group; the psycho/monster picks off the group one by one; people who have sex or take drugs or make jokes are usually rewarded with death; the 'final girl' survives to the end to dispatch the psycho/ monster after lengthy chases; the 'final girl' is a tomboy, virginal, a do-gooder, intelligent, resourceful; the 'final girl' has a 'masculine' name (Sidney, Will, Joey, Max, Stretch, Laurie, Terry, Marti, Stevie); gore; the weapon of choice is a knife, axe, or blade; combat is always hand-to-hand and up-close (no guns or poisons); the authorities (such as the police) are conspicuously absent; victims always run upstairs or into the basement to escape the killer, instead of outside; they never call the police or authorities; the attacks usually occur at night; the screams of the victim are never heard; the locations are labyrinthine, dark, threatening and devoid of people who can help (basements, colleges, schools, halls of residence, enormous empty houses);[31] the deaths are extravagant; there's some crime or evil act which in the past which needs to be righted (or some murder or mis-deed the psycho/ monster committed which resurfaces); the psycho/ monster always returns in the sequel; the sequels get increasingly louder and sillier; the proto-feminism (of the heroines) is countered by mindless frat boy, jock antics; the psycho/ monster is usually male and wears a mask or hood; the psycho/ monster is incredibly resilient and virtually indestructible (and often has supernatural powers); he (it's usually a 'he') is also unstoppable and keeps attacking relentlessly; the psycho/ monster can appear suddenly anywhere at any time; the psycho/ monster often becomes a cult figure (Jason Voorhees, Michael Myers, Hannibal Lecter, Norman Bates, Leatherface, Freddy Krueger, etc).

It's surprising just how many of those elements *White of the Eye* contains. The knife, the gun, the heroine locked in the attic, the point-of-view killer shots, the killer's disguise, Joan hides in a closet, the isolated locales, etc. And in *White of the Eye* the writers also deliberately subverted genre expectations: the murders take place during the day, in bright, white interiors, for instance.

For Robin Wood (in *American Nightmare: Essays On the Horror Film*), horror films are about 'all that our civilisation *represses* and *oppresses*: its re-emergence dramatised, as our nightmares'. Wood reckoned that there were two kinds of repression at work: the basic repression needed to live as an individual, and the 'surplus repression' of society, imposed by social forces, which creates the norm of 'monogamous heterosexual bourgeois patriarchal capitalists'. Anything outside that is other; the monster is a political 'return of the repressed', Wood noted in *Hollywood From Vietnam To Reagan.*

Roger Dadoun suggested (in "Fetishism in the Horror Film") that the monster offers a sign of totality, an illusory autonomy, that may be why horror films are popular in times of social unease.[32] For Linda Williams, the horror film monster is feminized; the monster's power derives from its sexual difference from the normal man; the monster is like a woman seen from a traumatized male viewpoint, with strange and disturbing hungers and needs.[33] The monster may be seen not as a castrated male, but as someone like the mother or a woman, someone whose sexual difference lies in not being castrated because they don't possess a penis; the woman's

---
[31] The Whites' house in *White of the Eye* is isolated.
[32] R. Dadoun: "Fetishism in the Horror Film", in Donald, 1989.
[33] L. Williams, in M. Doane, 1983

look at the monster in horror films is thus a recognition of their propinquity, as threats to the dominant patriarchal system.

For Barbara Creed, the monster in horror cinema is linked to the masochistic aspects of looking, because the monster is constructed as abject (irrational, perverse) and feminized. Thus, writes Creed, in *The Monstrous-Feminine* (using Julia Kristeva's theory of abjection), 'the male spectator is punished, as he looks at the abject body of the other – his monstrous, feminized gender counterpart' (131). In horror cinema, the abject body is aligned with the feminine and the 'socially denigrated', while the symbolic body is masculine and valorized (ibid.). Castration anxiety may be behind horror cinema's obsession with blood, especially bleeding women, reckons Creed (1986). Noël Carroll suggested (in *The Philosophy of Horror*) that monsters have two qualities: impurity and dangerousness; monsters are hybrids; they defy categorization, they cross boundaries.

White of the Eye is a slice of American Gothic – it's Jack the Ripper in the Arizonian desert.[34] The poetics of the Gothic, the horrific and the sublime have affinities with Julia Kristeva's psychoanalytic theory of the abject. Kristeva's abject relates to transgression, ambiguity and primal drives, all of which form the foundation of the horror film. However, despite the imagery of transgression, excess and taboo- and rule-breaking in horror cinema, they often end up endorsing Western, middle-class, mainstream values.[35] Thus, even those film directors who are celebrated by critics as producing ironic, postmodern or *avant garde* horror films (David Cronenberg, Tobe Hooper, Sam Raimi, Wes Craven *et al*) wind up with banal, melodramatic forms and petit bourgeois values. From transgressive to trivial, from horror movie to TV soap. Slasher horror films tend to be highly moralistic: the killer is dispatched, good and evil are clearly demarcated; there's no ambiguity about who are the heroes and who are the villains; even though the murderers kill victims throughout the films, there is always one person who will finally destroy the murderer. And when the psychopaths return in the sequel, there is always another hero/ine who'll confront them. (Or put it like this: American postmodern cinema may be 'postmodern', but it still upholds the American values of dualism, simplistic morality, good vs. evil, pro-militarism, and the American way of life).

---

[34] One of Donald Cammell's unmade projects was a script about Jack the Ripper that Cammell had co-written with critic Kenneth Tynan (U, 65).
[35] 'Although the popular tradition of horror and terror gestures towards the abject, the transgressive, the sublime, or whatever it is, its representation as morality tale or melodrama places it squarely on the side of a moralistic mass culture, or petit bourgeois kitsch', comments James Donald ("The Fantastic, the Sublime and the Popular", in J. Donald, 1989, 243).

(© Paramount)

This is like a 'guess the caption' picture.

You can't be a serial killer in movies unless you have a Really Big Knife: White of the Eye.

The happy, loving, white American couple.
Unfortunately, one of them is a serial killer.
(Note the not-so-subtle mise-en-scène of the
dead animal on the couch below, familiar tropes
of death—killing—hunting—victims—machismo).

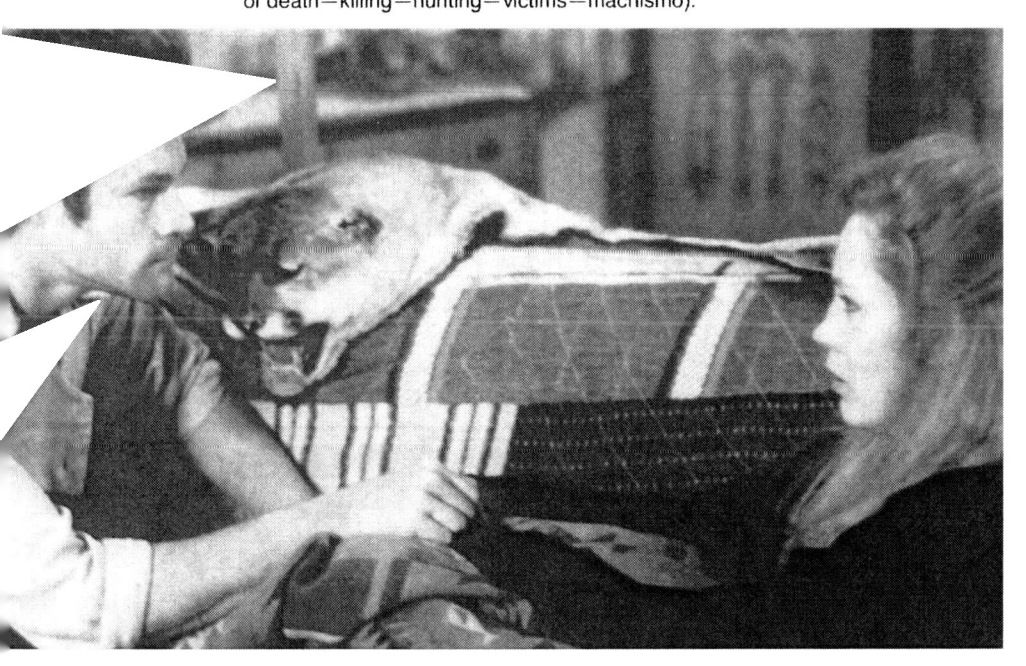

Someone once said of Citizen Kane that the Rosebud stuff was 'dollar-book Freud':
well, you've got the same psycho-silly thing going on here in White of the Eye:
a man with a big knife (plus a nod to Jean-Luc Godard's Pierrot le Fou).

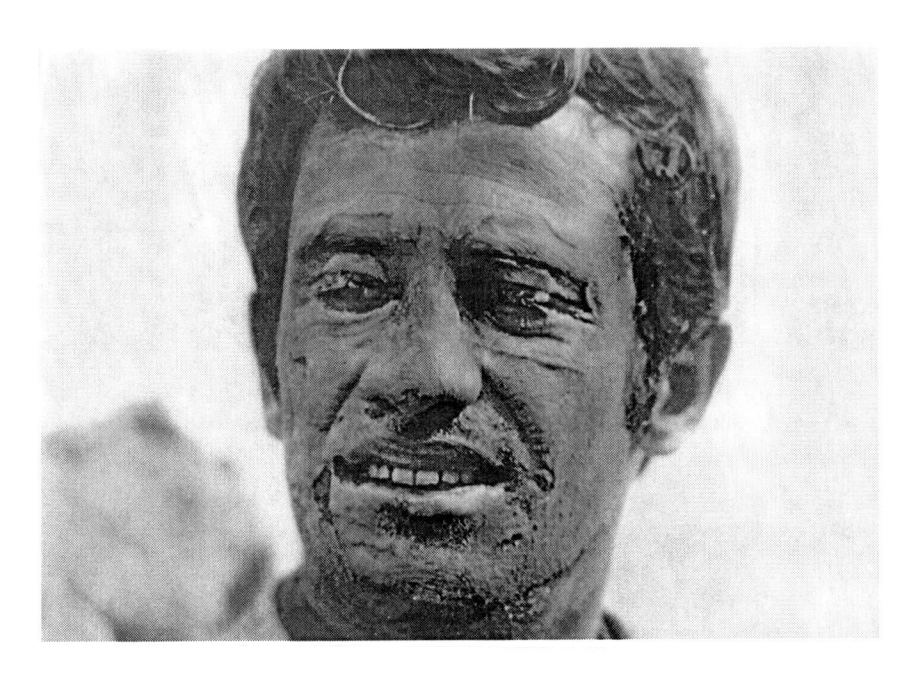

Jean-Paul Belmondo in the suicidal finale of Pierrot le Fou –
'What I wanted to say was… Shit!'

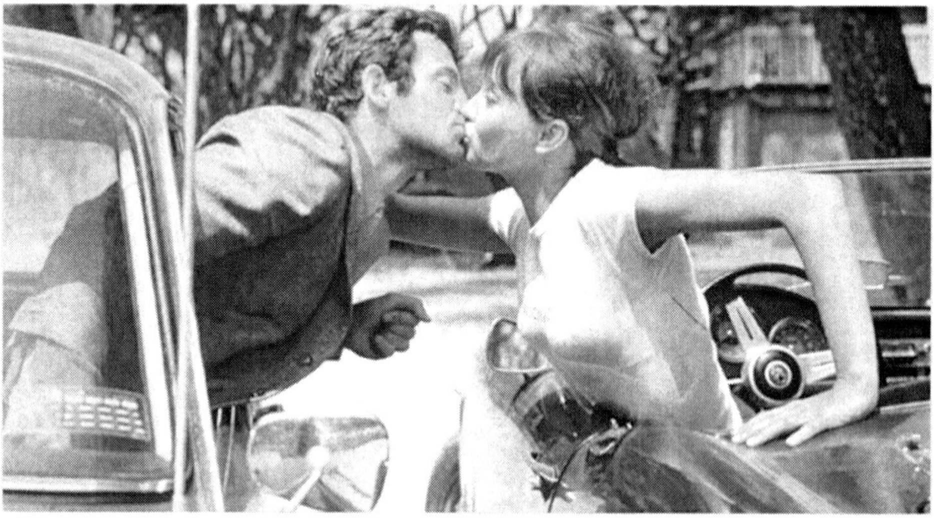

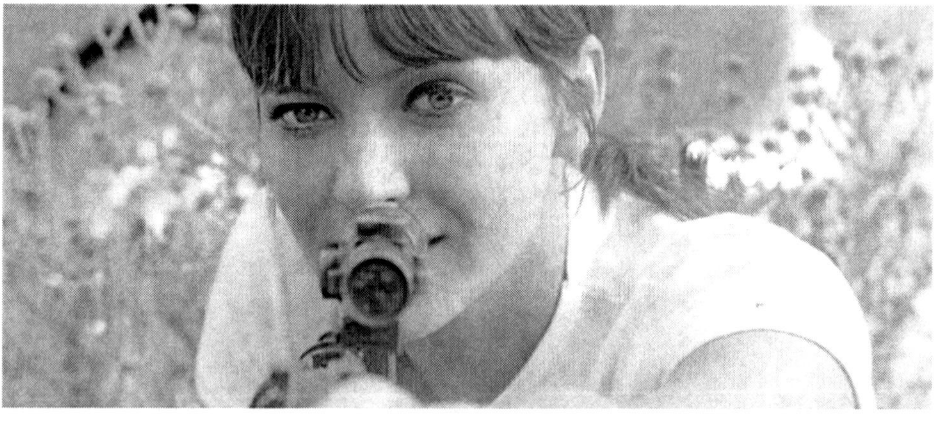

WILD SIDE

6
WILD SIDE
☆

Wild Side (1995/ 2000) was Donald Cammell's last film as director (but was restored in a 'director's cut' after his death).[1] *Wild Side* contains all of the usual Donald Cammell motifs and themes: death, violence, identity (and switching identities), sex, gangsters, guns, money, a contemporary, urban setting, rapid cutting, flashbacks, etc.

The budget for *Wild Side* was in the region of $3.5 million. The production had been announced as a $9 million project by Nakamura Goldman Productions in May, 1994,[2] but Nu Image scaled it back. The production company Nu Image was created by Avi Lerner, Danny Lerner, Danny Dimbort and Trevor Short. Its speciality was exploitation fare, for the new markets of video and cable television.

Wild Side was produced by Elie Cohn, Boaz Davidson, Donald Cammell, Joan Chen, China Kong, Nick Jones, John Langley, Hamish McAlpine. The xecutive producers were Danny Dimbort, Avi Lerner, Andrew Pfeffer, Danny Short, Trevor Short, Roger Trilling. Ryûichi Sakamoto composed the score; Sead Mutarevic was DP; casting was Pamela Guest; production designer was Claire Jenora Bowin; set decoration by Shana Sigmond; costume design by Alison Hirsch; Scott Williams was hair stylist; Ashley Scott was makeup artist; Paul Martin was first A.D.;and Benjamin Patrick was sound mixer.

The shooting schedule for *Wild Side* was short – from Feb 2 to March 3, 1995. Of course, that's only compared to a big Hollywood movie – because some filmmakers could shoot even quicker than that – Jean-Luc Godard and any Hong Kong movie once again being the obvious examples.

And when critics talk about short shooting schedules – such as the 23 days for Orson Welles' *Macbeth* (1948) – they are forgetting the months that go into the development of the script. And pre-production, in many ways the key production period, extends into months. And of course, a movie such as *Wild Side* requires an intensive editing period. Thus, the shooting can be the easiest or simplest bit.

THE CAST.

All of the actors in *Wild Side* are terrific, with the central foursome being particularly outstanding: Anne Heche, Christopher Walken, Steve Bauer[3] and Joan Chen.

---

1 Frank Mazzola and his wife oversaw this version of *Wild Side*; it was released in 1999, and Hamish McAlpine, Donald Cammell's friend, paid for it. The *Director's Cut* of *Wild Side* is 115 minutes; the Nu Image version is 95 minutes; excluding credits, about 18 minutes extra footage is included in the *Director's Cut*.
2 Nakamura Goldman Productions was formed by Ken Nakamura, Dai-Ichi Motion Pictures, and David Goldman, a former Hollywood agent.
3 Donald Cammell had admired Bauer in *Scarface* (1983). That movie is much loved, and has become a cult classic in the gangster and crime genres. Al Pacino's mannered, self-conscious turn as a gangster falling apart dominates the movie.

Every critic has drawn attention to the over-the-top performance of Christopher Walken in *Wild Side*, and he is truly amazing. But *Wild Side* is Anne Heche's film, through and through. Not really because she is the main character, but because she delivers a fabulously neurotic and, in its own way, quite bonkers performance. It's 'out there' like Walken's turn as Bruno Buckingham, but in a different way.

Prior to *Wild Side*, Anne Heche (born May 25, 1969) had appeared in *The Adventures of Huck Finn, The Juror* and *Milk Money*. After *Wild Side*, Heche was featured in *Volcano, Donnie Brasco, Wag the Dog, Psycho, Six Days Seven Nights* and *Superman*. But she's never been better than in *Wild Side* (parts like this are very thin on the ground for anybody – but especially for women). However, Heche wasn't the first choice: Donald Cammell wanted Lori Singer.

Off-screen, Anne Heche is a perfect actress for a Donald Cammell movie (or a Jackie Collins novel): she had a troubled upbringing (including being abused by her father), and had relationships with both men and women, including Ellen DeGeneres, Steve Martin, Richard Burg, David Forsyth and James Tupper (actors), Coleman Laffoon (a cameraman), and Lindsey Buckingham (of Fleetwood Mac). Inevitably, some people interpreted Heche's character in *Wild Side* biographically – particularly the lesbianism.

Allen Garfield has a cameo in *Wild Side* as Alex Lee's banker boss, Randall, at Long Beach Pacific Bank. (The scene between Alex and Randall is played the same as that police chief and cop scene that we've seen a zillion times: the police captain bawls out his underling.)

STYLE AND THEMES.

In *Wild Side*, everyone is on edge, highly neurotic, paranoid, fearful, and close to a nervous breakdown. No one is what they seem. The sarcasm, bitterness, irony, the put-downs, the swearing, the savagery of the social attitudes, the barely suppressed violence – these are routine elements of any thriller or cop show or *film noir* – going back to the Thirties. Yes, the 'bad language' and dialogue is cruder in the thrillers and cop shows of the 1990s, when *Wild Side* was produced, compared to the 1930s or 1940s, but in no way are the 1990s more cynical or more neurotic (in fact, you could argue that cinema of the 1990s and 2000s is more sentimental, more reactionary, less challenging, less radical and less edgy than the equivalents in the 1930s).

There is a welter of suppressed rage and violence in *Wild Side*, that threatens to erupt at any moment. Characters seem on the verge of lashing out at each other, even though most of the action is staged in rooms with two or three people talking to each other. *Wild Side* is a movie *thick* with dialogue, pages and pages of it, dialogue that rattles on and on throughout scenes. In that sense, *Wild Side* is certainly over-written and over-wrought, unless you think of it as a twisted, eroticized version of the screwball comedies of the 1930s and 1940s, the last period in North American cinema when dialogue was truly rapid.

The atmosphere of paranoia and neurosis is enhanced in *Wild Side* by the restless, prowling Steadicam camerawork.[4] This was *de rigeur* in crime and thriller movies of the 1990s set in contemporary urban worlds (*Pulp Fiction, Hard Eight, Natural Born Killers, Casino,* and films such as *Showgirls, Scream* and *Starship Troopers*). When in doubt, fling the Steadicam around: it gave movies a feeling of movement and dynamism, even when there was very little kinetic energy in the scripts, the blocking or the acting.

Although *Wild Side* is part of that trend, handheld camerawork was always a part of Donald Cammell's bag of tricks as a director – a large proportion of *Performance* is handheld, for instance. In the late 1990s and up to the present, the gimmick is to wave the camera around with a long lens, to give the impression that scenes are being filmed on the hoof, in a rush, and often from a distance, as if a documentary crew is observing the action from afar, zooming in.

I hate it! I hate this kind of wobbly camerawork!

This kind of filmmaking is just as irritating as the pointless waving around of the Steadicam. You can hear the producer or director issuing the requests on set: *oh, fuck it, wave the camera around a bit to liven things up.* And in post, they'll say, *cut cut cut, faster, faster, faster!,* as if audiences have the attention span of an insect that only lives for a few hours. But the *storytelling* and the *pace* of North American cinema and TV is *so slow*!

Although the editing in *Wild Side* is in Donald Cammell's and Frank Mazzola's customary rapid montage style, some of the scenes are actually quite long – or longer than they usually are in similar movies.[5] Rapid cuts: long scenes. Cammell and China Kong aren't in a hurry to get to the climax of the scene, script-wise, as similar movies usually are. They are going to take their time. So the script builds in pauses, and some of the pauses or miniature interludes are enhanced by the editing. Michael Kahn, Steven

---

[4] The Croatian cameraman, Sead Mutarevic, should be credited with almost being a third participant in some of the scenes; I think Donald Cammell indicated that Mutarevic was operating the Steadicam himself (it's not usually the DP who does that on a Hollywood production). Mutarevic is ducking and weaving with the actors throughout scenes, so that his choices of framing and movement are contributing much to the drama. Cammell had used Mutarevic to film some test footage for a project that never got made.

[5] The opening of *Wild Side* is a kind of *hommage* or reworking of *Performance*: there's a jet, red walls, some sex, a car, and a chauffeur, all delivered in flash cuts.

Spielberg's regular editor, said he likes to insert pauses in scenes, when characters are looking at each other, but not saying anything, and *Wild Side* has plenty of that.

Ryuchi Sakamoto's music composed for *Wild Side* is dreamy, oh so dreamy, so dreamy that at times it sounds like a New Age relaxation CD. It wouldn't count as classic film music, or one of the best soundtracks ever composed, but it fits the 1995 movie. Sometimes it doesn't sound like regular film music, but a series of drones and soft washes of sound.[6]

The dialogue in Donald Cammell's films has often been coarser than similar movies (though some thrillers and crime movies of the 1990s and after, like the gross-out comedies, have self-consciously coarsened their dialogue). In *Wild Side*, Cammell and co-writer China Kong have concocted their own version of the kind of fruity expressions found in other films of the period, such as *Boogie Nights* and *Pulp Fiction*. It doesn't always work, but the actors are so good they make it work.

There's quite a bit of musing on money and finance in *Wild Side*, as if Donald Cammell and China Kong are delivering their own commentary on the advanced capitalism of the North American system (and on the 1980s). The analysis of the American capitalist system is the fairly predictable one of left-liberalism, which you can find in the movies of Oliver Stone or Michael Moore (*Wild Side* was partly intended to be a satire on the financial world).

Wild Side once again explores the world of gangsters and crime – but this time it's the more refined world of money laundering, banks and high finance[7] (rather than the protection rackets and sleazy nightclubs of *Performance*). These people don't get their hands dirty – they do it via telephone calls and computers (the first time that Bruno Buckingham is depicted, he's on the phone, doing one of his money laundering deals).

On the one side, criminals involved in money laundering; on the other side, the FBI and the cops. But *Wild Side* happily subverts expectations, and turns the tables a number of times. For Bruno Buckingham, Tony plays the dumb chauffeur and aide who does whatever his boss asks; to Alex, Tony turns out to be an FBI agent, a bruiser (and one of his first acts is to rape her). Alex is a high-class call girl who turns out to be a banker, Johanna, who's hawking her body 'cos she wants to keep up the payments on her expensive beachside house. (The business with the wig that Alex uses in dressing up is classic Cammell – you can ee Anita Pallenberg doing the same things in *Performance*).

---
6 The 1995 Nu Image version of *Wild Side* had music by Jon Hassell, also associated with world music and New Agey, experimental music.
7 *Wild Side* is an urban film (it's set in Long Beach).

Alex Lee/ Johanna has a number of costume changes, and of course, this being a Donald Cammell movie, there's a scene where she's depicted dressing up (she puts on a black corset). At the beginning of the 1995 flick, she sports a sleek, call-girl outfit; she has different wigs; in the closing scenes, she is masculinized in a man's suit.

The rape in *Wild Sidde* is an extended scene of degradation, with Tony controlling everything and Alex Lee willing herself to endure it. The scene's staged like the most famous example of ass-fucking in the history of cinema ('the most famous sex scene in the history of the cinema', remarked Tom Matthews [211-2]), the notorious scene in *Last Tango In Paris* (1972), where Marlon Brando rutted on top of Maria Schneider, while raging on about the family.

MASCULINITY IN CRISIS.

Donald Cammell commented that *Wild Side* was meant to be a woman's view or a feminist view of a man's world (what China Kong called 'the boy's club'). Thus, as well as enshrining a proto-feminist viewpoint in the character of Alex Lee, *Wild Side* was also a deconstruction of contemporary masculinity. It's no surprise, for example, that the two main male characters in the movie, Bruno Buckingham and Tony, are highly exaggerated portrayals of masculinity under attack and on the verge of collapse. (Other movies of the Nineties also deconstructed and criticized masculinity – there are good studies of the 'masculinity in crisis' topic, including analyses of the 'hard body' films and action movies, by critics such as Yvonne Tasker).[8]

Wild Side is clearly meant to be an assault on masculinity: the narrative climaxes with Bruno Buckingham threatening to sodomize Tony, as if to express brutally the barely repressed homosexuality underneath male friendships (as well as satirizing the master-servant, employer-employee roles).

Both Bruno and Tony are very manly men in some respects (Tony, with his Cuban street kid persona and gym-honed body especially). Yet both are feminized. Bruno wafts around in colourful kimonos or dressing gowns, and has a beeezarre, jet black hair-do (Scott Williams did the hair). Bruno fidgets with his penis substitute, the gun, constantly. If he can't get it up and stay hard, his gun will do the job (the gay subtext continues when Bruno shoots Tony repeatedly, and Tony takes the shots lying on his back on the floor, disempowered, and being fucked over by his boss).

---

[8] See, for example, Y. Tasker, *Spectacular Bodies: Gender, Genre and the Action Cinema*, Routledge, London, 1993; S. Jeffords, *Hard Bodies: Hollywood Masculinity in the Reagan Era*, Rutgers University Press, New Brunswick, NJ, 1994; S. Cohan & I.R. Hark, eds., *Screening the Male: Exploring Masculinities in Hollywood Cinema*, Routledge, London, 1993

Tony, meanwhile, asserts his masculinity in the most excessive manner early in the movie, by raping Alex. Tenderness is nowhere in sight. And of course Alex's boyfriend is depicted as a weedy, white, American guy (though the filmmakers resist putting him in glasses with buck teeth, like the nerdy wimps that Jerry Lewis or Woody Allen sometimes play).

In *Wild Side*, it's a 'man's world', but it's the women who win, who come out of it all best. It's the women, not the men, who get the happy ever after ending, and drive off into the sunset.

THE SEDUCTION SCENE.

The main scene up front in *Wild Side* is the seduction scene between Alex Lee and Bruno Buckingham, played by two great actors, Anne Heche and Christopher Walken. Walken (born March 31, 1943) was the veteran of many movies by the time of *Wild Side*, but Heche, 25 when *Wild Side* was shot, easily matches him. (An actor can be great on their own, but in a scene like this it really helps if the other actor is also first class, and Heche certainly is).

It's the call girl and the powerful man in a hotel scene. Except writers Donald Cammell and China Kong don't play it straight, of course. How could they? And what would be the point of playing it straight? So there's plenty of playing around, of second guessing, of rapid dialogue masking God knows what. It's another of those scenes where the subtext seems to be changing every few minutes (or one actor's been told the subtext is X, while the other actor's been told it's Y. Meanwhile, the director really thinks of the subtext as Z!).

It's not a straight seduction scene, for a start: the characters are not going to get down to fucking instantly. (This is not porn, after all, and it's not even about sex. It's not the erotic thriller that the producers, Nu Image, seemed to want). The characters *talk* about sex (among other things), but they're not that interested in having sex. They play games; they role play, but they can't be bothered with going through with that, either. (Similarly, *Performance* is not a sexy movie in its sex scenes – it's sexy for other reasons).

One of the things the scene is about is money – it's a Godardian exchange of money that's at the heart of the scene (as Jean-Luc Godard depicted in *Vivre Sa Vie* and other films). It's prostitution in the Godardian sense of being the epitome of capitalism. Sex and money. (Bruno Buckingham brags about a big man in the financial world – big money equating with a big dick. Who's got the biggest wallet?). 'Dirty money' is one of the phrases used in the 1995 movie, with the rejoinder: 'all money is dirty'.

And when Alex Lee and Bruno do fuck it's not your regular intercourse – of course, being a Donald Cammell movie, there's S/M, with Bruno Buckingham winding up tied up (only to be discovered by his assistant, Tony).

GUNPLAY.

As with *Performance*, characters play with guns in *Wild Side*: there's a lengthy two-hander between Bruno Buckingham and Tony, where Bruno ponders killing Alex Lee for tying him up and sucking him dry, and Bruno's playing with a gun during the conversation (he also references suicide – ominous now, in relation to Donald Cammell's death).[9] In the big shouting scene which climaxes the 1995 movie, Bruno is again waving around a gun (Tony threatens Alex with a gun too). When Christopher Walken holds the gun to Tony's head, the allusion is clearly to the famous, harrowing scenes in *The Deer Hunter* (1978) of Russian roulette. Walken deservedly won an Oscar for his role as Nick, one of a group of Yanks who go to Vietnam.[10]

The Russian roulette scene in *The Deer Hunter* is powerful and unflinching: in a hut built over a river, Viet Cong soldiers pull up prisoners from their cell under the hut, where they wallow, hands tied, waist-deep in water, to play Russian roulette with a pistol and a bullet. The scene is full of brutality, men screaming at each other, people being slapped and tormented, and people dying, while the bets (dollars and wristwatches) pile up on the table.

Whatever the intentions of director Michael Cimino, the Russian roulette scenes can be seen as a metaphor or illustration of North America's involvement in Vietnam.[11] It's a pretty straightforward trope: the American soldiers are forced against their will to play Russian roulette by the Viet Cong soldiers (who were portrayed in a stereotypical fashion, as crude, jabbering and brutal). The scene demonstrates the idiocy of the Vietnam War, how the fate and survival of the soldiers is left up to chance, the spin of a gun's magazine. Cimino said the Russian roulette scene was a way of dramatizing the emotional reality of being in combat in Vietnam, the sense of waiting and waiting for weeks on end in a state of tension, then the sudden eruptions of horrific action. This was what the research and veterans had told the filmmakers the war in Vietnam was like, the waiting

---

[9] There are a number of references to suicide in the script and the movie – Virginia tries to kill herself, for instance.
[10] Prior to *The Deer Hunter*, Walken had already appeared in a memorable cameo in *Annie Hall* (1977), as Diane Keaton's kooky brother.
[11] The Russian roulette scene was associated with 31 real incidents involving Russian roulette with handguns between 1979 and 1982 (S. Prince, 2000). Michael Cimino said they did their homework, spoke to 100s of Vietnam veterans, and there were reports of Russian roulette.

then the violence.

In the final Russian roulette scene in *The Deer Hunter*, Michael (Robert de Niro) pays thousands of dollars to be able to play against Christopher Walken's Nick, now a glassy-eyed, burnt-out shell in a Saigon descending into turmoil. Nick's subsequent death seems inevitable, dramatically: he simply cannot return home to the U.S.A. with Michael. His death shows how the effects of the Vietnam ar last much longer than the soldiers' experience in battle.

SEX.

In *Wild Side*, sex is used as a power play between the four main characters: it's not eroticism, it's power – *power over* someone else. It seems as if everyone fucks everyone else, but never in the regular fashion. Instead, there's bondage, some kinky sex play, and rape. But the sexual practices aren't interesting: it's what they point towards – power – that counts.

No threesomes in *Wild Side*, but there is plenty of lesbian sex, when Alex Lee/ Johanna encounters Virginia Chow (Joan Chen),[12] who just happens to be Bruno Buckingham's wife. Virginia is a further complication to the already complex plot, which culminates in a series of betrayals and double crosses (this is still a thriller). It's typical of Donald Cammell's cinema that Alex and Virginia first get it on in a bathroom – again painted with deep red walls[13] (and later in a dressing room which contains one of the clothes racks from *Performance*).

As this is a Donald Cammell movie, the sex goes on for much longer than necessary in terms of the plot, but if *Wild Side* is a film about obsession and neurosis, and falling in love despite every signal screaming 'DON'T DO IT!', and about people who are ultra-neurotic and ultra-edgy, but also desperately lonely, then the sex scenes are fully justified. Besides, when the sex scenes are between two beautiful people like Anne Heche and Joan Chen, who's complaining? (Although *Wild Side* was co-written by a woman, China Kong,[14] and although there were women in the production team (in casting, production supervisor, music supervisor, assistant editors, props, costume, etc), the lesbian sex is still a guy's version of what lesbian sex might be).

---

[12] According to the Umlands, Virginia's character is inspired by China Kong (U, 235).
[13] *Wild Side* has the red walls of *Performance* (though Bruno's pad is decorated in a deliberately jarring green, which's taken up in Alex's place).
[14] The Screen Actors Guild got involved with the production when during auditions China Kong apparently took to kissing the actresses, to make sure they were right for the roles. There were complaints.

THE FINALE AND THE ENDING.

In the last third, *Wild Side* starts to lose its momentum; for me, the scenes become a little repetitive and unfocussed. It's partly to do with the narrative axis of the 1995 movie, which's a thriller involving undercover FBI agents (Tony), gangsters (Bruno), and a banker (Johanna) who has a double life as a high-class whore (Alex). But the plot starts to lose its impetus, or its appeal, or the film just isn't that interested in it anymore. It's a pity, for instance, that *Wild Side* isn't livened up by a couple of action sequences. Maybe the budget wouldn't stretch to that (but gunplay can be pretty cheap to shoot – Hong Kong action cinema does it all the time, on *tiny* budgets).

Instead, Donald Cammell and his team persuade Christopher Walken to go even further over-the-top, culminating in the crazy scene in Alex Lee's beachside home where there's a lengthy confrontation between the three principals (with Bruno Buckingham threatening to bugger Tony to punish him. According to critics Rebecca and Sam Umland, Bruno does sodomize Tony in this scene, but a two-second shot was cut out. But whether it's shown or not, the viewer doesn't need to see it: after all, there's Tony on his knees with Bruno waving a gun manically. If you can't show a hard cock in a movie, a handgun will do. And you don't need to see any ass-fucking because Bruno is whacking Tony, and suggesting a game of Russian roulette!).

But *Wild Side* isn't particularly about the thriller genre or the thriller narrative, it's about other things, such as characters and situations and relationships (as well as Donald Cammell's recurring themes of death, violence and sex). The problem with *Wild Side* is that for me it doesn't sustain its interest as a character piece or as a thematic piece. It still wants to explore the crime or thriller genre, but even a routine TV cop show handles crime narratives better than this.

The narrative elements of the finale of *Wild Side* don't add up or satisfy: Bruno Buckingham shoots Tony, but Tony doesn't die (he's wearing his armoured vest, which he only reluctantly put on); Tony doesn't get to nail Bruno; Bruno escapes in a helicopter, so the Feds don't capture Bruno. It's not that *Wild Side* has an 'ambiguous' ending, or an ending that lets the bad guys get away, it's that the ending isn't fulfilling. It's more of a character-based drama that kind of peters out instead of ending (quite a few movie endings celebrated as 'ambiguous' or 'open-ended' are in fact botched jobs, where the writers can't think of a decent finale).

After the climax, *Wild Side* ends with a surprisingly clichéd and uninspired scene: Alex Lee and Virginia are depicted happily riding on a bus down to Mexico.[15] Now all the darkness of the previous hour-and-a-half of the mid-1990s movie is forgotten, all of the paranoia, neurosis, threats and violence simply fades away in bright sunlight.

Virginia smiles. Alex smiles.

The bus moves through the border town to Tijuana,[16] and continues onward to dusty, sunny roads. Meanwhile, Alex Lee is narrating the Happy Ever After future she and her lover will enjoy (something about going to China).[17]

In fact, it's hard to believe this ending to *Wild Side*, because it's so sappy, so mushy, and so *bad*. It has the appearance of the kind of ending that Hollywood film studios enforce upon films, in order to deliver a more upbeat ending.[18] The bus journey, the lovers sitting happily together, the bright visuals (the sun, the light, the smiles), and the voiceover are all elements of the typical Hollywood re-shot ending.

Uhh, has *Wild Side* suddenly become *The Graduate*, with Dustin Hoffman and Katherine Ross heading out into the sunset on a bus while Simon & Garfunkel play 'The Sound of Silence'? Come on!

In short, the ending of *Wild Side* stinks. But that doesn't bother me, because I don't believe this ending at all. I don't invest in it. I don't want it. As Jean-Luc Godard suggests when you criticize a film: come up with your own ending. So I've written my own ending to *Wild Side*.

The ending of *Wild Side* has drifted in from some place else, but it's just too light and fluffy to alter the rest of the 1995 movie. It's the same with the 1982 theatrical version of *Blade Runner* (one of Donald Cammell's favourite movies): the famous ending where Deckard and Rachel fly off into the sunset far, far away from the rain-drenched, paranoid, dark streets of Los Angeles irritated many fans of *Blade Runner* (and was of course dropped from the two 'director's cuts' – the 1992 director's cut and the 2007 *Final Cut*).

But the flying-off-into-the-sunset ending of *Blade Runner* was very brief, and so lightweight, it didn't mar the movie at all for me. You can't sweep away two hours of dark, oppressive, claustrophobic (and brilliant) filmmaking with a lighter scene lasting one or two minutes. Besides, as J.R.R. Tolkien said of fairy tales, nobody really *believes* in those Happy Endings; they are a way of closing a fairy story, but you're not meant to believe the prince and princess will *really* live happily ever after.

The way that RKO, Robert Wise, Mark Robson, Jack Moss and others

---

[15] This scene, the last to be filmed, was apparently funded by Donald Cammell himself (U, 235).
[16] The kind of town where Orson Welles set *Touch of Evil*, although it was filmed partly in Venice, CA.
[17] Maybe there's an in-joke here, about China, because China was Donald Cammell's wife's name, and one of the co-writers of *Wild Side*.
[18] So it's odd, perhaps, that Donald Cammell apparently paid for this part of the shooting himself.

re-cut and re-shot the closing scenes of *The Magnificent Ambersons* is infinitely more serious, because they fucked up perhaps the greatest American movie yet made (and no 'director's cut' of Orson Welles' 1942 movie has emerged so far. And doesn't seem likely to).

EDITING *WILD SIDE*.

The idea was to take *Wild Side* to Cannes – but with shooting being completed in early March (with editing beginning on March 6, that wouldn't leave much time – Cannes being in May).

The first version of *Wild Side* attracted many criticisms from the producers, who wanted the characters and plot to be clearer, while *Wild Side* is ambivalence and complexity from its cynical base upwards. There are no clearly-defined heroes and villains in this piece.

The editors re-cut the movie, which was shown to the producers at Nu Image on April 18, 1995. But they still weren't happy with it. One issue was wanting to avoid an 'NC-17' rating, because the producers thought the cut was too graphic (producers and distributors prefer an 'R' rated movie every time – as 'NC-17' rated flicks such as *Showgirls* that same year and *Henry and June* before that demonstrated).

The editors re-worked *Wild Side*, and it was shown to Nu Image around May 10, 1995. The producers claimed that Donald Cammell and his editors had not incorporated many of their suggestions, and the movie would likely still get an 'NC-17' rating. Nu Image also didn't like the style of *Wild Side*, such as the editing – Cammell's trademark flashcuts and allusive, poetic montage.

In the end, the producers took Donald Cammell and Frank Mazzola and the editing team off the movie, and cut it themselves (they appointed Martin Hunter to re-cut the movie the way they wanted it). So when *Wild Side* was broadcast on HBO in February, 1996, it was not Cammell's version; Cammell took his name off it (using the pseudonym 'Franklin Brauner', rather than the more usual Allen Smithee). (The director's cut is some 18 minutes longer than the Nu Image version).

All of this is very familiar to anyone who knows anything about Hollywood and the contemporary film industry. Versions shuttling backwards and forwards between filmmakers and producers/ studios/ distributors and censors is all too common. Typically, the filmmakers resist, trying to keep their vision intact, while the producers and studios and distributors have a whole other agenda, which's shaping the movie into a saleable product.

Compromises are made all over the place. In the case of *Wild Side*, Donald Cammell's unusual editing style is clearly pivotal to the piece – if you change that, you alter the film fundamentally. It's the same with Tsui Hark or Jean-Luc Godard or any filmmaker with an instantly recognizable editing style.

Donald Cammell's resistance to the toning down of the sexuality is nowhere near as important as the editing of the overall movie. It's understandable that the producers would be wary of depicting male rape – a touchier subject in movies even than female rape. However, it does occur in a few movies – in *Pulp Fiction*, for instance, and *The Shawshank Redemption*, both released a year before *Wild Side*).

But Donald Cammell was not finished with *Wild Side:* he took up the editing of the picture again, hiring an editor (John Ganem)[19] to edit the movie on an Avid machine. A workprint was produced by April, 1996, not long before Cammell died.

Observers such as Drew Hammond reckoned that the debacle over *Wild Side* had deeply affected Donald Cammell: he felt he had let China Kong down over the movie, and that maybe he should've fought harder to retain his (their) vision. Hammond thought that Kong meant more to Cammell than filmmaking – 'she was the most important thing in his life' (B, 49), and much of what he did, including in filmmaking, was for her.

A 'director's cut' of *Wild Side* was produced in 1999. There is some confusion over what a 'director's cut' actually is; some are not made with the director's approval, or even involvement. And some, like *Wild Side*, are made after the director's death (as with restored versions of *Touch of Evil* and *Othello*, directed by Orson Welles). That creates problems, because no matter how closely the production team follow the director's intentions, it can never be a true director's cut, because the dead director hasn't *seen it* and *worked on it*. Even with collaborators who are totally sympathetic to the director's intentions and methods (like Frank Mazzola and China Kong with *Wild Side*), there still might be all sorts of elements which the director might alter, had s/he been alive to see it. No amount of written notes or guidelines or discussions can take the place of actually seeing the finished film. (Some critics have not accepted the 1998 restoration and re-editing of *Touch of Evil* as an Orson Welles 'director's cut' movie, for instance, even though it was clearly put together with immense care and attention by the team headed up by editor Walter Murch using written notes from Welles and other material).

---

[19] China Kong had left Donald Cammell in August, 1995. Ironically, she later had an affair with the young editor (John Ganem) that Cammell hired to re-cut *Wild Side*.

WILD SIDE AND THE 'EROTIC THRILLER' CYCLE.

Wild Side can be regarded as part of the cycle of a new sub-genre, the 'erotic thriller', 'neo-noir', *faux noir*, a fusion of *film noir* and softcore pornography. *Basic Instinct* (with *Fatal Attraction*) helped to launch the spate of 'suspense and suspenders' movies: *Body of Evidence, Night Rhythms, Disclosure, Sliver, Unlawful Entry, Night and the City, Single White Female, Kill Me Again, Red Rock West The Last Seduction, Damage, The Temp* and *Animal Instincts* (plus the usual hardcore porn spoofs). *Basic Instinct* was 'perhaps the most notorious example of sexual explicitness in the '*faux noir*' revival', as Steven Cohan put it.[20] *Basic Instinct* concerned a cop, Nick Curran (Michael Douglas) pursuing a murder suspect, Catherine Tramell (Sharon Stone), who supposedly writes novels about killing men, then proceeds to kill them.[21]

Basic Instinct was part of a group of 'erotic thrillers' of the 1980s and 1990s, which took the formulas of 'classic' Hollywood *film noir* movies, such as *The Big Sleep* and *Double Indemnity*, and spiced them up with sex scenes. The neo-noir films of the late 20th century looked back to mid-century classics, such as *Gun Crazy, To Have and Have Not, The Maltese Falcon, Kiss Me Deadly, Touch of Evil* and *They Live By Night*.

Catherine Tramell in *Basic Instinct* was seen as a postmodern version of the *femme fatales* in *film noirs*, though with a new irony, ambiguity and indeterminacy. The neo-noir *femme fatale* was a symbol of fear, desire and nostalgia, a figure of excess and spectacle.[22] There was an added dimension to Tramell's character: she was also a writer: she was in control in a new way: she wrote the books then supposedly acted them out; she decided who lived or died. 'Catherine can make Nick cease to exist in three ways: she can kill him; she can cease to love him; and she can cease to imagine him', as Robert E. Wood put it.[23]

Other 'psychofemmes' or *femme fatales* who refused male violence and did it their own way included Sigourney Weaver's Ripley in the *Alien* series, Linda Hamilton's Sarah Connor in the *Terminator* series, Demi Moore's Meredith Johnson in *Disclosure* (1994), Susan Sarandon and Geena Davis in *Thelma and Louise* (1991), Virginia Madsen's Dolly in *The Hot Spot* (1990), Madonna in *Body of Evidence* (1993), Nicole Kidman in

---

20 "Censorship and Narrative Indeterminacy in *Basic Instinct*", in S. Neale, 1998, 263.
21 On *Basic Instinct*, see R. van Scheers: *Paul Verhoeven*, Faber, London, 1997; D. Ansen: "Kiss Kiss Slash Slash", *Newsweek*, 23 March, 1992; G. Arnold: "Rating Erotic Thrillers", *Washington Times*, 17, January, 1993; T. Austin: "Gendered Displeasures: *Basic Instinct* and Female Viewers", *Journal of Popular British Cinema*, 2, 1999.
22 K. Stables. "The Postmodernist Always Rings Twice: Constructing the *Femme Fatale* in 90s Cinema", in E. Kaplan, 1998.
23 R. Wood: "Somebody Has To Die: *Basic Instinct* as White Noir", *PostScript*, 12, 3. For director Paul Verhoeven, Catherine Tramell was the Devil, not a 'real' woman so much as a moral dilemma for Nick, the seduction of the darker side of life.

Malice (1993) and *To Die For* (1995), Jamie Lee Curtis's Megan Turner in *Mother's Boys* (1993) and Jude in *Blue Steel* (1990), Kim Basinger in *Final Analysis* (1992), Theresa Russell and Debra Winger in *Black Widow* (1987), Jennifer Jason Leigh's Heddy in *Single White Female* (1992), Linda Fiorentino in *Jade* (1995) and as Wendy Kroy in *The Last Seduction* (1993), Kathleen Turner's Matty in *Body Heat* (1981), Lara Flynn Boyle in *Red Rock West* (1993), Joanna Whalley-Kilmer in *Kill Me Again* (1989), and Frances McDormand's Marge Gunderson in *Fargo* (1996). These women were bitch businesswomen (*Disclosure*), killers (*Singe White Female, The Hand That Rocks the Cradle*), unnatural mothers (*The Grifters, Mother's Boys*), and women whose actual bodies were weapons (*Body of Evidence*). Sartorial sophistication was a key part of the new *femme fatales*, with the women in films such as *The Hot Spot, Black Widow, Single White Female* and *Mother's Boys* going through multiple costume changes (narcissism is a key theme in *Wild Side*).[24] Ambiguity and indeterminacy was one of the hallmarks of these new female characters.

Another ancestor of the contemporary 'erotic thriller' were the films directed by Alfred Hitchcock: *Suspicion, Shadow of a Doubt, Notorious, Strangers on a Train, Vertigo, North by Northwest* and *Psycho. Psycho* contains not only the foundation of the 'erotic thriller', but also the contemporary horror film, with its series of manipulative shocks (*White of the Eye* is very Hitchcockian). *Psycho* combined sex and violence in a vivid, flamboyant and deliberately manipulative manner. *Psycho's* camera lingered over Janet Leigh undressing to a black and white bra while Anthony Perkins looked on, before she was murdered, naked in the shower. The influence of *Vertigo* and *North By Northwest*, plus *Psycho*'s slasher and serial killer elements, are obvious in the 'erotic thrillers' of the Nineties.

'Erotic thrillers' often emphasize voyeurism, as in Alfred Hitchcock's cinema: the 'pussy flash' in *Basic Instinct*, people spying on people having sex, replays of video footage of sex (*Body of Evidence, Jade*). Voyeurism is a significant ingredient in *White of the Eye* and *Demon Seed*. Many of the strategies of 'erotic thrillers' come from pornography: the variety of sex scenes (sexual positions, foreplay, sex in different locations), the use of voyeurism, and different kinds of sex (oral, anal, S/M, etc).

The 'explicit' language of *femme fatales* derives from porn too: Catherine Tramell's 'I wasn't dating him, I was fucking him' (*Basic Instinct*); Carlson's 'I fucked you, I fucked Andrew, I fucked Frank. That's what I do – I fuck' (*Body of Evidence*); and Bridget's 'I'm a total *fucking* bitch!' and 'fucking doesn't have to be anything more than fucking' (*The

---

[24] By contrast, the leads in *Basic Instinct, Body Heat* and *The Last Seduction* wore the same outfit at important moments (S. Bruzzi: *Undressing Cinema*, Routledge, London, 1997, 129).

Last Seduction). The new *femme fatales* appropriate the power of 'explicit' language, usually the preserve of men. They don't just swear, they use graphic language as a form of power, turning the tables on men: 'what are you? You are my designated fuck', says Bridget/ Wendy in *The Last Seduction*, or Demi Moore's retort to her male aggressor in *G.I. Jane*: 'suck my dick'.

Other erotic thrillers included the remake of *The Postman Always Rings Twice* (Bob Rafelson), with Jack Nicholson and Jessica Lange; *Body Heat* (Lawrence Kasdan) with William Hurt and Kathleen Turner (both 1981); *Unlawful Entry* (Jonathan Kaplan, 1992), *The Believers* (John Schlesinger, 1987), *Jagged Edge* (Richard Marquand, 1985), *Internal Affairs* (Mike Figgis, 1990), *Body of Evidence* (Uli Edel, 1992), *Body Double* (Brian de Palma, 1984), *Malice* (Harold Becker, 1993), *After Dark, My Sweet* (James Foley, 1990), *Dead Calm* (Philip Noyce, 1988), *Night and the City* (Irwin Winkler, 1992), *Red Rock West* (John Dahl, 1993), *Bitter Moon* (Roman Polanski, 1992), *Final Analysis* (Phil Joanou, 1992), *Black Widow* (Bob Rafelson, 1987), *Single White Female* (Barbet Schroeder, 1992), *The Last Seduction* (John Dahl, 1993), *Frantic* (Roman Polanski, 1988), *Poison Ivy* (Katt Shea Ruben, 1992), *The Crush* (Alan Shapiro, 1993), *The Hot Spot* (Dennis Hopper, 1990), *Mother's Boys* (Yves Simoneau, 1994), *Damage* (Louis Malle, 1993), *To Die For* (Gus van Sant, 1995), *The Temp* (Tom Holland, 1993), *Angel Heart* (Alan Parker, 1987), *Kill Me Again* (John Dahl, 1989), and *Fatal Attraction* (Adrian Lyne, 1987).[25]

All of these productions were marketed for their combination of eroticism and danger: the erotic thrill of potential violence, and the heightened sensation of violent sex. Also worth noting were 'neo-noir' films such as *LA Confidential* (Curtis Hanson, 1997), *The Grifters* (Stephen Frears, 1990), *sex, lies and videotape* (Steven Soderbergh, 1989), *Romeo Is Bleeding* (Peter Medak, 1993), *Guncrazy* (Tamra Davis, 1992), *Pulp Fiction* (Quentin Tarantino, 1994), *After Hours* (Martin Scorsese, 1987), and many of the Coen brothers' films (*Fargo, Blood Simple, Raising Arizona*).

The directors associated with the neo-noir and erotic thrillers of the 1980s and 1990s included John Dahl, Roman Polanski, the Coens, Martin Scorsese, Quentin Tarantino, Bob Rafelson and Paul Verhoeven, and writers such as James Ellroy, Jim Thompson, Raymond Chandler, and Dashiell Hammet. Actresses who played *femme fatales* and neo-noir women included Demi Moore, Susan Sarandon, Geena Davis, Sharon Stone, Michelle Pfeiffer, Cameron Diaz, Jamie Lee Curtis, Theresa Russell, Jennifer Jason Leigh, Linda Fiorentino, Nicole Kidman, Kathleen Turner, Lara Flynn

---

[25] Porn director Gregory Dark claimed he invented the 'erotic thriller' genre way before directors like Zalman King.

Boyle, Joanna Whalley-Kilmer, Kim Basinger and Frances McDormand. Anne Heche in *Wild Side* is part of this group.

A bunch of films of the mid-1970s constitute another cycle of *noirs*: *Chinatown*, most obviously, but also *The Long Goodbye*, *Marlowe* and *Farewell, My Lovely*. The early 1980s was the next period with *Body Heat, The Postman Always Rings Twice, Hammett, Dead Men Don't Wear Plaid* and *Union City*.

The 'erotic thrillers' of the 1980s and 1990s were more explicit in their depictions of sex and violence, as one would expect, but they were not darker or more cynical than the films of the 1940s and 1950s. In terms of attitudes such as world-weariness, seen-it-all-before, pessimism and darkness, the *film noir* and detective films of the 1940s and 1950s were just as strong as those of the 1980s and 1990s. Adding more explicit sex or violence did not make these films any better, or stronger. A Production Code era thriller of the 1940s could be just as desolate and bitter as a 'R' rated 'erotic' thriller of the 1990s. There are equally bleak views of humanity as corrupt, self-serving, stupid, greedy, lustful and narrow-minded in the 1940s-50s films as in the 1980s-90s films. Indeed, movies of the 1940s and 1950s were often more sarcastic, more bitter, and more vicious in their depiction of contemporary society. In fact, some directors said the Production Code had beneficial effects on filmmakers, because it forced them to think of new ways of getting across problematic information, such as sexuality or drugs.

The 'erotic thrillers' were marketed as thrillers, as genre pieces, but not as *film noirs*, not as historical pieces, and not as costume films. The 'erotic thrillers' were set in the present, in present day dress. Studio executives said that, in the Nineties, *film noirs* would be difficult to sell to audiences, because they were period pieces, and young people didn't want to see historical movies. The main audience for *film noirs* tended to be 'directors, film students, critics and the most ardent, generally upscale film enthusiasts' (and also the audience of the movies of Donald Cammell).[26]

Wild Side is, as expected from Donald Cammell and China Kong, a self-consciously eccentric and unusual take on the 'erotic thriller' genre, as well as a deconstruction of it, and a celebration of its more (potentially) radical elements.

---

[26] Warner Bros. exec, quoted in D. Ansen: 'The Neo-noir '90s", *Newsweek*, Oct, 27, 1997.

CHRISTOPHER WALKEN
ANNE HECHE
WILDSIDE
GOING TOO FAR
WAS JUST THE BEGINNING
DVD

CHRISTOPHER WALKEN
JOAN CHEN
ANNE HECHE
WILD
SIDE
GOING
TOO
FAR
WAS
JUST
THE
BEGINNING.

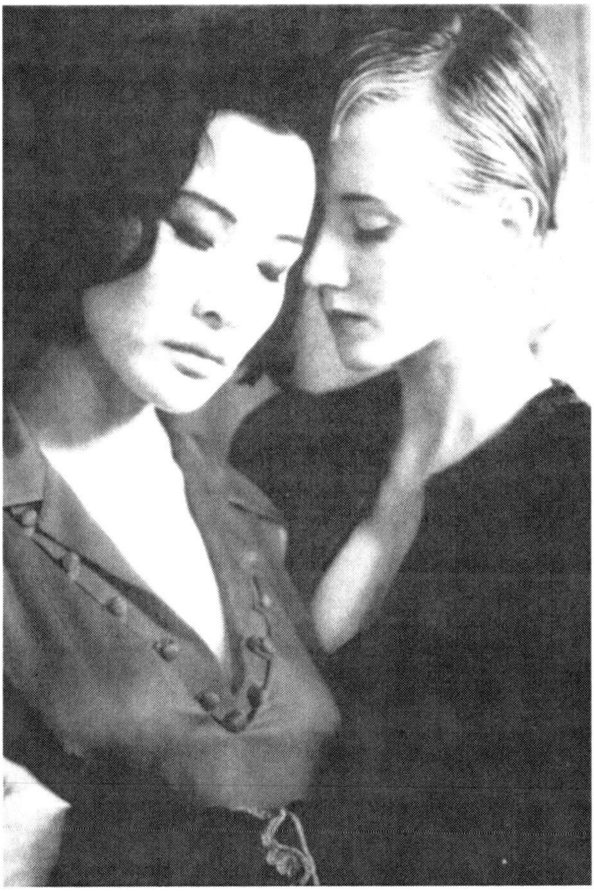

Christopher Walken in one of his best-known roles, in The Deer Hunter (1978), above, for which he won the best supporting actor Oscar.

And in Wild Side, below.

The most famous erotic thriller movie of the 1990s,
Basic Instinct (1992, Guild/ Carolco/ Canal).
Sharon Stone in the notorious 'pussy flash' scene.

Erotic thrillers in the 1990s: the wonderful Linda Fiorentino in
The Last Seduction (1994, ITC/ Jonathan Shestack), above.
and Madonna in Body of Evidence (1992, UIP/ Dino de Laurentiis)

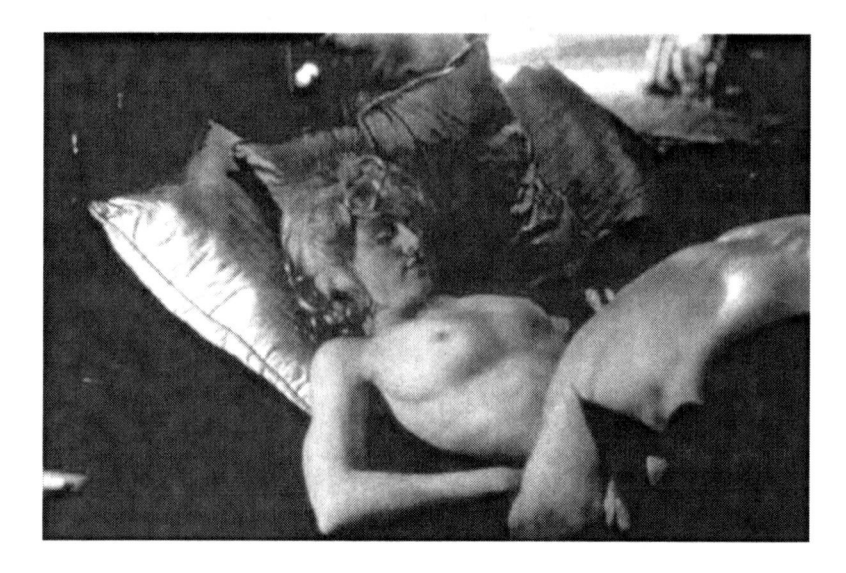

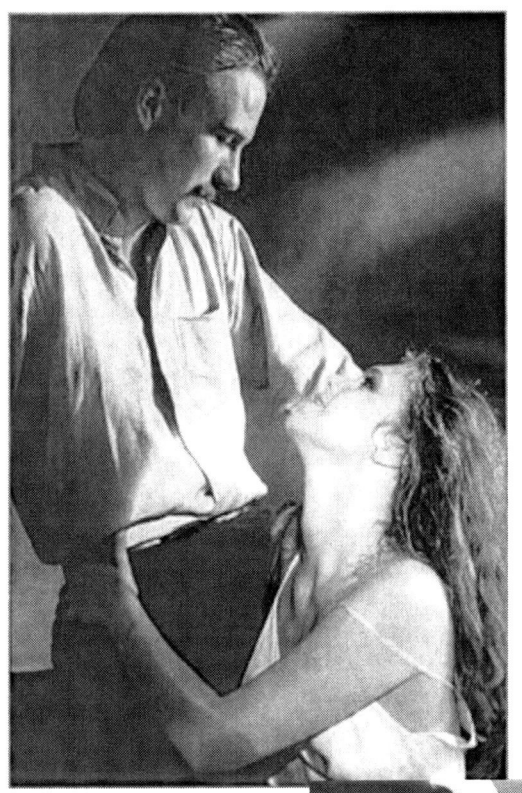

Earlier examples of erotic thrillers - famous films of the 1980s, Body Heat (1981) and Fatal Attraction (1987).

(Warner/ Ladd. Paramount/ Jaffe/ Lansing)

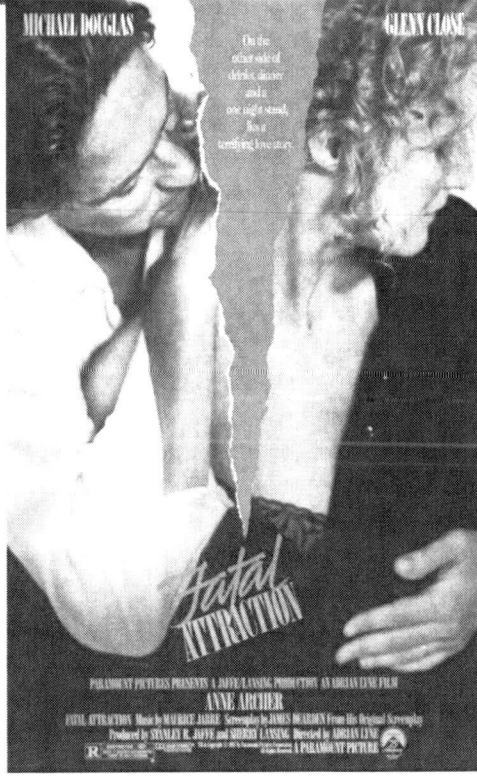

OTHER MOVIE PROJECTS

7

OTHER MOVIE PROJECTS

❋

UNMADE PROJECTS

Like most filmmakers, Donald Cammell had projects which weren't completed. After *Performance*, such a stunning début, Cammell wrote *Ishtar* (not the Warren Beatty-Dustin Hoffman disaster), in which a Supreme Court judge (apparently to be played by the novelist William Burroughs) is kidnapped in Morocco by terrorists.

About a film director called Nonus making a movie in Morocco, *Ishtar* (1970) was a script that Donald Cammell developed for Michael Butler. *Ishtar* tapped into the emerging interest in the Goddess, as incarnated in ancient goddesses such as Ishtar and Isis (in the screenplay, she's called Aissha). Linked to the project were actors such as Malcolm McDowell (who would have played the film director),[1] Mick Jagger, Orson Welles,[2] Dominique Sanda, Marlon Brando and William Burroughs. A pretty amazing cast, but it was not to be.

Donald Cammell revived the *Ishtar* concept in 1983-84, this time set in Jamaica, with Chris Blackwell of Island Records and Tim Deegan at Island Pictures. Same story, reworked, to be called *The Last Video*.

The Last Video was later taken up by EMI and Goldcrest, two of the main British film companies of the period, but the financial disaster of the historical epic *Revolution* (1985) and other films scuppered the project and it was dropped. Goldcrest, which had done well with *Chariots of Fire* and *Gandhi*, famously went to the wall in 1986, the large cost of the flop *Revolution* (budgeted at $19m) being largely the cause, though other people blamed the $8 million *AbsoluteBeginners* and *The Mission* ($17m). It wasn't just that Goldcrest embarked on three high budget movies at the same time (high, that is, for predominantly 'British' films), it was also that the pictures didn't do well at the box office, losing Goldcrest some £15 million ($23.4m).[3]

Donald Cammell may have worked on the concert movie *Gimme Shelter* (Maysles brothers, 1970), though it's not certain what he did (he said he'd been part of the editing [U, 147]).

The Beard (1972) was Donald Cammell's film adaption of Michael McClure's 1965 play about Jean Harlow and Billy the Kid. Cammell co-

---

[1] As McDowell proved in films such as *If...* and *A Clockwork Orange*, he was ideally suited to a Donald Cammell film.
[2] Orson Welles spoke highly of Robert Graves, calling him (in 1967, at the time of perhaps Graves's greatest popularity), 'the greatest living poet' (2002, 149). Robert Graves' White Goddess myth may be an influence on *The Lady From Shanghai*, according to Clinton Heylin, in particular the portrayal of Elsa Bannister, the Goddess as Muse, as inspiration, but also as the poet's destruction. Graves portrays the Goddess wielding a Cretan axe, and the poet as her hapless, devoted follower and lover. He has no choice but to act as she commands.
[3] In 1986, *The Mission* made $8.3 million in rentals in the U.S.A., but *Revolution* took a pitiful $1 million, and *Absolute Beginners* brought in a disastrous $0.3 million.

wrote the screenplay with McClure, and in the early 1970s hoped to set up the movie with Goodtimes Enterprises (with Sandy Lieberson). Actors such as Keith Carradine, Bud Cort, Tuesday Weld, Michelle Phillips, Mick Jagger, and Susan Tyrrell were considered.

Other projects included *Pale Fire*, from Vladimir Nabokov; *Pharaoh*, about Lord Nelson and Lady Hamilton; and a Mick Jagger vehicle, *Hot*. In the documentary *Donald Cammell: The Ultimate Performance*, the camera pans over a pile of scripts, the titles of which are *King of Heroin, Ishtar, The Beard, The Gull, Fan Tan, Thirty Three, The Last Video, Civil Unrest, Faro* and *Machine Gun Kelly*.

For his adaption in 1974 of *Pale Fire* (1962) by Vladimir Nabokov, Donald Cammell wrote a 60-page 're-telling' of the novel (Cammell had long admired *Lolita*, Nabokov's signature work).

In the mid-1970s, Donald Cammell wrote *The Lady Hamilton*, about Lord Nelson and Lady Hamilton, for producer Andrew Braunsberg, who found it a difficult project to sell in Hollywood. It was a historical drama, for a start, not the easiest movie to promote, and it had Donald Cammell attached to it: 'he was perceived as difficult,' Braunsberg recalled, 'and that didn't help the cause' (U, 167). The Nelson-Hamilton movie is one project I would've liked to have seen from Cammell – partly because it was a historical drama, a world away from Cammell's usual province of contemporary thrillers.

A script about Jack the Ripper had been written with critic Kenneth Tynan (U, 65). Created for producer Andrew Braunsberg between January and June, 1977, *Jack the Ripper* came to nothing in the end,[4] and Braunsberg fired Cammell in June, 1977.

The Changeling (Peter Medak, 1979) was a Canadian ghost story starring George C. Scott which Donald Cammell was approached to direct. Although Cammell was brought onto the project early, and probably did some location scouting in Canada, his concept of the movie didn't agree with that of the producers, so he left.

Producer Zalman King (best known for glossy Hollywood erotica such as *The Red Shoe Diaries* and *9 1/2 Weeks*), invited Donald Cammell to work on *Hot!*, as co-writer and possibly as director (U, 192). But *Hot* wasn't made. (Some US TV shows might've been ideal territory for Cammell: the sleazy, Louisiana vampire show *True Blood* of the mid-200s, for example. Cable and satellite channels, like HBO, seem to be an ideal working environment for a filmmaker like Cammell).

---

[4] Many movies have drawn on the Jack the Ripper mythology – among the more recent, *From Hell* (2000), seems particularly Cammellian: Johnny Depp's detective lounging around in opium dens would be quite at home in *Performance*.

Producer Steve Reuther, Donald Cammell's agent in the late 1970s, considered offering Cammell a script by J.F. Lawton, *Three Thousand*, when Reuther was at Vestron in the late 1980s.[5] Also a Don Johnson vehicle, *Centrifuge*.

Producer Brad Wyman and Donald Cammell kicked around ideas for a movie to follow *White of the Eye*: Wyman suggested Machine Gun Kelly, and Cammell went for it, turning in a script entitled *Machine Gun Kelly*, in which Kelly's wife was the orchestrator of the man and his legend.

El Paso was a script about gangsters and movies (originally called *Breakfast Included*), which Donald Cammell wrote for Armenian filmmaker Vartkes Cholakian at the end of the Seventies. *El Paso* took a while to get anywhere, but it did reach Sherri Lansing at Paramount. Later, in 1984, Cammell offered to write a screenplay for *El Paso* (his work in 1980 had been writing a treatment, as he often preferred to do). Cholakian gave Cammell $2,500, with more to follow when the script was delivered and finalized. But Cammell never wrote the script of *El Paso*.[6]

Alamogordo was a Jean-Claude van Damme sci-fi action vehicle which Donald Cammell would've directed for Columbia and Trans World Entertainment with a budget of $25m, to be shot in Spain (it was announced in early 1990 in the *L.A. Times*). Cammell was also suggested as a director for *Bad Influence* and *RoboCop 2*, two 1990 movies (U, 273). *Born Thief* was developed in the early 1990s: it was to star Mick Jagger and be produced by John Langley for Barbour/ Langely.

With his wife China Kong, Donald Cammell developed a project entitled *The Cull*, around 1993, dealing with the aftermath of the Iraq War and a Special Forces operation that goes badly wrong. It was going to be about a veteran of the Gulf War who plans to blow the whistle on the use of chemical weapons. Meanwhile, government agents are out to silence him. It was set mainly in Scotland. Sean Connery was interested (U, 233).

Johnny Depp was rumoured to be appearing in *The Cull*, to be directed by Donald Cammell, around September, 1995, in London. Cinefilm were due to produce the movie, but their production *Divine Rapture* was in trouble, so they had to cancel.

Donald Cammell wrote two scripts for Marlon Brando (he had met Brando in Paris in 1958, when Brando was filming *The Young Lions*). The first, *Fan Tan*, written in 1978, was a South Seas adventure, with a hero falling for a female pirate (with echoes of Brando's own life, of course – *The Mutiny On the Bounty* in the early 1960s). Cammell visited Brando at

---

[5] This script was later developed into *Pretty Woman*.
[6] But he remained interested in the project, and offered to buy it from Cholakian a year before his death in 1996 (U, 206).

his Tahitian island retreat, Tetiaroa, for weeks of discussions about the project, which was co-written with Brando. *Fan Tan*, a 133-page treatment, later appeared (in 2006) in book form, with David Thomson adding an afterword. Cammell and Brando planned further adventures on the high seas to follow *Fan-Tan*. Cammell in 1989 recalled that *Fan-Tan* would've been 'a saga of Conradian proportions' with 'a very enticing, very seductive premise'.

Fan-Tan would've been both a difficult project to sell to the producers and film studios, and a challenging movie to make. And it would've been very expensive, as filming on water always is (not to mention Marlon Brando's fee – for instance, at this time, for *Apocalypse Now*, was $3.5 million for three weeks' work (plus an extra day at $75,000); director Francis Coppola had knocked Brando down to $3m prior to Brando joining the production. He would also receive 11.5% of the adjusted gross profit from *Apocalypse Now*.)

The second Cammell-Brando project, *Jericho* (1989), in which Marlon Brando was to play a CIA assassin seeking revenge for his daughter's murder in the South American drug trade, would have been extremely violent (with the former CIA agent wreaking revenge on drug lords and CIA agents). Producer Elliott Kastner was involved, with Trans World Entertainment to produce for a budget of $14m.

Marlon Brando pulled out of both projects (*Jericho* went as far as preproduction in Mexico, and Donald Cammell spent 18 months on the project); one wonders just what a meeting between two talents (idiosyncratic, mercurial, temperamental, difficult) like Cammell and Brando would have produced.[7] Although Cammell visited Brando in Tahiti to work on the script, the project fizzled out by early 1989.

Donald Cammell had also planned an earlier film with Marlon Brando, entitled *The Liars*, one of the seeds of *Performance*. Brando was to play an American criminal, Cotrelli, on the run in *The Liars*, with Mick Jagger (Haskin) as the pop star he meets when he holes up in Earl's Court. There he also encounters Simon, a young, runaway woman, and Pherber. Cammell rewrote *The Liars*, which became *The Performers* (much closer to the final film of *Performance*).

One wonders what Marlon Brando would have been like in something like *Performance* or *The Liars*, but no one could disagree that James Fox turned in the performance of a lifetime, which can rank alongside Brando's best – and Brando is of course the best there is in cinema.[8]

---

[7] Elliott Kastner was sure it could have been something special.
[8] James Fox had appeared in *The Chase* (1965) with Marlon Brando, a cracking movie that Arthur Penn directed before *Bonnie & Clyde*.

Even if you don't know the details of why Marlon Brando pulled out of two of Donald Cammell's projects, pretty much everyone agrees that Brando could be - how to be put politely? - a tricky actor to work with. Brando was the greatest, and he knew it: his reputation was very powerful, and he often used that power in making deals, or turning around a production to suit his own ends. Stories of Brando's behaviour are legendary. (Maintaining Brando's interest in a project was certainly a challenge. With so many offers coming in, and with his restless personality, it took a lot to sustain Brando's involvement).

At the end of his life, Donald Cammell was working with Drew Hammond and China Kong[9] on a story about the heroin trade, entitled *Thirty Three*. Set in Marseilles in 1933, *33* involved a romantic triangle in the drug trade between Turkey and France. The debacle with Warners over *Performance* hadn't helped his standing in Hollywood; the studios didn't really know what to make of him, how to handle him, according to some onlookers, and Cammell wasn't going to play the Hollywood game, to do things the way Hollywood liked. Cammell wasn't going to leave, either, regarding Hollywood as the centre of the film world.

Bill Pullman had expressed an interest in appearing in the Cammells' drug film project (and Donald Cammell had heard this promising news days b4 he committed suicide). Attaching an actor like Pullman to the script would likely have helped it along: by Hollywood's standards, this was good news. (Pullman is a fine actor - I saw him in David Mamet's play *Oleanna* in L.A. in 2009, at the Mark Taper Forum, opposite Julia Stiles). At the time of *Wild Side* in the mid-1990s, Pullman's star was on the rise: he was appearing in movies such as *Independence Day* (Roland Emmerich, 1996), *Lost Highway* (David Lynch, 1997) and *The End of Violence* (Wim Wenders, 1997).

THE ARGUMENT

The Argument had been filmed in 1971, as a short, and a test piece for the unfinished *Ishtar* project. Donald Cammell's editor, Frank Mazzola, completed the film in 1999 (Mazzola was the chief driving force behind *The Argument*, acting in a producer role, putting together the crew, including paying them). In the end, producing *The Argument* took its toll on Mazzola

---
[9] This was after Kong had returned to live with Cammell after her affair with John Ganem.

– he said he had to sell his house and land in Laurel Canyon in L.A. to pay the crew and his debts. 'That film set me back a long way... I lost everything,' Mazzola recalled (U, 157). And *The Argument* wasn't even completed – it was another of those movies that's abandoned.

The Argument is distinctly a minor work; it starred Donald Cammell's then girlfriend, Myriam Gibril, as the witch Aisha, and Kendrew Lascelles as a film director, Nonus. *The Argument* constitutes primarily the witch and the film director arguing about making a film in the American desert.

The photography (credited to Vilmos Zsigmond, one of the great cinematographers of the era),[10] is beautiful.[11] But then, it'd be difficult to film those luscious locations and that incredible desert light and not have them come out romantic. This is the American West, a place of mythology, seen in countless Westerns and other movies (the setting was Arches National Park in Moab, Utah,[12] although the production also looked at Lone Pine in California).

The Argument looks like the kind of project that a bunch of film students might make if they went out into the desert from Los Angeles for the weekend and shot some footage. (I bet there are quite a few films that have been made with students in the Seventies driving out into the Mojave Desert, or Death Valley, or the Joshua Tree National Monument for the weekend, and shooting some silly stuff on Super-8, or with a 16mm, wind-up Bolex).

And there's nothing wrong with that at all: in fact, I'd say it enhances Donald Cammell's movies that some of them contain scenes which have the air of home movies or personal or autobiographical elements (such as *Performance*). So it's Cammell's lover Myriam Gibril up there on the hills, and it's Kendrew Lascelles dressed very much like Cammell at the time (the big floppy hat, for instance). Gibril is semi-naked, of course, and she sports an unusual costume and jewellery.

The witch Aisha standing up on the rocks in different places in the Californian desert and declaiming in a loud voice directly recalls the films of Kenneth Anger (in particular, *Lucifer Rising*, made around the same time).

But *The Argument* is really the bare bones of a movie, a movie that doesn't really go anywhere, that certainly doesn't have any kind of ending. It's a movie sketch, a test for something bigger and more fully realized.

The Argument is very much of its time, too, with its superimpositions, its visual effects of star fields, and 'cosmic' imagery (that came about,

---

[10] Vilmos Zsigmond's credits included *McCabe and Mrs Miller*, *The Long Goodbye*, *Close Encounters of the Third Kind*, *The Deer Hunter*, *Heaven's Gate*, and for Woody Allen, *Cassandra's Dream* and *Melinda and Melinda*.
[11] Vilmos Zsigmond opted to shoot in widescreen.
[12] Other movies which have shot here include *Indiana Jones and the Last Crusade*, *Austin Powers*, and *The Hulk*.

Frank Mazzola recalled, because the lab, Consolidated Film Industries, wanted to test the optical effects that the video switcher they'd bought could do).

In its portrayal of the main character as a witch, and its discourse on Goddesses, you could see *The Argument* as another contribution to the emerging Goddess movement, a neo-pagan trend in some areas of contemporary Western culture which drew on second wave feminism and the renewed interest in alternative beliefs like paganism and occultism (which Donald Cammell was certainly fascinated by).

The exaltation of the Goddess in *The Argument* is very familiar if you know anything about Robert Graves and *The White Goddess* (which also influenced filmmakers such as Orson Welles and John Boorman), or Robert Briffault, or Erich Neumann *et al.* The rebirth of Goddess cults was part of the resurgence of interest in all things pagan and hermetic in the mid-to-late twentieth century. Isis, Ishtar, Diana, Venus, and the Virgin Mary were evoked by these writers (and many others: Geoffrey Ashe, Xavière Gauthier, Monica Sjöö, Elinor Gadon, and Peter Redgrove).

And also artists such as Carolee Schneemann, Mary Beth Edelson, Judy Chicago, and Ana Mendieta, artists who were also feminists and took up ancient, female, religious deities in their art, re-enacting ancient, magical rituals, or performing acts affirming the 'eternal feminine', or creating paintings and sculptures and installations that explored 'feminine mysteries', women's empowerment, and women's issues (such as pregnancy, childbirth, child-rearing, menstruation, families, old age, etc).

While there is clearly plenty of exploration of femininity and masculinity (and the blending of the genders) in Donald Cammell's cinema, it's nowhere near as sophisticated or subtle or radical as explorations of the same issues in the writings of, say, Hélène Cixous, or the performance art of Anna Mendieta, or the philosophy of Julia Kristeva. But, to be fair, commercial cinema and also *avant garde* cinema have always lagged far behind radical philosophy and radical feminism. So even other Western filmmakers of Cammell's generation who explored similar territories of gender and desire and identity, such as Pier Paolo Pasolini, Bernardo Bertolucci, Nagisa Oshima, or Pedro Almodóvar, were far behind the radical philosophies of the Sixties through Nineties.

Besides, *The Argument* is a *movie*, not a philosophical treatise. If Donald Cammell and his team wanted to make a bundle of feminist statements, they might be better off publishing an essay in *Tel Quel* or *Diacritics*, or exhibiting some installations in the art galleries along West 57th Street in New York City. Only a very few filmmakers can put long and detailed lectures and essays and philosophical musings into their films and get away with it (the best being Jean-Luc Godard).

SIMONA

Simona (a.k.a. *Simone*, 1974)[13] was a Belgian-Italian film directed by Patrick Longchamps (filmed in 1972), for which Donald Cammell produced the English language version. *Simona* was based on Georges Bataille's *avant garde*, Surrealist fave among the intelligentsia, *The Story of the Eye* (a book which crops up in the cinema of Jean-Luc Godard and Walerian Borowczyk, for instance, and is an influence on writers such as William Burroughs and J.G. Ballard). The only actor you'll have heard of in *Simona* was Patrick Magee. Needless to say, *Simona* was subject to many cuts by censors (*The Story of the Eye* has lotsa sex, anal sex, and play involving eggs and eyes. It's very silly, juvenile erotica posing as Great Philosophy, but European intellectuals greedily lap it up like the milk from a saucer in the book).

Assisted by Frank Mazzola and five editing assistants, Donald Cammell put together the English language dub of *Simona* in L.A. in 1972 (U, 159). It meant rewriting the script in English, with lines that would match the Italian actors. There was also some extra shooting (at Bugsy Siegel's mansion, the Castillo del Lago, in L.A.. which Longchamps had bought in order to work on the movie). Although it was some of Cammell's 'best work, I think, he ever did', according to Mazzola, *Simona* is a rare piece, difficult to track down.

---
13 Not to be confused with a later movie, *Simone* (Andrew Niccol, 2002)

APPENDICES

NIC ROEG
THE MAN WHO FELL TO EARTH
SYD BARRETT
ONE PLUS ONE
FITZCARRALDO
BOOGIE NIGHTS

NIC ROEG

Nic Roeg (b. August 15, 1928) started out working as a cinematographer (on movies such as *Fahrenheit 451*, *The Masque of the Red Death*, *Petulia* and *Far From the Madding Crowd*), before co-directing *Performance* with Donald Cammell. Roeg would become known for quirky, international films, beginning with 1971's *Walkabout*. Roeg's highpoint as a filmmaker was probably *Don't Look Now* (1973) and *The Man Who Fell to Earth* (1975), both rightly lauded by film critics.

Then came the disastrous *Bad Timing* in 1980 (not helped by Art Garfunkel's wooden performance).[14] Nic Roeg followed *Bad Timing* with *Eureka* (1982), an interesting but flawed film; *Eureka* was the start of an Americanization and popularization in Roeg's cinematic œuvre, which watered down his idiosyncratic editing and camerawork. Though *Insignificance* (1985), *Castaway* (1987), *Track 29* (1988) and *The Witches* (1990) were successful in their own modest way, the edge of *Don't Look Now* was definitely lost. Roeg, like Alan Parker and Ridley Scott, seemed be parodying his own work. *Castaway*, for example, seemed to rehash ideas already used up in *Bad Timing* or *Don't Look Now*.

Later films directed by Nic Roeg included *Cold Heaven* (1992), *eart of Darkness* (1994), *Two Deaths* and *Hotel Paradise* (both 1995), *HFull Body Massage* (1995), *Samson and Delilah* (1996), and *Puffball* (2007).

Nic Roeg's trademarks included self-conscious and flashy camerawork and non-linear editing (clearly derived in part from *Performance*). His obsessions are the familiar ones of the masculinist, European *avant garde* – sex and death, by way of Sigmund Freud, Géorges Bataille, the Marquis de Sade *et al*. While some critics revere Roeg's movies (there's no one else quite like him in British cinema), others find his films pretentious and indulgent.[15]

Nic Roeg said his basic approach to film was melancholic – that is, proceeding from a form of reflection and introspection (J. Hacker, 368). Like Michelangelo Antonioni, Nic Roeg believed that the central fact of modern life was solitude, the fact of every individual being existentially alone. 'We are all so lonely really... Human beings are so lonely' (ib., 370). Consequently, films were a way of trying to make contact, a way of saying 'is anyone out there?' (ibid.).

The problem that Nic Roeg faces, as a filmmaker, is clearly finding the

---

14 *Bad Timing* reworked the sexual obsession of *Last Tango in Paris*, set in Vienna, but lacked the style, irony, eroticism and philosophical tautness of the 1972 film.
15 There was always a tendency in Nic 4Roeg's work too for pretending to be high art, or self-consciously arty – you can see it in *Bad Timing* or *Castaway*. In short, Roeg is not Pier Paolo Pasolini or Walerian Borowczyk.

right material, and combining his style of filmmaking with the right kind of subjects and scripts. When it works, it's wonderful – as in *Don't Look Now* and *The Man Who Fell To Earth*. But when the mix is off-balance, the results can be superficial, silly and flashy in the worst, MTV manner (*Castaway*). Roeg isn't a writer, and doesn't write his films.

THE MAN WHO FELL TO EARTH

There's a link between *The Man Who Fell to Earth* (1975) and Donald Cammell, not only that Nic Roeg directed the movie: Cammell's brother David had bought up the rights to Walter Tevis's novel from Metromedia (when they were developing it as a TV series). David Cammell recalled that although he spent 3 years negotiating the deal with Columbia, they dropped it quite far along in preproduction. British Lion picked it up, but David Cammell wasn't allowed to produce the movie (he did keep a share of the profits though) (U, 171). *The Man Who Fell to Earth* was produced by Michael Deeley and Barry Spikings and written by Paul Mayersberg from Walter Tevis's novel. It starred David Bowie in his finest screen role.

The Man Who Fell To Earth is a kind of follow-up to 1970's *Performance*, or at least displays its influence. And pretty much everybody agrees that David Bowie, at that point in his career, was terrific casting. *The Man Who Fell To Earth* is certainly an intriguing movie, a challenging movie, but much of its long-lasting appeal is surely due to Bowie in the lead role. Because too much of it is also trying too hard to be 'serious' or arty or self-conscious (the traits which scupper so much of Nic Roeg's work as a film director). However, *The Man Who Fell To Earth* was not conceived by Roeg – it was written by Paul Mayersberg (and based on Walter Tevis's novel). And the other appealing aspect of *The Man Who Fell To Earth* is its fascination with Americana – it's another example of a movie that celebrates pop culture Americana (forget the alien visiting Earth element and you have a lengthy exploration of Americana, combined with the portrait of an alienated young man. And some guff about big business and corporate North Amerika).

And it was a brave performance in another respect – there is a *lot* of nudity for David Bowie, and full nudity, too. And sex scenes. And in many scenes Bowie is stripped to the waist. There are many actors (indeed, probably most actors) who won't do full nudity.[16]

It seems odd that observers of the production such as writer Paul Mayersberg should have been so impressed with David Bowie's acting ability and concentration (the view at the time was that Bowie was a flaky, wasted rock star). The skinny, seemingly fragile body deceived them. Maybe they'd forgotten that Bowie had been learning acting chops from seasoned veterans such as Lindsay Kemp back in the 1960s, that he had already performed in numerous venues across Britain, Europe and the U.S.A. (and knew how to work an audience), that he had delivered the incendiary stage show *Ziggy Stardust*, that he had created characters such as Ziggy Stardust and Major Tom (and many more), that he was a ruthless operator who would even dismiss his entire band on stage (and at the height of their success), and that he was an incredibly ambitious and driven personality.

The Man Who Fell To Earth brought familiar accusations of David Bowie 'just playing himself', which have been hurled at numerous performers. Yeah, if only it were that simple! Those same critics seem to have forgotten that Bowie was by then a veteran of putting on masks and personas. However, there *were* elements drawn from Bowie's real life in his portrayal of Thomas Jerome Newton the alien – the limo he drives was one that Bowie used, and his bodyguard (Tony Mascia) was his real bodyguard.

If you know about the David Bowie Story, you'll find numerous in-jokes built into *The Man Who Fell to Earth*. Oliver Farnsworth says they'll be bigger than RCA (Bowie's record company), there's a traditional Japanese theatre show,[17] Thomas Jerome Newton declines shaking hands,[18] Bowie sings embarrassingly in the church,[19] someone wonders if Newton wants to put on some music, Bowie collapses in the elevator (Bowie apprently wouldn't even get into an elevator at this time),[20] Newton ends up in NYC (which Bowie has done since the 1980s), and so on.

John Phillips (of the Mamas and Papas) composed the music for the movie *The Man Fell To Earth*, altho' David Bowie had hoped he would be able to do it. Bowie worked with arranger Paul Buckmaster on some pieces (in the end, five songs). There were business reasons for the decision, but

---

16 But, I guess, Bowie would've been OK with the nudity – apart from being a major show-off and pop performer on stage (and in those revealing Ziggy costumes!), he had also had threesomes with Angie Barnett, and plenty of affairs with men and women.
17 Japanese culture has been a key ingredient in the David Bowie Legend: ever since Lindsay Kemp introduced the young actor and mime to kabuki theatre and noh theatre in the late 1960s, Bowie has been a passionate devotee of all things Japanese (he has visited the country many times).
18 Reflecting the (false) idea (inspired by Bowie's manager Tony DeFries) that Bowie didn't like being touched.
19 That scene seems included to capitalize on David Bowie's status – and Candy Clark steps out of character to giggle at the sight of Bowie, international pop superstar, pretending to fluff along to a hymn he would've known from way back in school: 'Jerusalem'.
20 That Bowie has a nose-bleed in this scene is reminiscent of Japanese animation, where a guy getting a nose-bleed occurs in humorous or embarrassing situations (sometimes with an erotic component).

the producers (Michael Deeley/ Barry Spikings/ British Lion) went with Phillips in the end. Seems absolutely mad now – in the age of synergy and cross-platform marketing, it'd be insane not to have Bowie deliver the soundtrack (or least a song or two). And you wish he had, because Phillips delivered some interesting textures and atmospheres, but it wasn't a patch on Bowie's music (yeah, and a hit theme song could've lifted the movie's media image immensely. Imagine a song as monumentally classic as 'Rebel Rebel' or 'The Jean Genie' being associated with the movie!).

David Bowie may have been conscious of some competition with Mick Jagger in taking on his first major movie role.[21] After all, Jagger had delivered an outstanding turn as the reclusive rock star Turner in Warners Brothers' *Performance*. Certainly both Jagger and Bowie watched each other's careers closely (as well as being friends). [22]

David Bowie could possibly have become a much bigger movie star than he was: he is acting up a storm in so many pop promos and videos. And he played prominent roles in movies such as *Labyrinth*, *The Hunger* and *Merry Christmas Mr Lawrence*. But how much higher he could've gone – to superstar status in cinema, perhaps.

But only in the right roles – David Bowie needed to be cast in the right sort of parts (generally, straight or serious drama). That he had the acting chops anyone could see from his stage performances as early as the *Ziggy Stardust* movie or earlier (and later in *The Elephant Man* on Broadway). A charismatic star that the camera adores, Bowie could have headlined many more movies. He might've become a strong romantic star, for instance, or a gently comedic actor in a romantic comedy in the mid-1980s.

✵

There isn't really a story in *The Man Who Fell to Earth*. Well, yes, of course there is – but this isn't a movie about a story: rather, it's a thematic picture, and it's about characters. It takes up themes like big business in contemporary North Amerika, the past haunting the present, and of course romantic love, perhaps Hollywood's number one theme.

And the central section of *The Man Who Fell to Earth* meanders somewhat, as it focusses on the relationship of Mary Lou and Thomas Jerome Newton. But later, in the final reels, it's wandering all over the place – by which time I would guess half the people in the theatre are either asleep or on their way to the bar.

The Man Who Fell to Earth is way, way too long. It's one of those movies that's made all the points it's going to make, that has shown us all

---

21 Mick Jagger apparently wanted Bowie's role in *The Man Who Fell To Earth*.
22 A number of ideas were mooted for David Bowie in movies: one idea was for Bowie to team up with Mick Jagger for two 1980s flicks: *Dirty Rotten Scoundrels* and *Ishtar*.

the spectacle, all the ideas, by two-thirds in. After that, it hobbles along drunkenly, having lost all notion of what it started out to achieve, just like Newton in his rock star/ Howard Hughes recluse phase.

If regarded as a conventional fiction film, *The Man Who Fell to Earth* suffers for having underwritten characters (you can see the actors floundering, too),[23] themes and issues that're confused and muddily presented, very little dramatic juice, a film which raises more questions than it answers, a movie searching for 'meaning'... But if you regarded *The Man Who Fell to Earth* as a movie of images, sounds and motifs, maybe it has more value. As David Bowie's first major acting job, it's far more interesting that anything in the story or the characters.

Candy Clark is charming, winsome, and delightfully gormless at times (and that hair! Who was the hairdresser on *The Man Who Fell to Earth* – it was Martin Samuel (Linda DeVetta did the make-up and May Roth was costume designer) – Bowie sports his red-orange-yellow hair of the time, but poor Clark gets a variety of 'bad hair' treatments). Unfortunately, Clark's Mary Lou is allowed to be played first whining then at really hysterical levels in the later scenes.

Meanwhile, Rip Torn's college professor in *The Man Who Fell To Earth* is a cliché of an ageing teacher who preys upon his students. The sex (again cut-up on the Movieola in the *Performance/ Don't Look Now* manner) is naff and unbelievable. The films directed by Nic Roeg often contain sex but it comes over as creepy and exploitative (but not as much fun as exploitation or underground or mondo cinema!). And Torn's professor banging his 18 year-old pupils is literally dirty old man material, as is the later frolicking on the bed with a gun with the ageing Mary Lou and Thomas Jerome Newton.[24]

The alien planet scenes are disappointingly unimaginative, cheesily low budget,[25] hopelessly bathetic (with a treacly sentimentality seemingly devoid of irony), and clearly filmed in the drier, desert parts of New Mexico (where other parts of the 1975 movie were shot).[26]

The Man Who Fell to Earth is a schizophrenic movie: it can't decide what (or who) it wants to be. The problems lie entirely with the script and the concept (tho' the filmmaking is also confused at times). It reminds me of movies such as *Zabriskie Point* (1970) or *Red Desert* (1964), in which

---

23 Rip Torn acts perpetually bemused in the later scenes, when he meets Newton.
24 From the same 1970s period, Nic Roeg is no match for masters of eroticism such as Walerian Borowczyk or Pier Paolo Pasolini.
25 That wedge-shaped transport with the sail! The concrete, breeze block monorail! The wilfully crude space suits (as if consciously apeing Bowie's 'Space Oddity' promo flick, which was the stand-out song in *Love You Till Tuesday*, where Bowie cavorts with two space-babes (played by Samantha Bond, a model, and Susie Mercer, the director Malcolm Thomson's girlfriend).).
26 *The Man Who Fell to Earth* was filmed in New Mexican locations such as Artesia (for the small town), Albuquerque, Madrid, Jemez Springs, the White Sands Missile Range, Alamogordo, and in Gotham.

lots *seems* to be happening, and Existential or philosophical issues *seem* to be explored (and there're nods of trendy pop culture, such as pop music or pop stars, and a'course some titillating but actually quite coldly portrayed nudity), and yet ... nuttin' much of anything is going on (it also resembles *The Passenger*, also released in 1975 – there's even a nod to *Blow-Up* in the darkroom scene. But Nic Roeg is no Michelangelo Antonioni, altho' both could be wilfully obscure and self-consciously 'arty' in their pursuit of the issues of identity and contemporary culture).

Pauline Kael dug her claws in to the 1975 movie, as she so often did, bless her. An uninvolving mess, which one can try looking at as a 'sci-fi framework for a sex-role-confusion fantasy', Kael opined. 'It's not just the grainy stock and bad sound – technically, we've come a long way. It's the cheesy sex, the awkward edits, the hammy symbolism, the mix of art-house aesthetics and exploitation cliché', remarked Steven Rea (*Philadelphia Inquirer*). For Marc Mohan in the *Portland Oregonian*, there was an 'inherent contradiction' in the movie: 'this sexually explicit motion picture, seemingly made by and for altered consciousness, is all about how an innocent newcomer falls prey to gin, sex, and television'.

SYD BARRETT

As well as Brian Jones, Mick Jagger and Jimmy Page, I also think of Roger 'Syd' Barrett in relation to the characterization of Turner in *Performance*. Poor Syd, the lead singer and founder of Pink Floyd, suffered a breakdown, exacerbated by drugs and other factors, and left the Floyd in 1968.

Towards the end, when Syd Barrett was still in the band, he was performing poorly; sometimes he would stand on stage and barely sing or play. Sometimes he would strum his Fender Telecaster incessantly and tunelessly (you can see Brian Jones disconnecting from the rest of the Rolling Stones in a similar way in the movie *One Plus One*). Other times, he would walk off stage. Once, he crushed Mandrax pills, mixing them with Brylcreem, and smeared it in his hair. As the goo melted, Nick Kent said (in *The Dark Stuff*) that Barrett 'looked like some grotesque waxwork of himself on fire, a blurred effigy of melting flesh and brain tissue coming apart in front of his peers, his fans and his followers.'

Syd Barrett was a nice bloke, apparently, who went mad. Nick Kent suggested that taking large amounts of LSD may have unhinged Barrett, creating a breakdown. More likely the drugs enhanced an already fragile mind, because not everyone who takes acid goes nuts (*Performance* charts the derangement of Chas Devlin brought on by mescalin and magic mushrooms). Certainly Barrett's drug-taking didn't help much, when it came to maintaining sanity.

When Syd Barrett & co. started taking LSD, things changed. Barrett moved to 101, Cromwell Road, 'the most notorious underground address in South Kensington', as Nicholas Schaffner put it in *Saucerful of Secrets: The Pink Floyd Odyssey* (76). It was here that Barrett began using LSD, Mandrax and other drugs regularly. The creative types at 101, Cromwell Road were 'heavily drug-orientated', as one of Barrett's Cambridge friends put it (ib., 76). At Earlham Street and Cromwell Road people would visit Barrett and give him acid, often when he didn't know it. Nick Kent claimed that some of the people Barrett associated with were really unstable themselves (very probable), and spiked his tea frequently (which seems especially cruel, as well as pathetically childish). Thus began Barrett's 'acid-fuelled derangement' (ib., 79).

June Child (later Bolan) recalled Barrett's acid trips:

> He used to come round to my house at five in the morning covered in mud from Holland Park when he'd freaked out. He used to go to the Youth Hostel in Holland Park, climb up on the roof and get wrecked and spaced, and he'd walk all the way to Shepherd's Bush, where I was living. [27]

Afterwards, the former Pink Floyd frontman lived as a recluse in Cambridge and Chelsea, moving between the two before returning to Cambridge in 1976 (and walking all the way, so legend has it), where he remained until his death from cancer in 2008. He sat for hours in front of television in his two-room flat in Chelsea Cloisters, with the curtains always drawn and the windows closed. He became fat and bald.[28] When John Marsh (Pink Floyd's lighting roadie) saw Barrett at South Ken tube, he was reminded of a 'picture of a middle-aged Aleister Crowley. Totally bald, about 15 stone, wearing a Hawaiian shirt and Bermuda shorts'.[29] There were other similar casualties in rock: Peter Green was in a mental hospital, and later became a hospital porter and gravedigger, while Danny Kirwan of Fleetwood Mac ended up in St Mungo's in Covent Garden amongst the

---

[27] In N. Kent, 1994, 109.
[28] Pink Floyd would bitterly satirize Syd Barrett (unfairly, I think) in *Wish You Were Here* and *The Wall* (altho' 1975's *Wish You Were Here*, like most o' Pink Floyd's darker material, is really about Roger Waters' paranoia and cynicism). In the film of *The Wall*, Bob Geldof's unhinged rock star shaves his head and acts weird in his hotel room.
[29] J. Green, 167.

drunks and derelicts.[30] At least Turner in *Performance*, though a recluse, has time to put on make-up and look attractive (note that Mick Jagger is never portrayed as horrible, or wasted from drug-taking, which would've been an obvious route to take).

Stories of Syd Barrett's crazy antics abound. He is supposed to have locked his girlfriend Lynsey Horner in a room for a week. He kept her alive with water and cookies. When she was rescued by June Child and Juliette Wright (Rick Wright's wife), Barrett proceeded to lock himself in the room (N. Schaffner, 78). Apocryphal or not, these stories all enhance the media legend. Poor Syd:

> Everyone is supposed to have fun when they're young – I don't know why, but I never did.[31]

In *Performance*, Turner hasn't gone that far yet. His problem, as Pherber and Lucy tell Chas, is that he is creatively blocked. It's art, and magic, for Turner, not drugs or sex. And it's Pherber, much more than Turner, who's into drugs (he tells her to watch out when she's injecting heroin into her butt; she says it's B-12; yeah, but a healthy woman – nay, a force of nature – like Pherber sure doesn't need vitamin shots!). As well as being Turner's lover, Pherber is his drug dealer, his fixer, preparing joints for him.

ONE PLUS ONE (a.k.a *SYMPATHY FOR THE DEVIL*)

A key intertext with *Performance*, cinematically and culturally, is Jean-Luc Godard's movie *One Plus One* (a.k.a. *Sympathy For the Devil*), made in 1968, in which the French New Wave *auteur* came to Britain to direct a film. Michael Pearson and Ian Quarrier produced for Cupid Productions; many in the crew were Brits: Tony Richmond[32] (DP), Arthur Bradburn and Derek Ball (sound); John Stoneman (AD), etc. Ken Rowles, Agnès Guillemot and Christiane Aya were the editors.

One Plus One is known now primarily for its documentation of the Rolling Stones in their prime in the recording studio working out one of the

---

30 G. Tremlett, 1990, 83.
31 Syd Barrett, interview, *Rolling Stone*, Autumn, 1971
32 Tony Richmond later worked on *The Man Who Fell To Earth*.

anthems of the time, 'Sympathy For the Devil'.[33] Mick, Keef, Charlie, Bill and Brian are shown rehearsing the song, trying out different grooves, and recording take after take. Sometimes they try it as a shuffle, or as a ballad, sometimes they get the bongos, shakers and tom toms out, sometimes they sit on the floor in a circle, all cosy and hippyish. They try it at different tempos.

The Rolling Stones come across as young professionals working at getting the song right, not the bad boys and rebels of Andrew Loog Oldham's marketing schemes. In between takes, they sit around and smoke (like everybody in a Jean-Luc Godard movie), but they're nice, middle-class boys from Dartford and Lewisham for the rest of the time.

Mick Jagger and Keith Richards are very much the ringleaders (it's always Richards who counts in the music), while Brian Jones strums an acoustic guitar in his own little corner. He seems to be lost in his own, private world, quite apart from the rest of the band (except when Richards gives him cigarettes during breaks), and Jones's guitar is not heard on the soundtrack. Indeed, the soundtrack is markedly different from the visuals – sometimes it appears as if the camera is picking up sound with the filmmakers' own mike – which unprofessionally swings into the shot from time to time – or as if they're getting a feed from the control room.

Jean-Luc Godard and his crew cover the recording session with lengthy, slow tracking shots. The camera not only captures the musicians, but also the engineers and people hanging about in the wings. It's a curious document of a rock 'n' roll band in the studio – not at all like the average rockumentary (the band are not interviewed, for a start, nor do they or the filmmakers provide a commentary, or even basic contextual information). And the 1968 film contains many pauses and halts which many other documentaries or films of a rock band would cut out. Moments where musicians fiddle around with guitars. The film dwells on moments when 'nothing happens'. The camera tracks around the flats to show friends of the band who aren't identified, and just seem to be hanging out (Anita Pallenberg is among the group). The 1968 film doesn't, for instance, go into the control room, where much of the real action in a recording session occurs. So the producers, the engineers and the hangers-on in the control room aren't heard or seen, except as vague figures behind the glass. Instead, the film stays resolutely on the floor of Olympic Studios.

A typical account of a recording session would automatically include

---

[33] Garry Mulholland found *One Plus One* 'an incredibly strange film': 'I love the clothes. Everyone in this film looks heartbreakingly cool... Most of all, I love the way Godard's camera prowls slowly, around the Stones, around his actors and locations. It lingers on something interesting, gets bored, moves on, and takes in every detail of its surroundings on its way to the next thing worth lingering upon. Godard's camera is as great an art thing as the Rolling Stones were in 1968, and that is a very good thing indeed' (76-77).

the producers, maybe an engineer, usually someone from the record company, maybe a journalist hanging around, but *One Plus One* does none of that. Yet it still works (it helps, of course, that this is a world-famous rock 'n' roll act – it wouldn't have quite the same resonance if it was a bunch of unknowns. But because it's Mick and Keef and the boys, it's fascinating).[34]

One Plus One had a troubled production history. Jean-Luc Godard said he hadn't wanted to come to England to make a picture, but he said he would if he could have either the Beatles or the Rolling Stones to film. The Rolling Stones agreed, and the maestro came to Blighty in 1968, with a budget of £180,000 ($280,000). The Stones were filmed at Olympic Studios in Barnes (one of the regular haunts of numerous pop acts), over three days (it was a former sound stage, with the space separated by baffle boards, and the windows shuttered against daylight. Glyn Jones was the house engineer).[35]

The initial idea was to interweave two stories: one of the Rolling Stones in the recording studio (a story of construction), the other about a white woman (played by Anne Wiazemsky, Jean-Luc Godard's young wife) who commits suicide when her black lover leaves her to join a Black Power group.

Problems Jean-Luc Godard encountered while shooting in London included the arrest of Brian Jones, and also Terence Stamp (who would have played Iain Quarrier's part – and he would have been far better; Quarrier doesn't seem to quite fit into a Godard film). The Black Power scenes were disrupted by rain.[36] The studio roof in Barnes caught fire.

One Plus One seems to have been one of Jean-Luc Godard's less than happy productions, and he was glad to return to France (it was May, 1968 when Godard left for Britain, and he might have preferred to stay in Paris, with so many things going on politically). In July, 1968, Godard returned to Blighty to complete the movie. Godard later said that 'the whole thing was a mistake', which's too harsh, though there is something in Wheeler Dixon's complaint (in *The Films of Jean-Luc Godard*) about 'a thinness of material' and Iain Quarrier's interference.[37]

Iain Quarrier, one of the producers, didn't see eye to eye with Jean-Luc Godard. When the Rolling Stones' manager and Quarrier added the completed version of 'Sympathy For the Devil' onto the end of his film, Godard attacked him at a public screening at the London Film Festival. You

---

[34] The hippy fashions are terrific in *One Plus One* – bright yellow, green and red trousers, pink and purple shirts.
[35] Godard's film crew were in Olympic Studios from the beginning of June.
[36] The weather threatens to scupper the shoot at Camber Sands: it's often very windy on the beach, and the day the production was there was another windy one.
[37] W. Dixon, 1997, 107; M. Goodwin, 28.

don't do that kind of thing to a great artist like Godard! (Quarrier was determined that a complete rendition of 'Sympathy For the Devil' would appear in the picture). Godard subsequently disowned Quarrier's version. The point was, Godard contended, that art and politics took years to develop, and the audience should only know a little of the song. The song was still developing, Godard said, and shouldn't be seen at the end. It was unfair to emphasize the Stones more than the group of black people. They were both as important as each other.[38]

One aspect of *One Plus One* that critics drew attention to, apart from its collage, non-narrative structure, its troubled production, and its account of the Rolling Stones in action, was that Jean-Luc Godard was shooting the film in English. Nearly all of Godard's films have been made in French (with English as the main secondary language). English has been used in many films (such as *Tout Va Bien*, *King Lear* and *JLG/ JLG*), but Godard was clearly much happier writing and filming in French.

One Plus One is a collage of other Godardian concerns: politics being number one, of course – this being 1968 and the height of Jean-Luc Godard's political cinema, and politicization of cinema. There are references to J.F. Kennedy, Mao Zedong, Communism, the FBI, the CIA, liberalism, democracy, trade unionism, all the usual Godardian political obsessions and *bête noirs*. Godard adds his political histories, of course, but slants them in some instances towards British history (citing Trafalgar, or El Alamein).

Anne Wiazemsky is seen spraying graffiti on cars, shops, walls, sidewalks, fences, billboards, embankments, doors and hotel windows (words like 'Stalin', 'Freudemocracy', 'Cinemarxism', and '(SO)VIETCONG') around London (she's playing the part of a Godardian political activist in a long coat and hat: a woman who's cute *and* into politics: it's the ultimate Godardian romantic fantasy! Wiazemsky plays a similar function to Pherber in *Performance* – a young, sexy woman who's also a muse, a guru, a tease, and a mystery).

One Plus One is a pæan to graffiti, the film as readymade, 20 years b4 it became fashionable (and there's plenty of graffiti in *Performance*). Some of the graffiti is wordplay and acrostics, which Godard has always loved:

```
        M
        A
        R
    S E X
```

---
38 Godard, in J. Cott, *Rolling Stone*, June, 1969.

```
M A O
    R
    T
```

If a bunch of media or film or drama or Eng. Lit. students went out and filmed themselves graffitying walls and doors with revolutionary word puzzles, a tutor might send them out again to do something *decent* and *interesting*. But Jean-Luc Godard can get away with it. Not because he 'means it', not because he 'believes' in this leftist, Maoist, Marxist, Freudian revolutionary politics, but because... well, he's *Godard*.

Jean-Luc Godard makes revolution *sexy*. Or at least *fun*. Soviet and Russian propaganda films can be so solemn, so serious. But Godard adds *humour* to revolutionary politics, which is extraordinary – and still extraordinary decades later. The world may be very different in the 2010s (is it, though?), but the additions of humour and verve mean that Godard's films don't appear as didactic, sombre, po-faced treatises. If you put Anne Wiazemsky or Anna Karina into a piece on pro-left-wing, anti-right-wing politics you have something automatically appealing (similarly, take away the playful, mercurial and humorous Pherber out of *Performance* and you have a much more sombre second half. Anita Pallenberg's wicked, playful presence helps to keep *Performance* sexy, exciting and unpredictable).

There are some extraordinary, very long takes in *One Plus One* (a master of montage, Jean-Luc Godard also features more long takes than most filmmakers. It's the opposite of the rapid montage style of *Performance*). One of the most amazing takes lasts some 10 minutes and thirty seconds, shot in a car scrapyard, beside the River Thames (and a railroad bridge), which appears to be the base of a Black Power group (all black, and all male). The camera tracks and pans constantly (it's one of Godard's 360° track-and-pans): past individuals reading from political texts, and newspapers, and a book about the history of popular music; another guy who hands out rifles to his comrades and later on in the shot fires his gun; a group of three white women in white dresses are brought into the compound in a red Mini (all the men are black); the women are prisoners and victims; a man strokes one woman who lies on the ground, while another guy next to him talks about black men's desire for white women; the other women are taken off camera (one appears to be raped, in the back of a car, another is shot dead; both are bloody). Sometimes the jets overhead or horns from boats on the river drown out the people reading aloud; sometimes the narration by Sean Lynch is faded up over the direct sound.[39] At the end of the sequence shot, the revolutionary leader says, 'it's not a question of left or right, it's a question of black'.

No one else in the world would produce a shot like that – and nobody else would *want to*! (As filmmakers Donald Cammell and Nic Roeg are certainly extraordinary, but they are not a patch, as they would admit, on Jean-Luc Godard; similarly, *Performance*, for all its artistry and would-be radicalism, is out-shone by the work of Godard. But then, Godard out-shines pretty much *everybody*!).

In the second black militant scene in *One Plus One* (the 'black syntax' scene), again at the junkyard by the River Thames, again covered in a track-and-pan shot around 360 degrees, the men are now arranged around the compound on cars, and throw the rifles and guns from one to another repeating phrases such as 'kill them!' Slogans such as 'Malcolm X' are sprayed on the cars. A Black Power leader is interviewed by two black, female journalists, voicing many of Jean-Luc Godard's revolutionary concerns. Near the Mini car a man lays the guns on the corpses of two white women – the symbolism of war and death needs no gloss. During this sequence, the 1968 film sets up a series of actions and rhetoric which it returns to. Here the actors are at the edge – either of corpsing, or of forgetting their lines.

This is very typical Godardian cinema, a slice of prime Sixties Godardania, but interesting for a British audience because it was filmed in Great Britain. In amongst the Marxist/ radical polemic are parts of contemporary Britain, which give *One Plus One* a particular flavour, quite different from Godard's French or Swiss films.

The British setting is endlessly fascinating for me – it's something to do with the way that Jean-Luc Godard and his team have filmed Britain. It's not the London of films made by Brits in London – the *Carry On* films, or *James Bond*, or 1960s musicals like *Oliver*. Godard is in London, but he avoids every single, major landmark, the ones that crop up in every film set in London: Big Ben, Buckingham Palace, Tower Bridge, the British Museum, red London buses, etc. Only the River Thames and parts of the river bridges are present. But it's still very much London: Godard's film provincializes London, turns it into a series of small roads... grey corrugated fences that hide industrial plants... a scrapyard... a row of small shops... In short, he Godardizes Britain, turning London into Godardland.

And this London, this Britain, in *One Plus One* hasn't changed one bit in four decades or more. Only the cars are different, and a bit of the street

---

[39] Sometimes the long sequence shots threaten to come unstuck – when actors nearly forget their lines, or botch up their readings from texts. Some of the actors were clearly not used to Godard's way of filmmaking.

furniture. Somehow Jean-Luc Godard and his collaborators have filmed Albion in 1968 and made it timeless and unchanging, whereas the comedies, the musicals, the spy thrillers and the 'Swinging London' films look incredibly dated, very much fixed in their time.

Similarly, London in *Performance* is still instantly recognizable today: and although there *are* scenes shot in central London (the car scenes at the beginning, which take in Trafalgar Square and Lincoln's Inn Fields, for instance), *Performance* creates a very different sort of London.

Another long take in *One Plus One* (entitled 'All About Eve') has Eve Democracy[40] (Anne Wiazemsky) being interviewed by Iain Quarrier and a film crew in a sunny, leafy, English wood. As Wiazemsky/ Eve and Quarrier wander around the trees, bushes and grass, Quarrier fires questions at Eve, who replies to everything with a one-word answer, yes or no (though it's mostly 'yes' – how can you say 'no' to Jean-Luc Godard's barrage of rhetoric? And what could democracy answer, Godard said, but yes *and* no).

Iain Quarrier's questions include classic Godard gems such as:
- 'do you have a theory about who killed Kennedy?'
- 'do you feel exploited by interviews?'
- 'orgasm is the only moment when you can't cheat life'
- 'is taking drugs a form of spiritual gambling?'[41]

Maybe it's Eve from the *Bible* in Paradise, a young woman in a lemon yellow dress in a sunny, green wood. That relates to the original concept for *One Plus One*, which was to have been a film about creation (the Rolling Stones at work in the studio), and destruction (the suicide of a young white woman when her lover joins a Black Power group). And it's Eve because one of Godard's concerns at the time was the notion of starting from zero.

Critics have complained that Jean-Luc Godard's cinema doesn't provide answers, but only asks questions. Of course. Ditto with Donald Cammell. And any artist. Godard loves to ask questions, and he doesn't have all the answers (or any answers). He wants to ask – he can't stop himself from asking – but he can't deliver pat answers to his own questions. And how many times have you seen have you seen filmmakers interviewed by people who ask, what does this or that scene mean, including Cammell? And filmmakers always deflect those sorts of questions.

The narration of *One Plus One* (read by Sean Lynch) was typical Jean-Luc Godard: scenes of fucking, *film noir* thriller, political observations, counter-culture activism, pop culture references, ruminations about

---

40 David A. Cook calls this character 'a lobotomized fairy godmother' (1996, 569). Eh?
41 It's London, 1968, so there are quite a few questions about drugs. Godard said he didn't use them because they had too strong an effect on him. He did partake of tobacco, of course, chain-smoking. The questions do not require an answer, and they all come from Godard. You could take all of those questions and publish them as a political pamphlet.

revolution, and allusions to Communism, Joseph Stalin, Mao Zedong, Russia, J.F. Kennedy, CIA, FBI, Walt Disney, etc.

It sounded like a combination of counter-culture faves such as Terry Southern (*Candy, Dr Strangelove, Blue Movie*), William Burroughs (*The Naked Lunch*), Tom Wolfe, Norman Mailer and Henry Miller. The voiceover is heard all of the way through the 1968 movie, including the final shot.[42]

The most amusing scene in *One Plus One* was constructed from more lengthy takes, set in a small bookstore that sold paperback novels, comic-books and soft porn magazines. Iain Quarrier wandered about (clad nattily in bright purple), reading aloud from *Mein Kampf* as he walks round the room, while a female secretary typed (maybe taking down Quarrier's words, maybe not – but why would you re-type *Mein Kampf*?), and customers perused the merchandize.

Tony Richmond's camera zoomed in and out of the rack of porno-graphic magazines, the comicbooks and the pulp softbacks. While Adolf Hitler's famous tract was read aloud, the camera panned along images of magazine covers showing half-naked women and coverlines like 'see Sophia Loren nude!', or American superheroes. This was, again, pure Godard. *8mm Magazine, Slaves To Sin, The Body,* Agatha Christie, Mickey Spillaine, Perry Mason, *Conan, Mayfair, Penthouse, Playboy* and *I Gave My Body To Hitler*. No other commentary was needed: this display of late 1960s publishing was unreal enough (the way the camera crawls across those wonderfully lurid book and magazine covers was like a history lesson or museum display in itself: it was Godard's own *Guide To Book Publishing In Late 1960s Britain*).[43]

If this wasn't silly enough, Jean-Luc Godard had each of the customers *seig heil* to Iain Quarrier after they'd bought their books. The customers also got to slap two hippy peaceniks sitting on one side (presumably meant to be some kind of political dissidents or activists – one has a head wound and a bloody bandage). They yelled out slogans: 'long live Mao!' + 'Peace in Vietnam!'. The scene was a pantomime of counter-culture discourse, very silly, very irritating, very didactic, very amusing, and very Godard.[44]

One Plus One closes with a bizarre sequence shot on the beach at Camber Sands in Sussex (it's the 'escape' scene, like 'going to Persia' in

---

[42] I would love to see Godard film the book of the narration, though! It would be the Ultimate Godard Movie - a twenty million dollar revolutionary call to arms (or a hundred and thirty million dollars by today's prices).
[43] Decades on, nothing has changed in dear, old Britain - there's simply loads more - the same book and magazine publishing, the same bookstores - those that haven't been squeezed out by the cultural imperialism of Borders or Waterstone's.
[44] It's the kind of scene that the Monty Python team might have made a year or so later in their TV shows at the Beeb: Adolf Hitler in his retirement running a porn mag and pulp paperback store, loudly declaiming from his own *Mein Kampf* while his customers happily *seig heil* him.

Performance). More guns, terrorists, films-within-films, self-conscious cinematic referencing, and Anne Wiazemsky racing around, stumbling a few times, before winding up on a camera crane, slumped beside a camera, and two flags (one red, one black). The final image of *One Plus One* has Wiazemsky on the camera crane raised in the air and framed against the sky. Jean-Luc Godard can be seen in a long coat and hat, running about directing the scene in high wind.

One Plus One is more a series of Godardian skits and sketches and essays with only the Rolling Stones sessions offering a through-line (the graffiti scenes are graphic punctuation, without a developing narrative).[45] And the dramatic blocks of the 1968 movie don't meld (but that was partly Jean-Luc Godard's point, of course, and one reason why the completed song 'Sympathy For the Devil' isn't heard – this is a film the viewer has to put together themselves). For that and other reasons, some Godardians find it a minor and not very satisfying work, and some barely mention it. Maybe. I really like it – for its British settings, its sense of fun, and its music and studio sessions. And, hell, this *is* the Rolling Stones!

There's also the pleasure of seeing Anne Wiazemsky skittering thru London trying to whip up revolutionary fervour with her slogans. Somehow, Marxist, Maoist Revolution and Quaint, Shabby, Provincial England don't go together. Yes, I know some of 1968's political demonstrations occurred in the U.K. (including inspiring Mick Jagger to write 'Street Fighting Maahhiiinnnn'), but, somehow, it's not quite the same as Paris or North America.[46]

And it's the same with the gangster lifestyle in Britain: somehow, it always comes across as parochial and suburban. Chas Devlin is impeccably dressed and cool and mean and charismatic and quite brilliant in the 1970 movie, but the gangster world of *Performance* is also quaint and provincial.

---

[45] Fredric Jameson wasn't impressed by *One Plus One*, complaining about: 'the low budget look of amateur actors, staged tableaux, and vaudeville-type numbers, essentially static and strung together' (1990).
[46] Godard was depressed by the apathy among the students he met at the University of Essex.

FITZCARRALDO

A film that Mick Jagger was cast in and partly filmed was *Fitzcarraldo* (1981), the epic of taking opera into the Amazonian jungle by steamboat, directed by Werner Herzog. *Fitzcarraldo* was dogged by controversy even before filming began. The lead actor was replaced twice: Jack Nicholson[47] was replaced by Jason Robards, and when he dropped out due to illness, Klaus Kinski was brought in (Herzog said he also wanted Warren Oates, but he died before filming).

Mick Jagger's part was written out of the script, because his character (as a sidekick) was conceived with Jason Robards in the lead (the surviving footage of Jagger with Robards is not particularly good; however, about 40% of the film had been shot, and director Werner Herzog was very reluctant to have to drop Jagger, who left for a Rolling Stones tour and album, and to change the script. 'Losing Mick was, I think, the biggest loss I have ever experienced as a film director', Herzog remarked later [2002, 173]).

Fitzcarraldo seemed to be a production of constant set-backs, with Werner Herzog vowing that he would walk into the jungle and never come back if he couldn't get his film made. *Fitzcarraldo* seemed to be one project that Herzog had invested so much of himself; it had to get done one way or another.

But *Fitzcarraldo* isn't a particularly good movie. Fascinating. Incredible. Spectacular. But not satisfying, dramatically or narratively (let alone emotionally). Perhaps the character Mick Jagger played would have enriched the piece, and given Fitzcarraldo the sidekick he requires for the audience to understand him. As it is, when Fitzcarraldo's on the boat, which's most of the 1981 movie, nobody understands his ultimate quest of creating a rubber industry and an opera house. He appears as a somewhat crazy loner (enhanced by the way that Klaus Kinski plays him), a visionary with no hope of attaining his vision. The lack of Jagger's character seems to create a gap in *Fitzcarraldo* which the other characters cannot fill. (It's an odd thing, hankering after Mick Jagger to appear in a film he's been written out of. Jagger was terrific in *Performance*, but I'm not sure I agree with Werner Herzog who reckoned that Jagger was a much-underrated actor. It may be that Jagger was the kind of actor or performer who could be amazing in the right role, but wasn't a versatile actor who could apply himself to any role. And certainly Turner in *Performance* was tailor-made for Jagger).

---

[47] Having Jack Nicholson and Mick Jagger on board no doubt helped financing the film.

BOOGIE NIGHTS

A movie with affinities to *Wild Side*, in terms of style, themes and setting (as well as to *Performance*), is *Boogie Nights* (1998), written and directed by Paul Thomas Anderson. *Boogie Nights* is a sensational and hugely enjoyable exploration and *hommage* to 1970s culture, concentrating on LA's pornography industry in the San Fernando Valley. It was made in a knowing, ironic, post-*Pulp Fiction* style, loose, somewhat erratic, mixing comedy with an endless round of sex, drugs, violence, arguments, disappointments, losses, affairs, drugs, and more drugs. *Boogie Nights* was a film of sleazy nightclubs, Seventies disco music, people snorting coke, dysfunctional characters, and simulated sex being filmed on cheap sets.

Director Paul Thomas Anderson saw his characters as 'stripped and raw and childlike', which was, he said, a truthful reflection of the porn industry as he knew it in the San Fernando Valley (P. Anderson, 175). At the centre of *Boogie Nights* was Eddie Adams, played by Mark Wahlberg, a young hustler who becomes a teenage porn star (dubbed 'Dirk Diggler'), partly due to the size of his weiner.[48] Diggler's character recalled Seventies porn stars such as John Holmes and his 'Johnny Wad' films (Holmes's rise to fame and subsequent fall into drugs and self-loathing).

Boogie Nights delighted in recreating mid-late 1970s culture (it began in 1977) – the discos, the music, the outrageous clothes, the shops and restaurants.[49] Like *Performance*, it got the *milieu* spot on. The scenes set in Don Cheadle's nightclub were a riot of flares, tank tops, platform boots and Seventies colours, and the characters chatting as they danced to classic disco cuts (the soundtrack of *Boogie Nights* is superb).

Burt Reynolds (the only star name in *Boogie Nights*, altho' the rest of the cast became names) played a sleazy porno *meister*, Jack Horner, and much of the action took place at his Hollywood home, with its swimming pool and parties (actually, Horner was less sleazy than his financier, the colonel, who's caught with an under-age girl, or the people around him who snort coke: Horner's only vice is his cigar and alcohol – he's an old-fashioned guy). Horner was a surrogate father to a family of child-like, damaged misfits, each with their own flaws or wounds to deal with (a little like Harry Flowers and his mob in *Performance*, which's also called a 'family').

The cast of oddballs in *Boogie Nights* included Rollergirl (Heather Graham), part of Jack Horner's coterie, a wide-eyed, naïf actress mature

---
[48] The Hitchcockian MacGuffin at the heart of the film, often discussed and looked at but only seen right at the end (in a flaccid state) was Eddie's twelve-inch weenie.
[49] *Boogie Nights* was part of a number of the 1990s which revisited the era of *Saturday Night Fever*, disco and Studio 54: the *Austin Powers* films, *54*, *Velvet Goldmine*, and *What's Love Got To Do With It?*.

beyond her teenage years (she keeps her skates on in every single scene, including the sex scenes); Horner's girlfriend, the ageing porn star Amber (Julianne Moore);[50] another porn actor (played by Anderson regular John C. Reilly), a clumsy wannabe who reckons he looks like *Star Wars'* Han Solo; William H. Macy's Little Bill, a hapless, middle-aged assistant whose wife cuckolds him right in his face with younger studs; and Scotty J. (Philip Seymour Hoffman), an overweight, neurotic soundman who lusts after Dirk Diggler.

Boogie Nights opted for melodrama, lightened by comic moments, a kind of postmodern, porn soap opera (but with its fair share of angst and suffering), instead of satire and ideas. *Boogie Nights* started to meander two-thirds of the way thru, and was half-an-hour too long – it was determined to explore each of the major characters right to the bitter end. Paul Anderson acknowledged that at times he was indulgent to his characters, allowing them longer on screen than would be good for the narrative. Even though he knew that the storytelling and pacing might suffer, he would indulge his characters and actors.

Donald Cammell is similarly indulgent – especially in *Wild Side*, where you can see him letting Christopher Walken and Anne Heche go to town: when you have actors that good, it's tempting to just sit back and let them fly. And in *Wild Side*, boy, do they fly!

Boogie Nights was shot in an energetic style, all mobile Steadicam shots (often in lengthy, circuitous takes), and freeze frames and titles. It recalled *The Player* (Robert Altman, 1992) with its ensemble acting caught in long, loose takes, or later Martin Scorsese (*GoodFellas*, *Casino*). And this was the approach that Donald Cammell took in *Wild Side* (you can see it in many other 1990s movies, such as *Starship Troopers*, *Pulp Fiction* and *Showgirls*.[51] *Boogie Nights* was a rare item – an in-depth Hollywood exploration of the (very) lucrative porn business.

---

[50] Based, Anderson remarked, on porn stars such as Veronica Hart, Marilyn Chambers and Seka.
[51] Paul Thomas Anderson said his stylistic influences were *GoodFellas*, *Nashville* and *The Battle of Algiers*. He was after something loose, and raw. Many of the camera moves were inspired by the music (P.T. Anderson. "Night Fever", in J. Hillier, 2001, 176). Whip pans and rapid camera movements were another stylistic device.

Donald Cammell,
U2, 'Pride', promo,
1984.

The Argument, featuring Myriam Gibril

The Argument, featuring Kendrew Lascelles as Nonus, the film director

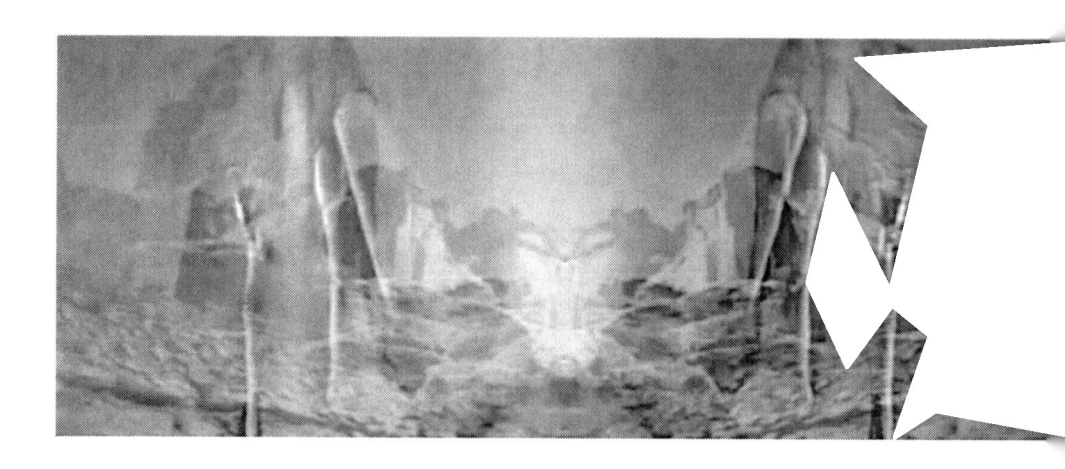

The Rolling Stones in the studio with Jean-Luc Godard for One Plus One

Mick Jagger in Peru for Fitzcarraldo

Syd Barrett (and with Pink Floyd, below).

Boogie Nights (1998)

Nic Roeg (above), co-director of Performance,
and two of his films: The Man Who Fell To Earth (below left),
and on the set of Don't Look Now (below right).

CRITICS

❄

Extracts from reviews of *Performance*.

The most disgusting, the most completely worthless film I have seen since I began reviewing.
Richard Schickel, *Time*

•

'Performance' is a bizarre, disconnected attempt to link the inhabitants of two kinds of London underworlds: pop stars and gangsters. It isn't altogether successful, largely because it tries too hard and doesn't pace itself to let its effects sink in.
Roger Ebert, *Chicago Sun-Times*

•

This hallucinogenic deconstruction of identity writhes with sex, substances, ultraviolence and good ol' rock 'n' roll.
Total Film

•

Mick Jagger? In a Brit gangster classic? Believe it. And believe that Performance is much, much more.
Jonathan Crocker, BBC

•

Clearly stands as one of the giant steps in freeing English-language film from the restrictions of Hollywood's standard narrative demands.
Andy Klein, *New Times*

•

Strange, confusing, and psychedelic, all are apt descriptions for this easy to follow story but most difficult film to keep track of.
Dennis Schwartz, *Ozus' World Movie Reviews*

FANS

✯

Extracts from online reviews of *Performance*.

AT AMAZON.COM

One of the most astonishing movies of all time.

•

Performance does upset audiences. It IS something.

•

Way ahead of its time, and in some ways ahead of ours, it's a movie that will make you yearn to have been there. In that mansion and in the 60's.

•

A must see movie that I've been viewing regularly for almost 30 years.

•

I see that most of the reviewers here give this film 5 stars... I must completely agree. This film is so radical and groundbreaking and Roeg is by far a genius... Mr. Jagger is just so perfect in this... It is one of MY top 10 films.

•

Amazing collaboration by Nic Roeg and Donald Cammell works best on film but is still captivating in VHS format. 30 years later it barely feels dated, and its dalliance with ambisexuality, drugs and rock n roll is a cut above all imitators. The blurring of identity, color and form comes as close to approximating psychedelic experience as any film ever produced.

•

What a watching experience! Performance is overwhelming In the way of how much it has to offer to its audience. Gangster melodrama, the ultimate chronicle of Swinging 60s London, the essential rock movie merges with the surreal bizarre nightmarish journey of switching and adopting personalities not unlike in Bergman's Persona to which Donald Cammell's and Nicolas Roeg's film openly refers more than once.

•

This is one of the best movies of all time. You have to watch it about thirty times to really understand it and even then I don't quite understand everything but that's the whole beauty of it. It's dark, complex and quite thrilling and beautiful. James Fox is a perfect Chas and Mick Jagger is gorgeous as Turner.

AT INTERNET MOVIE DATABASE

I don't know of any other movie where you see a Rolls Royce burning down in an acid bath, gangsters performing a strip-tease show, or a plunging view inside a skull as a bullet is shot through it, least all of them together. Besides, the recurring use of mirrors all throughout the picture, the constant play with colors and the superimposing of faces and images don't have many parallels either in film history.

•

I distinctly remember seeing this film on its initial release in Chicago. Roger Ebert at the time said he though it was either the best or the worst film he had ever seen, but that he was leaning toward the former!!! It is mind-bending, visually stunning, and chock-a-block with brilliant 'performances'! This film should not be missed by an cinema fan and it is my most eagerly awaited DVD release!

•

This film operates on multiple levels and in cultures that we barely knew existed in 1970. The East End London mobster culture being one and the London counter-culture of drugs and music another. To further lend a surreal air, Nicolas Roeg and Donald Cammell (who co-directed the film) present metaphors and psychological homologies – sadism, homosexuality, hierarchy in gangs and organizations – all stemming from central psychological needs for power and dominance combined with and expressed through sexuality

-

This superbly shot, deeply disturbing, complex, often pretentious, often brilliant parable of confused identity was the first feature directed by leading cinematographer Roeg, sharing the credit with artist Donald Cammell.

-

PERFORMANCE captured the perverse sub-culture of organized 'working class' gangsters with an unromanticized authenticity not matched until THE SOPRANOS came along three decades later. But it's not just a gangster movie; it's a heady brew overflowing with subtle and insightful intuitions about the power and dangers of the ego, the male-female equation, power structures, sex, drugs and rock 'n' roll.

-

Reading the various comments posted, I'm saddened to see that Nic Roeg is receiving the credit for this amazing film. Granted, Roeg did provide his always stunning camera work to the film, but it was Donald Cammell who wrote, directed the actors, and edited (along with Frank Mazzola) PERFORMANCE.

-

Technically the film is extraordinary, with stunning use of camera-work, editing and music throughout, and the conclusion is very ambiguous, leaving you to pose your own idea as to what really happens In the end.

-

Performance is no swinging Britain film, it's no Hard Day's Night or The Knack, there's no happiness and especially no happy ending. It's a bleak outlook on life with characters who are dark and flawed.

-

This is probably one of the best cult movies ever made. I have seen it about 20 times now and even the last time, it was still not boring and I stayed up late again to watch it at 3 In the morning (even though I have it on video).

FILMOGRAPHY
★

FILMS DIRECTED BY DONALD CAMMELL

Performance (1970)
The Argument (1972)
Demon Seed (1977)
White of the Eye (1987)
Wild Side (1995/ 2000)

SCRIPTS

The Bones of the Earth (earlier screenplay)
The Argument
RPM (as Franklin Brauner)
Wild Side
White of the Eye
Tilt
Performance
The Touchables
Duffy

OTHERS

U2: Love Is Blindness (video promo)
U2: The Best of 1980-1990 (video promo: *Pride*)
All You Zombies (the Hooters, video short)

PERFORMANCE

CREW

Directed by Donald Cammell and Nicolas Roeg
Written by Donald Cammell
Produced by Sanford Lieberson
David Cammell – associate producer
Music by Jack Nitzsche
Cinematography by Nicolas Roeg
Film Editing by Antony Gibbs, Brian Smedley-Aston, Frank Mazzola (uncredited) and Tony Palmer (uncredited)
Art Direction by John Clark
Helen Lennox – hairdresser
Linda DeVetta – makeup artist
Paul Rabiger – makeup artist
Deborah Dixon – costume consultant
Billy Jay and Emma Porteous – wardrobe
Kevin Kavanagh – unit manager
Robert Lynn – production manager
Richard Burge – assistant director
Peter Jaques – assistant director (uncredited)
Christopher Gibbs – design consultant: Turner's house
Peter Young – set dresser
Ron Barron – sound recordist
Alan Pattillo – sound editor
Gerry Humphreys – dubbing mixer/ sound re-recording mixer (uncredited)
Mike Molloy – camera operator
Paul Borg – electrician (uncredited)
Peter Hannan – first assistant camera (uncredited)
Annabel Davis-Goff – continuity
David Litvinoff – dialogue coach / technical advisor
Merry Clayton – music player (as the Merry Clayton Singers)
Ry Cooder – musician
Amiya Dasgupta – musician
Lowell George – musician
Milt Holland – musician
Bernard Krause – musician: Moog synthesisor
Randy Newman – music conductor
Gene Parsons – musician
Nasser Rastigar-Nejad – musician: santur
Buffy Sainte-Marie – music performer
Russ Titelman – musician
Bobby West – musician

CAST

James Fox – Chas Devlin
Mick Jagger – Turner
Anita Pallenberg – Pherber
Michèle Breton – Lucy
Ann Sidney – Dana

John Bindon – Moody
Stanley Meadows – Rosebloom
Allan Cuthbertson – Harley-Brown, the Lawyer
Anthony Morton – Dennis
Johnny Shannon – Harry Flowers
Anthony Valentine – Joey Maddocks
Kenneth Colley – Tony Farrell
John Sterland – the Chauffeur
Laraine Wickens – Lorraine
Reg Lye – Workman (uncredited)
Ian McShane – Noel - Black Musician (voice, uncredited)
Billy Murray – Thug 1 (uncredited)
Anthony Roye – Fraser (uncredited)

DEMON SEED

CREW

Directed by Donald Cammell
Written by Robert Jaffe and Roger O. Hirson
Dean R. Koontz – novel
Produced by Herb Jaffe and Steven-Charles Jaffe
Music by Jerry Fielding
Cinematography by Bill Butler
Film Editing by Frank Mazzola
Casting by Jennifer Shull
Production design by Edward C. Carfagno
Set decoration by Barbara Krieger
Don L. Cash and Lee Harman – makeup artist
Frank Griffin – special makeup
Dione Taylor – hair stylist
Sandy Cole – costume designer: Julie Christie
Joie Hutchinson – costumer: women
Bucky Rous – costumer: men
Michael I. Rachmil – unit production manager
Gary Bell – associate film editor
Freeman A. Davies – associate film editor
Edward Teets – assistant director
Alan Brimfeld – second assistant director
Bill Wainess – property master
Jerry Jost and William L. McCaughey – sound
John Riordan – sound editor
Tom Fisher – special effects
Terry W. King – special effects (uncredited)
Glen Robinson – special mechanical effects (uncredited)
Grant Bassett – genigraphics animator
Jordan Belson – special Proteus monitor footage
Richard L. Froman – electronic animator
Bo Gehring – synthavision animator
Ron Hays – electronic visuals designer / electronic visuals developer
Domenic Laia – technical associate
James F. Liles – optical supervisor
Julie Ann Johnson – stunts (uncredited)
Colin J. Campbell – gaffer
James R. Connell – camera operator
George Hill – key grip
John R. Shannon – still photographer (uncredited)
Dan Carlin Sr. – music editor
Harry V. Lojewski – music supervisor
Mary Meacham – title designer
Marshall J. Wolins – script supervisor

CAST

Julie Christie – Susan Harris
Fritz Weaver – Alex Harris
Gerrit Graham – Walter Gabler

Berry Kroeger – Petrosian
Lisa Lu – Soong Yen
Larry J. Blake – Cameron
John O'Leary – Royce
Alfred Dennis – Mokri
Davis Roberts – Warner
Patricia Wilson – Mrs. Talbert
E. Hampton Beagle – Night Operator
Michael Glass – Technician
Barbarao – Technician
Dana Laurita – Amy
Monica MacLean – Joan Kemp
Peter Elbling – Scientist
Georgie Paul – Housekeeper
Michelle Stacy – Marlene
Tiffany Potter – Baby
Felix Silla – Baby
Michael Dorn – Bit (uncredited)
Robert Vaughn – Proteus IV (voice) (uncredited)

WHITE OF THE EYE

CREW

Directed by Donald Cammell
Written by China Kong and Donald Cammell
Andrew Klavan and Laurence Klavan (as Margaret Tracy) – novel, *Mrs. White*
Produced by Sue Baden-Powell, Cassian Elwes, Elliott Kastner, Brad Wyman
Music by Rick Fenn and Nick Mason
Casting by Pamela Guest
Cinematography by Larry McConkey
Film Editing by Terry Rawlings
Set Decoration by Richard Rutowski
Costume Design by Merril Greene
George Fenton – music supervisor
Allan A. Apone – makeup effects supervisor
Nick Dudman – prosthetic supply
Sharon Ilson – key makeup artist
Jeanne Van Phue – makeup artist
Glenn Freemantle – sound editor
John Hayward – sound re-recording mixer
Bruce Litecky – sound mixer
Cliff Wallace – special effects makeup
Dan Bradley – stunt coordinator / stunts
Gary Dagg – key grip
Edward A. Gutentag – second assistant camera
Larry McConkey – Steadicam operator
John Murphy – grip
Sanford Hampton – transportation
Buddy Enright – location manager
Jan Evans – script supervisor
Matt Gatson – production assistant
Robert Shaw – assistant: Elliott Kastner (uncredited)

CAST

David Keith – Paul White
Cathy Moriarty – Joan White
Alan Rosenberg – Mike Desantos
Art Evans – Detective Charles Mendoza
Michael Greene – Phil Ross
Danielle Smith – Danielle White
Alberta Watson – Ann Mason
William G. Schilling – Harold Gideon
David Chow – Fred Hoy
Marc Hayashi – Stu
Mimi Lieber – Liza Manchester
Pamela Guest – Caryanne
Bob Zache – Lucas Herman
Danko Gurovich – Arnold White
China Kong – Ruby Hoy
Jim Wirries – Grunveldt
Katie Waring – Joyce Patell

Fred Allison – TV Newsman
Clyde Pitfarkin – Hairdresser
Richard Lester – Tucson Detective

WILD SIDE

CREW

Directed by Donald Cammell (as Franklin Brauner)
Written by China Kong and Donald Cammell
Produced by Elie Cohn, Boaz Davidson, Donald Cammell, Joan Chen, China Kong, Nick Jones, John Langley, Hamish McAlpine
Executive producers – Danny Dimbort, Avi Lerner, Andrew Pfeffer, Danny Short, Trevor Short, Roger Trilling
Frank Mazzola – producer (director's cut)
Music by Ryûichi Sakamoto
Cinematography by Sead Mutarevic
Film Editing by John Ganem and Frank Mazzola (director's cut)
Casting by Pamela Guest
Production Design by Claire Jenora Bowin
Set Decoration by Shana Sigmond
Costume Design by Alison Hirsch
Scott Williams – hair stylist
Elizabeth Rabe – additional hair stylist
Ashley Scott – makeup artist
Barbara Doyle – production supervisor
Steven Kevin Ogden – post-production supervisor
Paul Martin – first assistant director
Philip Gallegos – second assistant director
Rebecca Carriaga – property master
Mark Hutman – set dresser
Paul Isham – set dresser
Richard Redmond – assistant props
Tristano Solari – construction coordinator
Kaki Wall – art department coordinator
Craig Zumbroegel – propmaker (uncredited)
Darren Barnett – adr mixer / foley mixer / sound re-recording mixer
Geoffrey Haley – boom operator
Harry Harris – dialogue supervisor
Mark Korba, Pattie Lorusso, Peggy McAffee – sound effects editors
Benjamin Patrick – sound mixer
Christopher B. Reeves – dialogue editor (director's cut)
David Rodriguez – adr mixer / foley mixer
Mikael Sandgren – adr editor
Paul Schremp – sound re-recording mixer
Marsha Sorce – sound recordist
Eric Rylander – special effects coordinator
Spike Silver – stunt coordinator
Simone Boisseree and Eddie Yansick – stunts
James Carlton – grip
Collin S. Colberg – first assistant camera
David DeForest Keys – electrician
Mark Feijo – electrician
Dominik Feller – second assistant camera
Jason C. Fitzgerald – electrician
Philip Hurn – camera operator
Lisa Michele Jones – still photographer
Martin Leeper – gaffer

Doug Lively – dolly grip
David McLaughlin – best boy electric
Jennifer Perkins – electrician
Javier Pérez – key grip
Charles H.E. Richards – best boy grip
Marshall Stallings – grip
Jerry Conca – extras casting
Karen Meisels and Paige Scurti Sternin – casting assistant
Annette Dunford-Lewis – set costumer
Beverly Kline – costume supervisor
Elaine C. Andrianos – first assistant film editor
Dexter N. Adriano, Liam Baldwin, Arleen Beaty, Nicholas Edgar – second assistant film editor
Catherine Hader – assistant editor/ post-production coordinator: director's cut
Vivian Hengsteler – negative cutter
Mike Mertens – color timer
Roger Trilling – music` supervisor
Diane DeLouise Wessel – music supervisor
Ryûichi Sakamoto – music mixer / music recordist
Jeff Charbonneau – music editor
Jarvis Cocker – composer: additional music (director's cut)
Lee Curreri – composer: additional music
Steve Mackey – composer: additional music (director's cut)
Jamie Muhoberac – composer: additional music
Mark Webber – composer: additional music (director's cut)
Veronica Alweiss – production coordinator
Charles H. Coffman – set production assistant
Andre Gaudry – location manager
Ronit Ravich-Boss – script supervisor

CAST

Christopher Walken – Bruno Buckingham
Joan Chen – Virginia Chow
Steven Bauer – Tony
Anne Heche – Alex Lee / Johanna
Allen Garfield – Dan Rackman
Adam Novak – Lyle Litvak
Zion – Hiro Sakamoto
Richard Palmer – Cop Driver
Randy Crowder – Federal Agent
Marcus Aurelius – Agent James Reed
Michael Rose – Agent Morse Jaeger
Lewis Arquette – the Chief
Rolando De La Maza – Steward
Candace Kita – Lotus Ita
Ian Johnson – Philip Hamlyn
Gena Kim – Massage Girl
Robert Mazzola – Gilberto

BIBLIOGRAPHY

Y. Allom et al, eds. *Contemporary British and Irish Film Directors, A Wallflower Critical Guide*, Wallflower, London, 20001
G. Andrew. *The Film Handbook*, Longman, London, 1989
—. *Stranger Than Paradise: Maverick Filmmakers in Recent American Cinema*, Prion, 1998
K. Anger. *Hollywood Babylon*, Dell Publishing, New York, NY, 1975
R. Armes. *A Critical History of British Cinema*, Secker & Warburg, London, 1978
J. Arroyo. *Action/ Spectacle Cinema*, British Film Institute, London, 2000
J. Ashby & A. Higson, eds. *British Cinema, Past and Present*, Routledge, London, 2000
M. Auty & N. Roddick, eds. *British Cinema Now*, British Film Institute, London, 1985
S. Bach. *Final Cut: Dreams and Disaster In the Making of Heaven's Gate*, Pimlico, London, 1996
T. Balio, ed. *Hollywood In the Age of Television*, Hyman, Boston, MA, 1990
M. Barker, ed. *The Video Nasties: Freedom and Censorship In the Media*, Pluto Press, London, 1984
—. & J. Petley, eds. *Ill Effects: The Media/ Violence Debate*, Routledge, London, 1997
—. *From Antz to Titanic*, Pluto Press, London, 2000
P. Biskind. *Easy Riders, Raging Bulls: How the Sex 'n' Drugs 'n' Rock 'n' Roll Generation Saved Hollywood*, Bloomsbury, London, 1998
—. *Down and Dirty Pictures: Miramax, Sundance and the Rise of Independent Film*, Bloomsbury, London, 2004
V. Bockris. *Keith Richards*, Omnibus Press, London, 2002
D. Bordwell & K. Thompson. "Art cinema as a mode of film practice", *Film Criticism*, 4, 1, 1979
—. & K. Thompson. *Film Art: An Introduction*, McGraw-Hill Publishing Company, New York, NY, 1979
—. et al. *The Classical Hollywood Cinema: Film Style and Mode of Production to 1960*, Routledge, London, 1985
—. *Narration In the Fiction Film*, Routledge, London, 1988
—. *Making Meaning*, Harvard University Press, Cambridge, MA, 1989
—. & N. Caroll, eds. *Post-Theory: Reconstructing Film Studies*, University of Wisconsin Press, Madison, WI, 1996
—. *The Way Hollywood Tells It*, University of California Press, Berkeley, CA, 2006
D. Breskin. *Inner Voices: Filmmakers In Conversation*, Da Capo, New York, 1997
R. Brody. *Everything Is Cinema: The Working Life of Jean-Luc Godard*, Faber, London, 2008
P. Brooker, ed. *Modernism/ Postmodernism*, Longman 1992
—. & W. Brooker. *Postmodern After Image*, Arnold, London, 1997
J. Brosnan. *Future Tense: The Cinema of Science Fiction*, St Martin's Press, New York, NY, 1978
—. *Primal Screen: A History of Science Fiction Film*, Orbit, London, 1991
M. Brown, *Performance*, Bloomsbury, London, 1999
S. Bukatman. *Terminal Identity: The Virtual Subject in Postmodern Science Fiction*, Duke University Press, Durham, NC, 1993
I. Butler. *Religion In the Cinema*, A.S. Barnes, New York, NY, 1969
—. *Horror In the Cinema*, Zwemmer, London, 1970
Judith Butler. *Gender Trouble: Feminism and the Subversion of Identity*, Routledge 1990
—. & J.W. Scott, eds. *Feminists Theorise the Political*, Routledge 1992
C.R. Cammell. *Aleister Crowley*, Richards Press, 1951
D. Cammell. *Performance*, ed. C. MacCabe, Faber, London, 2001
N. Carroll. *Mystifying Movies: Fads and Fallacies of Contemporary Film Theory*, Columbia University Press, New York, NY, 1988
—. *The Philosophy of Horror*, Routledge, London, 1990
J. Caughie & A. Kuhn, eds. *The Sexual Subject: A Screen Reader in Sexuality*, Routledge, London, 1992
S. Chibnall & R. Murphy, eds. *British Crime Cinema*, Routledge, London, 1999
C. Clover. "Her Body, Himself: Gender In the Slasher Film", *Representations*, 20, Fall, 1987
—. *Men, Women and Chain Saws: Gender In the Modern Horror Film*, Princeton University

Press, Princeton, NJ, 1992

J. Collins et al, eds. *Film Theory Goes to the Movies*, Routledge, New York, NY, 1993

D.A. Cook. *A History of Narrative Film*, W.W. Norton, New York, NY, 1981, 1990, 1996

—. *Lost Illusions: American Cinema In the Shadow of Watergate and Vietnam*, Scribners, New York, NY, 2000

R. Corman. *How I Made a Hundred Movies in Hollywood and Never Lost a Dime*, New York, NY, 1990

B. Creed. *The Monstrous-Feminine*, Routledge, London, 1993

J. Curran & V. Porter, eds. *British Cinema History*, Weidenfeld & Nicolson, London, 1983

D. Dalton, ed. *The Rolling Stones*, Star, London, 1975

S. Davis. *Hammer of the Gods: The Led Zeppelin Saga*, Sidgwick & Jackson, London, 1985

M. Deeley. *Blade Runners, Deer Hunters and Blowing the Bloody Doors Off: My Life In Cult Movies*, Faber & Faber, London, 2008

D. Del Valle. "Memo From Cammell", *Video Watchdog*, 35, 1996

W.W. Dixon, ed. *Re-viewing British Cinema*, State University of New York Press, Albany, NY, 1994

—. *The Films of Jean-Luc Godard*, State University of New York Press, Albany, NY, 1997

M. Doane et al, eds. *Re-Visions: Essays in Feminist Film Criticism*, University Publications of America, Frederick, MD, 1983

—. *The Desire to Desire: The Woman's Film of the 1940's*, Macmillan, London, 1988

—. *Femmes Fatales: Feminism, Film Theory*, Routledge, London, 1991

J. Donald, ed. *Fantasy and the Cinema*, British Film Institute, London, 1989

R. Durgnat. *Films and Feelings*, Faber, London, 1967

—. *A Mirror For England: British Movies From Austerity to Affluence*, Faber, London, 1970

R. Dyer. *Stars*, British Film Institute, London, 1979

J. Eberts. *My Indecision Is Final: The Rise and Fall of Goldcrest Films*, Faber, London, 1990

J. Eszterhas. *The Devil's Guide to Hollywood*, Duckworth, London, 2006

M. Faithfull. *Faithfull*, Michael Joseph, London, 1994

S. Farber. "Performance – The Nightmare Journey", in D. Dalton, 1975

J. Finler. *The Movie Directors Story*, Octopus Books, London, 1985

—. *The Hollywood Story*, Wallflower Press, London, 2003

C. Fleming. *High Concept: Don Simpson and the Hollywood Culture of Excess*, Bloomsbury, London, 1998

J. Fox. *Comeback*, Hodder & Stoughton, London, 1983

K. French, ed. *Screen Violence*, Bloomsbury, London, 1996

L. Friedman, ed. *Fires Were Started: British Cinema and Thatcherism*, UCL Press, London, 1993

J. Gallagher. *Film Directors On Directing*, Praeger, New York, NY, 1989

P.C. Gibson & R. Gibson, eds. *Dirty Looks: Women, Pornography, Power*, British Film Institute, London, 1993

H. Mark Glancy. *When Hollywood Loved Britain*, Manchester University Press, Manchester, 1999

J.-L. Godard. *Jean-Luc Godard*, ed. T. Mussman, Dutton, New York, NY, 1968

—. *Godard on Godard*, eds. J. Narobi & T. Milne, Da Capo, New York, NY, 1986

—. *Interviews*, ed. D. Sterritt, University of Mississippi Press, Jackson, 1998

R. Goldberg. *Performance: Live Art Since the 60s*, Thames & Hudson, London, 1998

M. Goodwin & G. Marcus. *Double Feature*, Outerbridge & Lazard, New York, 1972

B.K. Grant, ed. *Film Genre*, Scarecrow Press, Metuchen, NJ, 1977

—. ed. *Planks of Reason: Essays on the Horror Film*, Scarecrow Press, Metuchen, NJ, 1984

—. *Film Genre Reader II*, University of Texas Press, Austin, TX, 1995

—. ed. *The Dread of Difference: Gender and the Horror Film*, University of Texas Press, Austin, TX, 1996

J. Green. *Days In the Life: Voices From the English Underground 1961-1971*, Heinemann, London, 1988

N. Griffin & K. Masters. *Hit & Run: How Jon Peters and Peter Guber Took Sony For a Ride in Hollywood*, Simon & Schuster, New York, NY, 1996

E. Grosz. *Volatile Bodies*, Indiana University Press, Bloomington, IN, 1994

J. Hacker & D. Price, eds. *Take 10: Contemporary British Film Directors*, Oxford University Press, Oxford, 1991

M. Haskell. *From Reverence to Rape: The Treatment of Women In the Movies*, University of Chicago Press, Chicago, IL, 1973

W. Herzog. *Herzog On Herzog*, ed. P. Cronin, Faber & Faber, London, 2002

C. Heylin, ed. *The Penguin Book of Rock & Roll Writing*, Penguin, London, 1993

—. *Despite the System*, Canongate, London, 2005

A. Higson. *Waving the Flag: Constructing a National Cinema in Britain*, Oxford University Press, Oxford, 1995

—. ed. *Dissolving Views: Key Writings on British Cinema*, Cassell, London, 1996

J. Hillier. *The New Hollywood*, Studio Vista, London, 1992

—. *American Independent Cinema: A Sight & Sound Reader*, British Film Institute, London, 2001

W. Hughes. *Performance*, Award Books, 1970

M. Jagger. "Jagger On *Performance*", in D. Dalton, 1975

F. Jameson. *Signatures of the Visible*, Routledge, London, 1990

D. Jarman. *Modern Nature*, Century, London, 1991

E. Kaplan, ed. *Psychoanalysis and Cinema*, Routledge, London, 1990

—. ed. *Women in Film Noir*, British Film Institute, London, 1998

N. Kent. *The Dark Stuff*, Penguin, London, 1994

P. Keough, ed. *Flesh and Blood: The National Society of Film Critics on Sex, Violence, and Censorship*, Mercury House, San Francisco, CA, 1995

P. Kolker. *The Altering Eye: Contemporary International Cinema*, Oxford University Press, New York, NY, 1983

—. *A Cinema of Loneliness: Penn, Stone, Kubrick, Scorsese, Spielberg, Altman*, Oxford University Press, New York, NY, 2000

D. Koontz. *Demon Seed*, Bantam, 1973/ Corgi, London, 1977

P. Krämer. *The Big Picture: Hollywood Cinema From Star Wars to Titanic*, British Film Institute, London, 2001

—. *The New Hollywood*, Wallflower Press, London, 2005

J. Kristeva. *Desire in Language: A Semiotic Approach to Literature and Art*, ed. L.S. Roudiez, tr. T. Gora *et al*, Blackwell 1982

—. *Revolution in Poetic Language*, tr. M. Walker, Columbia University Press, New York, NY, 1984

—. *The Kristeva Reader*, ed. T. Moi, Blackwell, Oxford, 1986

A. Kuhn. *Women's Pictures: Feminism and the Cinema*, Routledge & Kegan Paul, London, 1982

—. ed. *Alien Zone: Cultural Theory and Contemporary Science Fiction*, Verso, London, 1990

—. *Family Secrets*, Verso, London, 1995

—. ed. *Alien Zone 2*, Verso, London, 1999

J. Lanza. *Fragile Geometry: The Films, Philosophy and Misadventures of Nicolas Roeg*, PAJ, New York, NY, 1989

—. *Phallic Frenzy: Ken Russell and His Films*, Aurum Pres, London, 2008

R. Lapsley & M. Westlake, eds. *Film Theory: An Introduction*, Manchester University Press, Manchester, 1988

E. Levy. *Cinema of Outsiders: The Rise of American Independent Film*, New York University Press, New York, NY, 1999

J. Lewis. *The Road to Romance and Ruin: Teen Films and Youth Culture*, Routledge, London, 1992

—. ed. *New American Cinema*, Duke University Press, Durham, NC, 1998

—. *Hollywood v. Hard Core: How the Struggle Over Censorship Created the Modern Film Industry*, New York University Press, New York, NY, 2000

—. ed. *The End of Cinema As We Know It: American Film In the Nineties*, New York University Press, New York, NY, 2002

R.J. Libin. "Don Cammell's Performance Pluperfect", *Interview*, 23, July, 1972

V. LoBrutto. *Sound-On-Film*, Praeger, New York, NY, 1994

—. *Stanley Kubrick*, Faber, London, 1997
R. Manvell. *New Cinema in Britain*, Dutton, New York, NY, 1968
E. Marks & I. de Courtivron, eds. *New French Feminisms: an anthology*, Harvester Wheatsheaf, Hemel Hempstead, 1981
G. Mast et al, eds. *Film Theory and Criticism: Introductory Readings*, Oxford University Press, New York, NY, 1992
—. & B Kawin. *A Short History of the Movies*, Macmillan, New York, NY, 1992
T.D. Matthews. *Censored*, Chatto & Windus, London, 1994
—. "Donald Cammell: Shoot To Kill", *The Guardian*, May 1, 1998
C. McCabe. *Performance*, British Film Institute, London, 1998
B. McFarlane, ed. *An Autobiography of British Cinema*, Methuen, London, 1997
R. McKee. *Story: Substance, Structure, Style and the Principles of Screenwriting*, Methuen, London, 1999
B. Miles. *Paul McCartney*, Secker & Warburg, London, 1997
M. Miles. *Seeing and Believing: Religion and Values In the Movies*, Beacon, Boston, MA, 1996
F. Miller. *Censored Hollywood: Sex, Sin and Violence On Screen*, Turner Publishing, Atlanta, 1994
T. Modleski, ed. *Studies in Entertainment*, Indiana University Press, Bloomington, IN, 1987
—. *The Women Who Knew Too Much: Hitchcock and Feminist Theory*, Methuen, London, 1988
T. Moi. *Sexual/Textual Politics: Feminist Literary Theory*, Methuen, London, 1983
G. Mulholland. *Popcorn: Fifty Years of Rock 'n' Roll Movies*, Orion Books, London, 2011
L. Mulvey. *Visual and Other Pleasures*, Indiana University Press, Bloomington, IN, 1989
S. Munt, ed. *New Lesbian Criticism: Literary and Cultural Readings*, Harvester Wheatsheaf, Hemel Hempstead, 1992
R. Murphy. *Realism and Tinsel: British Cinema and Society, 1939-48*, London, 1989
—. *Sixties British Cinema*, British Film Institute, London, 1992
—. ed. *The British Cinema Book*, Palgrave/Macmillan, London, 2nd edition, 2009
R. Murray. *Images In the Dark: An Encyclopedia of Gay and Lesbian Film and Video*, Titan Books, London, 1998
S. Neale. *Cinema and Technology*, Macmillan, London, 1985
—. & B. Neve. *Film and Politics in America*, Routledge, London, 1992
—. & M. Smith, eds. *Contemporary Hollywood Cinema*, Routledge, London, 1998
—. *Genre and Hollywood*, Routledge, London, 2000
—. *Genre and Contemporary Hollywood*, Routledge, London, 2002
J. Nelmes, ed. *An Introduction to Film Studies*, Routledge, London, 1996
K. Newman. *Nightmare Movies*, Harmony, New York, NY, 1988
—. *Millennium Movies*, Titan Books, London, 1999
—. ed. *Science Fiction/Horror: A Sight & Sound Reader*, British Film Institute, London, 2002
P. Norman. *The Stones*, Elm Tree, 1972
—. *Sympathy For the Devil: The Rolling Stones Story*, Linden Press, New York, NY, 1984
—. *Mick Jagger*, HarperCollins, 2012
Novalis. *Hymns to the Night and Other Selected Writings*, tr. C.E. Passage, Bobbs-Merrill Company, Indianapolis, 1960
—. *Novalis Schriften. Die Werke Friedrichs von Hardenberg*, ed. R. Samuel et al, Stuttgart, 1960–88
—. *Pollen and Fragments: Selected Poetry and Prose*, tr. A. Versluis, Phanes Press, Grand Rapids, 1989
M. O'Pray, ed. *The British Avant Garde Film, 1926-1995*, University of Luton Press/John Libbey, London, 1996
—. *Avant-Garde Film*, Wallflower Press, London, 2003
C. Paglia. *Sexual Personae: Art and Decadence From Nefertiti To Emily Dickinson*, Penguin, London, 1992
—. *Sex, Art and American Culture*, Viking, London, 1992
—. *Vamps and Tramps: New Essays*, Penguin, London, 1995
J. Park. *Learning to Dream: The New British Cinema*, Faber, London, 1984
—. *British Cinema*, B.T. Batsford, London, 1990

D. Petrie. *Creativity and Constraint In the British Film Industry*, Macmillan, London, 1991
—. ed. *New Questions of British Cinema*, British Film Institute, London, 1992
—. *The British Cinematographer*, British Film Institute, London, 1996
G. Phelps. *Film Censorship*, Gollancz, London, 1975
J. Phillips. *You'll Never Eat Lunch In This Town Again*, Heinemann, London, 1991
M. Powell. *A Life In the Movies*, Heinemann, London, 1986, 1992
—. *Million-Dollar Movie*, Heinemann, London, 1992
S. Prince. *Savage Cinema: Sam Peckinpah and the Rise of Ultraviolent Movies*, University of Texas Press, Austin, TX, 1998
—. ed. *Screening Violence*, Athlone Press, London, 2000
—. *A New Pot of Gold: Hollywood Under the Electronic Rainbow*, Scribners, New York, NY, 2000
M. Pye & Lynda Myles. *The Movie Brats: How the Film Generation Took Over Hollywood*, Faber, London, 1979
J. Pym. *Film On Four*, British Film Institute, London, 1992
S. Reynolds. *Blissed Out: The Raptures of Rock*, Serpent's Tail, London, 1990
—. & Joy Press. *The Sex Revolts: Gender, Rebellion and Rock 'n' Roll*, Serpent's Tail, London, 1995
Adrienne Rich. *Blood, Bread and Poetry*, Virago 1980
—. *Of Woman Born: Motherhood as Experience and Institution*, Virago 1977
J. Richards, ed. *Films and British National Identity*, Manchester University Press, Manchester, 1997
K. Richards. *Life*, Weidenfeld & Nicolson, London, 1997/ 2009
W.H. Rockett. *Devouring Whirlwind: Terror and Transcendence In the Cinema of Cruelty*, Greenwood Press, New York, NY, 1988
J. Romney & A. Wootton, eds. *Celluloid Jukebox: Popular Music and the Movies Since the 50s*, British Film Institute, London, 1995
R. Roud. *Jean-Luc Godard*, Thames & Hudson, London, 1970
K. Russell. *A British Picture: An Autobiography*, Heinemann, London, 1989
—. *Fire Over England: The British Cinema Comes Under Friendly Fire*, Hutchinson, London, 1993
—. *Directing Film*, Brassey's, Washington DC, 2001
V. Russo. *The Celluloid Closet: Homosexuality In the Movies*, Harper & Row, New York, NY, 1981
T. Ryall. *Alfred Hitchcock and the British Cinema*, Croom Helm, 1986
C. Sanford. *The Rolling Stones: 50 Years*, Simon & Schuster,London, 2013
N. Schaffner. *Saucerful of Secrets: The Pink Floyd Odyssey*, Sidgwick & Jackson, London, 1991
T. Shaw. *British Cinema and the Cold War*, I.B. Tauris, London, 2001
T. Shone. *Blockbuster: How the Jaws and Jedi Generation Turned Hollywood Into a Boom-Town*, Scribner, London, 2005
K. Silverman. *The Subject of Semiotics*, Oxford University Press, New York, NY, 1983
—. *The Acoustic Mirror: The Female Voice in Psychoanalysis and Cinema*, Indiana University Press, Bloomington, IN, 1988
—. *Male Subjectivity at the Margins*, Routledge, London, 1992
—. & H. Farocki. *Speaking About Godard*, New York University Press, New York, NY, 1998
P. Adams Sitney, ed. *The Film Culture Reader*, Praeger, New York, NY, 1970
—. ed. *The Avant-Garde Film: A Reader of Theory and Criticism*, New York University Press, New York, NY, 1978
—. *Visionary Film: The American Avant-Garde, 1943-1978*, 2nd ed., Oxford University Press, New York, NY, 1979
J. Smith. *Withnail and Us: Cult Films and Film Cults in British Cinema*, Tauris, London, 2010
V. Sobchack. *The Limits of Infinity: The American Science Fiction Film*, A.S. Barnes, New York, NY, 1980
—. *Screening Space: The American Science Fiction Film*, Ungar, New York, NY, 1987/1993
—. *The Address of the Eye: A Phenomenology of Film Experience*, Princeton University Press, Princeton, NJ, 1992
—. ed. *The Persistence of History: Cinema, Television, and the Modern Event*, Routledge,

London, 1995
D. Sterritt. *The Films of Jean-Luc Godard*, Cambridge University Press, Cambridge, 1999
J. Still & M. Worton, eds. *Textuality and Sexuality: Reading Theories and Practices*, Manchester University Press, Manchester, 1993
S. Street. *British National Cinema*, Routledge, London, 1997/ 2009
Y. Tasker. *Spectacular Bodies: Gender, Genre and the Action Cinema*, Routledge, London, 1993
K. Thompson. *Exporting Entertainment: America In the World Film Market, 1907-1934*, British Film Institute, London, 1985
–. *Breaking the Glass Armor: Neoformalist Film Analysis*, Princeton University Press, Princeton, NJ, 1988
–. & D. Bordwell. *Film History: An Introduction*, McGraw-Hill, New York, NY, 1994
–. *Storytelling In the New Hollywood*, Harvard University Press, Cambridge, MA, 1999
D. Thomson. *A Biographical Dictionary of Film*, Deutsch, London, 1995
Time Out, Performance issue, 1970
M. Tracy. *Mrs White*, Dell, 1983
G. Tremlett. *The David Bowie Story*, London, 1976
–. *Rock Gold: The Music Millionaires*, Unwin Hyman, London, 1990
G. Vincendeau, ed. *Encyclopedia of European Cinema*, British Film Institute, London, 1995
–. ed. *Film/ Literature/ Heritage: A Sight & Sound Reader*, British Film Institute, London, 2001
A. Walker. *The Celluloid Sacrifice: Aspects of Sex In the Movies*, Michael Joseph, London, 1966
–. *Sex In the Movies*, Penguin, London, 1968
–. *National Heroes: British Cinema In the Seventies and Eighties*, Harrap, London, 1985
–. *Hollywood, England: The British Film Industry In the Sixties*, Harrap, London, 1986
J. Walker. *The Once and Future Film: British Cinema In the 1970s and 1980s*, Methuen, London, 1985
J. Wasko. *Movies and Money*, Ablex, NJ, 1982
–. *Hollywood In the Information Age*, Polity Press, Cambridge, 1994
P. Webb. *The Erotic Arts*, Secker & Warburg, London, 1975
E. Weiss. & J. Belton, eds. *Film Sound: Theory and Practice*, Columbia University Press, New York, NY, 1989
O. Welles. *This is Orson Welles*, HarperCollins, London, 1992
–. *Orson Welles: Interviews*, ed. M. Estrin, University of Mississippi Press, Jackson, 2002
Colin Wilson. *The Occult*, Granada, 1971
–. *Mysteries*, Granada, 1979
M. Wolf. *The Entertainment Economy*, Penguin, London, 1999
J. Wolmark. *Aliens and Others: Science Fiction, Feminism and Postmodernism*, Harvester Wheatsheaf, Hemel Hempstead, 1993
–. ed. *Cybersexualities: A Reader on Feminist Theory, Cyborgs and Cyberspace*, Edinburgh University Press, Edinburgh, 1999
L. Wood, ed. *British Films, 1971-1981*, British Film Institute, London, 1983
R. Wood & R. Lippe, eds. *American Nightmare: Essays On the Horror Film*, Festival of Festivals, Toronto, 1979
–. *Hollywood From Vietnam To Reagan*, Columbia University Press, New York, NY, 1986
–. *Hollywood From Vietnam To Reagan... and Beyond*, Columbia University Press, New York, NY, 2003
T. Woods. *Beginning Postmodernism*, Manchester University Press, Manchester, 1999
R. Yorke. *Led Zeppelin*, Virgin, 1999
J. Zipes. *The Enchanted Screen: The Unknown History of Fairy-tale Films*, Routledge, New York, NY, 2011
S. Zizek. *Enjoy Your Symptom Jacques Lacan in Hollywood and Out*, Routledge, New York, NY, 1992
–. ed. *Everything You Always Wanted to Know About Lacan (But Were Too Afraid to Ask Hitchcock)*, Verso, London, 1992
–. *The Fright of Real Tears: The Uses and Misuses of Lacan in Film Theory*, British Film

Institute, London, 1999

WEBSITES

mickjagger.com
keithrichards.com
rollingstones.com

Jeremy Robinson has written many critical studies, including *Hayao Miyazaki, Walerian Borowczyk, Arthur Rimbaud,* and *The Sacred Cinema of Andrei Tarkovsky*, plus literary monographs on: William Shakespeare; Samuel Beckett; Thomas Hardy; André Gide; Robert Graves; and John Cowper Powys.

It's amazing for me to see my work treated with such passion and respect. There is nothing resembling it in the U.S. in relation to my work.
Andrea Dworkin (on *Andrea Dworkin*)

This model monograph – it is an exemplary job, and I'm very proud that he has accorded me a couple of mentions... The subject matter of his book is beautifully organised and dead on beam.
Lawrence Durrell (on *The Light Eternal: A Study of J.M.W. Turner*)

Jeremy Robinson's poetry is certainly jammed with ideas, and I find it very interesting for that reason. It's certainly a strong imprint of his personality.
Colin Wilson

Sex-Magic-Poetry-Cornwall is a very rich essay... It is a very good piece... vastly stimulating and insightful.
Peter Redgrove

Thomas A. Christie

JOHN HUGHES
& EIGHTIES CINEMA
Teenage Hopes & American Dreams

John Hughes (1950-2009) is one of the best-loved figures in 1980s American filmmaking, and considered by many to be among the finest and most celebrated comedy writers of his generation. His memorable motion pictures are insightful, humanistic, culturally aware, and paint a vibrant picture of the United States in a decade of rapid social and political change.

Bibliography, notes, illustrations   372pp.
ISBN 9781861713896 Pbk   ISBN 9781861713988 Hbk
Also available: *Ferris Bueller's Day Off: Pocket Movie Guide*

WILLIAM MALPAS
the art of andy goldsworthy

This is the most comprehensive and detailed account of the art of Andy Goldsworthy available.

This study of Andy Goldsworthy discusses all of Goldsworthy's major exhibitions, books and projects, including the *Sheepfolds* project; *Garden of Stones* in New York; TV and dance collaborations; and the books *Wood, Stone, Time* and *Passage*. William Malpas surveys all of Goldsworthy's output, and analyzes his relation with other land artists such as Robert Smithson, the Christos, Walter de Maria, Chris Drury, Richard Long and David Nash; women sculptors; sculpture in the modern era; and Goldsworthy's place in the contemporary British art scene.

The book has been updated and revised for this new edition.

ISBN 9781861714107 Pbk   ISBN 9781861714114 Hbk
Fully illustrated   www.crmoon.com